D1520778

Research Guide to
the Turner Movement in
the United States

Recent Titles in
Bibliographies and Indexes in American History

Research Guide to the Turner Movement in ___the United States___

Compiled by
ERIC L. PUMROY and
KATJA RAMPELMANN

Bibliographies and Indexes in American History,
Number 33

Greenwood Press
Westport, Connecticut • London

1996

ISBN: 0-313-29763-0

Library of Congress Cataloging-in-Publication Data

Pumroy, Eric.
  Research guide to the Turner movement in the United States /
compiled by Eric L. Pumroy and Katja Rampelmann.
      p.   cm.—(Bibliographies and indexes in American history,
ISSN 0742–6828 ; no. 33)
  Includes bibliographical references and index.
  ISBN 0–313–29763–0 (alk. paper)
  1. American Turners (Organization)—History—Bibliography.
2. German Americans—Societies, etc.—Bibliography.   3. Physical
education and training—United States—History—Bibliography.
I. Rampelmann, Katja.   II. Title.   III. Series.
Z6121.P85   1996
[GV203]
016.796′06—dc20   96–5846

British Library Cataloguing in Publication Data is available.

Library of Congress Catalog Card Number: 96–5846
ISBN: 0–313–29763–0
ISSN: 0742–6828

First published in 1996

Greenwood Press, 88 Post Road West, Westport, CT 06881
An imprint of Greenwood Publishing Group, Inc.

Printed in the United States of America

The paper used in this book complies with the
Permanent Paper Standard issued by the National
Information Standards Organization (Z39.48–1984).

10 9 8 7 6 5 4 3 2 1

For Kenneth and Karl-Heinz

Contents

Introduction and Acknowledgments

In many cities and large towns of the East and Midwest it is still possible to find the grand, Germanic-style public buildings that the Turners built a century ago to serve as their meeting halls. A few of them are still being used as Turner halls, while the rest have been converted to other purposes: a church in Chicago, an apartment building in Indianapolis, a law office in Louisville and even a car dealership in Tell City, Indiana. Most of the old Turner halls are gone now, victims of the urban renewal and downtown redevelopments of the last half century. Many of those that remain, though, have a size and former elegance that testify to the prosperity and prominence the Turner societies once enjoyed. At the height of the movement in the 1890s there were more than three hundred societies across the country affiliated with the national organization, the American Turnerbund, boasting a total membership of more than 40,000. At that time the Turner halls served as community centers for the large German population in American cities, providing meeting rooms and assembly halls for neighborhood groups to gather, for music and theater societies to perform, for unions and political groups to organize, for new immigrants to learn American ways and the English language, and for older ones to speak German and teach it to their children.

The surviving buildings are the most visible signs of the Turners' former glory, but the significance of the Turners extended far beyond their halls. During the years from the establishment of the first Turner society in 1848 to the crisis for German-America brought on by World War I, Turner societies exerted political leadership that extended far beyond the German community. Their founding generation included most of the leading political exiles from Germany's failed democratic revolutions of 1848, including Carl Schurz, Franz Sigel, Sigismund Kaufmann and August Willich, all of whom later achieved prominent positions in American political and military affairs. The next generation included business and community leaders and leaders in the German radical labor movement, reflecting both the increasing prosperity of the German immigrants from the 1850s and the rapid increase in the number of German industrial workers as a result of the immigration of the 1870s and 1880s. The athletic interests of the Turners meant that they were leaders in the effort to make physical education a standard part of public school curriculum in the late nineteenth century, but Turners were also engaged on a much wider group of issues, including opposing temperance and Sabbath-Day laws, promoting the development of public parks and playgrounds and supporting legislation to improve conditions for working people.

The passage of time, the natural assimilation of Americans of German descent and the anti-German atmosphere generated by both World War I and World War II have reduced the Turners in the United States to a small number of societies, most of them struggling to survive. The decline of the Turners parallels the disappearance of the prosperous, self-confident German-American community that played such an important part in American urban life from the mid-nineteenth century through World War I, but which is now almost completely forgotten. One of the reasons for our fading awareness of German-American life is that so much of the written record has been lost. For most of this century, very few libraries made an effort to collect the publications and historical records of German-Americans, and a few libraries even destroyed those materials they already owned, either out of anti-German zeal at the end of World War I, or, more recently, as part of programs to remove little-used books from their collections. As a result, very little documentation on the Turners, as well as on other important German-American organizations, has been available for people to use. This book is the result of a project which tried to find out how much documentation on the Turners still existed, and to ensure its survival by arranging for its transfer from attics and storerooms to historical libraries.

TURNER SURVEY PROJECT

The origins of this book date back to 1978 when the newly opened University Archives at Indiana University-Purdue University Indianapolis (IUPUI) acquired a large collection of historical records of the Normal College of the American Gymnastic Union, the private college founded by the Turners in the late nineteenth century and the forerunner of the IUPUI School of Physical Education. The records were stored in the Athenaeum, an impressive Wilhelmenian-style building in downtown Indianapolis where the school had been housed until 1970. The records included not only those of the school, but also those of the numerous Indianapolis German organizations that had used the building, in particular the Athenaeum Turners, the principal occupant of the building. In addition, the collection included many national records since the Athenaeum had housed the Turner national headquarters during the movement's most successful years at the beginning of the century. By the time the preliminary processing of the records had been completed in the mid-1980s it had become clear that the Athenaeum Collection was not only an extraordinarily rich source of documentation on the influential German community in Indianapolis, but that it also constituted the largest single collection of national records from the Turner movement available in any repository. In the late 1980s the IUPUI University Archives began working with the campus's growing German-American Studies program, under the direction of Professor Giles Hoyt, to develop original research collections to support work in the field. At that time connections were made with the American Turners national office in Louisville and with the president of the American Turners, Eldon Zahm of Fort Wayne, Indiana, to determine if additional historical records had survived. In 1989 the American Turners agreed to make IUPUI the repository for its national records, and a substantial volume of records were transferred. The records from the national office were immediately exciting but also frustratingly incomplete. They included, for example, letter books from the years 1864-1866 when the national organization was being re-established at the end of the Civil War, but no other correspondence until the 1930s. Perhaps most intriguing, though, were the district and local publications which showed how extensive and prosperous Turner societies once were across the country, and how rich the movement's publishing history had been.

From this beginning, we began discussions with the Turners about a large-scale project to preserve local and district records as well as national ones. Searches of the National Union Catalog of Manuscript Collections and library online catalogs indicated that there was very little Turner material already in repositories, or if it had been deposited, was still uncataloged. At the same time, Turner societies in Louisville, New York City, and Covington, Kentucky, reported that they still held extensive sets of historical records. As a result of this preliminary work, we saw the need for a project that would both locate surviving Turner records and arrange to have them transferred to appropriate archives or libraries where their preservation could be assured. In 1990 we submitted a proposal for the project to the National Endowment for the Humanities. After some revisions and resubmissions, the project was funded at the end of 1992.

The project formally started in August 1993 when Katja Rampelmann began work as project archivist, and it ran through March 1995. During the course of the project, the staff contacted every existing Turner society that could be identified and visited most of them to inventory their historical records. The staff also contacted or visited historical societies and public and academic libraries in areas where Turner societies had been active. The survey findings confirmed our initial impression that only a small amount of historical documentation was preserved and accessible in institutions. That situation has partially changed as a result of the project's work. More than a dozen Turner societies have transferred their historical records to libraries and archives in the last few years, and several more are considering a transfer. In addition, several hundred publications were donated to the Turner national archives at IUPUI during the course of the project, many of which are the only known copies or the only copies in a public institution.

As a result of the project, approximately two thousand publications and archival collections were identified for inclusion in this guide. Most of these items have surfaced only as the result of the work done since the mid-1980s, and so represent a substantial expansion of the available sources on the Turners. Nonetheless, this guide is far from being definitive. The entries in this guide demonstrate the scale and quality of the Turners' publishing activity in the late nineteenth and early twentieth centuries, but they also suggest how much more once existed but has now been lost. It is our hope that this guide will lead those who own the rare surviving copies of Turner and other German-American publications to see to it that they are saved.

PROJECT METHODOLOGY

The following methods were used to locate Turner publications and collections. First, the major printed bibliographies on German-Americana were searched, most notably Henry A. Pochmann and Arthur R. Schultz's Bibliography of German culture in America to 1940 (Millwood, NY: Kraus International Publishers, 1982), Don Heinrich Tolzmann's German-Americana: a bibliography (Metuchen, NJ: Scarecrow Press, 1975) and Catalog of the German-Americana Collection, University of Cincinnati (München and New York: K.G. Saur, 1990) and Karl Arndt and May Olson's The German language press of the Americas/ Die deutschsprachige Presse der Amerikas (München: Verlag Dokumentation, 1976-1980). In addition, Turner publications, particularly Mind and Body and the Amerikanische Turnzeitung, were searched for announcements of Turner publications and notices of Turner societies not identified elsewhere.

Second, on-line catalogs for academic and research libraries were systematically searched, as well as the national bibliographic databases, OCLC and RLIN. Online catalogs made it possible to search library collections that could never have been visited in person. Nonetheless, they are not without drawbacks, the most important one being that substantial parts of the collections of major research libraries have not yet been cataloged in machine-readable form and so cannot be found through the on-line catalogs.

Third, inquiries were sent to libraries and historical societies throughout the country, and many were visited in person by project staff during the course of visits to Turner societies. In many cases, pamphlets and other printed items were found not through the library catalogs, but as parts of Turner archival collections or miscellaneous collections of uncataloged German-language pamphlets. Libraries in Germany were not searched systematically but contacts with scholars in the field and a search of the German Gesamtverzeichnis des deutschsprachigen Schrifttums (GV) indicated that holdings on American Turners in German institutions were very limited. Nonetheless, whenever items were found in German institutions the institution has been indicated.

Fourth, about seventy-five Turner societies were visited and their records inventoried. The society collections frequently included older pamphlets and anniversary books, even if there were few other historical records. By far the largest group of printed items was found in the files of the American Turners national office in Louisville; those materials have now been transferred to the IUPUI University Library. Important collections can also be found in the files of the Milwaukee Turner Foundation, the American Turners New York and the New Ulm (MN) Turnverein.

The accessibility of materials at Turner societies is uncertain and researchers are strongly advised to contact societies before attempting to use their collections. A list of societies with their addresses can be found in Appendix 2 of this book.

SCOPE OF THE GUIDE

This guide focuses on the Turner movement in the United States, and as such it includes only those works which were created by the Turners or were written specifically about them in the form of books, book chapters, articles and dissertations. There are, of course, many other sources that should be consulted for background and context, particularly works on the Germans in the United States in general and specifically on German Forty-Eighters, German immigration, the German-American labor and radical movements and the Freethinkers. The literature on these topics is far too voluminous to be included in this work, although a number of the most important works are cited in the footnotes to the historical sketch. Anyone interested in Turner activities in a particular state or city will also find references in city and county histories and the local German-language newspapers.

STRUCTURE OF THE GUIDE

The guide consists of the following sections:
1) Historical essay on the Turner movement in the United States.
2) Guide to publications and historical records, subdivided into the following categories:
   a) National publications and historical records, consisting of materials created, published or sanctioned by the national office of the American Turners;
   b) District publications and historical records, listed alphabetically by district name.
   c) Society publications and historical records, arranged alphabetically by state and city. Entries for each society consist of a brief history of the organization, a description of the surviving historical records, and a bibliography of publications issued by the society.
   d) Normal College of the American Gymnastic Union publications and historical records.
   e) Publications on physical education published by the Turners or written by people active in the Turner movement.
   f) Writings on the American Turners, consisting of scholarly books, pamphlets, articles, theses and dissertations on the Turner movement in general or on individual societies. In order to distinguish works written by contemporaries from more recent works by scholars, the section is subdivided into publications issued before 1920 and those issued since 1920.

3) List of all Turner societies that have been active in the United States, arranged by
    state, city and date of founding.
4) Addresses of Turner societies in the United States, arranged by district.
5) Location codes for repositories, arranged by state.
6) Index

USE OF THE GUIDE

Principles of Inclusion

Publications were included if they were at least eight pages in length and included
substantive information about the activities, history or philosophy of the Turners.
Items with fewer than eight pages were included if the content was significant, such
as convention proceedings. Larger items with little content, such as programs
containing only schedules and advertising, were not included. Chapter 6, "Writings
on the American Turners," contains books, book chapters, articles, doctoral
dissertations and master's theses on the Turners. Unpublished conference papers,
undergraduate papers, photographs or newspaper clippings were not included.

   Archival collections were included if they contained records of a Turner
society or of the national organization. Personal papers of people involved in the
Turner movement were not included unless the collection contained a substantial
amount of Turner-related material.

Entries

Publications

Entries for published items are based on the Chicago Manual of Style guidelines and
consist of the following information:

   1. *Author*. The author is listed as found in the publication except when there
are multiple items by the same author. In this case either a consistent version of the
name has been used or, if the entries appear together, the full name is given only for
the first entry and subsequent entries have dashes in the author field. Except for the
entries in the "Writings" and "Publications on Physical Education" chapters, most
publications do not have authors.
   2. *Title*. Titles are transcribed as they appear on the title page or on the cover
if there is no title page. When there is both a title page and a cover title and the two
are substantially different, the title page has been used for the entry and the cover title
transcribed in the annotation.
   3. *Publication information*. Place of publication, publisher and date of
publication are given as found. Approximate dates are given in brackets for undated
items that were examined.
   4. *Pagination*. The number of pages are given where the information was

available. An approximate page count is given in brackets for unpaged items that were examined.

5. *Location.* Locations for known copies are listed using codes based upon those used in the National Union Catalog. The list of codes and institutions can be found in Appendix 3. Turner societies and private collections are listed as locations only when they hold the only known copy. Inquiries about the exact location for private collections can be sent to IUPUI's Special Collections and Archives. In cases where no copies were located, the source of the citation is noted. The principal sources for unlocated items were Henry A. Pochmann's Bibliography of German culture in America to 1940 (noted as 'Pochmann'); Karl Arndt and May Olson's The German language press of the Americas (noted as 'Arndt/Olson'), and Ralf Wagner's Zwischen Tradition und Fortschritt: Zur gesellschaftspolitischen und kulturellen Entwicklung der deutschamerikanischen Turnbewegung am Beispiel Milwaukee und Chicagos, 1850-1920 (Ph.D. dissertation, Ludwig-Maximilians Universität, München, 1988) (noted as 'Wagner').

6. *Annotations.* Annotations include transcriptions of cover titles, English-language summaries of German titles, descriptions of contents, and language of the publication where the language is not clear from the title or the item is in both German and English.

Archival Collections

Entries for archival collections consist of the following information:

1. Collection name. The name was either provided by the institution owning the records or supplied by the project staff.
2. Inclusive dates of the records.
3. Extent of the collection, usually expressed either in linear feet or number of boxes.
4. Location.
5. Availability of finding aids.
6. Description of the records.

ACKNOWLEDGMENTS

The success of a project of this scale depends upon the help of many people. We want to thank the numerous librarians, archivists and historians who responded to our questionnaires and telephone calls. The number is too great to list here, but their help allowed us to fill many gaps, saved us from some unnecessary visits and made others much more profitable than they would otherwise have been. We also want to thank the numerous Turners who warmly welcomed us to their societies, sent us information and provided much of the background information on the recent history of the Turners. Critical to the success of the project were former American Turners presidents Eldon Zahm and Ed Colton and national historian Forrest Steinlage, all of whom put a great deal of energy and imagination into the work. The project would never have gotten off of the ground without the support and encouragement of Barbara Fischler, Director of the IUPUI University Library, and the financial support of the National Endowment for the Humanities, and particularly program officer Barbara Paulson. We appreciate the friendly and critical advice of all members of the advisory board, Joseph Anderson, American Institute of Physics; Professor Robert Barney, University of Western Ontario; Professor John Bodnar, Indiana University; Dr. John Grabowski, Western Reserve Historical Society; Professor Giles Hoyt, IUPUI; Dr. Hartmut Keil, Universität Leipzig; Dr. Jörg Nagler, Kennedy Haus Kiel; Michael Palmer, German Genealogical Society of America; Forrest Steinlage, American Turners; Dr. Don Heinrich Tolzmann, University of Cincinnati; Joel Wurl, Immigration History Research Center; and Eldon Zahm, American Turners. We also want to thank Dr. Dolores Hoyt at the IUPUI University Library who served as an unofficial but highly valued advisor to the project. We are deeply indebted to the IUPUI Special Collections staff, particularly Sandra Hartlieb, Barbara Mondary and Gregory Mobley for all their patience, encouragement and support during the time of the project. Our gratitude also goes to the helping hands of the project, Stephen Fisher and Anette Dau, and especially to Jill Mechelke, whose energy and good work added greatly to the success of this project. Finally, the book could not have been completed without the heroic editorial work of Eric's wife, Ann Koopman.

Historical Overview of the Turner Movement in the United States

The Turner movement began in Germany in response to the country's humiliation following Napoleon's shattering defeat of the Prussian army in 1806. Friedrich Ludwig Jahn, the founder of the Turners, was a teacher whose books, _Deutsches Volksthum_ (1810) and _Deutsche Turnkunst_ (1816), argued that a revived, independent Germany could come into being only through national unification, democratic reforms, and young Germans trained in a program of vigorous physical exercise, patriotic ideals and love of liberty. In 1811 he set up an athletic field, or _Turnplatz,_ in Berlin where he trained young men both physically and mentally for the liberation and unification of Germany under a reformed government. Jahn attracted a large number of followers, and in the years following Napoleon's defeat the movement continued to grow, becoming closely associated with the _Burschenschaften,_ the student fraternities that agitated for democratic reforms. The Turners' activities were tolerated by the German governments for a time, until the assassination of reactionary writer August von Kotzebue in 1819 by Carl Sand, a student fraternity member and a Turner. Using the assassination as a pretext, the German governments suppressed the Turners and Jahn spent most of the next twenty years under police surveillance. In spite of the ban on Turner activities throughout the German states, the movement continued to operate underground. In 1842 the government restrictions were lifted, largely as a result of the growing public interest in Turner ideas about physical education. Once they were allowed to operate freely, the Turner movement grew rapidly, attracting support both from those interested in the Turners' athletic program and from those who used Turner competitions as vehicle for political organizing on behalf of democratic and social reforms. After the outbreak of the Revolution of 1848, the Turners formally split into conservative and reformist camps. The former, supporting a constitutional monarchy and interested primarily in Turner athletic and social programs, formed the _Deutsche Turnerbund_ in Hanau in April 1848. In early July the more radical Turners organized the _Demokratischer_

Turnerbund under the leadership of Friedrich Hecker and Gustav Struve. The radical Turners played a prominent role during the Revolution and fought alongside the democratic forces in Baden. After the revolution failed, many of the members of the *Demokratischer Turnerbund* went into exile, primarily in the United States. From that point, the German Turner movement came under the control of conservatives who focused its energies on gymnastics and physical exercises, a course which led to the *Deutsche Turnerbund* becoming the leading athletic organization in Germany.[1]

It is not certain when the first Turner society was formed in the United States. Jahn's physical exercises had been known in the United States since the 1820s due to the influence of his students Karl Beck, Karl Follen and Franz Lieber, but their work was with schools in Massachusetts and had little impact on German immigrant society. German immigrants probably brought knowledge of Turner exercises with them in the mid-1840s, and there appear to have been Turner activities in New York and Louisville in early 1848, and there may have been activities in Galveston, Texas prior to 1848.[2] Nonetheless, the beginning of the Turners as a national movement directly followed from the failure of the 1848 uprising in Germany and the arrival in the United States of political exiles who had been active in the German Turner movement. The society traditionally identified as being the first in the United States was the Cincinnati Turnverein, organized in October 1848 during a meeting with the exiled revolutionary leader Friedrich Hecker. The movement grew quickly over the next few years, particularly in the cities of the East and Midwest where large numbers of German immigrants and exiles settled. By 1855 seventy-four societies had been formed with a total of about 4500 members, and there were perhaps 10,000 Turners by 1860. Exiled revolutionaries from Germany, known as Forty-Eighters, played key roles in the establishment of many societies. August Willich, a leader of the Communist League in Cologne and of republican military forces during the revolution, helped organize the Milwaukee Turnverein in 1853; Gustav Struve, a leader of the Baden uprising, helped to form the New York Turnverein; Theodor Hielscher, prominent in the Berlin uprising, was active in the early years of the Indianapolis Turngemeinde; and Hans Reimer Claussen and twenty other veterans of the uprising in Schleswig-Holstein formed the Davenport, Iowa Turnverein.[3]

While the leadership during the pre-war years consisted of many former teachers, journalists and other educated professionals from Germany, the majority of the members were drawn from the class of skilled crafts workers, part of the approximately one million Germans who came to the United States during the years 1847-1857. Recent works by Bruce Levine and Ralf Wagner have demonstrated the close association of the Turners in many cities with labor interests.[4] The New York Turnverein, for example, was active in support of the 1850 tailors' strike and affiliated with the *Amerikanische Arbeiterbund* in its call for reform of working conditions in 1853. The connection with labor causes found support throughout the country, for within a year of the founding of the national association of Turner societies, the national convention in Philadelphia changed the organization's name from the *Vereinigte Turnvereins Nordamerika* (United Turner Societies of North America) to the *Socialistische Turnerbund von Nord Amerika* (the Socialist Turner Federation of North America), with the goal of advancing the cause of socialism. Societies in

Philadelphia, Baltimore, Indianapolis, Davenport and other cities demonstrated their commitment to social reform by including the word *'socialistischer'* in their name.

The Turner commitment to liberty and equality brought them into conflict with the powerful pro-slavery and anti-immigrant forces in American society. In their 1855 national convention in Pittsburgh, the Turners declared that opposition to slavery, nativism and prohibition were the cornerstone principles of the movement. The events of the 1850s showed that the Turners were prepared to fight for these principles. Turners were involved in clashes with anti-German gangs throughout the 1850s, and they were at the center of anti-German riots in Philadelphia, Cincinnati, Columbus, Ohio, Covington, Kentucky and Hoboken, New Jersey. The Turners' radical views, distinctive white uniforms and militaristic mass drill exercises made them obvious targets for nativist rowdies, particularly in the border states where the Turners' anti-slavery stance provided a further aggravation. But the Turners were not simply targets of anti-German gangs. Following Jahn's teachings, they engaged in physical training not as an end in itself, but as a means of preparing themselves to defend the principles of liberty and equality. To that end, the *Socialistische Turnerbund* recommended that all Turner societies possess arms in 1851, and in 1852 arranged for the publication of Franz Sigel's "Drill Regulations" in order to ensure that Turners received proper training.[5] As a result, Turners frequently played the role of security guards for their political allies. During the turmoil over the Kansas-Nebraska Act Turners ejected pro-slavery rowdies from a New York City protest meeting in 1854, Turners in Cincinnati and Boston served as security forces during speeches by abolitionist Wendell Phillips, and Turners in Leavenworth, Kansas fought against pro-slavery raiders during the Kansas conflict.[6]

The Civil War won the Turners a position of prominence in the German community. During the late 1850s the Turners had become increasingly active supporters of the new Republican Party because of its anti-slavery stance, and played an important role in leading significant numbers of urban German voters away from the Democrats during the 1860 election. With the threat of secession and war looming after the election, a number of Turner societies formed military units and began training in anticipation of the need to defend the Union. Their opportunities for action came quickly. Turners and other German volunteers helped to save St. Louis at the outset of the war by holding the federal arsenal and capturing Fort Jackson from a pro-Confederate militia. Turner companies in Chicago and Washington provided bodyguards for President Lincoln, and a company of Baltimore Turners rushed to Washington to help defend the city. In retaliation for this last action, Confederate sympathizers looted the Baltimore Turner hall and the adjoining offices of the Turner national newspaper, the Turn-Zeitung. Throughout the country, Turners were among the first to volunteer for military service. More than two-thirds of Turners in America served in the Union Army, compiling a distinguished record of military service. Regiments such as the 20th New York and the 9th Ohio, made up principally of Turners, suffered heavy casualties during the war but earned their members a reputation for discipline and courage. Many German troops saw action under Forty-Eighters who had received military training in Germany and were now active in the Turner movement. Friedrich Hecker raised the 24th and 82nd Illinois Regiments,

August Willich commanded the 32nd Indiana, and Franz Sigel, after leading the Turners in St. Louis, ultimately rose to the rank of major general. The demands of the war depleted the memberships of most Turner societies, and some, such as the Indianapolis *Socialistische Turngemeinde*, suspended operations entirely during the war. In other cases, though, enough members remained for the societies to continue operations and, in the case of the Chicago Turngemeinde, even open a new hall during the war years.[7]

Although the Turners built their reputation on their staunch defense of the Union, there were also Turner societies in the South whose members had to reach accommodation with slavery and secession. By the mid-1850s Turner societies were active in Richmond, Charleston, New Orleans, Mobile, Houston and other towns in the South and Texas where German immigrants had settled. Although most of these societies had Forty-Eighter connections, they found that the political climate in the South made it impossible for them to take the strong anti-slavery positions that dominated the thinking of Turners in the North. One of the few Turners who tried, Adolf Douai, founder of the San Antonio Turnverein and editor of the San Antonio Zeitung, was forced out of Texas in 1856 after several threats of mob violence against him. All of the Turner societies in the Deep South resigned from the national Turnerbund after it made opposition to slavery a central plank in its political platform in 1855. When the war came, Turner societies in New Orleans and Houston organized regiments to serve in the Confederate army.[8]

A national revival of the movement began in late 1864 behind the leadership of the New York and Baltimore Turnvereins, culminating in a national convention in Washington at the beginning of April 1865. The convention chose the politically neutral *Nordamerikanische Turnerbund* as a name for the revived organization, as opposed to the pre-war *Socialistische Turnerbund*, but the positions adopted by the national conventions over the next decades showed that the political fires were still very much alive among the Turner leadership. Immediately after the war the national convention endorsed the Reconstruction plan of the Republican Congress, including voting rights for ex-slaves, and in the early 1870s the convention debated voting and legal rights for women. Throughout the period the Turners were becoming increasingly concerned about the social conditions for industrial workers, culminating in a new statement of principles adopted at the 1878 convention in Cleveland calling for the government to protect industrial workers against exploitation and unsafe working and housing conditions, and for the prohibition of child labor in industrial work. In addition, the platform called for the breaking up of monopolies, the public ownership of utilities, and the adoption of the recall and referendum to provide for greater public oversight of government.[9]

In the 1878 platform the Turners also took a strong stand against laws which favored religion. These positions came out of the Turners' longstanding connections with the German Freethinkers, an antireligious movement that included many of the Forty-Eighters. Through their meetings and lectures, the Freethinkers advocated rationalism, science and history as the proper guides for living, and harshly criticized established religions for promoting superstition and bigotry. Connections between the Freethinkers and Turners were extensive for nearly a century. Freethinker articles were routinely published in the pre-Civil War Turn-Zeitung, and continued to be published in Turner newspapers until the demise of The American Turner in the early 1940s. Turner societies in Cleveland and Philadelphia co-sponsored programs with freethinker schools, and Turner societies throughout the country regularly hosted freethinker lecturers. The connections between the two groups were particularly strong at the national level. The owners and editors of the Freidenker Press in Milwaukee, Carl Doerflinger and C.H. Boppe, were active at the national level in the American Turnerbund in the late nineteenth century, and the Press handled most of the American Turnerbund's publishing from the mid-1880s until World War I, including the weekly Amerikanische Turnzeitung, the Turner national newspaper. From 1880 to 1900 the Freidenker Press also published an annual almanac for the Turners, the Turner-Kalendar, which included many Freethinker articles. Freethinkers also dominated the Turnerbund's governing board during the years 1898-1923 when the Indianapolis *Socialer Turnverein* served as the Turner national headquarters. Many of the leaders of the *Socialer Turnverein* also served on the national board during those years, and most of them had been members of the Indianapolis *Freidenker Verein*, a freethinker society active in the 1870s and 1880s. The *Socialer Turnverein* carried on the work of the *Freidenker Verein* by sponsoring freethinker lectures and a freethinker Sunday school for children into the 1910s.[10]

It is difficult to determine how accurately the political and philosophical positions of the national leadership reflected the thinking of individual Turners, but the regular reaffirmation and publication of the Turner political platform suggests that its progressive ideas were at least tolerated at most societies. Serious local political activism, though, seems to have been limited to a small number of societies, particularly those closely associated with the labor movement. The most militant of these societies were ones in Chicago and Milwaukee which attracted large numbers of working class immigrants active in the industrial labor movement. The Turnverein Milwaukee provided offices for the editor of Der Socialist in the late 1870s and later provided office space for the Social Democratic Party in the city, while the working class Southside Turnverein, known as the *'roter* (red) Turnverein' was closely involved with the Socialist Party.[11] In Chicago the Aurora Turnverein and the *Vorwärts* Turnverein were centers of labor organizing in the 1870s and 1880s. The Aurora Turnverein was particularly significant, hosting many meetings and rallies of the anarchist International Working Peoples Association, the *Lehr- und Wehr-Verein* and other union and radical groups. One of the Aurora Turnverein's leaders, August Spies, was editor of the Chicago Arbeiter-Zeitung and one of the leading speakers for the anarchist International Working Peoples Association. Along with Albert Parsons, he was also one of the radicals arrested and hanged as a result of the Haymarket bombing. The Aurora Turnverein raised money for his legal defense and for his family, marched *en masse* in his funeral procession and provided a chorus to sing at the gravesite. The *Vorwärts* Turnverein also regularly hosted union and radical meetings. In both 1877 and 1891 the hall was the scene of labor violence when the Chicago police attempted to break up meetings being held there.[12]

The radical societies were the exception, though. Most societies focused their energies on their athletic, social and cultural programs and considered politics as an area for debate rather than organized action. Whenever efforts were made to mobilize a society on behalf of a particular position, the result was frequently to split the organization. In Indianapolis the *Socialisticher Turngemeinde* expelled a quarter of its members in 1868 for opposing voting rights for ex-slaves. The expelled members formed a new society, and four years later the two groups rejoined under the name *Socialer Turnverein*, emphasizing that the society had changed from a political organization to a social one.[13] In a number of societies the Haymarket Affair exposed the growing tensions between the conservative middle class members and the working class union activists. A large group of members left the Aurora Turnverein in protest over its financial support for August Spies, and founded a new, social society, the Central Turnverein.[14] The opposite happened in Louisville, where virtually the entire athletic team quit the society in protest over its refusal to support the Haymarket defendants.[15]

Turner societies may have reduced their organized political activities by the late nineteenth century, but individual members still had strong convictions and were actively engaged in political affairs. During the late nineteenth and early twentieth centuries Turners were elected mayors in Kansas City, Milwaukee, St. Louis and other cities, Richard Bartholdt of St. Louis and the socialist Victor Berger of Milwaukee were elected to Congress, and Turners routinely served in state legislatures, city councils and school boards. Moreover, the Turners did not abandon organized political activity when vital interests were at stake. Throughout the late nineteenth century the Turners collaborated with other German-American organizations to fight Temperance laws, Sabbath-Day laws and other attempts to restrict the German way of life. The Turners also took an interest in foreign affairs, particularly when people of Germanic origin were involved. In 1902 the national executive board raised funds for the relief of the Boers in South Africa and corresponded with Clara Barton of the American Red Cross about the failure of the Red Cross to participate in such relief efforts.[16]

The field in which the Turners had their greatest influence on the non-German community was physical education. At the core of the Turner philosophy is the belief that physical fitness is essential to an active and productive life. Accordingly, gymnastic and exercise programs have been central parts of the Turner movement since the founding of the first societies. Even in the politically active years of the 1850s, the Turners held annual athletic competitions called *Turnfests*, published articles in the Turn-Zeitung on gymnastic exercises, and sponsored the publication of a gymnastics training manual, Das Turnen (1853) by New York Turner instructor Eduard Müller. After the Civil War, gymnastics took on an increasing prominence in Turner affairs. The national Turnfests grew in size and stature, so that by the beginning of the twentieth century they were attracting several thousand competitors and turning into grand social occasions marked by parades, receptions, and musical and theatrical performances . During the 1850s most societies offered gymnastics for young men, but these were gradually expanded after the Civil War to include programs for boys and girls, older men (known as *Bären*, or Bears) and adult women. The Turners were among the first organizations in the country to offer athletic training for women. The Louisville Turngemeinde had a women's class as early as 1871, and most other societies started classes over the following twenty years.[17]

Because of the importance of their physical training programs to the success of the societies, the Turners saw the need to have professionally-trained instructors in charge of the programs. During the 1850s there was discussion at the national level of the need for a school to train gymnastics instructors, and the national Turnerbund made the establishment of an instructors' school a priority at the April 1865 convention. The school opened in November 1866 as the *Turnlehrer-Seminar* in New York City under the direction of the New York Turnverein. The school moved to Milwaukee in 1874 and to Indianapolis in 1907 where it operated as the Normal College of the American Gymnastic Union until 1941, when it was acquired by Indiana University. Because of the school, most of the larger societies had professionally-trained instructors by the late nineteenth century who were able to expand and upgrade their gymnastic programs.[18]

As early as the 1865 national convention the Turners had called for physical education to become a standard part of the public school curriculum, and during the following years they played leading roles on the local and state levels to accomplish this goal. When Ohio made physical education compulsory in the public schools in the early 1890s, for example, the legislation was written by Anton Leibold, a Turner instructor, and introduced by legislator John Molter, a member of the Sandusky Turnverein. Kansas City adopted physical education for its public schools in 1885 through the leadership of Turner instructor Carl Betz, and Indianapolis introduced physical education in the public schools in the 1890s while Turners Clemens Vonnegut and John P. Frenzel served on the city's school board. In many cities the school districts' physical education programs were designed and directed by people who had been trained at the Turner Normal College or who were working as instructors in local Turner societies, such as Henry Suder in Chicago, William Stecher in Philadelphia, Carl Betz in Kansas City and Curt Toll in Indianapolis. Even as late as the 1950s, the directors of physical education programs in New York, Chicago, St. Louis, Los Angeles and other cities had received their training at the Turners' Normal College.[19]

Beginning in the mid-1880s, the Turner movement experienced an extraordinary growth in membership and facilities. In 1880 the national membership was approximately 13,000, only slightly larger than it had been on the eve of the Civil War, and was spread among 186 societies. Over the next decade the Turnerbund more than tripled in size, reaching a high point of 42,000 in 1893, with most of the growth coming in the late 1880s and early 1890s. The dramatic growth in membership was the result of the growth and maturation of the German communities in American cities by 1890. More than four million German immigrants came to the United States between the early 1840s and the severe depression of 1893 that ended large-scale German immigration. Turner societies clearly benefitted from this influx of Germans, but even in the period of most rapid growth, most of their new members were people who had been in the United States long enough to have become settled and acquire citizenship. This was true for the urban working class societies, as well. The percentage of non-citizens among the memberships of the Aurora and *Vorwärts*

Turnvereins in Chicago, for example, was never higher than twenty-five percent, and dropped to below ten percent by the mid-1890s.[20]

       The growth and prosperity of both the German communities and the Turner societies produced a building boom in Turner halls as most societies built their largest facilities during the years between 1885 and World War I. Many of the Turner halls built during the late nineteenth century served not just as meeting places and gymnasia for the Turners, but also as cultural and political centers for the local German community. In Chicago, for example, the Aurora Turner Hall was the largest public facility in the German neighborhoods of the northwest side during the 1870s and 1880s, and as a result it was in constant use for neighborhood meetings, labor rallies, plays, concerts, balls and banquets sponsored by various German organizations in the city.[21] In Indianapolis the Socialer Turnverein sponsored the building of a community center for the city's Germans in the 1890s. The building, known as *Das Deutsche Haus* (now on the National Register of Historic Places) included a restaurant, theater, ballroom and meeting rooms for numerous other German-American organizations, including the German-English School Society, the *Musikverein*, the German-American Veterans Society, the German Ladies Aid Society and the *Deutsche Klub*.[22]

       World War I provoked a crisis for the Turners, as it did for most German-American organizations. During the first years of the war the national Turnerbund collaborated with other German-American organizations in lobbying the United States government to maintain a strict neutrality toward the combatants. In a circular issued in both German and English in the fall of 1914, the Turnerbund's National Executive Committee condemned governments on both sides as being responsible for the war, and urged the American government to treat them in an even-handed way. At the same time, many individual Turners had personal ties to people in Germany and Austria that made them anxious to relieve the suffering of civilians in those countries. In the same 1914 circular, the National Executive Committee announced a national drive for money and supplies to help refugees, widows and orphans in Germany, and over the following two years many individual Turner societies sponsored similar fund raising efforts.[23] Once the United States entered the war, however, Turners strongly supported the American military effort, and the national organization pointed to the low rejection rate of Turner army recruits as proof of their patriotism and the value of the Turner way of life. Nonetheless, the powerful anti-German propaganda put extraordinary pressures on the Turners and other German-American organizations to prove their loyalty. Many Turner societies came under the surveillance of local, state and national authorities. The Portland, Oregon, Turnverein received regular visits from a federal Bureau of Investigation agent throughout most of 1917, and the Hartford, Connecticut, Turnverein was searched by federal agents investigating reports that crates of weapons were being carried into the Turner hall (they were actually crates of beer).[24] In many cities German organizations abandoned the use of the German language and adopted English names in an effort to show their commitment to the United States. In Indianapolis, for example, the Socialer Turnverein changed the name of its home from *Das Deutsche Haus* to the Athenaeum, and the *Unabhängigen Turnverein* became the Hoosier Athletic Club. World War I has often been thought of as the point at which connections were broken between German-

Americans and their home countries, but in fact the Turners quickly reestablished ties following the war. From 1919 to 1921 the national Turnerbund raised more than $18,000 for German relief, and individual societies undertook their own relief activities as well. The Women's Auxiliary of the Athenaeum Turners, for example, helped to support orphanages and children's hospitals in Germany through the early 1920s.[25]

The American Turners came through the anti-German hysteria of World War I surprisingly intact. Membership had dropped from the pre-war levels, but only by a bit more than ten percent, from 39,000 in 1917 to 34,000 in 1920. The number of societies affiliated with the Turnerbund dropped by about fifteen percent during the war years, from 214 to 186, but this is only a slightly accelerated version of the process of society consolidations and dis-affiliations that had been going on since the mid-1890s and would continue well into the 1950s. The Germanness and the political radicalism of the organization were still in evidence, but both were clearly waning as the membership became increasingly assimilated and apolitical. The national convention proceedings and the Amerikanische Turnzeitung continued to be issued in German into the 1930s, but the proceedings were also issued in English after 1921 and the Turnzeitung ran an increasing number of English-language articles during the 1920s. Language usage at the local level varied considerably from society to society, with some being predominately English even before World War I, and others maintaining German dominance until World War II. The most prominent of the latter was the New York Turnverein, which in 1940 issued its 90th anniversary publication in German. For most societies, though, the language transition came during the late 1910s and early 1920s and was the result of both external pressure to demonstrate loyalty to the United States and internal pressure to abandon impediments to active membership by the growing number of non-German speaking members. Politically the national organization continued its official support for progressive social and political reforms and its opposition to Prohibition, Sunday blue laws and other constraints on German-American life. The lifestyle issues were clearly of interest to most Turners, but the political platform appears to have been an active concern of only a small number of societies, principally the Milwaukee Turners who were closely associated with the Social Democratic Party, and the Pittsburgh Turnverein, which had responsibility for the national headquarters from 1923 to 1937. The president of the American Turnerbund during the Pittsburgh years was George Seibel, director of the Carnegie Library in Pittsburgh and a contributor of articles to The Progressive and other left-wing publications. Outside of the national leadership, though, Turner societies were involved in very little political or pro-labor activity.[26]

The 1920s are generally considered to be the beginning of the decline of the Turners, but in fact these were prosperous years for many societies. Total national membership stabilized in the low 30,000s through the end of the decade. The number of societies continued to decline, but this reflected the closing or merging of small societies that lacked the facilities and resources to be competitive with the larger Turner societies, the YMCAs and other sports organizations. Many Turner societies became leading social clubs in their cities. The Philadelphia Turngemeinde was the largest, with a membership of more than two thousand and a calendar of social and cultural events that attracted the families of many successful businessmen. Societies in other cities may have had smaller memberships, but this was often the result of a conscious decision to limit the number of members. Prohibition has sometimes been cited as contributing to the decline of Turner societies, but anecdotal evidence indicates that at least some societies may have attracted members during those years because of their ability to circumvent the anti-liquor laws. The Turner influence in physical education was also at its high point during the 1920s. The enrollments at the Turner Normal College were at their peak, and Normal College graduates occupied positions of leadership in school physical education departments and city recreation programs throughout the country. Turner instructors William Stecher of Philadelphia and Emil Rath of the Normal College were among the most prolific of writers on physical education, and their ideas were promoted in the Turner-sponsored physical education journal, Mind and Body. The 1920s were also the beginning of a thirty-year period in which Turner-trained athletes appeared regularly on the United States Olympic teams, principally on the gymnastics squads.[27]

The most difficult time for the Turner movement was not World War I and its aftermath, but the Depression and World War II. Between 1929 and 1944 the organization lost more than one-third of its members and one-third of its societies, with most of the membership loss coming in the first few years of the Depression. The economic troubles were succeeded by political ones as the Nazi rise to power in Germany re-awakened anti-German sentiment in America. In order to remove any question of loyalty, the American Turnerbund changed its name to the American Turners in 1938, followed by conversion of most remaining 'Turnvereins' and 'Turngemeindes' into 'Turners' by the time the United States entered World War II. In spite of the name changes and a distinguished record of military service, the Internal Revenue Service investigated the American Turners as a potential enemy sympathizer and revoked its tax-exempt status.[28] As the war neared its end, the leadership of the American Turners held a meeting in Detroit to discuss the future of the organization. The central theme of the discussion was the issue of identity, for it had become clear that an organization that celebrated its German origins and socialist principles could no longer be successful in the United States. In 1948 the American Turners adopted a new set of principles, one that had abandoned calls for specific social reforms in favor of general statements supporting liberty and equality and emphasizing the athletic, cultural and social programs of the Turners.[29]

The Turners made a recovery during the late 1940s and 1950s. The membership rose to 25,000 in 1950 as societies attracted members through a combination of sports programs and social activities. The Turners continued to have strong gymnastics programs, as demonstrated by their success in placing a number of Turner-trained gymnasts on the 1956 U.S. Olympic team. By the 1960s, though, declining fortunes were unmistakable. The institution of rigid eligibility requirements for high school athletes in most states deprived private clubs like the Turners of their best athletes, and increasing competition with the better-equipped YMCAs and private sports clubs made it difficult for many societies to attract new members. Many societies were also burdened with the grand Turner halls built at the beginning of the century, but which were now located in undesirable neighborhoods and imposed crushing maintenance and utilities costs on the societies. By the early 1990s, the total membership had dropped to about 13,000 in sixty societies, and many of those societies are small, social ones that offer few programs and may not survive another generation. A number of societies, though, such as those in South Bend, St. Paul, Louisville and Kansas City, have been successful in making a break with the past by becoming more sports-oriented and building new facilities in the suburbs. With their continued success, the Turners show signs of prospering well into the next century.

NOTES

1.   For an overview of the Turner movement in Germany, see Horst Ueberhorst, Turner unterm Sternenbanner: Der Kampf der deutsch-amerikanischen Turner für Einheit, Freiheit und Soziale Gerechtigkeit (München: Heinz Moos, 1978) and Ralf Wagner, "Turner societies and the Socialist tradition," in German workers' culture in the United States, 1850 to 1920, ed. by Hartmut Keil (Washington: Smithsonian Institution Press, 1988). For a biography of Jahn in English, see Ueberhorst's Friedrich Ludwig Jahn, 1778-1978 (Bonn-Bad Godesberg: Inter Nations, 1978).

2.   Robert Knight Barney, "America's first Turnverein: commentary in favor of Louisville, Kentucky," Journal of Sport History, 11, no. 1 (1984): 134-137; Stanley Nadel, Little Germany: ethnicity, religion, and class in New York City, 1845-80, (Urbana, IL: University of Illinois Press, 1990), p.120; K.B. Wamsley, "A home in the South: the Turners of Galveston, Texas, 1840-1865," in Ethnicity and sport in North American history and culture, ed. by George Eisen and David K. Wiggins (Westport, CT: Greenwood Press, 1994).

3.   There is an extensive literature on the Forty-Eighters in the United States. Much appeared during the late nineteenth century, often in the form of memoirs or in articles in contemporary German-American historical journals, notably Der Deutsche Pionier and the Deutsch-Amerikanische Geschichtsblätter. The most comprehensive work on the Forty-Eighters is Carl Wittke's Refugees of revolution: the German Forty-Eighters in America (Philadelphia: University of Pennsylvania Press, 1952. Also useful from that period is Adolf Zucker's The Forty-Eighters: political refugees of the German revolution of 1848 (New York: Columbia University Press, 1950). More recent works are Bruce Levine's The Spirit of 1848: German immigrants, labor conflict, and the coming of the Civil War (Urbana, IL: University of Illinois Press, 1992) which focuses on the Forty-Eighters during the 1850s, and the collection of essays edited by Charlotte Brancaforte, The German Forty-Eighters in the United States (New York: Peter Lang, 1989) which shows the range of Forty-Eighter activities. On the Turners in the United States, the only recent full-length scholarly works are in German: Horst Ueberhorst's Turnen unterm Sternenbanner and Ralf Wagner's Ph.D. dissertation Zwischen Tradition und Fortschritt: Zur gesellschafts-politischen und kulturellen Entwicklung der deutsch-amerikanischen Turnbewegung am Beispiel Milwaukees und Chicagos, 1850-1920, Ludwig-Maximilians Universität, München, 1988. The best

overviews in English are the chapters on the Turners in Wittke's and Zucker's works on the Forty-Eighters, Wagner's "Turner societies and the Socialist tradition," and Robert Knight Barney's "Forty-Eighters and the rise of the Turnverein movement in America," in Ethnicity and sport in North American history and culture, pp.20-41. The American Turners published an official history in 1911, Henry Metzner's A brief history of the North American Gymnastic Union (Indianapolis: North American Gymnastic Union, 1911). This work is a reprint and translation of Metzner's 1874 history of the Turners in the United States. New editions of this work were issued in 1924, 1974 and 1989 (See entries **N202-N205**).

4.   Levine, Spirit of 1848, especially pp. 91-93; Wagner, Zwischen Tradition und Fortschritt.

5.   Wagner, "Turner societies and the Socialist tradition," p.229

6.   Levine, Spirit of 1848, p.163; Metzner, A brief history of the American Turnerbund, 2nd ed. (Pittsburgh: American Turnerbund, 1924), pp.13-19.

7.   For the Forty-Eighters' and Turners' service in the Civil War, see Wittke, Refugees of revolution, chapter 16 "In defense of the Union," pp.221-243.

8.   For Turners in the South, see Robert Knight Barney, "German -American Turnvereins and socio-politico-economic realities in the Antebellum and Civil War upper and lower South," Stadion 10 (1984): 135-181; Mary Lou LeCompte, "German-American Turnvereins in frontier Texas, 1851-1880," Journal of the West 26 (1987): 18-25; and Wamsley, "A home in the South: the Turners of Galveston, Texas, 1840-1865."

9.   See Offizielles Protokoll der Tagsatzung des Nord-Amerikanischen Turnerbundes for 1878.

10. For the Freethinkers, see Wittke, Refugees of revolution, chapter 10 "Freethinkers and personal liberty," pp.122-146, and Bettina Goldberg, "*Deutsch-Amerikanische Freidenker in Milwaukee 1877-1890: Organization und gesellschaftspolitische Orientierung*," (*Staatsarbeit, Ruhr Universität Bochum*, 1982). For Indianapolis, see the minutes of the Freidenker Verein, Athenaeum Turners Collection, IUPUI Special Collections.

11. See Wagner, Zwischen Tradition und Fortschritt; also anniversary books for the Milwaukee Turners, particularly the fiftieth anniversary book, Goldenes Jubiläum des Turnvereins Milwaukee, 1853-1903, and the ninetieth anniversary book, 90 Years of Service: 1853-1943.

12. Keil, Hartmut and John Jentz, German workers in Chicago: a documentary history of working-class culture from 1850 to World War I, (Urbana, IL: University of Illinois Press, 1988), especially pp.166-168 on the Aurora Turnverein, and pp.231-233 and 362-371 on the *Vorwärts* Turnverein.

13. Stempfel, Theodor, Fünfzig Jahre unermüdlichen Deutschen Strebens in Indianapolis (Indianapolis: Pitts & Smith, 1898); an English translation was published by the German-American Center and the Indiana German Heritage Society in 1991.

14. Keil and Jentz, German workers in Chicago, p.167.

15. M.M. Kling, "A Reminiscence," The Turner 2, no.8 (October 1917): 8. The Turner was the magazine of the Louisville Turngemeinde.

16. See the American Turnerbund's annual report (*Jahresbericht*) for the year 1901/1902, p.xxxi; Boer War Files, Athenaeum Turners Collection, IUPUI Special Collections.

17. Barney, "Forty-Eighters and the rise of the Turnverein movement," pp.30-37.

18. For the history of the *Turnlehrer Seminar* and Normal College, see Emil Rinsch, History of the Normal College of the American Gymnastic Union of Indiana University, 1866-1966 (Bloomington: Indiana University, 1966).

19. Rinsch, History of the Normal College, pp.146-149; Walter C. Eberhardt, The American Turners: their history, philosophy, and contributions to American democracy (Bloomington: Indiana University, 1955), 16 p.

20. See the statistical sections of the American Turnerbund's annual reports for the years 1880-1900.

21. Keil, German workers' culture, p.47.

22. For a contemporary description of the building and its purposes, see Stempfel, Fünfzig Jahre.

23. "To the Members of the North American Gymnastic Union, Greetings," [1914], Athenaeum Turners Collection, IUPUI Special Collections; for examples of fundraising for German relief at the local level, see the programs for events in Wilmington, Delaware (**De4**) and in Davenport, Iowa (**Ia5**).

24. Records of the Bureau of Investigation, Files 80140 and 19524, National Archives.

25. See the American Turnerbund's annual reports for 1919/1920 and 1920/1921; and file of postcards from Germany to the Women's Auxiliary, Athenaeum Turners Collection, IUPUI Special Collections.

26. See the American Turnerbund's annual reports for the 1920s.

27. See list of Turner Olympians in History of the American Turners (Louisville: American Turners, 1989).

28. See American Turnerbund's annual reports for the 1930s; minutes of the National Executive Committee of the American Turnerbund, American Turners Collection, IUPUI Special Collections.

29. Minutes of the American Turners Round Table Conference held at Detroit, Michigan on January 22 and 23, 1944, American Turners Collection, IUPUI Special Collections; Proposed revised principles and statutes of the American Turners [1948].

Chapter 1

National Publications
and Historical Records

ARCHIVAL COLLECTIONS

N1   American Turners Collection, 1855-present. 38.5 linear feet.
Finding aid available from repository.
Location: Indiana University-Purdue University Indianapolis.
Description: The American Turners records include minutes of the National Council (*Bundesvorort*), 1858-1978 (incomplete); financial records, 1866-1970s; officers' correspondence and papers, 1872-1923; two letter books of correspondence on the reorganization of the Turnerbund following the Civil War, 1864-1868; correspondence with council members and societies, 1927-1980s; correspondence and papers relating to physical education, 1920s-1970s; news releases, 1951-1970; papers relating to Turner sporting events and national festivals, 1913-1987; investigation files, 1938-1942, concerning involvements of Turner members or societies with pro-German activities; Turner pioneer records, 1924-1943; and women's auxiliary records, 1921-1976.

N2   Carl May Wiedeman Papers, 1921-1972. 4 boxes.
Location: University of Michigan, Bentley Historical Library.
Description: Carl Wiedeman was national president of the American Turners from 1937 to 1952, member of the 73rd Congress and a federal judge. The papers include three Turner scrapbooks with newspaper clippings from 1936-1937 and 1948-1949 and information on the 1948 commemorative stamp and the Turners' 100th anniversary celebrations; address by the U.S. Secretary of Commerce Charles Sawyer before the 100th anniversary celebration at the Francis Field Stadium, St. Louis, and correspondence, 1959. For photographs see Carl May Wiedeman photograph series, ca. 1900-1970s.

ANNUAL REPORTS

The National Executive Committee (*Vorort*) began publishing annual reports as supplements to the Turnzeitung and as part of the convention proceedings in the mid-1850s. The first separately published annual reports seem to have been issued only after the Civil War, beginning with a half-year report in late 1865. Reports from the late 1860s and early 1870s were 4 to 8 pages in length and consisted primarily of narrative reports of the Turnerbund's activities and discussions of social issues of concern to the Turnerbund's members. The 1872 report, for example, consists almost entirely of a discussion of women's rights.

The National Executive Committee began issuing more substantial annual reports in 1880, and issued them continuously until 1966. From 1884 through 1941 the reports followed the Turnerbund's fiscal year of April 1 through March 31; from 1942 through 1966 the reports covered the calendar year. During World War II and after 1953, the reports were issued only every two years or longer.

The reports issued since 1880 typically included the following:

1. Report from the Executive Committee or President. This was an overview essay on the condition of the organization, and usually included information on membership, district and national festivals, the *Turnlehrer Seminar* and other educational programs. Through the 1930s the reports also discussed political issues of interest to Turners, such as prohibition, Sabbath-Day laws, working conditions, women's rights, immigration, and World War I. The reports were published in German through 1917/1918, and in English thereafter.

2. Report of the Technical Committee on regulations and standards for athletic events.

3. Report of the Cultural Committee, usually including debate and essay topics for the year and reporting on the development of local cultural programs.

4. Reports on the *Turnlehrer Seminar*/Normal College through 1941.

5. Treasurers' Reports.

6. Lists of gymnastics instructors.

7. Names and addresses of districts, societies and officers.

8. Statistical reports on societies and districts, published in tables. The number of categories of information requested by the national office varied from a low of sixteen in 1879/1880 to a high of forty-six in 1890/91. The reports contained statistics for each society on the numbers and types of members, the types of athletic and cultural programs offered, and the type and value of property owned by the society.

Publications

N3   Halbjahrs=Bericht des Vororts des Nord=Amerik. Turner=Bundes. n.p. [1865?]. 8 p.
Note: Prepared in the late fall of 1865. The half-year report describes the organization's activities and plans following the April 1865 reorganization, and

includes statistical information on the districts and societies belonging to the Turnerbund.
Location: InlU.

N4 Jahres-Bericht des Vorortes des Nordamerikanischen Turnerbundes: 1868-1919.
Note: Varies slightly in title. Reports for the years 1868, 1870, and 1872 were reprinted from the convention proceedings; no publication information found. Report for 1871 published by the Office of the Zukunft in Indianapolis; report for 1880 published by Doerflinger Book & Publishing Co. in Milwaukee; reports for 1884-1916 published by the Freidenker Publishing Co. in Milwaukee; reports for 1917-1918 published by the Turner Publishing Co. in Minneapolis.

N5 Annual Reports of the National Executive Committee: 1920-1966.
Note: Varies slightly in title; beginning in 1952 the reports were from the National Council. Issued by the American Gymnastic Union, 1920-1923; by the American Turnerbund, 1924-1938; and by the American Turners, 1939-1966. Reports for 1919-1923 published by the Turner Publishing Co., New Ulm, MN; remaining reports published by the American Turners in Pittsburgh (1924-1937), Detroit (1938-1955), and Rochester, NY (1957-1966).

Locations for Jahres-Berichte and Annual Reports:
> DLC: 1924, 1926, 1927.
> IaDP: 1948, 1952.
> In: 1902, 1906, 1914, 1917, 1919.
> InlU: 1868, 1870, 1871, 1872, 1880, 1884-1917, 1920-1966.
> OClWHi: 1923-1933.
> PPG: 1872-1884, 1899.
> WHi: 1939-1940, 1946-1950.
> WMCHi: 1890, 1891, 1895, 1907-1910, 1912, 1914, 1915, 1917, 1925, 1927, 1928.
> WMT: 1918, 1933, 1936-1938, 1940, 1947-1949, 1952, 1957, 1966.

NATIONAL CONVENTIONS

Turners held their first national convention in Philadelphia in 1850 and met every year through 1860. Between 1855 and 1859 the Turnerbund split into eastern and western sections and each held separate conventions. At the end of the Civil War, the Turnerbund was reorganized at an April 1865 convention in Washington, D.C., and since 1866 has met every other year. Convention minutes (*Tagsatzungs-Protokolle*) have been published by the national governing board (*Bundesvorort*) since at least the 1854 meeting. Minutes appeared in double- or triple-column newspaper format (approx. 9" x 11.75") until 1872, and in smaller pamphlet form from 1874 through

1964. The minutes were published exclusively in German through 1915, in both English and German to 1931, and exclusively in English since 1933.

The conventions are used to set policies and conduct the business of the American Turners. In the years prior to World War I, the conventions routinely debated and passed resolutions on social and political issues, ranging from slavery and the nativist movement in the 1850s, to women's rights, working conditions, and the elimination of church-inspired laws in the post-Civil War years. Since the 1930s the conventions have focused on the internal business of the organization and rarely addressed public issues.

Convention minutes have typically included reports and resolutions presented by the following committees:

1. Financial Committee. Reports on the organization's finances.

2. Cultural Committee. Reports on society libraries, Sunday Schools, German and English language classes, essay and cultural contests, and debating, dramatic and music clubs.

3. Publications Committee. Reports on the newspapers and magazines serving the national organization.

4. Committee on National Affairs. Prior to World War I this committee presented social and political issues for discussion. It has also been responsible for the business of the national organization, particularly the selection of Turnfest and convention sites.

5. Committee on Physical Education. Reports on issues relating to physical education instruction, teachers, exhibitions, and Turnfests. Through 1880 the committee was also responsible for oversight of the *Turnlehrer Seminar*.

6. Committee on the *Turnlehrer Seminar*/Normal College. Reports on the activities and finances of the school. It was active from 1882 to 1948.

7. Committee for Complaints and Appeals. The committee handled disputes involving more than one society or district. Reports included from 1874 to 1915.

8. Committee on Platform and Statutes. Reports on proposed revisions to the principles and regulations of the national organization.

9. Committee on Turner Youth Movement. Reports on programs designed to recruit children and teenagers. Reports included from 1935 to 1948.

Convention Proceedings

N6   Die Verhandlungen der Turner-Tagsatzung zu Pittsburgh, im Auszuge herausgegeben vom Vorort. n.p., [1854]. 6 p.
Note: Title from first page. Minutes of the national convention, held September 11-13, 1854 in Pittsburgh.
Location: InIU.

N7   Die Verhandlungen der Turner-Tagsatzung zu Buffalo, vom 24. bis 27. September 1855. Im Auszuge herausgegeben vom Vorort. Philadelphia: King and Braid, [1855]. 8 p.

Note: Title from first page. Includes "*Satzungen des socialistischen Turner-Bundes in Nord Amerika,*" the constitution and principles for the national organization.
Location: InIU; NN.

N8 Die 6. Tagsatzung des sozialistischen Turnerbundes von Nord-Amerika zu Pittsburg, Pa. vom 1. bis 5. September 1856. n.p. [1856]. 14 p.
Note: Title from first page.
Location: InIU; NN.

N9 Verhandlung der Turner Tagsatzung des sozialistischen Turnerbundes zu Washington, D.C.. n.p. [1856].
Note: Title given. Cited in Wagner, p. 338.

N10 Protokoll und Satzungen für den sozialistischen Turnerbund von Nord-Amerika. 7. Bundesjahr, vom 1. October 1857 bis 30 September 1858. Berathen und beschlossen auf der 7. Tagsatzung in Detroit, Mich., September 1857. Cincinnati: Office des Hochwächters, [1857]. 18 p.
Note: Title from cover. Title on first page: "*Die 7te. Tagsatzung des sozialistischen Turnerbundes von Nord Amerika zu Detroit, Mich. vom 4. bis 7. September, 1857.*"
Location: DLC; InIU (incomplete); NN.

N11 Verhandlungen der Turner Tagsatzung zu Paterson, N.J., vom 7. bis 11. September 1857, im Auszuge herausgegeben vom Vorort Williamsburgh. Williamsburgh, N.Y.: E. Röhr, 1857. 12 p.
Note: Title from first page. Convention was attended by delegates from fourteen societies in New York and New Jersey. Includes the constitution and principles of the *Socialistische Turnerbund* and a letter from the eastern societies to the *Socialistische Turnerbund* requesting that the next national convention be held in the east rather than in Indianapolis.
Location: DLC (incomplete).

N12 Die 8. Tagsatzung des sozialistischen Turnerbundes von Nord-Amerika zu Indianapolis, Ind., vom 4. bis 8. September 1858. [Cincinnati]: *Office des Hochwächters*, [1858]. 8 p.
Note: Title from first page.
Location: InIU; NN.

N13 Verhandlung der Turner Tagsatzung des sozialistischen Turnerbundes zu Bloomingdale, N.Y.. n.p. [1858].
Note: Title given. Cited in Wagner, p. 338.

N14 Offizielles Protokoll der 10. Tagsatzung des nordamerik. Turnerbundes, zu Chicago, Ill., vom 5. bis 9. September inclusive des Jahres 1859. n.p. [1859]. 16 p.

Note: Title from first page.
Location: InIU; NN.

N15   Verhandlung der Turner Tagsatzung des sozialistischen Turnerbundes zu Dubuque, Ia. n.p. [1859].
Note: Title given. Cited in Wagner, p. 338.

N16   Satzungen des nordamerikanischen Turnerbundes von 1860-61. Baltimore: W. Schnauffer (Baltimore Wecker), [1860]. 14 p.
Note: Title from first page. Convention minutes begin on page five under title *"Offizielles Protokoll der 11. Tagsatzung des nordamerikanischen Turnerbundes zu Rochester, N.Y. vom 30. Juli bis 12. August 1860."*
Location: InIU.

N17   Offizielles Protokoll der Beschlüsse, welche von der am 3. April 1865 in Washington D.C. zusammengetretenen Tagsatzung des Nord-Amerikanischen Turnerbundes angenommen wurden. n.p. [1865]. 3 p.
Note: Newspaper format (10.5" x 17"). Includes *"Protokoll der Tagsatzung des Nordamerikanischen Turnerbundes, 1-3 April, 1865"* and *"Platform und Statuten des nord=amerikanischen Turnerbundes."* The April 1865 convention re-established the North American Turnerbund following its period of dormancy during the Civil War.
Location: InIU; NN.

N18   Offizielles Protokoll der Verhandlungen der Tagsatzung des Nord-amerikanischen Turnerbundes. 1866-1872.
Note: Title varies, and includes the convention city, the meeting dates, and the number of the convention, beginning with no. 2 in 1866. The national convention was held every two years beginning in 1866. Through 1870 the publications contained minutes of the meetings and the annual report of the Executive Committee (*Vorort*). In 1872 the minutes also included statistical information on the societies and districts. The following minutes were issued:
    1866 (2nd), St. Louis, pub. by Adolf Frey, Cincinnati. 8 p.
    1868 (3rd), Boston, pub. by Fr. B. Teuthorn, Boston. 10 p.
    1870 (4th), Pittsburgh, pub. by the Volksblatt, Pittsburgh. 10 p.
    1872 (5th), Louisville, pub. by R. Gelpke, New York. 21 p.

N19   Offizielles Protokoll der Tagsatzung des Nord-Amerikanischen Turnerbundes. 1874-1921.
Note: Title varies, and includes convention city, meeting dates, and number of the convention. From 1884 through 1915, all convention proceedings were published by the Freidenker Publishing Company of Milwaukee. No convention was held in 1917 due to World War I.
    1874 (6th), Rochester, NY, pub. by Max Stern, Chicago. 40 p.

1876 (7th), New Ulm, MN, pub. by Justus Löhr, Chicago. 30 p.
1878 (8th), Cleveland, pub. by Hermann Zippe, Chicago. 28 p.
1880 (9th), Indianapolis, pub. by Doerflinger, Milwaukee. 38 p.
1882 (10th), Newark, pub. by Doerflinger, Milwaukee. 68 p.
1884 (11th), Davenport, IA, pub. by Freidenker Pub. Co., Milwaukee. 51 p.
1886 (12th), Boston. 52 p.
1888 (13th), Chicago. 88 p.
1890 (14th), New York. 80 p.
1892 (15th), Washington. 126 p.
1894 (16th), Denver. 48 p.
1896 (17th), Louisville. 49 p.
1898 (18th), San Francisco. 54 p.
1900 (19th), Philadelphia. 54 p.
1902 (20th), Davenport, IA, 40 p.
1904 (21st), Pittsburgh. Cited in Wagner, but no copies found.
1906 (22nd), Newark. 41 p.
1908 (23rd), Chicago. 43 p.
1910 (24th), St. Louis. (no copies found)
1912 (25th), Indianapolis. 67 p.
1915 (26th), San Francisco. 24 p.
1919 (27th), Louisville. (no copies found)
1921 (28th), Chicago, pub. by Turner Pub. Co., New Ulm, MN, 22 p.

N20   Official minutes of the convention of the American Turnerbund. 1923-1994.
Note: Title varies, and includes convention city, meeting dates, and number of the convention. The organization was known as the American Turnerbund through the 1938 meeting, and as the American Turners thereafter. The proceedings for 1925, 1927, and 1931 were issued in both English and German editions, with the German-language editions having the title "*Offizielles Protokoll der [no.] Tagsatzung des Amerikanischen Turnerbundes.*" The American Turnerbund/American Turners was responsible for publishing the proceedings, and no separate publisher was listed. The proceedings were published as printed pamphlets through 1964, and thereafter as packets of 8.5" x 11" mimeographed or photocopied pages.

1923 (29th), St. Louis. 22 p.
1925 (30th), Elkhart Lake, WI. 16 p.
1927 (31st), Cleveland. 16 p.
1929 (32nd), Philadelphia. 19 p.
1931 (33rd), Elkhart Lake, WI. 22 p.
1933 (34th), Elkhart Lake, WI. 23 p.
1935 (35th), Rochester, NY. 26 p.
1937 (36th), Los Angeles. 29 p.
1938 (37th), Detroit. 21 p.
1940 (38th), Elkhart Lake, WI. 32 p.
1942 (39th), Moline, IL. 26 p.
1944 (40th), Johnstown, PA. 32 p.

1946 (41st), Indianapolis. 40 p.
1948 (42nd), Lawrence, MA. 43 p.
1950 (43rd), New York. 53 p.
1952 (44th), Davenport, IA. . 52 p.
1954 (45th), Cleveland. 55 p.
1956 (46th), Louisville. 55 p.
1958 (47th), Kansas City. 43 p.
1960 (48th), Rochester, NY. 47 p.
1962 (49th), Toledo, OH. 34 p.
1964 (50th), New York. 33 p.
1966 (51st), Chicago. 62 p.
1968 (52nd), Buffalo. 51 p.
1970 (53rd), McKeesport, PA. 52 p.
1972 (54th), St. Louis. 51 p.
1974 (55th), Springfield, MA. 56 p.
1976 (56th), Moline, IL. 73 p.
1978 (57th), Louisville. 53 p.
1980 (58th), St. Louis. 56 p.
1982 (59th), Clinton, MA. 60 p.
1984 (60th), Monaca, PA. 45 p.
1986 (61st), South Bend, IN. 60 p.
1988 (62nd), Toledo, OH. 59 p.
1990 (63rd), South Bend, IN. 64 p.
1992 (64th), Aurora, IL. 36 p.
1994 (65th), Baltimore. 50 p.

Locations for Tagsatzungsprotokolle and Minutes:

DLC: 1866-1872.
IU: 1931 (English).
IaDP: 1950.
In: 1912.
InIU: 1866-1902, 1906, 1908, 1912, 1915, 1921-1994.
MnU: 1912.
MoSHi: 1931 (English), 1935, 1937, 1946, 1950, 1954, 1956.
NN: 1866-1872.
OClWHi: 1933.
WHi: 1882, 1890, 1892, 1935, 1937, 1940, 1946, 1948.
WMT: 1931 (German & English), 1937, 1938, 1942-1956, 1974, 1976,
    1984, 1986, 1990, 1992.

Convention Programs

Substantial convention programs began appearing on a regular basis in the late
1930s, and through the 1950s they normally included information about the history

and activities of the host society. In several cases the national convention was timed to coincide with the centennial anniversary celebration of the host society, with the result that the program doubled as the 100th anniversary publication of that society. After 1958 the programs only included advertising and schedules of events, and so have not been listed in the bibliography.

N21 Program, 27th National Convention, North American Gymnastic Union and Turntag Indiana District, June 22 - 25, 1919, Louisville, Ky. Louisville: Anzeiger, 1919. 155 p.
Note: Special issue of The Turner (newsletter of the Louisville Turners), vol. 4, no. 4, June 1919. Includes program for the 27th national convention and articles on physical education, the Turner movement, and the history of the Louisville Turners.
Location: InIU; Louisville Turners.

N22 The Detroiter Turner: the American Turners 37th National Convention Issue, July 1-2-3-4 1938. [Detroit]: n.p., 1938. 26 p.
Note: Includes a message from the president, program of events, photographs of the Detroit Turnverein, and lists of all national conventions and festivals.
Location: InIU; MoSHi.

N23 American Turners Thirty-Ninth National Convention, June 25th-June 28th, Moline Turner News. Moline: Moline Gazette, 1942. 24 p.
Note: Includes convention program and news of Moline Turners activities.
Location: InIU.

N24 American Turners, Fortieth National Convention, Johnstown Turnverein, Johnstown, Pennsylvania, June 29-30 and July 1-2, 1944. Johnstown: Schubert Press, 1944. 38 p.
Note: Includes convention program and brief historical sketch of the Turners in Johnstown.
Location: InIU.

N25 Forty-Second National Turner Convention, 1948, Lawrence, Massachusetts. Lawrence: Eagle-Tribune, 1948. [44 p.]
Note: Includes convention program and brief history of the Lawrence Turnverein.
Location: InIU.

N26 One Hundredth Anniversary, 1852-1952, 44th National Convention, Central Turners, Davenport, Iowa. n.p., 1952. 112 p.
Note: One hundredth anniversary publication of the Davenport Central Turners and program for the national convention. Includes detailed history and photographs of the Central Turners.
Location: InIU.

N27 Souvenir Program, the Kansas City Turners Centennial and 47th National Convention of the American Turners, Kansas City, Mo., June 29-July 2, 1958. n.p., 1958. 39 p.
Note: Includes convention program, history and photographs of the Kansas City Turners, and list of national conventions and festivals.
Location: InIU; MoSHi; WMT.

Women's Auxiliary Convention Proceedings

The Women's Auxiliary of the American Turners was organized at the Louisville convention in 1919 to unite local auxiliaries and cooperate with the American Turnerbund. The auxiliary established a scholarship fund, later transformed into a student loan fund, to provide financial assistance to students of the Turner Normal College. Other projects included raising funds for banners and flags, cottages at Camp Brosius, furniture and books for the women's dormitory at the Normal College, and for the Instructors and Leaders courses. Auxiliary members were also active in the Red Cross, contributing their time and money to relief work. In 1921 the women's auxiliaries began to hold national conventions alongside the American Turnerbund's conventions. The Women's Auxiliary convention minutes were published separately until 1966 when they began to be included in the American Turners convention minutes.

N28 Official Proceedings of the Biennial Convention of the Ladies Auxiliary of the American Turnerbund. 1921-1964(?).
Note: Title varies, and normally includes the number, date, and location of the convention.
Locations:
    InIU: 1938, 1948, 1956.
    Dayton Liederkranz Turners: 1927.

NATIONAL COUNCIL MEETING MINUTES

N29 American Turners, National Council Meeting, 1971-1994.
Note: Title varies. Mimeographed or photocopied pages, bound together. Typically consists of about sixty pages of the minutes of the annual National Council meeting, held in the fall.
Location: InIU.

NATIONAL DIRECTORIES AND STATISTICS

N30 American Turners, Directory and Statistics of National, Districts, Societies.

1970-1993.
Note: Title varies. Issued every other year, except for mid-1970s when it was issued annually. Issued in printed, mimeographed, or photocopied formats. Includes names and addresses of national, district, and society officers and addresses of Turner societies. Through the 1970s the directories also included statistical information on individual societies.
Location: InIU.

NATIONAL CONSTITUTIONS AND BY-LAWS

The national constitutions and by-laws *(Grundsätze und Forderungen)* laid out both the principles of the movement and the governing rules for the organization. These documents have changed dramatically since the 1850s, reflecting the transformation of the politically-engaged *Sozialistischer Turnerbund* of the mid-nineteenth century into the sports-minded American Turners of the last fifty years. In the 1854 statement of principles the Turnerbund announced its support for radical social, political, and religious reforms in general, and its opposition to slavery, temperance laws, and anti-immigration activities in particular. The Turnerbund's principles continued to be heavily political throughout the late nineteenth century, with the Turnerbund taking positions in support of the eight-hour day, progressive income taxes, the defense of the environment, and the strict separation of church and state, among other issues. Although the Turnerbund became less radical and politically active in the twentieth century, the fundamental principles continued to support progressive political positions into the late 1940s. By 1951 the American Turners had eliminated all political statements from their principles.

The following is a list of the separately published constitutions and by-laws for the national Turnerbund. Constitutions were also published in the convention minutes as early as the mid-1850s, and they were included in printed society and district constitutions, as required by a resolution passed at the 1872 national convention.

N31   Platform und Statuten des Nordamerikanischen Turnerbundes, nebst einem Anhang, enthaltend die Turnfestordnung, sowie das Reglement für das Turnlehrerseminar. [Angenommen im Juni 1886 in Boston]. n.p., [1886]. 29 p.
Note: Constitution, Turnfest rules and regulations for the *Turnlehrer Seminar*, adopted in Boston in 1886.
Location: In.

N32   Platform, Principielle Beschlüsse und Statuten des Nordamerikanischen Turnerbundes. St. Louis: Grassmee Printing Co., 1892. 16 p.
Note: Cover title: *"Angenommen und amendirt durch die im Juni 1892 in Washington, D.C., abgehaltene fünfzehnte Bundestagsatzung."* Statutes and by-laws

were also published by the Freidenker Publishing Company in Milwaukee in the same year.
Location: InIU.

N33   Grundsätze und Forderungen des Nord-Amerikanischen Turnerbundes angenommen von der 19. Tagsatzung abgehalten in Philadelphia, Pa., am 17., 18., 19., und 20. Juli 1900. n.p., [1900]. 31 p.
Location: IaHi.

N34   Grundsätze und Forderungen des Nord-Amerikanischen Turnerbundes. Milwaukee: Freidenker Publishing Co., 1900. 37 p.
Location: InIU.

N35   Allgemeine Grundsätze des Nord-Amerikanischen Turnerbundes angenommen am 28., 29. und 30. Juni 1908. n.p., [1908].
Note: Cited in Pochmann # X7744 c.

N36   Statutes of the North American Gymnastic Union, May 1909. n.p., [1909]. 30 p.
Location: InIU.

N37   Allgemeine Grundsätze und Statuten des Nord-Amerikanischen Turnerbundes, Januar 1915. n.p., [1915]. 32 p.
Location: InIU.

N38   Allgemeine Grundsätze und Statuten des Amerikanischen Turnerbundes, 1919. n.p., [1919]. 32 p.
Location: InIU; MnHi.

N39   Principles and Statutes of the American Turnerbund, 1924. n.p., [1924]. 31 p.
Location: InIU; WHi.

N40   Principles and Statutes of the American Turnerbund, 1926. n.p., [1926]. 31 p.
Location: MnHi; OH.

N41   Fundamental Principles, American Turnerbund. Pittsburgh: National Executive Committee, [1930]. [6 panel brochure]
Location: InIU.

N42   Principles and Statutes of the American Turnerbund. n.p., [1931]. 30 p.
Location: WHi.

N43   Principles and Statutes of the American Turnerbund, October 1935. n.p., [1935]. 32 p.
Location: InIU; MnHi; WHi; WMT.

N44   Principles and Statutes of the American Turners, 1941. n.p., [1941]. 29 p.
Location: InIU; WM.

N45   Principles and Statutes of the American Turners, revised 1942. n.p., [1942].
Location: WM.

N46   Principles and Statutes of the American Turners, 1947. n.p., [1947]. 28 p.
Location: InIU.

N47   Proposed Revised Principles and Statutes of the American Turners. n.p., [1948]. 29 p.
Location: InIU.

N48   Principles and Statutes of the American Turners, 1951. n.p., [1951]. 40 p.
Location: InIU; MnHi.

N49   Principles and Statutes of the American Turners. Revised 1957. Detroit: American Turners, 1957. 39 p.
Location: InIU.

N50   Principles and Statutes of the American Turners. Revised August 1972. Rochester, N.Y.: American Turners, 1972. 41 p.
Location: CSDHi; InIU; WM.

N51   Principles and Statutes of the American Turners. Revised August 1976. Rochester, N.Y.: American Turners, 1976. 41 p.
Location: InIU; WMT.

N52   Procedural Guide. An extension of the statutes of the American Turners. Reprinted 1984. n.p., [1984]. 7 p.
Location: WMT (Wiedemann Collection).

Statutes and By-laws of the Women's Auxiliary

N53   Constitution and By-Laws of the Women's Auxiliary of the American Turners. Organized June 24, 1921 at Louisville, Ky. n.p., [1946]. 23 p.
Location: InIU.

N54   Constitution and By-Laws of the Women's Auxiliary of the American Turners. n.p., [1946]. 12 p.
Location: InIU.

Statutes and Principles of the American Boy Turners

The American Boy Turners was organized in 1933 as a youth group for boys between the ages of 10 and 18 years. The group's purposes were to teach Turner principles to boys and young men and to encourage future membership in the American Turners. The by-laws outline the group's rules and administrative structure.

N55   A.B.T. Principles and Statutes of the American Boy Turners of the American Turnerbund. n.p., 1933. 16 p.
Note: Cover title: "(Motto) F.F.S.T. Freedom, Friendship, Strength, Truth."
Location: InIU.

NATIONAL TURNFEST PUBLICATIONS

Since 1851 national Turnfests have played an important role in the Turner movement, giving members the opportunity to display their skills, compete, and socialize with fellow Turners around the country. The first Turnfest was held in Philadelphia in 1851, only one year after the *Sozialistische Turnerbund* was founded. Teams from most societies were sent to participate in the event and exhibit their physical exercises. From 1852 to 1860 Turnfests were celebrated annually both in the western and eastern parts of the country. After the Civil War the Turnerbund decided to hold Turnfests every two years to ease the financial burden on hosting societies, and in 1881 the interval was changed to every four years. Although women were allowed to participate in the exhibition performances as early as 1893 it was not until 1921 that women were admitted to the competitions.

For each festival the host society and the national office published a wide variety of materials publicizing or commemorating the event, establishing rules for the competitions, and providing schedules, songs and other information needed during the event. The period from the 1880s through the 1920s saw the most substantial publications, many of which contained lengthy essays on the histories of the Turner societies and the German element in the host cities, and large numbers of illustrations of the Turner societies and festival events. For the 1893, 1896, 1900, and 1917 Turnfests the host societies also published monthly newspapers, or *Turnfest-Zeitungen*, beginning a year before the event. The newspapers publicized the event, the host city and the host societies, and contained schedules, competition rules and other information about the event. Festival publications have been limited to programs since the 1960s.

Archival Collection

N56   Louisville Turnfest Collection, 1926. 150 black and white photographs.
Location: University of Louisville, Photographic Archives, Ekstrom Library.
Description: The collection contains 150 black and white photographs taken during
the 33rd National Turnfest in Louisville in 1926.

Publications

N57   Chicagoer Turngemeinde. Geschichte der Turnerei, bis zum 17. Bundes-
Turnfest, abgehalten zu Chicago, Ill., vom 7.-11. Aug. 1869. Chicago: Abendzeitung,
1869. 68 p.
Note: Cited in Pochmann, # X3794 a.

N58   Wegweiser für das 22. Bundes Turnfest des Nord Amerikanischen
Turnerbundes zu Milwaukee, Wis., vom 18. bis 23. Juli 1877. Milwaukee:
Löwenbach & Sohn, 1877. 99 p.
Location: WHi.

N59   Wegweiser für das 23. Bundes-Turnfest des Nordamerikanischen
Turnerbundes zu St. Louis, vom 4. bis 7. Juni 1881. St. Louis: n.p., [1881]. 64 p.
Location: MoSHi.

N60   Bericht über das 24. Bundesturnfest, abgehalten in Newark, N.J., vom
20.-25. Juni 1885. Milwaukee: Freidenker Publishing Co., 1886. 116 p.
Note: Cover title: *"Bericht über das 24. Bundesturnfest, abgehalten in Newark, N.J.,
vom 20.-25. Juni 1885. Erster Teil: Bericht des Beobachtungsausschusses. Zweiter
Teil: Die Turnübungen, umfassend den Aufmarsch und die Massenfreiübungen, die
Pflichtübungen der Wettturner, statistische Angaben, die Wett-Frei-und
Ordnungsübungen, die Übungen der Musterriegen, sowie der Schüler und
Schülerinnen des 'Newark Turnvereins.'"* Report of the 24th national Turnfest held in
Newark, June 20-25, 1885, published in two parts. The first part is the report of the
Observation Committee. The second part includes statistical reports and descriptions
of exercises, mass drills, obligatory exercises and exercises for the students of the
Newark Turnverein.
Location: InIU (included in the bound annual reports for 1885/86).

N61   Gilmore's Great Cincinnati Musical Festival for the Benefit of the 25th
National Turnfest of North America will be held in the Music Hall, May 3, 4, and 5,
with Matinees on the 4th and 5th. [Cincinnati]: n.p., [1889]. [ca. 30 p.]
Note: Promotional brochure of the Gilmore's Band. Includes biographical sketches of
the singers and schedule of their national tour.
Location: OCHP.

N62   Cincinnati Turnfest-Führer. Festschrift, herausgegeben mit Autorisierung des
Fest-Komittees für das 25. Bundes-Turnfest des Nordamerikanischen Turnerbundes,
abgehalten in Cincinnati vom 21.-26. Juni 1889. Cincinnati: Press of M & R
Burgheim, 1889. 208 p.
Note: Includes the program of the 25th Turnfest, histories of Turnerism in the United
States and the Turnverein in Cincinnati, and historical sketches of Cincinnati and its
environs by Carl Wolffradt.
Location: DLC; OCHP (microfilm); MWA (microfilm, pp. 167-206 only).

N63   Nordamerikanischer Turnerbund. Festzeitung für das 26. Bundesturnfest
abgehalten in Milwaukee, Wis., Juli 1893. Milwaukee: Becker & Rattinger, 1893.
Note: Title page: "Nordamerikanischer Turnerbund, Official Organ for the 26th
National Tournament, July 21 to 25, '93. Published under the Auspices of the Press
Committee by Becker & Rattingen, Printers, 151 West Water Street, Milwaukee
Wisconsin." The 12 issues of the *Festzeitung* were published monthly prior to the
Turnfest. Every issue includes details on the preparations for the festival, program of
events, exercises to be studied, news on the host societies and Milwaukee, and
practical advise for Turnfest participants. Articles are in German and English.
Location:
     InIU: no. 10, 11, 13 (May-June 1893).
     WHi: Feb.-July 1893.

N64   Nord Amerikanischer Turner Bund. 26tes Bundes Turn Fest, Milwaukee,
Wis. Milwaukee: The Evening Wisconsin Company, 1893. 64 p.
Note: Page 15 reads: "*Offizielles Festprogramm für das 26ste Bundes-Turn-Fest des
Nord-Amerikanischen Turnerbundes, 21., 22., 23., 24. und 25. Juli,* 1893,
Milwaukee, Wisconsin." The program includes a list of committee members, program
of events, facts about the city of Milwaukee and a list of exercises.
Location: InIU; MnBCHI. Also included in "The Immigrant in America," microform
publication of Research Publications, Inc., 1984. Reel 148, item 6.

N65   Allgemeine Bestimmungen giltig für das 26. Bundes-Turnfest in Milwaukee,
Wisconsin, am 21., 22., 23. und 24. Juli 1893: Zusammengestellt vom Technischen
Ausschuß des Bundes-Vororts, St. Louis, Mo., 1893. St. Louis: Henry Rauth, 1893.
38 p.
Note: Includes regulations and guidelines for the 26th national festival.
Location: InIU.

N66   Twenty-Sixth National Festival of the North American Gymnastic Union
(Turnerbund). Held at Milwaukee, Wis., July 21st to 25th, 1893. Reports of the
Special Committee on Observation. St. Louis: Executive Board of the Union, 1893.
20 p.
Note: Reports by three independent judges (Dr. E. Hitchcock, Dr. D. A. Sargent, and
Dr. E. M. Hartwell) who had been asked to attend the festival and comment on the

Turnfest and the performance of the participating members. Also includes photographs of mass exercises.
Location: InIU.

N67 Übungen des 26sten Bundes-Turnfests des N.A.T.B. abgehalten zu Milwaukee den 21, 22, 23, 24, 25 Juli 1893. Milwaukee: Art Gravure and Etching Co., 1893. [ca. 50 p.]
Note: Includes results of competitions and approximately 35 photographs taken at the Turnfest.
Location: InIU; MnV; MoU (Louis Kittlaus Collection); WHi; WMCHi; WMT.

N68 Festzeitung: 27stes Bundesturnfest. St.Louis, Mo., 6., 7., 8. und 9. Mai 1897. Herausgegeben vom Festausschuß des Nord-Amerikanischen Turnerbundes. St. Louis: Hermann Ruppelt, 1896.
Note: The 12 issues of the *Festzeitung* were published monthly prior to the 27th Turnfest. Every issue includes details on the preparation for the festival, programs of the event, exercises to be studied, news on the hosting societies and St. Louis, and practical advice for Turnfest participants. Articles are in German and English.
Location: InIU.

N69 Programme, 27th National Festival of the N.A. Gymnastic Union, Turnerbund, May 6,7,8,9, 1897, St. Louis, Mo. St. Louis: Western Engraving Co., 1897. [20 p.]
Note: Includes daily program of the 27th National Turnfest in English and German.
Location: InIU.

N70 Illustrated Souvenir of the 27th National Festival of the North American Gymnastic Union. Nord Amerikanischer Turnerbund and the City of St. Louis, MO. St. Louis: Western Engraving Company, 1897. 63 p.
Note: Cover title: "The 27th National Gymnastic Festival illustrated Bundesturnfest, May 6, 7, 8, 9, 1897, St. Louis." Includes program, results of competition, and many photographs of the city of St. Louis, the St. Louis Turnerhall, and the 27th Turnfest.
Location: InIU; MnHi; MoU (Louis Kittlaus Collection).

N71 Arbeitsplan für das Vereinsturnen, Einzelturnen und Musterturnen. St. Louis: Henry Roth Printing Co., 1897. 16 p.
Note: Title page: "*27. Bundes Turnfest, 6.- 9. Mai 1897, St. Louis, Mo., Arbeitsplan für das Vereinsturnen, Einzelturnen und Musterturnen.*" Work plan for exercises.
Location: PPB.

N72 Official Programme and Guide. For the 28th National Festival and Golden Jubilee of the North American Gymnastic Union (Turnerbund). To be held in Philadelphia, Pa., June 18-23, 1900. [Philadelphia]: n.p., [1900]. 60 p.
Note: Cover title: "*Festausschuss für das 28. Turnfest des Nordamerikanischen*

Turnerbundes, 1900. Official Programme and Guide for the 28th National Festival and Golden Jubilee of the North American Gymnastic Union (Turnerbund) to be held in Philadelphia, PA, June 18.-23., 1900."
Location: InIU; MnHi.

N73   Festzeitung für das 28. Turnfest des Nordamerikanischen Turnerbundes, 1900 abgehalten in Philadelphia. Philadelphia: Union Printer, 1899-1900.
Note: The *Festzeitung* was published monthly prior to the 28th Turnfest. Every issue includes details on the preparation for the festival, programs of events, exercises to be studied, news on the hosting societies and Philadelphia and practical advice for Turnfest participants. Articles are in German and English.
Location: InIU; PPG.

N74   Obligatorische Stabübungen für das 28ste Bundesturnfest in Philadelphia, 1900. Zusammengestellt von R. Pertuch (Festleiter). n.p., [1900]. 12 p.
Note: Includes description and photographs of exercises.
Location: InIU.

N75   Bericht des Beobachtungs-Ausschusses beim 28. Bundesturnfest des Nord Amerikanischen Turnerbundes abgehalten in Philadelphia, Pa., in den Tagen vom 21. bis 24. Juni 1900. Milwaukee: Freidenker Publishing Co., 1900. 124 p.
Note: Report of the Observation Committee for the 28th Turnfest. Includes detailed criticism and evaluation of the Turnfest, photographs of Turnfest events, and locations, reports and explanations of exercises.
Location: InIU; MnV; NBuU; PPB. Also included in "The Immigrant in America," microfilm publication of Research Publications, Inc., 1984. Reel 148, item 4.

N76   Das Neunundzwanzigste Turnfest des Nord-Amerikanischen Turnerbundes in Indianapolis im Juni 1905. Ein Gedenkbuch. Indianapolis: Gutenberg Co., 1906. [50 p.]
Note: Title page: "*Das Neunundzwanzigste Turnfest des Nordamerikanischen Turnerbundes in Indianapolis im Juni 1905. Ein Gedenkbuch. Mit 47 Ganzseitigen Bildern und Bildergruppen in Autotypiedruck. Herausgegeben von der Vorortsbehörde des Turnerbundes.*" Cover title: "*Nordamerikanischer Turnerbund, Neunundzwanigstes Bundesturnfest, Indianapolis, 1905.*" Includes program and many photographs depicting the Turnfest parade and athletic and cultural events.
Location: In; InIU; WMCHi.

N77   Nordamerikanischer Turnerbund. 29. Bundesturnfest, 21.-25. Juni 1905. Übungen und nähere Bestimmungen, Indianapolis, Indiana. [Indianapolis]: n.p., [1905]. 20 p.
Note: Includes program with descriptions and photographs of exercises.
Location: InIU; WMT.

N78   Twenty-Ninth National Gymnastic Festival of the North American Gymnastic Union at Indianapolis, Indiana, June 21-25 1905. Indianapolis: Hollenbeck Press, 1905. 20 p.
Note: List of committee members and program of events.
Location: InIU.

N79   Das 29. Bundesturnfest des Nordamerikanischen Turnerbundes abgehalten vom 21.-25. Juni 1905 in Indianapolis, Ind. Obligatorische, Muster- und Kür-Übungen, Arbeitsplan, Leistungstabellen und Beobachtungs-Berichte. Zusammengestelt von Dr. Karl Zapp, Cleveland, OH. Milwaukee: Freidenker Publishing Co., 1906. 200 p.
Note: Includes work plan, diagrams of exercises, reports of Observation Committee, results of competitions and photographs.
Location: InIU.

N80   Official Souvenir Program. 30th National Gymnastic Festival of the North American Gymnastic Union. To be held at Cincinnati, Ohio, June 19th to 28th, 1909. Cincinnati: Roessler Bros., 1909. 40 p.
Note: Includes a brief history of the North American Gymnastic Union written by Adolf Varrelmann, program of events and photographs of the committee members of the American Turnerbund.
Location: InIU.

N81   Liederschatz gewidmet dem N.A. Turnerbunde zum 30. Bundesturnfest, Juni 1909. Cincinnati: The Baldwin Company, 1909. 32 p.
Note: Song book.
Location: RPB.

N82   Souvenir des 31. Bundesturnfestes, North American Gymnastic Union, June 25th to 29th, 1913 in Denver. n.p., [1913]. 32 p.
Note: Contains photographs of the Turnfest parade and events.
Location: WMCHi.

N83   31. Bundesturnfest, Denver, Colo. 25.-29. Juni, 1913. n.p., 1913. 14 p.
Note: Cover missing; title taken from heading on first page. Includes guide to Denver and other places of interest in the surrounding area.
Location: InIU.

N84   Stabübungen, Hantelübungen, Freiübungen und Tanzschritte. Für das 31. Bundes Turnfest in Denver, Colorado, 25-30 Juni 1913. Denver: Colorado Herald, 1913. 47 p.
Note: Includes explanations and photographs of exercises and dance steps.
Location: InIU.

N85   Bundes-Turnfest Zeitung. 32. Bundes-Turnfest des Nordamerikanischen
Turnerbundes Brooklyn, N.Y., Juni 1917. Officielles Organ der Bundes Festbehoerde
unter den Auspicien des Turn-Verein Brooklyn E.D.. New York: Max Schmetterling,
1916-1917.
Note: Newspaper for the 1917 national Turnfest planned for Brooklyn, but cancelled
due to the American entry into World War I.   The issues contain articles on
gymnastics, Turnfest plans and Germans and Turners in New York City.
Location: InIU: no.3 (October 1916).

N86   Official Souvenir Program of the Thirty-Second National Tournament of the
American Gymnastic Union. To be held at Riverview Athletic Field from June 29th
to July 3rd Nineteen Twenty-One. Chicago: Executive Committee of the American
Gymnastic Union, 1921. 112 p.
Note: Program includes articles on Chicago, the American Gymnastic Union, the
Normal College, and essays on Turnerism and physical education in the United States.
Articles are in English.
Location: ICHi (Lincoln Turner Collection); InIU.

N87   Physical Educator: Official Monthly, published by the Executive Committee
of the 32nd National Tournament of the American Gymnastic Union in the interest of
the 32nd National Tournament of the American Gymnastic Union, held June 29th to
July 3rd, incl., 1921. Chicago: Executive Committee of the American Gymnastic
Union, 1921.
Note: Monthly publication issued by the Committee on Publicity. Includes essays on
Americanization, lists of committee members, and description and photographs of
exercises for men and women.
Location: InIU: v.1, no.1 (March 1921).

N88   Working Plan. 32nd National Festival of the American Gymnastic Union.
Chicago, Ill. June 29, 30, July, 1, 2, 3, 1921. Indianapolis: National Executive
Committee, 1921. 42 p.
Location: InIU.

N89   Results of Competition of the 32nd National Gymnastic and Athletic
Tournament at Chicago, Ill, June 29 - July 3, 1921. n.p., [1921]. 8 p.
Location: InIU.

N90   Official Souvenir and History, Thirty-Third National Turnfest, American
Turnerbund, Louisville, Kentucky, June 15 - 20, 1926. Louisville: The Standard
Printing Co., 1926. 71 p.
Note: Includes photographs, schedule of events and articles on the Normal College,
the development of gymnastics, Camp Brosius and the German Turner team in
America. Articles are In German and English.
Location: InIU.

N91   Turner Prize Essays. Turnfest of 1926 at Louisville, Ky. Being the Literary Work Submitted in the Contest and Awarded Diplomas. Pittsburgh: National Executive Committee, [1926]. 77 p.
Note: Includes 15 essays and poems submitted in the cultural competition at the 32nd Turnfest. Essays are written on the topics of physical education, Turnerism, science, music, progress and relations between the United States and Europe.
Location: InIU.

N92   Mass Exercises for the 33rd National Turnfest of the American Turnerbund, Louisville, Ky, June 16-20, 1926. n.p., [1926]. 32 p.
Note: Contains explanations and photographs of different exercises.
Location: InIU.

N93   Apparatus Exercises for Men and Women for the 33rd National Gymnastic Festival of the Amerian Turnerbund to be held in Louisville, Ky, June 16th to 20th, 1926. n.p., [1926]. 12 p.
Location: Madison Turners; American Turners Louisville.

N94   Work Plan. 33rd National Festival of the American Turnerbund Gymnastic Union. Louisville, Ky, June 16, 17, 18, 19 and 20, 1926. Pittsburgh: National Executive Committee, 1926. 56 p.
Location: InIU.

N95   Rang-Ordnung und Leistungstabellen im Vereins-und Einzel-Wetturnen beim 33. Bundes-Turnfest des Amerikanischen Turnerbundes. Abgehalten vom 15. bis 20. Juni 1926 in Louisville, Kentucky. n.p., [1926]. 30 p.
Note: Competition results. Title page in German but text in English.
Location: InIU.

N96   The Turner: National Turnfest Number. Published by the Buffalo Turnverein. n.p., [1930]. 79 p.
Note: Green cover with golden disc thrower and Buffalo. Includes program of the 1930 Turnfest and a long article on Turnerism.
Location: InIU.

N97   Buffalo Turners: National Turnfest-Celebration Number. n.p., [1930]. 31 p.
Note: Commemorative publication for the 1930 Turnfest. Includes many photographs and comments on the events.
Location: InIU; WMT.

N98   Buffalo Turner: Published Monthly by the Buffalo Turn Verein, Vol. XII-No. 9, June 1930: 34th National Turnfest, Buffalo, N.Y. June 24-29, 1930. [Buffalo]: n.p., [1930]. 20 p.

Note: Extra issue of the Buffalo Turners' newsletter. Includes national and society news and program of events.
Location: InIU.

N99   Turner Prize Essays. Turnfest of 1930 at Buffalo, N.Y. Being the Literary Work submitted in the Contest and Awarded Diplomas. Pittsburgh: National Executive Committee, 1930. 87 p.
Note: Includes 19 essays and poems submitted in the cultural competition at the 34th Turnfest. Essays address Turnerism, physical education, science and fine arts.
Locations: InIU; NBuHi.

N100   Preisgekrönte Aufsätzte vom Turnfest 1930 in Buffalo, N.Y.: die im literarischen Wettbewerb eingesandten und mit Diplom ausgezeichneten Arbeiten. Pittsburgh: Bundesvorort Amerikanischer Turnerbund, [1930]. 30 p.
Note: German-language award-winning essays submitted in the cultural competition at the 1930 Turnfest.
Location. DLC.

N101   Society and Mass Exercises for the Thirty-Fourth National Turnfest of the American Turnerbund, Buffalo, N.Y., June 24-29, 1930. Pittsburgh: National Executive Committee, 1930. 16 p.
Location: InIU; MoSHi.

N102   Work Plan. 34th National Festival of the American Turnerbund. Buffalo, New York, June 23, 24, 25, 26, 27, 28, 29, 1930. Pittsburgh: National Executive Committee, 1930. 64 p.
Location: InIU; MoU (Louis Kittlaus Collection).

N103   Results of the of Events held at the 34th National Turnfest of the American Turnerbund, Buffalo, N.Y., June 24th-29th, 1930. n.p., [1930]. 30 p.
Location: InIU; MoSHi; WMT.

N104   Official Program. National Turnfest, Cleveland, Ohio, June 29th-July 4th, 1936. Under the Auspices of Germania Turn-Verein Vorwärts, Socialer Turn-Verein of Cleveland. [Cleveland]: n.p., [1936]. 48 p.
Note: Cover title: "Thirty-Fifth National Turnfest, June 29th 1936 to July 3rd, Cleveland, Ohio, Official Souvenir Program." Includes histories of the *Germania Turnverein Vorwärts* and the *Socialer Turnverein*, a guide to the city of Cleveland, festival program, history of Turnerism and photographs.
Location: InIU; OClWHi; WMT.

N105   35th Annual Turnfest, 1936, Compliments of Germania Turnverein Vorwärts, 1608-1622 East 55th Street, Cleveland, Ohio. Cleveland: n.p., [1936]. 32 p.

Note: Promotional brochure for the *Germania Turnverein Vorwärts*.
Location: InIU.

N106 Work Plan. Thirty-Fifth National Turnfest, American Turnerbund. Cleveland, Ohio, June 29th-July 3rd, 1936. Pittsburgh: National Executive Committee, 1936. 64 p.
Note: The work plan consists primarily of schedules of events and sport exercises.
Location: InIU.

N107 Results of the Events held at the 35th National Turnfest of the American Turnerbund, June 29th to July 3, 1936. Cleveland, Ohio. [Cleveland]: n.p., [1936]. 32 p.
Location: InIU.

N108 Society Mass and Apparatus Exercises for the Thirty-Fifth National Turnfest of the American Turnerbund. Cleveland, Ohio, June 29th to July 3rd, 1936. Pittsburgh: National Executive Committee of the American Turnerbund, 1936. 20 p.
Location: InIU.

N109 Official Program. American Turners 36th National Tournament, June 24-25-26-27-28 1941, Springfield, Mass. Holyoke-Springfield: Wisly-Brooks Co., 1941. [40p.]
Note: Title page: "American Turners Thirty Sixth National Tournament, June 24-28, 1941, Springfield, Mass." Includes histories of the Springfield Turnverein, Adams Turners, Clinton Turners, Detroit Turners, Holyoke Turnverein, Cleveland East Side Turners, *Turnverein Vorwärts*, Holyoke, and program of events.
Location: InIU; MiU (Wiedeman Papers).

N110 Society Mass and Apparatus Exercises for the Thirty-Sixth National Festival of the American Turners. Springfield, Mass., June 24 to 28, 1941. Detroit: National Executive Committee of the American Turners, 1941. 19 p.
Note: Instructions for different types of exercises using gymnastic apparatus.
Location: InIU.

N111 Work Plan. Thirty-Sixth National Tournament, American Turners, Springfield, Mass., June 24 to 28, 1941. n.p.: National Physical Education Commission, 1941. 27 p.
Note: Includes program of events, competition schedule, and lists of judges.
Location: InIU.

N112 American Turners Celebrating A Century of Health. 1848[-]1948. 37th National Festival, June 30-July 4, 1948, St. Louis, Missouri. [St. Louis]: n.p., [1948]. 128 p.
Note: Includes an extensive history of Turnerism in the United States, program of

events, history of the Ladies Auxiliary, essay on mental training and a list of life members of the American Turners.
Location: IaDa; InIU; MoSHi; MoU(Louis Kittlaus Collection); WMT.

N113   Society Mass and Apparatus Exercises for the Thirty-Seventh National Festival of the American Turners. St. Louis, Mo., June 30 - July 4, 1948. Detroit: National Executive Committee. 1948. 19 p.
Location: InIU; MoSHi.

N114   Work Plan. Thirty-Seventh National Festival. American Turners, St. Louis, MO., June 30 to July 4, 1948. n.p.: National Physical Education Committee of the American Turners, [1948]. 31 p.
Location: InIU.

N115   American Turners. 38th National Festival, June 29th-July 3rd 1951, Buffalo, New York. n.p., 1951. 48 p.
Note: Cover title: "103 Years of Physical Education, 1848-1951, American Turners, 38th National Festival, June 29-July 3 1951, Buffalo, New York. Souvenir Program."
Location: InIU.

N116   Society Mass and Apparatus Exercise for the Thirty-Eighth National Festival of the American Turners at Buffalo, New York, June 29 to July 4, 1951. Detroit: National Executive Committee, 1951. 24 p.
Note: Includes compulsory apparatus exercises for men and women.
Location: InIU.

N117   Work Plan. 38th National Festival, American Turners, Buffalo, N. Y., June 29th to July 3rd, 1951. n.p.: National Executive Committee of American Turners, [1951]. 28 p.
Location: InIU.

N118   American Turners. 39th Quadrennial National Festival, June 29-July 3 inclusive 1955, Milwaukee, Wisconsin. n.p., [1955]. 60 p.
Note: Includes schedule of events, pictures of national officers, brief history of the Normal College, list of all life members, and brief historical sketches of several Turner societies nationally.
Location: InIU; MoSHi; WMCHi; WMT.

N119   Work Plan. 39th National Festival, American Turners, Milwaukee, Wisconsin, June 29th to July 3rd, 1955, arranged by the National Health and Physical Education Committee. n.p., [1955]. 24 p.
Location: InIU.

N120   Results of Events of the 39th Turnfest, June 29-July 3, 1955. n.p., [1955].
Location: Dayton Liederkranz Turners.

N121   American Turners One Hundred and Eleventh Year, 40th National Festival,
June 28th - July 2nd, 1959, Louisville, Kentucky. [Louisville]: n.p., [1959]. 58 p.
Note: Cover title: "40th National Festival, June 28 thru July 2, 1959, Louisville,
Kentucky." Includes articles and pictures of the Louisville Turnverein and their indoor
circus, history of the Ladies Auxiliary, brief historical abstracts of a number of Turner
societies throughout the country and the Turnfest program.
Location: InIU; KYHi; KYLOF; MN; WMT.

N122   American Turners Celebrating 115 Years of Physical Education, 1848 [-]
1963, 41st National Festival, June 19-23, 1963, Cleveland, Ohio. n.p., 1963. 48p.
Note: Cover title: "American Turners 41st National Festival, June 19 thru 23, 1963,
Cleveland, Ohio." Includes schedule of events and article "Heritage of Turnerism."
Location: InIU.

N123   42nd National Festival, June 28.-July 2., 1967, Moline, Ill. n.p., [1967].
Location: InIU; MoSHi; WMT.

N124   43rd National Festival in Milwaukee, WI, June 24-27, 1971. n.p., [1971].
[50 p.]
Location: WMT.

N125   43rd National Festival Gymnastic and Cultural Competition, Milwaukee,
June 24-27, 1971. n.p., [1971]. 40 p.
Location: Kansas City Turners; Madison Turners.

N126   Meet me in St. Louie Louie: Welcome Turners to the 44th National Festival,
1875[-]1975. n.p., [1975]. [25 p.]
Note: Lists program of events and participating Turners.
Location: InIU; WI; WMT.

N127   45th National Festival at the Moline Turners, July 4-8, 1979. n.p., [1979].
[25 p.]
Location: WMT.

N128   47th National Turnfest, June 24-28, 1987, Adams, Massachusetts. n.p.,
[1987]. [20 p.]
Note: Cover title: "Adams is Heaven in '87. 47th National Turnfest, June 24-28,
1987, Adams, Massachusetts."
Location: InIU.

N129   48th National Turnfest, June 21-24, 1991, Indianapolis, IN. n.p., [1991].
[28 p.]
Location: InIU; Covington Turner Society.

Festival Rules

The National Technical Committee sets the rules (*Festordnung*) which regulate
the organization and conduct of national festivals and individual and team
competitions. Rules for the early festivals can be found in the national convention
minutes. The 1886 platform and statutes of the North American Turnerbund also
includes regulations for national Turnfests.

N130   Turnfestordnung des Nordamerikanischen Turnerbundes. Milwaukee:
Freidenker Publishing Co., 1893. 61 p.
Note: Rules governing the 26th National Turnfest in Milwaukee.
Location: InIU.

N131   Revidierte Festordnung des Nordamerikanischen Turnerbundes. Milwaukee:
Freidenker Publishing Co., 1898. 30 p.
Note: Cover title: "*Revidierte Festordnung des Nordamerikanischen Turnerbundes.
(Angenommen von der Bundestagsatzung zu San Francisco, Cal., 5. bis 8. Juli
1898).*" Revised festival rules adopted at the 1898 convention in San Francisco.
Location: InIU.

N132   Nix, Robert. Festordnung des Nordamerikanischen Turnerbundes.
Indianapolis: Hollenbeck Press, 1903. 73 p.
Note: Cover title: "*Festordnung des Nordamerikanischen Turnerbundes. Auf Grund
der Beschlüsse der zwanzigsten Tagsatzung im Auftrag des Bundesvororts.
Neuerarbeitet und erweitert von Robert Nix.*" Festival rules adopted by the 20th
national convention, revised and enlarged by Robert Nix.
Location: DLC; InIU.

N133   Turnfestordnung des Nord-Amerikanischen Turnerbundes angenommen von
der 26. Bundestagsatzung, San Francisco, Cal., 1915. Milwaukee: Freidenker
Publishing Co., 1915. 75 p.
Location: American Turners Louisville.

N134   Rules Governing National Festivals of the American Turnerbund. Pittsburgh:
National Executive Committee, [1925]. 59 p.
Note: Cover title: "Rules Governing National Festivals of the American Turnerbund.
Revised at the National Convention, Elkhart Lake, Wis. June 1925."
Location: InIU.

N135 Rules Governing National Festivals of the American Turnerbund. Pittsburgh: National Executive Committee, [1929]. 60 p.
Note: Cover title: "Rules Governing National Festivals of the American Turnerbund. Revised at the National Conventions, Cleveland and Philadelphia, 1927-29."
Location: InIU.

N136 Rules Governing National Festivals of the American Turnerbund. Revised to January 1st, 1936. Pittsburgh: National Executive Committee, 1936. 64 p.
Location: InIU.

N137 National Festival Rules of the American Turners. Revised to January 1, 1941. Detroit: National Executive Committee, [1941]. 60 p.
Location: InIU.

N138 National Festival Rules of the American Turners. Revised to January 1, 1948. Detroit: National Executive Committee, [1948]. 71 p.
Location: InIU; MoSHi.

N139 National Festival Rules of the American Turners. Revised to January 1, 1951. Detroit: National Council, [1951]. 79 p.
Location: InIU; WMT (Wiedemann Collection).

Rules for Cultural Competitions

N140 Rules Governing Mental Contests at National Festivals of the American Turnerbund. Revised at the National Conventions, Cleveland and Philadelphia, 1927-29. Pittsburgh: National Executive Committee, [1927]. 8 p.
Location: Private collection.

N141 Rules Applying to Cultural Educational Activities of the American Turners. Revised June 1, 1941. Detroit: National Executive Committee, [1941].
Location: Kansas City Turners.

N142 Rules Applying to Cultural Educational Activities of the American Turners. Revised to January 1, 1948. Detroit: National Executive Committee, [1948]. 32 p.
Location: InIU; MoSHi.

N143 Rules Applying to Cultural Educational Competition of the American Turners. Revised to July 1, 1949. Detroit: National Executive Committee, [1949]. 36 p.
Location: InIU.

N144   Rules Applying to Cultural Education Competition of the American Turners.
Detroit: North American Turners, [1953]. 40 p.
Location: Northwest Davenport Turners.

N145   Rules Applying to Cultural Education Competition of the American Turners.
Revised 1962. n.p., [1962]. 29 p.
Location: InIU.

N146   Rules Applying to Cultural Education Competition of the American Turners.
Revised 1974. n.p., [1974]. 23 p.
Location: Covington Turners, Covington, KY.

NATIONAL NEWSPAPERS, MAGAZINES AND CALENDARS

In order to communicate with its members the North AmericanTurnerbund selected a series of newspapers to serve as the national organization's official publication. Only the first newspaper, the Turn-Zeitung, and the current one, Turner Topics, were under the direct control of the Turnerbund. The other papers were independent publications that received subsidies and subscriptions from the Turners in return for printing Turner news.

N147   Turn-Zeitung. 1851-1861.
Note: Subtitles: 1) *"Organ des Sozialistischen Turnerbundes."* 2) *"Organ des Sozialistischen Turnerbundes von Nordamerika."* Monthly, Nov. 1851 - Oct.1853, weekly thereafter. Includes supplements. Place of publication varies: New York City (Nov. 1851 - Oct. 1853), Philadelphia (Nov. 1853 - Oct. 1854), Cincinnati (Nov. 1854 - Nov. 1858), Dubuque, Iowa (Dec. 1858- Oct. 1859), Baltimore (Nov. 1859 - April 1861). Among the editors were Sigismund Kaufmann, William Ehrmann, William Rapp, Godfried Becker, Wilhelm Rothacker, Dr. George Edward, Dr. Adolph Wiesner. Radical newspaper which took strong positions against slavery, nativism and temperance laws. Includes articles on politics and social conditions, national Turner news, reports on physical education and health and announcements of the national officers. On April 21, 1861 the office and the printing equipment of the Turn-Zeitung were destroyed by a mob of southern sympathizers in Baltimore.
Location:
    DLC: v.1-v.2 (1851?-1852?).
    In: v.4 (Nov. 1855) - v.6 (Sept. 1857).
    InIU: v.1(1851) - v.6 (1857). Microfilm (incomplete)
    MB: v.6 (Oct. 1857) - v.10 (Feb. 1861).
    MH: v. 8 (Oct. 1859) - v.9 (Mar. 1860).
    MnHi: v.1 (Dec. 1851) - v.3 (Oct. 1854); v.4 (Nov. 1855) -v.8 (Nov. 1859).
    MoS: v.6 (Mar. 1857 - Sept. 1857).
    NN: v.1 (Nov. 1851) - v.3 (Oct. 1854); v. 10 (April 1861).

PPG: v.3 (Nov. 1854) - v.4 (Oct. 1855).
WHi: v.1 (1851) - v.6 (Jan. 1857). Original and microfilm (incomplete)

N148   Turn-Blatt. Für die Vereine des Socialistischen Turnerbundes von
Nord-Amerika. Williamsburgh: Williamsburgh *Vorort*, 1856-1858.
Note: Monthly. When the national Turnerbund split into the East and West sections
in 1855, Williamsburgh (Brooklyn) became the headquarters (*Vorort*) for the eastern
Turnerbund. Since the Turn-Zeitung had been at the center of many disputes between
the two sides, the eastern Turnerbund started its own publication, the Turn-Blatt. A
four page paper, it includes reports on the dispute and negotiations between the two
factions, official news, and scientific articles.
Location:
   NN: no. 1-24, (Oct. 1856-Sept. 1858).

N149   Unsere Zeit. Ein unabhängiges Wochenblatt für Politik und öffentliches
Leben; Kunst, Wissenschaft und Literatur. Organ des Nord-Amerikansichen Turner-
Bundes. Cincinnati: A. Frey & Co., 1865-1867.
Note: Weekly. Beginning with v.2, # 21 (April 21, 1866), the long subtitle was
dropped, and the masthead read: "*Unsere Zeit. Organ des Nord-Amerikanischen
Turner-Bundes.*" The newspaper was edited by Adolph Frey and W. Stängel. This
eight-page paper typically included foreign and domestic news, political commentary
and reports on Turner societies, festivals and meetings. The last issue (10/6/67) notes
that Frey was joining the Telegraph Company and that Unsere Zeit and the Freie
Presse von Indiana were being consolidated under the new name Die Zukunft and
moving to Indianapolis. The note assures readers that the radical tendencies of the
paper would continue.
Location:
   In: v.1, no.36 (August 5, 1865) - v.3, no.48 (Oct. 25, 1867).

N150   Die Zukunft: Organ des Nord-Amerikanischen Turner-Bundes. Indianapolis:
1867-1882.
Note: Weekly ; published by the Telegraph Company (1867-1868) and the Gutenberg
Company (1868-1882). Edited by Carl Beyschlag (1867-1868), R. Goebel (1870-
1872) and Adolph Seidensticker (ca. 1873-1878). The newspaper contained national
and international news, articles on Turner societies and activies, and opinion pieces,
particularly on socialism and freethought issues. During the 1876 national convention
in New Ulm, the North American Turnerbund prohibited the newspaper from
supporting any political parties or candidates or printing articles discussing party
politics. Nevertheless, Die Zukunft printed numerous articles favoring the Democratic
Party presidential candidate Samuel Tilden, with the result that many societies
demanded the replacement of Die Zukunft by a newspaper that would follow the
decisions of the national conventions. In 1878, Der Freidenker was chosen as the new
national newspaper.
Location:

DLC: v.2 (Dec. 1868) - v.3 (Nov. 1869).
ICHi (Rowell Collection): v.9, #38 (July 6, 1876).
In: v.2 (1868-1869); v.4 (1870) - v.5 (1872); v.7 (1873) -v.10 (1877).
InIU: v.7 (April 1874)-v.14 (Feb. 1881). Incomplete.
TxU: v.3 (July 1869)-v.7 (Oct. 1873); v.9 (Oct. 1875)-v.12 (Jan. 1879).

N151   Der Freidenker: Freiheit, Bildung und Wohlstand für Alle! 1872-1942.
Note: During the national convention of 1878, the Turnerbund selected Der Freidenker as the new official newspaper, replacing Die Zukunft. Der Freidenker was a weekly published in Milwaukee (April 1, 1872-May 7, 1916), Minneapolis (May 14. 1916-Sept. 8, 1918), and New Ulm, MN., (Sept. 15, 1918-Oct. 25, 1942), and for most of its life was the official newspaper of the *Freidenker Gemeinden* (Freethinker Societies). It began publication under owner and editor Michael Biron in 1872. In November 1876 it was taken over by the Carl Doerflinger Publishing Company (1876-1882), followed by the Freidenker Publishing Company (1883-1916?), and the Turner Publishing Co. of New Ulm (1916?-Oct. 1942). During the time it served as the national publication of the Turnerbund, the Swiss-born Hermann Boppe was its principal editor. Beginning in January 1880 Der Freidenker included a 4-page supplement entitled Turnzeitung: Beilage zum Freidenker containing news about gymnastics and activities of the Turnerbund, individual Turner societies and districts. Publishing information in Der Freidenker (p.4) contains a note that the Turnerbund bore the sole responsibility for its official news and for other Turner-related articles. In 1879, Karl Heinzen's paper, Der Pionier, merged with Der Freidenker and Heinzen became one of its editors until his death 1880. Although it includes the subscription price for European subscribers, Der Freidenker was banned from the German market in 1879 for its critical views of Bismarck's reform policies. Demand for more Turner news finally led to the separate publication of the supplement as an independent paper called the Amerikanische Turnzeitung.
Locations:
DLC: v.36 (1906) - v.42 (1912); v.45 (1916) - v.46 (1917).
GyAIZ: July 11, 1886; Jan. 12, 1890; March 6 & 13, 1892.
ICHi (Rowell Collection): v.5, # 26 (Sept. 24, 1876).
IU: v.47 (1918) - v.71 (1942). Incomplete.
In: v.9 (Jan. 1880) - v.13 (December 1884).
MnHi: v.46 (1917) - v.71 (1942). Incomplete.
MWA: v.8 (1879) - v.13 (1884). Incomplete.
NN: v.5 (1876), v.28 (1889) - v.36 (1907), v.43 (1914) - v.71 (1942).
    Incomplete.
TxU: v.7 (1878) - v.13. (1884). Incomplete.
WaSp: 1907-08.
WHi: v.1 (1872) - v.38 (1909); v.43 (1914) - v.71 (1942). Microfilm available.
WM: v.1 (1872), v.3 (1874), v.8 (1879) - v.13 (1884), v.17 (1888), v.19
    (1890) - v.48 (1916). Incomplete.
WMCHi: v.1 (1872) - v.71 (1942).

N152   Amerikanische Turnzeitung. 1885-1943.

Note: Sub-titles: 1) *"Turnerische Ausgabe der "Freidenker": Organ des Nordamerikanischen Turner-Bundes"* 2) *"Offizielles Organ des Nordamerikanischen Turner-Bundes;"* 3) *"Offizielles Organ des Nordamerikanischen Turner-Bundes* and Organ of the American Gymnastic Union: American Independent Periodical for Rational Physical and Mental Education." The paper was published weekly as the national publication of the North American Turnerbund from 1885-1937, bi-weekly from 1938-1939, and semi-weekly from 1940-1943. Place of publication varies: Milwaukee (Jan. 4, 1885-May 7, 1917); Minneapolis (May 14, 1917-1918) and New Ulm, MN (Jan. 1919-1943). Among the editors of the Amerikanische Turnzeitung were Hermann Boppe, Heinrich Huhn, Gustav Schäfli, Willibal Fleck, and Albert Steinhauser. The paper reported on the activities of the Turnerbund and individual societies. The paper's motto was *"Freiheit, Bildung und Wohlstand für Alle,"* and in 1917 it added the phrase *"Gegen alle patriotische und religiöse Hysterie - Für eine ruhige, klare, vernünftige Weltanschauung!"* The German government banned the importation of the newspaper in 1885 for its radical views. In August 1918 the newspaper was suppressed by the United States government on suspicion of pro-German sentiments. It resumed its publication in New Ulm with v. 35, no.1, Jan. 19, 1919. On October 4, 1936, the Amerikanische Turnzeitung changed its name to The American Turner; subtitle: *"Amerikanische Turnzeitung."* The American Turner's publishing information states that the paper is "A Radical Periodical of Free Thought for Progress, Liberty and Justice to All; Official Organ of the Free Thought League of North America." The paper continued to print German and English articles on physical education, Turner news, and Free-thought issues until 1943.

Locations:

   CC: v.33 (1917) - v.48 (1931). Incomplete.

   DLC: v.23 (1907) - v.34 (1918). Incomplete.

   GyAIZ: v.1, no.40 (Oct.4, 1885), v.2, no.28 (July 11, 1886), v.6, no. 2-3 (Jan. 12-19, 1890), v.7, no.30 (July 26, 1891), v.8, no.1 (Jan.3, 1892).

   ICN: v.10 (1894) -v.20 (1904). Incomplete.

   InIU: v.1 (1885) - v.33 (1917); v.48 (1932) - v.54 (1938). Incomplete.

   MB: v.1 (1885) - v.3 (1887). Incomplete.

   MWA: v.2 (1885) - v.8 (1892). Incomplete.

   NN: v.16 (1900) - v.24 (1908). Incomplete.

   OO: v.21 (1905), v.34 (1918)

   TxU: v.1 (1885-1886), v.5 (1888) - v.7 (1891). Incomplete.

   WHi: v.1 (1885) - v.33 (1917). Available on microfilm.

   WM: v.1 (1885) - v.48 (1933).

N153   Für Unsere Jugend: Beilage zum Freidenker und der Amerikanischen Turnzeitung. Milwaukee: Freidenker Publishing Co., 1889-1906.

Note: Monthly youth magazine that was supplement to Der Freidenker and to the Amerikanische Turnzeitung. The four-page paper was edited by Maximilian

Grossmann with H.H. Fick as associate editor, April 1889-?; by F.W. Dodel, ?-Nov. 1906. Beginning with 1907, the paper was continued as a section of the Freidenker.
Location:
GyAIZ: v.1, no. 12 (Feb., March 1890); v.3, no. 1 (April 1891).
ICN: v.6 (1895) - v.16 (1904). Incomplete.
NN: v.1 (1889) - v.18 (1906). Incomplete.
WHi: v.1 (1889) - v.18 (1906). Bound with Amerikanische Turnzeitung.

N154   Turner Topics, 1936-present.
Note: Subtitles: "Official Organ of the American Turnerbund," 1936-Jan. 1939; "Official Organ of the American Turners," Feb. 1939-present. Monthly from 1936-May 1950; bi-monthly, June 1950-present. Place of publication varies: Philadelphia, Detroit, Rochester, NY, Buffalo, NY and Indianapolis. Among the editors and contributing editors have been George Seibel (1936-1939), Karl Schaltenbrand (1939-1948), Emil Pletz (1949-1950), Dr. E.A. Ecklund (1950-1970), William Huth (1970-1978), Betty Dau (1978-1981), Bob Dau (1981-1988) and Bob Swan (1988-present). Magazine format. Contains essays on physical education and Turner history, news of national and district conventions and competitions, news of individual societies and their members and photographs.
Location:
InIU: 1936-present. Incomplete.
WMCHi: July/Aug, 1943-June 1948.

N155   Amerikanischer Turner Kalender. Milwaukee: 1880-1901.
Note: The Turner *Kalenders* were first published by Carl Dörflinger Book & Publishing Co.; later by the Freidenker Publishing Co. In addition to being a calendar, the books include poems, essays, songs, and short stories by prominent Turner members and free thinkers, such as Max Hempel, Robert Nix, Henry Metzner, Hermann Boppe, Johann Straubenmüller, Otto Sourbon, E. Zündt, and Carl Heinzen. In 1901 the Turner Kalender was published together with the Freidenker-Almanach. Each volume has approximately 130 pages.
Location:
GySIA: 1880-1900.
IU: 1901
InIU: 1880- 1897.
NN: 1880-1900.
PPG: 1880-1900.
WMCHi: 1890-1900.

N156   Mind and Body: A Monthly Journal devoted to Physical Education, 1894-1936.
Note: Monthly physical education magazine supported by the American Turnerbund. Publisher and place of publication varies: Freidenker Publishing Co., Milwaukee (1894-April 1916), Turner Publishing Co. (May 1916-Sept. 1917), and Mind and

Body Publishing Co., New Ulm, MN (Sept. 1917-1936). Numerous Turners and faculty members of the Turner Normal College were members of the editorial committee, including Karl Kroh, William Stecher, Hans Ballin, W. Ocker, and Dr. Pfister. Includes articles on physical education, health and hygiene and outlines of exercises, games, plays, drills, and dances.
Location:
InIU: 1894-1936; frequently available in large academic and public libraries.

TURNER SCHOOLBOOKS

After the Civil War the American Turnerbund sponsored the publication of several schoolbooks for use as teaching materials in Turner schools. Among the authors of these books were Adolf Douai and William Grauert. Douai had come to the United States in 1852, settled in Texas and became a leading advocate of Friedrich Froebel's education system. He was the author of a number of works on education but wrote only one book for the Turner series. Volumes two to four were written by William Grauert, also an author of many German school books in the United States. Although it can be assumed that volumes five and six were also published, they have not been located. Whereas the first four volumes focus on German language, the seventh book, written by Joseph Deghuee, is a textbook for geography classes.

N157 Douai, Adolf. Turner Schulbücher I: Bilder-Fibel und erstes deutsches Lesebuch. Herausgegeben durch den Vorort des Nord-amerikanischen Turnerbundes unter Begutachtung einer Commission von Schulmännern. New York: E. Steiger, 1866.
Note: First German reading book, published by the North American Turnerbund under the direction of a committee of teachers. Includes pictures, handwriting exercises for German script, poems, and reading exercises.
Location: DLC; NN; WaU.

N158 Grauert, William. Turner Schulbücher II. Zweites deutsches Lesebuch. Herausgegeben durch den Vorort des Nordamerikanischen Turnerbundes unter Begutachtung einer Commission von Schulmännern. New York: E. Steigert, 1867.
Note: Pochmann mentions the 12th edition in 1873. Second German reading book published by the North-American Turnerbund. Includes reading exercises.
Location: DLC.

N159 ---. Turn Schulbücher III. Drittes Deutsches Lesebuch. Herausgegeben durch den Vorort des Nordamerikanischen Turnerbundes unter Begutachtung einer Commission von Schulmännern. New York: E. Steiger, 1868. 236 p.
Note: Pochmann mentions an edition published in 1872. Third German reading book published by the North American Turnerbund. Includes poems and short stories.
Location: DLC; InIU.

N160   ---. Turn Schulbücher IV. Viertes deutsches Lesebuch. Herausgegeben durch den Vorort des Nordamerikanischen Turnerbundes unter Begutachtung einer Commission von Schulmännern. New York: E. Steiger, 1871. 404 p.
Note: Fourth German reading book published by the North American Turnerbund. Includes poems and short stories.
Location: DLC; MnSH; TxSMS.

N161   Deghuee, Joseph. Turner Schulbücher VII. Leitfaden für den Geographischen Unterricht in deutschen Schulen der Ver. Staaten. Herausgegeben durch den Vorort des Nord-amerikanischen Turnerbundes unter Begutachtung einer Commission von Schulmännern. New York: E. Steiger, 1871. 181 p.
Note: Seventh Turner schoolbook published by the North-American Turnerbund for the study of geography in German schools.
Location: DLC; InIU; NB; RPB.

TURNER INSTRUCTOR MEETING PUBLICATIONS

As the training of gymnastics instructors became more rigorous, the instructors began holding conventions to discuss standards and teaching methodology. The meetings appear to have been held on a regular basis from the late 1880s to the 1910s.

N162   Die Turnlehrerversammlung in Cincinnati, O., am 27., 28., 29., 30. und 31. Juli 1887. Bericht über die Vorträge und Verhandlungen. Zusammengestellt auf Wunsch des Bundesvororts von Wm. A. Stecher auf Grund der geführten Protokolle. Milwaukee: Freidenker Publishing Co., 1887. 70 p.
Note: Minutes of the Turner instructors' convention in Cincinnati in 1887.
Location: InIU.

N163   Protokoll des Turnlehrertages zu Put-in-Bay, Ohio, vom 14-17. August, 1890. n.p., 1890. 59 p.
Note: Title from page one; bound with 1887 convention minutes. Minutes of the Turner instructors' day in 1890.
Location: InIU.

N164   Vorträge von Turnlehrern auf dem Turnlehrertage in Indianapolis, Ind., 6. und 7. Juli 1912. n.d. [1912]. 24 p.
Note: Essays and lectures given at the 1912 Turner instructors' conference.
Location: InIU.

N165   Second Annual Meeting of the Instructors and Turnwarts of the American Turnerbund at the Normal College, Indianapolis, Ind. Friday, November 30, and Saturday, December 1, 1928. n.p., [1928]. 45 p.

Note: Minutes of the second teachers' convention.
Location: InIU.

N166   Instructor's Fund of the American Turnerbund. [Cleveland]: n.p., [1938?].
4 p.
Note: Cover title: "The Instructors' Fund was established by the American Turnerbund
for the purpose of aiding instructors who have served the American Turnerbund
faithfully and who are seriously in need of financial assistance."
Location: InIU.

AMERICAN TURNERS AND GERMAN TURNERS

During the 19th and early 20th centuries, contacts between the American Turners
and the German Turners were frequent and both groups sent teams to the other's
Turnfests. A team of Milwaukee Turners under the direction of George Brosius was
the first American team to visit Germany, participating in the 1880 Turnfest in
Frankfurt am Main and winning several prizes. After World War II the ties between
both sides weakened but have been revived in recent years.

N167   Metzner, Heinrich. "Christian Müller, *der Sieger beim Frankfurter
Turnfest*." Der Deutsche Pionier v.12 (1880): pp. 283-84.

N168   Rattermann, Heinrich. "*Der Sieg der deutsch-amerikanischen Turner in
Deutschland*." Der Deutsche Pionier v.12 (1880): pp. 281-83.

N169   Zur Erinnerung an den Besuch des nordamerikanischen Turnerbundes.
Wiesbaden: n.p., 1908. 64 p.
Note: Travelling schedule and songs in memory of the journey of the North American
Turnerbund to Wiesbaden, Germany.
Location: KHi.

N170   Obermeyer-Stuttgart, Dr. Mit der Riege der Deutschen Turnerschaft in
Amerika. Heilbronn: C. Rembolt, 1926. 123 p.
Note: Account of the German team's participation in the Turnfest in Louisville in
1926.
Location: InIU.

N171   American Turners at Cologne, 1928. 14. Deutsches Turnfest, 21.-30. Juli
1928, Köln am Rhein. n.p., 1928. 24 p.
Note: Includes articles by Emil Rath, "The American Turners at Cologne" and
Richard Turnt, "Those Days in Cologne." Also includes results of competitions and
photographs.
Location: InIU.

PROMOTIONAL LITERATURE

N172   American Turners National Executive Committee. Who these Turners are.
[Detroit]: [1940]. [8 panel brochure]
Note: Brief history of the American Turners.
Location: InIU.

N173   Bernicke, L. O. Turnerism: An Outline of its Study. Buffalo: n.p., 1929.
Location: InIU.

N174   North American Gymnastic Union. [Recommendations of the Committee on
Physical Training]. New Ulm, MN: Turner Publishing Company, 1919. 35 p.
Note: On cover: "North American Gymnastic Union, Indianapolis, Indiana, April
1919," and table of contents. Collection of essays on Turnerism in English and
German. Includes recommendations for improvements for Turner societies.
Location: InIU.

N175   Seibel, George. Who are these Turners? Pittsburgh: National Executive
Committee, 1935. 7 p.
Note: Radio address delivered at Rochester, NY on Station WHAM, June 29, 1935,
in which Seibel speaks about the history and achievements of the Turner movement
in the United States.
Location: InIU.

N176   Turn with the Turners. n.p.: American Gymnastic Union, 1922. 12 p.
Note: Includes description of national organization and outline of classes for various
age groups.
Location: IaHi; InIU; OClWHi.

N177   Weier, Ernst. The Work of the Turner Societies (American Turnerbund). A
Handbook by Ernst Weier. Indianapolis: Executive Committee of the American
Gymnastic Union, 1919. 19 p.
Note: Includes a history of the American Turners and an outline of their principles.
Location: InIU; MWT.

N178   ---. The Work of the Turner Societies (American Gymnastic Union). A
Catechism by Ernst A Weier. Indianapolis: National Executive Committee, American
Gymnastic Union, [1919]. 27 p.
Note: Cover title: "A Sound Mind and a Sound Body." Consists of an historical
overview of the American Turners in the form of questions and answers and the
principles of the American Gymnastic Union, p. 25-27.
Location: DLC; InIU; MnMSU; MoS; NcGU; PPB; WU; WUO.

N179 ---. The Work of the American Turner Societies (American Turnerbund) A Handbook by Ernst Weier. Detroit: National Executive Committee of the American Turnerbund, [1940]. 18 p.
Note: Includes a historical overview in the form of questions and answers, and the principles of the American Turnerbund, p. 16-18.
Location: InIU; MnBCHi; MnU.

MEMBERSHIP PUBLICATIONS

N180 Initiation of Candidates for Membership in the American Turnerbund. Pittsburgh: National Executive Committee, 1932. 14 p.
Note: In English and German.
Location: InIU.

N181 Initiation of Candidates for Membership in the American Turnerbund. Detroit: National Executive Committee, n.d. [3 panel brochure]
Location: InIU.

N182 Official Program for Membership Introduction Ceremony and Orientation of New Society Members to be used by the Turner Societies Affiliated with the American Turners on and after January 1, 1971. n.p., 1971. [10 p.]
Location: InIU.

N183 Official Catalog: Organization Insignia, Trophies, Awards and Accessories. Detroit: American Turnerbund, National Executive Committee, 1938. 15 p.
Note: Catalog of Turner memorabilia.
Location: InIU.

N184 Official Catalog: Organization Insignia, Trophies, Awards and Accessories. Detroit: American Turners, National Executive Committee, 1950. 8 p.
Location: InIU.

N185 American Turnerbund Medal. n.p., n.d. 15 p.
Note: Requirements to achieve a Turner medal.
Location: InIU.

N186 American Turnerbund Medal, revised to Nov. 1, 1935. n.p., 1935. 4 p.
Note: Requirements to achieve a Turner medal.
Location: InIU.

MISCELLANEOUS PUBLICATIONS

This section consists of publications written by Turners or works issued by the national office as official publications.

N187   The American Turners: A Splendid Tribute to the Turner Idea from an Outside Source. Pittsburgh: National Executive Committee of the American Turnerbund, [1927?]. 7 p.
Note: Brief introduction written by George Seibel, national president. Includes historical essay on the American Turners which was originally printed in The Interpreter, a publication by the Foreign Language Information Service.
Location: InIU.

N188   Aßmy, Ernst. Friedrich Ludwig Jahn: Eine Gedenkschrift aus den Jahren 1809-1819. Milwaukee: Freidenker Publishing Co., 1887. 46 p.
Note: Biographical sketch of Friedrich Jahn.
Location: MnSHi; WMCHi.

N189   Bary, Charles. The Turners' Organization. Milwaukee: Freidenker Publishing Company, 1906. 8 p.
Note: On cover, Charles Bary is identified as the president of the World's Fair Commission of the North American Turner Bund. Pamphlet describes the structure of the Turner organization. This is one of the informational pamphlets handed out at the World's Fair.
Location: ICN; InIU.

N190   Brosius, George. Fifty Years Devoted to the Cause of Physical Culture. Milwaukee: Germania Publishing Company, 1914. 127 p.
Note: Cover Title: "*Brosius: Goldenes-Jubiläum*, 1864[-]1914." Includes a biography of George Brosius, one of the leading gymnastic teachers in the Turner movement and director of the *Turnlehrer Seminar* in Milwaukee, poems, historical essays of Milwaukee Turners and American Turners and many photographs. In English and German.
Location: In; InIU; WHi; WM; WMCHi; WMT.

N191   Bundesvorort. Die bürgerliche Gleichstellung der Geschlechter. Im Auftrag der 21. Tagsatzung des Nordamerikanischen Turnerbundes, hrsg. Vom Bundesvorort. Milwaukee: Freidenker Publishing Co., 1905.
Note: Cited in Wagner, p. 346.

N192   Dapprich, Emil. Turnerische Fortbildungsschule. Plan für Einrichtung und Leitung derselben. Milwaukee: Freidenker Pub. Co., 1900.
Note: Cited in Wagner, p. 346.

N193   Die Deutsch Amerikanischen Turner: An das Amerikanische Volk. Williamsburgh, L.I.: Long Island Anzeiger, 1871.
Note: Cited in Pochmann #2099, and in Wagner, p. 340.

N194   Eberhardt, Walter C. The American Turners: their history, philosophy, and contributions to American democracy. Bloomington: Indiana University School of Health, Physical Education and Recreation, 1955.

N195   Geschichte der Turnerei bis zum 17. Bundes Turnfest abgehalten in Chicago, Illinois, vom 7. bis 11. August 1869. Mit einem Brustbilde Jahn's, und den Abbildungen der Festhalle, des Triumphbogens, u.s.w. Chicago: Chicago Abendzeitung, 1869. 68 p.
Note: Title translation: "The history of Turnerism up to the 17th National Turnfest in Chicago held August 7-11, 1869, with a portrait of Jahn and pictures of the festival hall and the triumphal arch." Includes an essay on Turnerism, brief reports on individual societies and districts and their development in 1869.
Location: InIU.

N196   Gollmer, Hugo. Namensliste der Pioniere des Nord-Amerikanischen Turnerbundes der Jahre 1848 - 1862. St. Louis: Henry Rauth, 1885. 34 p.
Note: List of early members of the American Turnerbund.
Location: InFA; InIU; WHi.

N197   Heintz, Jacob. Aus meinem Tagebuch: Eine Californien Reise zur 18ten Tagsatzung des Nordamerikanischen Turnerbundes in San Francisco, July 1898. New York: J. Goldmann, 1898. 80 p.
Note: Title translation: "From my diary: A Trip to California to the 18th national convention of the North American Turnerbund in San Francisco, July 1898."
Location: NN.

N198   Kuecken, Arthur. Turnerism is Americanism. Detroit: National Executive Committee of the American Turners, 1938. 19 p.
Note: Illustrated history of the Turner movement in the United States, with biographical sketches of Turner leaders.
Location: InIU.

N199   Metzner, Heinrich. Jahrbücher der Deutsch-Amerikanischen Turnerei: Dem gesammten Turnwesen mit besonderer Berücksichtigung der Geschichte des Nordamerikanischen Turner-Bundes gewidmet. 3 vols. New York: 1890-1894.
Note: Heinrich [Henry] Metzner immigrated to the United States in 1846, settled in New York and became an active member of the New York Turnverein as well as the national organization. As self-elected historian of the Turners, he published several books describing the development and goals of the organization. The Jahrbücher der Deutsche Turnerei were published every two months, with each set of six booklets

being gathered into a volume. In all, three volumes (18 booklets) were published. Metzner served as editor of the series and wrote many of the articles. Includes articles on the history of the American Turners, reports on individual societies and prominent members, political opinion pieces, songs, poems and general information. In German.
Location: DLC; InIU; MiU; MnU; NjR; OCU; WMCHi.

N200   ---. Deutsch-Amerikanische Dichtung mit besonderer Berücksichtigung des Turnerliedes. Vortrag im New Yorker Turn-Verein. New York: n.p., 1909. 30 p.
Note: "*Sonder-Abruck aus dem Organ des N.Y. Turn-Vereins Bahn Frei*, 1909." Survey of German-American literature with particular emphasis on Turner lyrics.
Location: DLC (microfilm); MdU; NN (microfilm); OCU.

N201   ---. Geschichte des Turnerbundes. Indianapolis: Office der Zukunft, 1874. 112 p.
Note: History of the North American Turnerbund, 1848-1874.
Location: IaDP; InIU; InU; OCU; WHi.

N202   ---. "*Die prinzipiellen Bestrebungen der Turner.*" Der deutsche Vorkämpfer [N.Y.] v. 3 (1909).
Note: Cited in Pochmann #7116.

N203   ---. A Brief History of the North American Gymnastic Union: In Commemoration of the One Hundredth Anniversary of the Opening of the First Gymnastic Field in Germany by Friedrich Ludwig Jahn. Stempfel, Theodore, trans. Indianapolis: National Executive Committee of the North American Gymnastic Union, 1911. 62 p.
Note: Revised edition of the Geschichte des Turnerbundes.
Location: CLU; DLC; IaHi; InI; InIU; InU; MiU; MnU; MoSW; PPiU; WHi.

N204   ---. A Brief History of the American Turnerbund. Theodore Stempfel, trans. rev. ed. Pittsburgh: National Committee of the American Turnerbund, 1924. 56 p.
Location: InIU; frequently available in large academic and public libraries.

N205   ---. History of the American Turners. 3rd rev. ed. Rochester, NY: National Council of the American Turners, 1974. 59 p.
Location: InIU; widely available.

N206   ---. History of the American Turners. 4th rev. ed. Louisville, KY: National Council of the American Turners, 1989. 67 p.
Location: InIU.

N207   North American Turnerbund. Erinnerungs-schriften, Nord-Amerikansichen Turner-Bundes, Gewidmet von dessen Vertretern bei der Weltausstellung den Freunden und Förderern des deutschen Turnwesens in den Vereinigten Staaten,

Chicago, 1893. Chicago: Edward Beeh, Jr., 1893. 116 p.
Note: Published for the celebration of the Columbian Exposition in Chicago, 1893. Includes poetry, humor and articles on health and fitness, the history of the Turners, the Normal College and free thought.
Location: InIU.

N208   Reuter, Hans C. [Reminiscences] n.p., 1969. 66 p.
Note: Transcription of a tape recording of Hans Reuter, in which he relates his experiences in the American Turner organization as a pupil, an adult member, and a teacher. Includes discussion of physical education in the public schools and teacher training at Wisconsin State University at La Crosse. Recorded in 1969.
Location: WHi.

N209   Seibel, George. Fifteen Years of Turner History in Pittsburgh. Pittsburgh: Jahn Educational Fund, 1954. 32 p.
Note: George Seibel was national president, 1923-37. Includes history of Turners, principles, and description of the Jahn Educational Fund.
Location: InIU; WM.

N210   ---. "The Turners in our History." Progressive World: The Thinker's Magazine v.9, no.8 (1955), pp. 30-34.

N211   Seventieth Anniversary of the American Gymnastic Union, Historical Sketch and Suggestions for Celebrations, 1850[-]1929. n.p.: American Turners National Executive Committee, [1920]. 10 p.
Note: Includes historical sketch of the Turner movement.
Location: InIU.

N212   Stempfel, Theodore. Ghosts of the Past: Autobiographical Sketches. Indianapolis: Privately Published, 1936. 101 p.
Note: Theodore Stempfel was national president, 1910-18.
Location: InFA; InHi; InI; InIU.

N213   Wiedeman, Carl. A Reply to Seibel's Fifteen Years. n.p., 1954.
Note: Carl Wiedeman was national president, 1937-1952.
Location: InIU.

Chapter 2

Circuit and District Publications and Historical Records

Below the national level, Turner societies have been organized into regional circuits (*Kreise*) and districts (*Bezirke*). These organizations have provided opportunities for societies in a region to meet on a regular basis to address issues of common concern, to influence national policy and to sponsor Turnfests and other athletic competitions. Several districts, most notably Illinois and St. Louis, have also maintained summer camps where members engage in outdoor activities. Most regional activity has taken place at the district level. The larger districts kept to a regular schedule of conventions and festivals beginning in the late 1860s, and were responsible for publishing a substantial number of convention proceedings and festival souvenir books, as well as special publications on physical education and gymnastics. The number of districts has ranged from sixteen in 1865, to a high of thirty-five in 1890, to the current fourteen. Circuits consisted of several districts, and were much more ephemeral organizations than the districts. The circuits were in existence from the late nineteenth century through the 1930s, but they seem to have been used only irregularly to sponsor Turnfests and other regional events. Neither districts nor circuits had fixed headquarters, but instead the leadership rotated among the member societies. As a result, the number of surviving publications and archival collections is very small and most of what has survived was intermixed with the records of individual societies. The amount and quality of surviving documentation, though, is suggestive of the amount of publishing that was probably done. The Indiana District and its predecessors, the Ohio Valley and Cincinnati *Turnbezirke*, published proceedings for most of their biennial conventions from 1869 to 1945, but this is the only district for which such a complete file of convention proceedings exist.

A list of circuits active in the 1930s follows the list of circuit publications, and a list of districts follows the district publications.

CIRCUITS

Publications

C1   Erste Tagsatzung des IV. Kreises des Nord=Amerikanischen Turner-Bundes, abgehalten zu Indianapolis, Ind., am Sonntag, den 21.Juni 1891, anlässlich des 1. Turnfestes obigen Kreises. Indianapolis: Indiana Tribüne, 1892. 8 p.
Note: The West-Central Circuit included the Indiana, Lake Erie, Ohio and Southern Central districts. Minutes and program for the circuit's first convention and festival.
Location: InIU.

C2   Kreis Turnfest, Fort Wayne, Ind., am 16.-19. Juni, 1911. Arbeitsplan für das körperliche Turnen. n.p., [1911].
Note: Work plan for the West-Central Circuit Turnfest.
Location: InIU.

C3   Working Plan for the Kreis Turnfest (Circuit Tournament) Sponsored by Lake Erie District, Detroit, Michigan (Belle Isle) July 5-6-7th, 1929. Judges and Instructors' Program for Competitive Events, Arranged by the Technical Committee of Lake Erie District. n.p., 1929. 14 p.
Note: Work plan for West-Central Circuit. Includes program of events.
Location: InIU.

C4   Official Program, Circuit Turnfest, Belle Isle Athletic Field, July 5-6-7, 1929, Detroit, Michigan. n.p., 1929. 21 p.
Note: Includes list of participating societies and districts. Published as July 1929 issue of the Detroit Turner, the newsletter of the *Detroiter Socialer Turnverein.*
Location: InIU.

C5   Souvenir Program of the Mid-West Turnfest at Moline, Illinois, June 24, 25, 26, 1932. n.p.: National Council of American Turners, 1957. 32 p.
Location: St. Paul Turners.

C6   Working plan for Central States Turnfest, Indiana District, Turners Park, Louisville, Kentucky, June 22-23-24, 1934. Judges' & Instructors' Program for Competitive Events Arranged by Turnfest Technical Committee. Mimeographed. n.p., 1934.
Note: Program of competitions and list of judges.
Location: InIU.

C7   24. Jahresbericht der Turner Gegenseitigen Unterstützungsgesellschaft des Nordwestens. Milwaukee: Freidenker Publishing Co., 1908. 7 p.
Note: Twenty-fourth annual report of the Turner Mutual Aid Society of the Northwest.
Location: MnHi.

Circuits in the 1930s

I. *Östlicher Kreis* (Eastern Circuit): Included New York, Philadelphia, and New Jersey Districts.

II. *Nordöstlicher Kreis* (Northeastern Circuit): Included New England, Connecticut and Central New York Districts.

III. *Östlicher Zentralkreis* (East-Central Circuit): Included Pittsburgh and West New York Districts.

IV. *Westlicher Zentralkreis* (West- Central Circuit): Included Indiana, Lake Erie, Ohio and South-Central Districts.

V. *Südwestlicher Kreis* (Southwestern Circuit): Included St. Louis, Upper Mississippi, Kansas-Missouri and New Orleans Districts.

VI. *Nordwestlicher Kreis* (Northwestern Circuit): Included Wisconsin, Illinois, and Minnesota Districts.

VII. *Westlicher Kreis* (Western Circuit): Included Rocky Mountain, Pacific, North Pacific and Southern California.

DISTRICTS

Central States District

Archival Collection

D1   Central States District, 1975-1976.
Location:InIU.
Description: Mimeographed minutes of the Central States District meetings, 1975-1976.

Publications

D2   Official Minutes of the Central States District of the American Turners.
1945-1957; 1977-1984.
Note: District minutes include reports of the district president, vice-president, financial secretary, treasurer and physical education committee, as well as individual society reports on their activities.
Location:
        InIU: 1946-1948, 1951-1954, 1977-1980, 1984.
        Dayton Liederkranz Turners: 1945, 1948, 1951-1955.
        American Turners Louisville: 1949.

D3   Constitution and By-Laws of the Central States District of the American Turners. n.p., n.d. 50 p.
Location: Covington Turners.

Chicago District (Chicago Turnbezirk)

Publications

D4   Fest-Zeitung für das 17. Bezirks-Turnfest des Turnbezirks Chicago, abgehalten am 20., 21., 22., und 23. Juni 1901, in Gardner's Park, Kensington, Ill. [Chicago], Columbia Printing Co., 1901. 40 p.
Note: Festival program for the 17th Chicago District Turnfest. Includes program for the festival, poems, humorous stories and photographs of sport activities. Essays in German; program in German and English.
Location: InIU.

D5   Gut Heil! Offizielles Organ des Chicago Turn Bezirks. Chicago: Chicago Turnbezirk, 1904-1916?
Note: Weekly. Newsletter of the Chicago district; possibly published until 1916.
Location:
     NN: v.1 (Dec. 1904) - Apr. 1906. Microfilm (incomplete).
     DLC: same as above. Microfilm.

Cincinnati District (Cincinnati Turnbezirk)

Archival Collections

D6   Cincinnati Turnbezirk, 1864-1869. 2 volumes.
Records are in German.
Location: American Turners Louisville.
Description: Financial records of the district, including records relating to competitions. The district included societies in Indiana, Ohio, and Kentucky.

Publications

D7   Protokoll der Verhandlungen und Beschlüsse der am 14. und 15. März abgehaltenen Bezirks-Tagsatzung in Columbus, Ohio. Indianapolis: *Office der Zukunft*, 1869. 7 p.
Note: Minutes of the district convention in 1869.
Location: InIU.

D8   Protokoll der Verhandlungen und Beschlüsse der am 26. und 27. März 1871 abgehaltenen Bezirks-Tagsatzung in Terre Haute, Indiana. Indianapolis: *Office der Zukunft*, 1871. 7 p.
Note: Minutes of the district convention in 1871.
Location: InIU.

Connecticut District (Connecticut Turnbezirk)

Publications

D9   Turn Fest Zeitung zum 15. Turnfest des Connecticut Turn Bezirks. [New Haven]: Herausgegeben vom New Haven Turn Verein, 1893.
Note: Newsletter for the 15th Connecticut District Turnfest.
Location: Cited in Eldredge, Wentworth H. "The New Haven German Community: A Field and Historical Study of German-American Institutions and Group Life." Ph.D. dissertation, Yale University, 1935.

D10   Einundzwanzigstes Turnfest des Connecticut Turn-Bezirks abgehalten im Schützen Park zu New Haven vom 3. bis 6. Juli 1902. n.p.: H. Bussmann, 1902.
Note: Includes programs of events, list of officers and committees, and concert program.
Location: NN (Metzner Collection., v. 5).

Illinois District (Illinois Turnbezirk)

Publications

D11   Official Song Book of the Illinois Turner District. n.p.,[1920].75 p.
Note: Includes lyrics and music to Turner songs and German folk songs. In English and German.
Location: InIU.

D12   Grosser Familien-Abend veranstaltet von der Vereinigten Alters-Riegen des Illinois Turnbezirks in der Lincoln Turnhalle, Samstag den 28. März 1925. n.p., 1925. [30 p.]
Note: Program of events for family evening held at the Lincoln Turner hall. Includes a history of the Illinois Turner camp and an article "*Warum sind wir Turner?*"(Why are we Turners?)
Location: ICHi.

D13   Songs of the American Boy and Girl Turners Issued by the Illinois District of the American Turnerbund, Season 1938. Mimeographed. n.p.,1938. [25 p.]
Note: Includes lyrics to German and American folk songs.
Location: InIU.

D14   100th Anniversary, American Turners Illinois District: 1865[-]1965. Aurora Turners, Chicago Turners, Eiche Turners, Lincoln Turners, Northwest Turners and the Illinois Turner Camp. n.p., 1965. [20 p.]
Note: Includes Illinois District calendar for 1965 and Illinois District Invitational

Turnfest program for June 25th and 26th, 1965.
Location: InIU.

D15   Illinois District of the American Turners Presents its Invitational Turnfest,
1968, June 28-29-30, at Our Beautiful Turner Camp Located on the Fox River
between Algonquin and the Fox River Grove. n.p., 1968. [15 p.]
Note: Includes Illinois District calendar for 1968 and Illinois District Invitational
Turnfest program for June 28th to 30th, 1968.
Location: InIU.

Illinois Turner Camp

The Illinois District Camp began in 1914 when Alfred Wild, the instructor of the
Eiche Turners, leased five acres on the north bank of the Fox River near Cary, Illinois,
to establish a summer camp for his gymnastic students. In 1919 the district purchased
a larger area on the opposite side of the river to which the camp was moved. The
district made the camp available to its members and allowed them to erect tents, and
later, cottages. More land was bought in 1925 and 1927, extending the area to over
120 acres. Over the years the camp has added a large community dining hall, kitchen,
dormitories, and other buildings. For physical exercises members have access to the
ball fields, tennis courts, gymnastic areas, and the swimming pool. The Illinois Turner
camp continues to be used as a weekend and summer recreation camp by members of
the district and it has long been the largest Turner camp in the United States.

Archival Collection

D16   Illinois Turner Camp, 1915-ca.1920.
Location: InIU.
Description: Alfred Wild's photograph album containing photographs of the Illinois
Turner Camp, 1915-ca.1920.

Publications

D17   Illinois Turner Camp. n.p., 1933. 16 p.
Note: Promotional brochure. Includes a history of the camp and camp regulations.
Location: InIU.

D18   Fifty Golden Years, 1914[-]1964, Illinois District Turner Camp.
Mimeographed. n.p., 1964. 5 p.
Note: Includes letter of the district president and a brief history of the Illinois District
camp.
Location: InIU.

D19   Glaser, Henry A. The Early Days: Illinois Turner Camp. n.p.: Illinois District Council, 1987. 24 p.
Note: Includes detailed history of camp, photographs, and reminiscences of Henry Glaser.
Location: InIU; WMT.

D20   Backer, Jim. "History, 1914-1994." Videotape, 1994.
Note: Video on the history of the Illinois Turner Camp.
Location: InIU.

Indiana District (Indiana Turnbezirk)

Archival Collection

D21   Indiana District Records, 1890-1910, 3 volumes.
Location: American Turners Louisville.
Description: Minutes of meetings, 1890-1910. In German. The Indiana District included societies in Indiana, northern Kentucky and Illinois.

Publications

D22   Offizielles Protokoll der [no.] Tagsatzung des Indiana Turn-Bezirks. 1880-1918?
Note: Title includes number of convention and meeting dates and place. Place of publication and publisher varies: Indianapolis: Indiana Tribüne, 1880-1885; Evansville: Indiana Post, 1886-1895, 1897; South Bend: South Bend Courier, 1896. Minutes of the years 1880-1885, 1887-1888 also include the district's statutes. Ladies Auxiliary minutes are included in the volumes for 1881, 1883 and 1887.

       1880 (9th), New Albany, IN., 20 p.
       1881 (10th), Evansville, IN, 24 p..
       1882 (11th), Lafayette, IN, 17 p..
       1883 (12th), Louisville, 22 p.
       1884 (13th), Danville, IL., 17 p.
       1885 (14th), Indianapolis, 12 p.
       1886 (15th), Evansville, 14 p.
       1887 (16th), Terra Haute, IN, 15 p.
       1888 (17th), Louisville, 14 p.
       1889 (18th), Danville, 13 p.
       1890 (19th), Indianapolis, 14 p.
       1891 (20th), Tell City, IN, 15 p.
       1892 (21st), Louisville, 18 p.
       1893 (22nd), South Bend, IN, 21 p.
       1894 (23rd), Indianapolis, 20 p.

      1895 (24th), Danville, 23 p.
      1896 (25th), Chicago Süd-Seite, 20 p.
      1897 (26th), Evansville, 19 p.
      1908 (37th). Location not identified.
Location:
      In: 1881, 1908.
      InIU: 1880-1897.

D23   Minutes of the [no.] Convention of the Indiana District of the American Gymnastic Union. 1921-1944.
Note: Title includes number of convention and meeting dates and place. No place of publication or publisher given.
      1921 (50th), Evansville, 8 p.
      1922 (51st), Evansville, 7 p.
      1923 (52nd), Louisville, 6 p.
      1924 (53rd), South Bend, 7 p.
      1927 (56th), Louisville, 8 p.
      1928 (57th), Indianapolis, 8 p.
      1929 (58th), Evansville, 12 p.
      1931 (60th), Indianapolis, 12 p.
      1932 (61st), Fort Wayne, 12 p.
      1933 (62nd), Louisville, 15 p.
      1934 (63rd), Evansville, 16 p.
      1935 (64th), Athenaeum, Indianapolis, 12 p.
      1938 (67th), Fort Wayne, 12 p.
      1939 (68th), Evansville, 8 p.
      1940 (69th), Athenaeum, Indianapolis, 18 p.
      1942 (71st), Louisville, 23 p.
      1943 (72nd), Fort Wayne, 19 p.
      1944 (73rd), South Side Indianapolis, 19 p.
Location:
      InIU: 1921-1944.
      Dayton Liederkranz Turners: 1940, 1944.

D24   Turnfest-Programm für das 18. Indiana Bezirks-Turn-Fest unter der Leitung des Südseite Turn-Vereins von Indianapolis, Ind., den 27., 28., 29. und 30. Juni 1903. Indianapolis: Gutenberg Co., [1903]. 20 p.
Note: Souvenir program for the 18th Indiana District Turnfest in 1903. Includes a brief history of the South Side Turners, list of committee members, statistical information on other societies in the district, and a brief article on women's exercises.
Location: InIU.

Kansas District (Kansas Turnbezirk)

<u>Archival Collection</u>

D25   Kansas Turnbezirk, 1887-1912. 1 volume
Location: MoKU.
Description: Minute book (*Protokollbuch*) of the Kansas Turnbezirk, 1887-1912.
In German.

<u>Publication</u>

D26   <u>Verfassung des Turn-Bezirks Kansas nach der Revision vom 6. und 7.</u>
<u>Dezember 1874</u>. n.p., 1874. broadsheet: 35.5 X 21.5 cm.
Location: InIU (photocopy); KHi.

Kansas-Nebraska-Missouri District

<u>Archival Collection</u>

D27   Kansas-Nebraska-Missouri District, 1888-1905. 1 volume.
Location: MoKU.
Description: Minute book of the Kansas-Nebraska-Missouri District, 1888-1905.
Includes list of members and dues.

Lake Erie District (Lake Erie Turnbezirk)

<u>Publications</u>

D28   <u>Protokoll der Dreizehnten Tagsatzung des Lake Erie Turnbezirks abgehalten</u>
<u>zu Akron, Ohio, am Sonnatg, den 29 April 1888</u>. n.p., 1888. 12 p.
Note: Minutes of the 13th convention of the Lake Erie Turnbezirk.
Location: Private collection.

D29   <u>Protokoll der Sechzehnten Tagsatzung des Lake Erie Turnbezirks,</u>
<u>abgehalten am 10. Mai 1891 in Erie, Pennsylvania</u>. Cleveland: Schmidt, Mugler &
Kraus, 1891. 20 p.
Note: Minutes of the district's 16th convention.
Location: InIU.

D30   <u>Protokoll der 26. Tagsatzung des Lake Erie Turnbezirks, abgehalten in</u>
<u>Akron, Ohio, den 12. Mai 1901</u>. n.p., 1901. 22 p.

Note: Minutes of the district's 26th convention.
Location: Private collection.

D31   Protokoll der 28. Tagsatzung des Lake Erie Turnbezirks, abgehalten in der
Germania Halle, Cleveland, O., am Sonntag, den 10. Mai 1903. Cleveland: Chas.
Lezius Print, 1903. 56 p.
Note: Includes a membership directory for the Germania Turnverein.
Location: InIU.

D32   Verhandlungen und Beschlüsse der [no.] Tagsatzung des Lake Erie
Turnbezirks. 1908-1947.
Note: Place of publication and publisher varies: Cleveland: West Side Printing House,
1925; Cleveland: Glenville Times, 1926-1932; thereafter no publishing information.
Until 1926 the minutes are exclusively in German; from 1927 to 1930 reports are in
German and English; after 1930 the minutes are predominantly in English. From 1931
to 1947 the convention minutes include the proceedings of the Ladies Auxiliary of the
Lake Erie District [1931 (4th Lake Erie District Ladies Auxiliary convention) - 1947
(20th Lake Erie District Ladies Auxiliary convention)].

    1908 (33rd), Akron Turnverein, 24 p.
    1913 (38th), Akron Turnverein, 24 p.
    1914 (39th), *Germania Turnverein*, Cleveland, 23 p.
    1925 (50th), *Sozialer Turnverein*, Cleveland, 12 p.
    1926 (51st), Akron Turner Club, 12 p.
    1927 (52nd), *Socialer Turnverein*, Detroit, 11 p.
    1928 (53rd), Toledo *Turn-und Sport Verein*, 12 p.
    1929 (54th), Akron Turner Club, 23 p.
    1930 (55th), *Germania Turnverein Vorwärts*, Cleveland, 18 p.
    1931 (56th), *Socialer Turnverein*, Detroit, 24 p.
    1932 (57th), *Sozialer Turnverein* Cleveland, 28 p.
    1933 (58th), *Turn-und Sport Verein*, Toledo, 26 p.
    1934 (59th), *Germania Turnverein Vorwärts*, Cleveland, 26 p.
    1935 (60th), Akron Turner Club, 24 p.
    1936 (61st), *Socialer Turnverein*, Detroit, 27 p.
    1937 (62nd), *Sozialer Turnverein,* Cleveland, 25 p.
    1938 (63rd), Toledo Turners, 25 p.
    1939 (64th), *Germania Turnverein Vorwärts*, Cleveland, 27 p.
    1940 (65th), Akron Turner Club, 28 p.
    1941 (66th), Detroit Turner Club, 31 p.
    1942 (67th), American Turners S.T.V., Cleveland, 31 p.
    1943 (68th), Toledo Turners, 21 p.
    1944 (69th), Cleveland East Side Turners, 17 p.
    1945 (70th), Akron Turner Club, 18 p.
    1946 (71st), American Turners Detroit, 21 p.
    1947 (72nd), American Turners S.T.V., Cleveland, 27 p.

Location:
  InIU: 1925-1947.
  Private collection: 1908, 1913-1914.

D33   Souvenir, 10tes Bezirks Turnfestes des Lake Erie Turnbezirks, Detroit, Mich., July 8, 9, 10 & 11, 1898. Detroit: John Bornman & Son, 1898. 40 p.
Note: Title page: "Tenth Grand Athletic Tournament of the Lake Erie Circuit of the North American Gymnastic Union, July 8, 9, 10 and 11, 1898, held at Detroit, Mich." Includes program of events, list of committee members, photographs of committee members, brief history of the Detroiter Socialer Turn-Verein and brief essay on the necessity of physical education in the public schools. In English and German.
Location: InIU.

D34   Allgemeine Bestimmungen für das Zehnte Bezirks Turnfest des Lake Erie Turnbezirks in Detroit, Michigan, am 9, 10, 11 Juli 1898. Detroit: John Vorman, 1898. 12 p.
Note: Festival rules for the 10th district Turnfest.
Location: Private collection.

D35   Bericht des Technischen Kommittees über die Leistungen der Turner auf dem 13. Bezirks Turnfest in Saginaw, Mich., vom 3. bis 5. Juli 1910. n.p., 1910. 6 p.
Note: Report of results for the 13th district Turnfest.
Location: Private collection.

D36   Program, 14th District Turn Fest of the Lake Erie Turn District, June 19th until June 22nd, 1914 at Akron, Ohio. Akron: n.p., [1914]. 52 p.
Note: Includes festival program, essay on the North American Gymnastic Union, and photographs of the Akron Turners' activities and hall. In English and German.
Location: InIU.

D37   Allgemeine Bestimmungen für das 14. Bezirks Turnfest des Lake Erie Turnbezirks in Akron, Ohio, am 19, 20, 21, und 22 Juni 1914. n.p., 1914. 23 p.
Note: Festival rules for the 14th district Turnfest.
Location: Private collection.

D38   Official Souvenir Book of the Lake Erie District Turnfest, June 18, 19, and 20, 1937. At the University of Toledo and German-American Athletic Club. n.p., 1937. 20 p.
Note: Includes a brief history of the German Athletic Club in Toledo, Ohio, and a program of events.
Location: InIU.

D39   Official Souvenir Book of the Lake Erie District Turnfest, Toledo, Ohio, June 21-23, 1940. Libbey High School, Gymnasium and Stadium, Toledo Turners, 3304

Collingwood Ave. n.p., 1940. 15 p.
Note: Includes list of committee members, program, a message to the Turners, and information about the Normal College.
Location: InIU.

D40   Lake Erie District Turnfest, Toledo, Ohio, June 16, 17, 18, 1950. n.p., 1950. 20 p.
Note: Program for the district Turnfest.
Location: InIU.

D41   N.A.T.B. Turnbezirk Lake Erie, Turnverein Vorwärts, Cleveland, O. n.p., 1907. 22 p.
Note: Includes list of national officers, principles and political platform of the Turnerbund, and list of members of the *Turnverein Vorwärts*, Cleveland.
Location: InIU.

D42   Verfassung des Lake Erie Turnbezirks gegründet am 7. Mai 1876, revidiert in der 37. Bezirks Tagsatzung des Lake Erie Turnbezirks abgehalten am Sonntag, den 19. März 1912 in der Halle des Sozialen Turnverein, Cleveland, Ohio. n.p., 1912. 10 p.
Note: Constitution of the Lake Erie Turnbezirk adopted at the 1912 convention.
Location: OCIWHi.

D43   Lake Erie Turn-Zeitung. 1889?-1918?
Note: Monthly.
Location: Cited in Arndt/Olson, v.1, p. 465.

Long Island District (Long Island Turnbezirk)

Publications

D44   Souvenir and Programme of the Exhibition of Physical Culture at the Academy of Music, Brooklyn, on Monday, March 25th, 1895. Arranged by the Long Island District of the North American Gymnastic Union. New York: Louis Weiss & Co., 1895. 8 p.
Note: Includes articles on physical education in Brooklyn and the value of physical training.
Location: InIU.

D45   Der Turnwart. Long Island Turnbezirk.
Note: Newsletter for the Long Island Turnbezirk. Discontinued before 1894.
Location: Cited in Metzner's Jahrbücher, v.3, no. 4, p. 282.

Minnesota District (Minnesota Turnbezirk)

Publications

D46   36. Tagsatzung und Turntag des Turnbezirks Minnesota abgehalten am 18. und 19. Januar 1902, in der Halle des West Seite Turnvereins, St. Paul, Minn. n.p., 1902. 4 p.
Note: Program for the 38th district convention. Includes German songs.
Location: MnHi.

D47   Protokoll der 36. Tagsatzung, abgehalten am 18. und 19. Januar 1902, in der Halle des Westseite Turnvereins, St. Paul, Minn. n.p., 1902.
Note: Minutes of the 36th district convention.
Location: MnHi.

D48   Turnbezirk Minnesota, Protokoll (Auszug) der 40. Tagsatzung, St. Anthony (Minneapolis) 1906. n.p., 1906. 4 p.
Note: Minutes of the 40th district convention.
Location: MnHi.

D49   Statuten des Turnbezirks Minnesota und Beschlüsse der 28. Bezirkstagsatzung, abgehalten den 22. Juni 1894. n.p., 1894. 12 p.
Note: Regulations of the Minnesota Turnbezirk and resolutions approved at the 28th annual district convention.
Location: MnHi.

D50   Grundsätze und Forderungen und Statuten des Nordamerikanischen Turnerbundes, angenommen von der 19. Tagsatzung zu Philadelphia im Juli 1900. Statuten des Turnbezirks Minnesota, wie von der 28. Tagsatzung angenommen und von der 29. bis 35. Tagsatzung verändert. New Ulm: The District, 1901. 40 p.
Note: Includes the principles and regulations of the North American Turnerbund and the regulations of the district.
Location: MnHi.

D51   Turnbezirk Minnesota, Turnfest Ordnung, 1906. n.p., 1906. 8 p.
Note: District festival rules.
Location: MnHi.

D52   Allgemeine Grundsätze und Statuten des Nordamerikanischen Turnerbundes, angenommen von der 23. Bundestagsatzung in Chicago am 28., 29. und 30. Juni und 1. Juli 1908: Statuten des Turnbezirks Minnesota, wie von der 28. Tagsatzung angenommen und von der 29. bis 43. Tagsatzung verändert. St. Paul: The District, 1909. 34 p.

Note: National and district regulations.
Location: MnHi.

D53   General Principles of the American Turnerbund. Statuten and By-Laws of the Turnbezirk Minnesota. n.p., [1925]. 11 p.
Location: InIU.

Middle Atlantic District

Publication

D54   Statutes of the Middle Atlantic District of the American Turners, Middle Atlantic District Founded 1868, Revised 1973. n.p., 1973. 7 p.
Location: InIU.

Missouri Valley District (Missouri Valley Turnbezirk)

Archival Collection

D55   Missouri Valley District, 1872-1902. 1 volume.
Location: MoKU.
Description: Minute book (*Protokoll*) of the Missouri Valley Turnbezirk, 1872-1902. In German.

Publication

D56   Offizielles Protokoll der 25sten Tagsatzung des Missouri Valley Turn-Bezirk abgehalten in Omaha, Nebraska, am 13ten und 14ten November 1887. Omaha: Schnellpressendruck von F.C. Festner, 1888. 30 p.
Note: Minutes of the 25th convention of the Missouri Valley Turnbezirk in Omaha.
Location: InIU; KU (Max Kade Institute).

Missouri-Kansas District (Missouri-Kansas Turnbezirk)

Archival Collection

D57   Missouri-Kansas District Records, 1887-1919.
Location: MoKU.
Description: Includes minutes of the district meeting, 1912-1919; financial records, 1887-1906; records of the *Kreis Turnfest*, 1911; and district correspondence, 1904 and 1917. In German and English.

New England District (New England Turnbezirk)

Publications

D58 Convention Minutes of New England District.
Note: Title includes place and date of meeting. Since 1961 the minutes have been mimeographed or photocopied.
> 1946 (72nd), Providence, RI, 4 p.
> 1960 (86th), Clinton, MA, 7 p.
> 1961 (87th), Lawrence, MA, 13 p.
> 1962 (88th), Adams, MA, 15 p.
> 1964 (90th), Holyoke, MA, 5 p.
> 1965 (91st), Providence, RI, 7 p.
> 1969 (96th), Lawrence, MA, 13 p.
> 1970 (97th), Adams, MA, 15 p.
> 1970 (semi-annual), Holyoke, MA, 3 p.
> 1971 (98th), Springdale, MA, 19 p.

Location: InIU: 1946, 1960-1971 [not complete].

D59 Round Table Convention, New England Turn District, Providence, R.I., May 2, 1971. Mimeographed. n.p., 1971. 3 p.
Note: Title from page 1. Convention minutes.
Location: InIU.

D60 Round Table Convention Report of the New England Turn District, Fitchburg, Massachusetts, May 7, 1972. Mimeographed. n.p., 1972. 6 p.
Note: Convention minutes.
Location: InIU.

D61 Gymnastic Festival New England, July 2-4, 1904, Turn Verein Lawrence, MA. n.p., 1904.
Note: Includes history of the Lawrence Turn Verein and many photographs of the society's members and hall.
Location: MLIA.

D62 Souvenir of the 27th New England Turn District Turnfest, Friday-Saturday-Sunday, June 14-15-16-1935, Under the Auspices of Springfield Turnverein, Springfield, Mass. n.p., 1935. 40 p.
Note: Includes histories of the Springfield Turners, officer list, program, and poems.
Location: InIU.

D63 29th Turnfest, New England District, under Auspices of the Deutsche Turnerschaft, July, 1, 2, 3, 4, 1939, Providence, Rhode Island. n.p., 1939. 52 p.

Note: Includes histories of the *Deutsche Turnerschaft*, its ladies auxiliary and band, a list of committee members, and festival program.
Location: InIU.

D64   Souvenir Program, Thirty-fourth Gymnastic Tournament of the New England District, Friday, Saturday, and Sunday, June 27-28-29, 1867-1947. Sponsored by the Clinton Turn Verein, Inc. Clinton, Massachusetts. n.p., 1947 28 p.
Note: Includes brief history of the Clinton Turn Verein and program.
Location: InIU.

D65   36th Annual Gymnastic Turnfest Tournament, New England District, June 23-24-25, 1950, Turners Athletic Field, Adams, Mass. n.p., 1950. 70 p.
Note: Includes article on the principles of the American Turners, program for the festival, and photographs.
Location: InIU.

D66   New England District, 44th Annual Turn Fest, June 23, 24, 25, 1961, Holyoke, Mass. n.p., 1961. 28 p.
Note: Includes program and picture of Holyoke Turner Society.
Location: InIU.

D67   46th New England District Turnfest, June 19, 20, 21, 1964, Lawrence Turn Verein Host Society. n.p., [1964].
Note: Includes history of the Lawrence Turn Verein and program of events.
Location: MLIA.

D68   53rd New England Turnfest, June 22, 23, 24, 1973. Hosts Clinton Turn Verein, Clinton, Mass. n.p., 1973. 47 p.
Note: Includes festival program and photographs of Clinton Turn Verein.
Location: InIU.

D69   New England District, American Turners, Constitution and By-Laws as Amended 1964. Springfield: Print Craft, Inc, 1964. 10 p.
Location: InIU.

D70   New England District, American Turners, Constitution and By-Laws as Amended 1984. n.p., 1984. 8 p.
Location: InIU.

D71   Rules Governing American Turner Gymnastic Tournaments Conducted by New England Turn District. n.p., 1959. 4 p.
Location: InIU.

D72   First Combined Gymnastic and Singing Festival of the New England Gymnastic and Singing Societies, July 2,4,5, and 6, 1924 at Lawrence, Massachusetts. n.p., 1924.
Note: Includes poems, songs, history of singing societies, and photographs of Lawrence Turner hall.
Location: MLIA.

D73   New England Candle Pin Championship Matches.
       1963 (10th), Fitchburg, MA, 10 p.
       1965 (12th), Manchester, NH, 18 p.
       1967 (14th), Lawrence, MA, 4 p.
Note: Title includes place and date of tournament. Includes competition results.
Location: InIU: 1963, 1965, 1967.

New Jersey District (New Jersey Turnbezirk)

Publication

D74   Die Zukunft. Offizielles Organ des Deutsch Amerikanischen Central Vereins der Stadt Newark, New Jersey, und des New Jersey Turnbezirks . 1904-1909
Note: Monthly publication.
Location: NN: v.1 (1904) - v.6 (1909). Scattered issues.

New York District (New York Turnbezirk)

Publications

D75   Gedenkschrift zur Feier des Fünfzigjährigen Jubiläums des Turn-Bezirks New York, am 13. und 14. April 1913, New York. [New York]: n.p., [1913]. 48 p.
Note: Cover title: *"Fest Programm, Goldenes Jubiläum des Turn-Bezirks New York am 13. April 1913 im New York Hippodrome."* Souvenir program of the 50th anniversary of the New York District. Includes principles of the North American Gymnastic Union, summary of the Olympic games and gymnastic festivals, history of the New York District and festival program. In German and English.
Location: InIU.

D76   Souvenir Program, Gymnastic Tournament of the New York District of the American Turners to be held in Schenectady 21, 22, 23 June 1946. n.p., 1946. 40 p.
Note: Includes essay on the principles of the American Turners, brief history of the American Turners, historical notes on the Schenectady Turnverein, festival program, and photographs of the Schenectady Turners.
Location: InIU.

D77   Statuten des Turn Bezirks New York. New York: Geo. J. Speyer, 1900.
10 p.
Location: InIU.

D78   Constitution and By-Laws, New York District of the American Turners,
1951 as amended through March 7, 1987. n.p., 1987.14 p.
Location: InIU.

Ohio District (Ohio Turnbezirk)

Publications

D79   Liederbuch für Turner gewidmet dem Ohio Turnbezirk, von den Turnlehrern
Wilhelm A. Stecher, Anton Leibold und Julius Stemmler. Zweite Auflage. Cincinnati:
John Church & Co., 1885. 64 p.
Note: Music and lyrics to seventy-two German and English songs.
Location: InIU; MnHi.

D80   Songs of the Ohio District, American Turnerbund. 1st ed. Cincinnati: n.p.,
1925. 26 p.
Note: Includes sixty-three English songs.
Location: InIU.

D81   A Symposium of Papers dealing with Turner Activities by the Ohio District
Turners. n.p., 1928. 24 p.
Note: Includes essays on "What is a Turnverein?", "Budgeting a Turnverein,"
"Society Meetings-When, What, How!" and "Committee Work."
Location: InIU.

D82   Reck und Barren: Offizielles Organ des Ohio Turnbezirks, 1890?-1891?
Note: Newsletter of the Ohio district; probably started in 1890. Includes national and
local Turner news, advertisements, and reports on physical culture. The ending date
is unknown.
Location: OCHi: v.2, no. 47 (Feb. 21, 1891).

Ohio Valley District (Ohio Valley Turnbezirk)

Publications

D83   Revidierte Statuten, Verhandlungen und Beschlüsse der zweiten Tagsatzung
des Ohio Valley Turn-Bezirks gehalten zu Lafayette, Ind., am 12. und 13. Januar
1873. Indianapolis: Die Zukunft, 1873. 14 p.

Note: Proceedings, resolutions and revised statutes from the 2nd convention of the Ohio Valley District, held at Lafayette, IN.
Location: InIU.

D84 Revidierte Statuten, Verhandlungen und Beschlüsse der Tagsatzung des Ohio Valley Turn-Bezirks gehalten zu Indianapolis, Ind., am 12. und 13. April 1874. Indianapolis: Die Zukunft, 1874. 16 p.
Note: Proceedings, resolutions and revised statutes from the district convention held at Indianapolis.
Location: InIU.

D85 Offizielles Protokoll der [no.] Tagsatzung des Ohio Valley Turn-Bezirks. 1875-1879.
Note: Published in Indianapolis by the Zukunft from 1875-1877, by the Gutenberg Co., 1878 and by the Indiana Tribüne, 1879.
     1875 (4th), New Albany, 23 p.
     1877 (6th), Lafayette, 18 p.
     1878 (7th), Louisville, 21 p.
     1879 (8th), Indianapolis, 16 p.
Location: InIU: 1875, 1877-1879.

Pacific District (Pacific Turnbezirk)

Publications

D86 Minutes of the third annual convention of the Pacific Turners, held January 30th, 1949 at the California Hall, San Francisco, California. Mimeograph. 1949. 7 p.
Location: InIU.

D87 Sixth Turnfest of the Pacific Circuit. Combined with Sängerfest. Souvenir Program, June 23 to 26, 1911. Los Angeles: n.p., 1911.
Location: CSmH.

Philadelphia District (Philadelphia Turnbezirk)

Archival Collection

D88 Progress Turnverein Records, 1865-1875. 2 volumes.
Location: PPB.
Description: Includes the minutes of the 1874 convention of the Philadelphia Turnbezirk; handwritten in German.

Publications

D89   Protokoll der Tagsatzung des Philadelphia Turn-Bezirks, abgehalten am 24. März 1895, zu Trenton, N.J. Philadelphia: Thos. Pfizenmayer, 1895. 48 p.
Note: Convention minutes.
Location: InIU.

D90   Protokoll der Tagsatzung des Philadelphia Turn-Bezirks, abgehalten am 22. März 1896, zu Wilmington, Del. Philadelphia: William Franck, 1896. 45 p.
Note: Convention minutes.
Location: InIU.

D91   Protokoll der Tagsatzung des Turn-Bezirks Philadelphia, abgehalten am 27. und 28. März 1897, zu Philadelphia, PA. Philadelphia: William Franck, 1897. 53 p.
Note: Convention minutes.
Location: InIU.

Pittsburgh District (Pittsburgh Turnbezirk)

For archival collection, see Western Pennsylvania District.

Publication

D92   Plattform des Nordamerikanischen Turnerbundes und Statuten des Turnbezirks Pittsburg, sowie Protokoll der 32. Bezirks=Tagsatzung abgehalten in der Halle des "Columbia-Turnvereins," nebst Jahresberichten der Bezirksbeamten. Steubenville: Steubenville Germania, 1896. 28 p.
Note: Includes statutes of the American Turnerbund and the Pittsburgh District, and district convention minutes for 1896.
Location: InIU.

D93   Statuten des Pittsburg Turn-Bezirks sowie Protokoll der 40sten Bezirks-Tagsatzung abgehalten in der Halle des Jeannette Turn-Vereins, Jeanette, Pa, am Sonntag, den 10. April 1904, nebst Jahres-Berichten der Bezirks-Beamten. Allegheny, Pa: Max Schwartz, 1904. 33 p.
Note: Includes statutes of the American Turnerbund, Pittsburgh District, and district convention minutes for 1904.
Location: InIU.

D94   Statuten des Pittsburg Turn-Bezirks und das Protokoll der 44. Bezirks-Tagsatzung abgehalten in der Halle der Charleroi Turn-Vereins zu Charleroi, Pa., Sonntag, 12. April 1908, nebst den Jahresberichten der Bezirksbeamten. Pittsburgh: Karl Schwarz, 1908. 34 p.

Note: Includes statutes of the American Turnerbund, the Pittsburgh District, and district convention minutes for 1908.
Location: InIU.

D95 Leistungs-Tabellen und Rangordnung am Schau-und Preis-Turnfest abgehalten am 10. und 11 Juni 1906 in McKeesport, Pa. n.p., 1906. 8 p.
Notes: Results of competitions at the 1906 district Turnfest.
Location: InIU.

D96 Leistungs-Tabellen und Rangordnung vom Bezirks-Turnfest des Pittsburg Turn-Bezirks abgehalten am 7., 8. und 9. Juni 1908 in Monongahela City, Pa. Pittsburgh: Allied Printing, 1908. 8 p.
Note: Results of competitions at the 1908 district Turnfest.
Location: InIU.

D97 Invitational Turnfest Arranged by the Johnstown Turnverein and Sponsored by the Pittsburgh Turn District, June 23-26, 1938, Johnstown, PA. Johnstown: Schubert Press, 1938. 32 p.
Note: Includes historical sketch of the Johnstown Turnverein, program of events, and historical sketch of the American Turners by George Seibel.
Location: InIU.

D98 Work Plan, Program, and Schedule of Events (A Guide for Officials and Participants), Invitational Turnfest, Johnstown, PA., June 23, 24, 25 and 26, 1938, Auspices of Pittsburg Turn District. All Events are Scheduled on Eastern Standard Time, E.S.T. Johnstown, Pa.: Local Technical Committee, 1938. 20 p.
Location: InIU.

D99 Mass, Class and Apparatus Exercises (Revised Tentative Program). For the Invitational Turnfest, June 23-26, 1938, Johnstown, Pa. n.p., 1938. 28 p.
Location: InIU.

D100 Amerikanischer Turnerbund, Statuten des Pittsburg Turn=Bezirks, angenommen in Monessen 1925. American Turnerbund, Statutes of the Pittsburgh District Turners, adopted at Monessen, 1925. n.p., 1925. [24 p.]
Note: Separately paged sections for German and English statutes.
Location: InIU.

D101 Pittsburgh District of the American Turners, Constitution and By-Laws. Pittsburgh: n.p., 1946. 21 p.
Location: InIU.

Rocky Mountain District (Rocky Mountain Turnbezirk)

<u>Publications</u>

D102   Protokoll der Fünfzehnten Tagsatzung des Rocky Mountain Turnbezirk, abgehalten am 24. April 1887 in der Vorwärts Turnhalle, Denver, nebst Statuten und Turnfestordnung des Rocky Mountain Turnbezirks. n.p, 1887. 8 p.
Location: IaDP.

D103   Souvenir Programme of the Twenty-First Gymnastic Tournament of the Rocky Mountain District Turner Society to be held at Leadville, Colorado, June 29 and 30, and July 1, 1907. n.p., 1907. 36 p.
Location: CoD.

St. Louis District (St. Louis Turnbezirk)

<u>Publications</u>

D104   Protokoll des 36sten Bezirks-Tagsatzung des St. Louis Turnbezirks, abgehalten in der Rock-Spring Turnhalle, am Sonntag, den 17ten April 1898. n.p.: Herman Ruppelt, 1898. 28 p.
Note: Convention minutes.
Location: InIU.

D105   77th Biennial Convention, St. Louis District· American Turners. Mimeographed. n.p., 1945. 13 p.
Note: Cover title: "Report, American Turners, 77th Biennial Convention, St. Louis District American Turners, 1944-1945." Convention minutes.
Location: InIU.

D106   Golden Jubilee, St. Louis Turn-Bezirk, History, 1862[-]1912 in German and English. St. Louis: C. Schreiner, 1912. 35 p.
Note: Title page: "*Gedenkschrift und Geschichtlicher Rückblick über die Entwicklung der Turnerei in den Vereinigten Staaten und der Tätigkeit des St. Louis Turnbezirks zu seinem fünfzigjährigen Bestehen verfasst von Otto Kallmeyer in German und Englisch.*" Detailed history of the St. Louis Turnbezirk; pages 1-23 written in German, pages 23-35 written in English.
Location: InIU; MoU.

D107   St. Louis Turner: Published Monthly. Official Organ of the St. Louis District of the American Gymnastic Union.
Note: Monthly newsletter of the St. Louis District. May have been published in two series: 1) 1891-??; 2) ca.1913-1932?

Location:
IU (University Archives): v.17 (1930) - v.19 (1932). Scattered issues.
MoSHi: Jan. 31-Dec.26, 1891. Cited in Arndt/Olson, v.1, p. 271.

South California District (Süd California Turnbezirk)

Publication

D108   Protokoll der 44sten Tagsatzung des Süd-California Turnbezirks am 29.
April 1934. n.p., 1934.
Location: CSDHi (San Diego Turner Collection).

Upper Mississippi District (Oberer Mississippi Turnbezirk)

Publications

D109   Protokoll der [no.] Tagsatzung des Oberen Mississippi Turnbezirks
abgehalten am [loc.], nebst Verfassung des Bezirks.
Note: Place of publication and publisher: Davenport: Iowa Reform. Proceedings are
in German and English, and include the district's statutes and by-laws.
        1916 (51st), Burlington Turngemeinde, IA, 34 p.
        1917 (52nd), Ottawa Turnverein, IL, 39 p.
        1918 (53rd), Rock Island Turngemeinde, IL, 55 p.
Location: InIU: 1916-1918.

D110   Proceedings of the [no.] annual convention of the Upper Mississippi
Gymnastic District, 1920?-1955?
Note: Publisher varies: 1921-1930 and 1932 printed by the Peterson Printing Co.;
1931, 1933 and 1939-1941 by the Blackhawk Printing Co.; and 1934, 1949, 1951,
1953 by the Model Printing Company in Moline, IL. The 1934 minutes also include
the proceedings of the 15th annual convention of the women's auxiliary of the Upper
Mississippi District.
        1921 (56th), East Davenport Turner Society, 33 p.
        1922 (57th), *Vorwärts* Turner Society, Clinton, IA, 31 p.
        1924 (59th), *Concordia-Germania Turnverein*, Moline, 15 p.
        1925 (60th), Keystone Turnverein, IA, 15 p.
        1926 (61st), Burlington Turngemeinde, 16 p.
        1927 (62nd), Northwest Davenport Turner Society, 15 p.
        1928 (63rd), East Davenport Turner Society, 15 p.
        1929 (64th), Clinton Turners & Benevolent *Verein Vorwärts*, 15 p.
        1930 (65th), Keystone Turnverein, 14 p.
        1931 (66th), Davenport Turngemeinde, 16 p.

1932 (67th), *Concordia-Germania Turnverein*, Moline, 16 p.
1933 (68th), Northwest Turner Society, Davenport, 16 p.
1934 (69th), East Davenport Turner Hall, 23 p.
1935 (70th), Keystone Turner Hall, 19 p.
1936 (71st), Clinton Hall, 21 p.
1937 (72nd), Davenport Turn-Gemeinde, 19 p.
1938 (73rd), Davenport Turner Hall, 15 p.
1939 (74th), East Davenport Turner Hall, 19 p.
1940 (75th), Moline Turner Hall, 19 p.
1941 (76th), Keystone Turner Hall, 19 p.
1942 (77th), Eldridge Turner Hall, IA, 20 p.
1943 (78th), Central Turner Hall, Davenport, 19 p.
1944 (79th), Northwest Davenport Turner Hall, 20 p.
1945 (80th), Clinton Turner Hall, 23 p.
1948 (82nd), Keystone Turner Hall, 16 p.
1949 (83rd), Moline Turners, 18 p.
1950 (84th), Central Turners Davenport, 18 p.
1951 (85th), Northwest Turner Society, Davenport, 17 p.
1952 (86th), Clinton Turner Society, 16 p.
1953 (87th), East Davenport Turner Society, 16 p.
1954 (88th), Keystone Turner Society, 15 p.
1955 (89th), Moline Turner Society, 16 p.

Location:
    IaDP: 1921-1928, 1930-1936, 1938-1944, 1948-1953.
    InIU: 1929-1934, 1937, 1940-1944, 1946-1949, 1951, 1953-1955.

D111   The American Turners. Upper Mississippi District Convention, Davenport, Iowa, April 27th and 28th, 1963. n.p., 1963. [30 p.]
Note: Cover title: "The American Turners. 111th Anniversary in the Quad Cities, Central Turners Organized 1852." Program to the 97th convention of the Upper Mississippi district, 1963.
Location: InIU.

D112   Constitution of the Upper Mississippi Turner District. n.p., n.d. 8 p.
Location: IaHi.

D113   Constitution of the Upper Mississippi Turner District, Revised 1943. n.p., 1943. [8 p.]
Location: Northwest Davenport Turners.

D114   Constitution of the Upper Mississippi District, revised 1953. n.p., 1953. 12p.
Location: Northwest Davenport Turner Society.

Upper Missouri District (Oberer Missouri Turnbezirk)

D115 Verhandlungen der Dreizehnten Tagsatzung des Oberen Missouri-Turnbezirks, Sioux Falls, Süd-Dakota, 6. und 7. April 1895. Yankton, SD: Dakota Freie Presse, 1895. 15 p.
Location: InIU.

West New York District (Western New York Turnbezirk)

Publications

D116 82nd Annual Convention, Western New York District, Rochester, New York, October 6-7, 1945. Mimeographed. n.p., 1945. 13 p.
Note: Convention minutes.
Location: InIU.

D117 95th Annual Convention, Western New York District, Buffalo, New York, May 2-3, 1959. Mimeographed. n.p., 1959. 22 p.
Note: Convention minutes.
Location: InIU.

D118 96th Annual Convention, Western New York District, Buffalo, New York, May 7 & 8, 1960. Mimeographed. n.p., 1960. 22 p.
Note: Convention minutes.
Location: InIU.

D119 Offizielles Fest-Programm für das 26ste Bezirks-Turn-Fest, 18., 19., 20. und 21. Juli, 1896, Syracuse, New York. n.p., 1896. 116 p.
Note: Title page on page 19. Cover: "1896, West New York *Turn-Bezirk, 26stes Bezirks Turn Fest*, Syracuse, N.Y." Includes photos of members and classes of societies belonging to the district, list of exercises and program.
Location: InIU.

D120 West New York Turn Bezirk. Siebenundzwanzigstes Bezirks-Turnfest, 13.-16. August, 1898, Buffalo, NY. Buffalo: n.p., 1898.
Note: Cited in Pochmann #11611.

D121 Souvenir Book of the Thirty-first Turnfest of the West New York District, North American Gymnastic Union, Rochester, N.Y., June twenty-ninth, thirtieth and July first, Nineteen Hundred Six. n.p.: Walsh & Kramer Printing Company, 1906. 32 p.
Note: Cover title: "'*Gut Heil*' 31st Turnfest of the West New York District. North American Gymnastic Union, June, 29th-30th and July 1st. Rochester, N.Y. Souvenir

1906." Includes essays on the American Turnerbund and the Rochester Turnverein, a list of officers, class schedule, and photographs of the Rochester Turners.
Location: InIU.

D122   32nd Turnfest of the West New York District, North American Gymnastic Union, Buffalo, N.Y., June 28th-30th, 1907 held under the Auspices of the Columbia Turnverein, Buffalo, N.Y. n.p., 1907. 49 p.
Note: Program of the 32nd West New York District Turnfest in Buffalo. In English and German.
Location: Private collection.

D123   Souvenir Program of the 35th Turnfest of the Western N. Y. District, North American Gymnastic Union, June 14, 15, 16, 17, 1912. Held under the Auspices of the Buffalo Turn Verein at Buffalo, N.Y., U.S.A. Buffalo: Courier Company, 1912. 56 p.
Note: Cover Title: "35th Turnfest of the Western New York District at Buffalo, June 14, 15, 16, 17, 1912. North American Gymnastic Union." Includes brief history of the Buffalo Turners and the city of Buffalo, program of events, and photographs of the Buffalo Turners and Buffalo.
Location: InIU.

D124   Gau-Turn-Fest der Östlichen Turn-Bezirke. Goldenes Jubiläum des West New York Turn Bezirks und 60. Jubiläum des Syracuse Turn-Vereins abgehalten in Syracuse, N.Y. Juni 12-15, 1914. n.p., 1914. [50 p.]
Note: Includes articles on physical education, history of the Syracuse Turnverein, program of events, and photographs of Syracuse gym classes.
Location: InIU.

D125   Souvenir Program of the 37th Bezirks Turnfest of the Western New York District of the North American Gymnastic Union. June 16th, 17th, 18th, 19th, 1916 at Buffalo, N.Y. Under the Auspices of the Columbia Turn Verein. Buffalo: Quality Press, 1916. 48 p.
Note: Cover title: "North American Gymnastic Union. 37th Turnfest, June 16, 17, 18, 19, 1916, Buffalo, NY, Western New York Turn Bezirk Auspices Columbia Turn Verein." Includes brief history of the Columbia Turnverein, program of events, committee members, and pictures of Buffalo and Columbia Turnverein gym classes.
Location: InIU.

D126   38th Field Day and Athletic Carnival, June 14, 15, 16, 1918, Auburn, New York, Western New York District, Auspices of the Auburn Turn Verein, Inc. n.p., 1918. 16 p.
Note: Cover title: "North American Gymnastic Union, 38th Field Day and Athletic Carnival, June 14, 15, 16, 1918, Auburn, New York, Western New York District,

Auspices of the Auburn Turn Verein, Inc." Includes program, brief history, and photographs of the Auburn Turnverein.
Location: InIU.

D127   41st Field Day and Athletic Carnival, June 20, 21, 22, 1924, Auburn, N.Y. Western New York District, Auspices of the Auburn Turn Verein, Inc. n.p., 1924. 14p.
Note: Cover title: "North American Gymnastic Union, 41st Field Day and Athletic Carnival, June 20, 21, 22, 1924, Auburn, N.Y. Western New York District, Auspices of the Auburn Turn Verein, Inc." Includes program, brief history, and photographs of the Auburn Turnverein.
Location: InIU.

Western Pennsylvania District (Western Pennsylvania Turnbezirk)

Archival Collection

D128   Western Pennsylvania\Pittsburgh District Collection, 1916-1975.
Records prior to the 1930s are predominantly in German.
Finding aid available from repository.
Location: PPiHi
Description: The collection includes minutes of the Pittsburgh Turn Bezirk and its successor, the Western Pennsylvania Turnbezirk, 1916-1924; district correspondence and financial records, 1924-1949, 1956-1975; and dues records, 1970.

Publications

D129   First Annual Circuit Turnfest, Friday-Saturday-Sunday, June 13,14, 15, 1958 at Turner Hall & Cochran Field. n.p., 1958. 4 p.
Note: Cover title: "Johnstown Turners, Oscar N. Simmen Memorial. First Annual Circuit Turnfest, Friday-Saturday-Sunday, June 13, 14, 15, 1958 at Turner Hall & Cochran Field." Includes program of events.
Location: InIU.

D130   100 District Convention of the Western Pennsylvania Turners, Sunday, May 17, 1964 at Turners Hall, 127 E. Main Street, Monongahela, PA, 1864[-]1964. n.p., 1964. [32 p.]
Note: Includes brief histories of the member societies.
Location: InIU.

D131   Western Pennsylvania District of the American Turners, Constitution and By-Laws. Rochester: Henderson Print, 1968. 35 p.
Location: InIU.

D132   Revision of Constitution of the Women's Auxiliary to the Western Penna. District of the American Turners, Revised and Adopted January 26, 1969. n.p., 1969. 12 p.
Location: InIU.

Wisconsin District (Wisconsin Turnbezirk)

Archival Collection

D133   Wisconsin Turnbezirk Records, 1865-1916.
Location: WMCHi
Description: Minutes of the Wisconsin district conventions (*Verhandlungen der Tagsatzung des Turnbezirk Wisconsin*), 1865-1875, and statistical reports, 1873-1916 (reports cited in Wagner, pp. 338).

Publications

D134   Protokoll der [no.] Tagsatzung des Turnbezirks "Wisconsin", abgehalten in [loc.], 1895-1916.
Note: Varies slightly in title. Convention minutes for the years 1895-1915 printed by the Freidenker Pub. Co. of Milwaukee. Minutes for 1916 printed by the Moebius Printing Co. of Milwaukee.
   1891, Milwaukee. Cited in Wagner, p.338.
   1895 (31st), Manitowoc. 40 p.
   1900, New Holstein. Cited in Wagner, p.338
   1901, Fond du Lac. Cited in Wagner, p.338.
   1915 (51st), Mayville. 30 p.
   1916 (52nd), Kenosha. 32 p.
Location:
   InIU: 1895.
   WMCHi: 1915.
   WM: 1916.

D135   Minutes of the 82st District Convention of the Wisconsin Turn District convened at Milwaukee Turner Hall on Sunday, May 5, 1946. Mimeographed. n.p., 1946. 8 p.
Location: InIU.

D136   Obligatorische Übungen für das 22. Turnfest des Turnbezirks Wisconsin am 13. bis 17. August 1886 zu La Crosse, Wis. Milwaukee: Freidenker Publishing Co., 1886.
Note: Exercises for the district's 22nd Turnfest in La Crosse.
Location: WMT.

D137   Fest Zeitung des Monroe Turn Vereins zum 24. Bezirksturnfest des Wisconsin Turnbezirks. n.p., 1888. [broadside]
Note: Announcements for the 24th district Turnfest.
Location: WMHi.

D138   Fest-Zeitung des Turnfest des Turnbezirks Wisconsin. n.p., 1892.
Note: Monthly publication issued before the 1892 Wisconsin District Turnfest.
Location: WHi (bound with Wisconsin Botschafter, Monroe, WI).

D139   Die Turnerei. Festprogram: allgemeine Bestimmungen und Übungen für das 34. Bezirks-Turnfest des Turnbezirks "Wisconsin," am 24. - 27. Juni 1904, in La Crosse, Wisconsin. Milwaukee: n.p., 1904.
Note: Cited in Pochmann #11036.

D140   Souvenir zum Goldenen Jubiläum des Turnbezirks Wisconsin, 1865 - 1915 am 5. und 6. Juni 1915. Milwaukee: n.p., 1915. [70 p.]
Note: Includes a history of the Wisconsin District and photographs.
Location: WHi; WM; WMCHi; WMT (Wiedemann Collection).

D141   Wisconsin State Turn Fest. Official Program and Memorial Edition, Eighty-Fifth Anniversary, Turn Verein Milwaukee, June 18 and 19, 1938. n.p., 1938. 20 p.
Note: Includes Turnfest program, the history of the Turner movement in the United States, history of the Milwaukee Turners, and the principles of the American Turners.
Location: InIU; WHi; WMCHi.

D142   Verfassung des Turnvereins Milwaukee nebst Plattform und Statuten des Nord-Amerikanischen Turnerbundes und des Turnbezirks Wisconsin, sowie Freibrief (Charter) des Vereins und Statuten der Unterstützungssektion. Milwaukee: Freidenker Publishing Co., 1884. 51 p.
Location: WM.

D143   Verfassung des Turnvereins der Nordseite nebst Plattform und Statuten des Nordamerikanischen Turner-Bundes und des Turnbezirks Wisconsin, sowie Freibrief des Vereins. Milwaukee: Hugo Schubel, 1890. 87 p.
Location: InIU.

LIST OF DISTRICTS, 1865 - PRESENT

District Name	Beginning Date	Ending Date	Comments
Arkansas	1885	1890	renamed *Südlicher*
Boston	1864	1885	joined with New England
Central Illinois	1871	1914	merged with Chicago to become Illinois
Central Michigan	1883	1897	joined Chicago
Cent. New York	1868	1920	Hudson River joined in 1872; not listed 1903-1915; joined New England in 1920
Central States	1945	pres.	formed from Indiana; South Central joined in 1949
Chicago	1865	1914	Central Michigan joined in 1897; merged with Central Illinois to form Illinois
Cincinnati	1864	1885?	renamed Ohio
Connecticut	1868	1929	joined New England
Florida	1885	1904	
Hudson River	1866?	1872	joined Central New York
Illinois	1914	pres.	made up of Chicago and Central Illinois
Indiana	1883	1945	renamed Central States in 1945, formerly part of Ohio Valley; added Ohio in 1940
Kansas	1866?	1905	joined Missouri Valley in 1885; independent again from 1888-1905 when it joined the Kansas-Missouri-Nebraska.
Kansas-Missouri	1913	1950	formed when Nebraska left Kansas-Missouri-Nebraska, renamed Midwest in 1950
Kansas-Missouri-Nebraska	1905	1913	formed by merger of Nebraska Kansas, Missouri Valley; renamed Kansas-Missouri in 1913 when Nebraska left.
Lake Erie	1883?	pres.	formerly Michigan
Long Island	1888	1898	joined New York
Lookout Mountain	1868	1884	
Michigan	1870	1883?	renamed Lake Erie
Middle Atlantic	1937	pres.	formerly Philadelphia
Midwest	1950	pres.	formerly Kansas-Missouri
Minnesota	1866?	pres.	
Missouri	1873	1885?	renamed *Nordwest*
Missouri	1953	1973?	joined St. Louis
Missouri Valley	1883?	1905	formerly Missouri, added Kansas 1885?, joined Kansas-Missouri-Nebraska

District Name	Begin-ning Date	Ending Date	Comments
Montana	1887	1897	changed to *Oberer* Rocky Mountain
Nebraska	1889	1933	became part of Missouri Valley in 1897; part of Kansas-Missouri-Nebraska, 1905-1913; reappears as separate district 1913-1916; 1931-1933.
New England	1872	pres.	Boston added in 1885; Connecticut added in 1929; Central New York added in 1920.
New Jersey	1866?	pres.	Passaic added 1885
New Orleans	1870	1929	
New York	1863	pres.	Long Island joined in 1898.
Nord Iowa	1872	1885	renamed *Nordwest*
Nord Mississippi	1866	1867	renamed *Oberer* Mississippi
Nord-Pacific	1885	1956	
Nordwest	1885	1895	formerly known as *Nord* Iowa; joined *Oberer* Mississippi
Oberer Mississippi	1867	pres.	*Nordwest* joined in 1895
Oberer Missouri	1883	1897	renamed *Süd* Dakota
Oberer Rocky Mountain	1897	1900	formerly Montana
Ohio	1885	1940	joined Indiana
Omaha	1870	1884	joined Missouri Valley
Pacific	1872	1886	split off to form *Süd*- and *Nord* Pacific
Passaic	1869	1885	joined New Jersey
Philadelphia	1866?	1937	became part of Middle Atlantic
Pittsburgh	1866	1955	renamed Western Pennsylvania
Red River	1887	1890	
Rocky Mountain	1869	1992	not listed from 1941-1952; merged with Southern California to form Western U.S. District
Savannah	1866?	1883	renamed *Süd* Atlantic
South Bend	1975	1976	joined Central States
St. Louis	1862	pres.	
Süd California	1886	1992	formed by part of Pacific; joined Rocky Mountain to form Western District
Süd Atlantic	1883	1916?	formerly Savannah
Süd Central	1891	1949	formerly *Südlicher*; joined Central States
Süd Dakota	1897	1900	formerly *Oberer* Missouri
Südlicher	1890	1891	formerly Arkansas; renamed *Süd* Central
Südöstlicher	1866?	1897	joined Philadelphia

District Name	Beginning Date	Ending Date	Comments
Texas	1872	1885	no longer listed
West New York	1864	pres.	
Western Pennsylvania	1955	pres.	formerly Pittsburgh
Western United States	1992	pres.	formed by merger of Southern California & Rocky Mountain
Westlicher Massachusetts	1901	1905	formerly part of New England; joined New England in 1905
Wisconsin	1866?	pres.	

Chapter 3

Society Publications
and Historical Records

Entries are listed alphabetically by state, then by city. The entries for each society begin with a brief historical sketch, followed by descriptions of the archival collections and publications. The order of listings for the publications is generally 1) festival, anniversary, or other publications containing historical information about the society; 2) constitutions and by-laws; 3) programs, library catalogs and other miscellaneous publications; and 4) newsletters. Within each category, the publications are arranged chronologically. This section contains only those publications issued by the societies. Scholarly articles written about societies will be found in Chapter 6, "Writings on the American Turners." Publications prepared for national or district festivals or conventions also frequently contain historical information about the host societies. The *Festzeitung* for the 1900 Turnfest in Philadelphia, for example, contained historical articles on all of the societies in the city. These publications are not listed in this section, but instead are with the national or district publications.

ALABAMA

Birmingham: Deutscher Turnverein

Organized in 1887; involved with local Mardi Gras celebrations; reached peak membership in early 1900 with two hundred members; disbanded in 1915.

Archival Collections

Ab1   Fred. Grambs Scrapbooks, 1882-1938. 12 volumes.
Finding aid available from repository.
Location: AB

Description: The early scrapbooks contain material on the activities of the Birmingham Turnverein in which Grambs was a prominent member and musician.

Ab2   Milner, H. Key. Mardi Gras Scrapbook, 1899. 1 volume.
Finding aid available from repository.
Location: AB
Description: The scrapbook documents the activities of the Birmingham Turnverein which sponsored several Mardi Gras celebrations.

Mobile: Mobile Turnverein

Organized in 1851; left *Socialistischer Turnerbund* with other southern societies over the anti-slavery views of the Turnerbund in 1855; established Sick Relief Section in 1870 which later became the German Relief Association; renamed Mobile Relief Association in 1918 and active until 1941; closing date of Turnverein unknown.

Archival Collection

Ab3   The German Relief Association Papers, 1870-1941. 28 boxes.
Records prior to 1918 are predominantly in German.
Finding aid available from repository.
Location: AMU (University Archives).
Description: The records include minute books, 1870-1941; financial records containing the complete reports of the secretary, 1892-1937; reports of the treasurer, 1935-1938; reports of the officers of the sick, 1935-1939; membership lists and reports, 1870-1937; correspondence, 1899-1941; and papers relating to the Association's building. The extent of the Turnverein's records within the collection is unclear.

CALIFORNIA

Los Angeles: Los Angeles Turners

Organized in 1870-1871 as the Los Angeles Turnverein; several members broke away and joined the *Teutonia* Singing Society to form the *Teutonia Concordia Verein*; the two societies merged in 1871 under the name *Turn-Verein Germania*; built or occupied series of halls on Spring St. (1871), Main St. (1894), S. Figueroa St. (1906), Washington Boulevard (1926), West St. (1944) and S. Georgia St. (1959); first hall was city's first theater and the drama section included German professional actors; suffered financial setbacks and loss of members due to World War I, Prohibition and the Depression; hosted the national convention, 1937; changed name to Los Angeles Turners, 1943; still active.

Archival Collection

Ca1   Los Angeles Turners Collection, 1870-present. 46 volumes.
Preliminary inventory available from Indiana Univ.-Purdue Univ. Indianapolis.
Location: Los Angeles Turners, Los Angeles.
Description: The Los Angeles Turner Collection includes minute books of the
society, 1870-1940; membership records, 1872-1938; financial records, 1912-1941;
records of the building committee and Building Association, 1925, 1951; class rosters,
1929-1942; Turner library record from 1892 and library catalog from 1905, and
miscellaneous scrapbooks, newspaper articles, diplomas, photos, and awards. The
collection also includes the minute books of the ladies auxiliary, 1891-1910, and
minute books of the Turner Singers, 1906-1957.

Publications

Ca2   Diamond Jubilee, Los Angeles Turners: The History of the Turners in Los
Angeles, California. [Los Angeles]: n.p., [1946]. 32 p.
Note: Includes a detailed history of the society.
Location: CsmH; InIU.

Ca3   One Hundredth Anniversary, 1871-1971, Los Angeles Turners: The History
of the Turners in Los Angeles, California. [Los Angeles]: n.p., [1971]. 70 p.
Note: Includes numerous photographs and detailed histories of the organization, its
singing section, and the ladies auxiliary.
Location: InIU.

Ca4   Konstitution und Nebengesetze des Turn Vereins Germania, Gegründet am
12. Juni 1871, Incorporiert am 19. Juni 1871: Constitution and By-laws of the Turn
Verein Germania, Los Angeles, California, Founded 1871. (rev. ed.) [Los Angeles]:
n.p., [1932]. 110 p.
Note: Published in 3 sections: Constitution and By-laws of the *Germania* Turnverein,
in German, pp. 1-44; in English, pp. 46-80; principles and statutes of the American
Turnerbund, pp. 1-30.
Location: InIU.

Ca5   Constitution and By-Laws (Adopted June 13th, 1944) of the Los Angeles
Turners, Founded 1871. Los Angeles: n.p., 1944. 12 p.
Location: InIU.

Ca6   Turnverein Germania, Los Angeles. Schlußtheil des Berichts des ersten
Sprechers des Turnvereins Germania, gegeben am 13. Januar 1872. Los Angeles: n.p.,
1872. [broadside].
Location: CSmH.

Ca7   Los Angeles Turnverein Topics. Los Angeles Turnverein, 1925-??
Note: Newsletter of the Los Angeles Turnverein. No issues located.

Oakland: Oakland Turnverein

Organized in 1867; built *Germania* Hall in 1877 with Sons of Hermann and *Rothmänner*, two German fraternal organizations; lost hall in 1914 due to financial problems and location of hall in section of the city that had become predominantly Chinese; purchased hall on 12th and Alice Streets in 1919; membership peaked at 135 in 1935 but declined thereafter; left American Turners in 1948 and closed in 1952.

Publication

Ca8   Konstitution des Oakland Turn Vereins, Gegründet am 20. Februar 1867. n.p.: Emil Gerlach, 1935. 35 p.
Note: In German and English.
Location: InIU.

Sacramento: Sacramento Turnverein

Organized in 1854; first hall erected on K Street in 1859; among its sections were the dramatic section (1878), rifle club (1878), and ladies auxiliary (1882); played leadership role in introducing physical education to the public schools in 1892; erected new hall on 34th and J streets in 1926; rifle range installed in basement in 1936; started sponsorship of Boy Scout Troop in 1948; still active.

Archival Collection

Ca9   Sacramento Turnverein Collection, 1854-1974. 34 volumes.
Records in English can be found as early as 1903 and records in German as late as 1938. The majority of records changed from German to English in the mid-1920s.
Location: Sacramento Turnverein, Sacramento.
Description: The records include the minutes of the society, 1854-1968; minutes of the board of directors, 1854-1934; minutes of the entertainment committee, 1895-1905; membership records, 1854-1979; dues, 1902; financial records, 1905, 1937-1956; class roster, 1887-1906; book containing the handwritten amendments to constitutions, 1886-1936; and publications.

Publications

Ca10   Gedenkblatt zum goldenen Jubiläum am 2. Juni 1904, Sacramento Turn-Verein, Souvenir of the Golden Jubilee June 2, 1904. [Sacramento]: n.p., [1904].

76 p.
Note: Fiftieth anniversary book of the Sacramento Turnverein. Includes an historical overview of Turnerism in the United States, description of the first Turnfest in Philadelphia, a detailed history of the Sacramento Turnverein, list of 50-year members, photographs and brief biographies of members.
Location: C; InIU (photocopy); Sacramento Turners.

Ca11 Sacramento Turn Verein, Fest-Schrift, Souvenir Album, "Mens sana in corpore sano", May 15.- 23, 1954. [Sacramento?]: n.p., [1954]. 44 p.
Note: Cover title: "100 Years Sacramento Turn-Verein, 1854-1954." The anniversary publication includes a detailed history of the society, program of events, and photographs.
Location: C; InIU.

Ca12 125 Anniversary, 1854-1979, Sacramento Turn Verein, 3349 Jay Street, Sacramento, California, Friday, Saturday and Sunday, June 15, 16 and 17, 1979. [Sacramento]: n.p., [1979]. 29 p.
Note: Includes a brief history of the Sacramento Turnverein and photographs.
Location: InIU; Sacramento Turnverein.

Ca13 Konstitution und Nebengesetze, Revidiert am 5 Juli 1922, Sacramento Turn-Verein, Gegründet am 2. Juni 1854, Organized June 2, 1854, Constitution and By-Laws, Revised Juli 5, 1922. San Francisco: The Hansen Co., 1923. 75 p.
Note: Published in 3 sections: constitution in German, pp. 7-43; constitution in English, pp. 7-35, membership list of December 1, 1923, pp. 42-43.
Location: InIU.

San Diego: San Diego Turners

Organized in 1884 as *Eintracht* Turnverein; changed name to San Diego Turnverein in 1886; erected hall on 8th Street in 1887 which was lost in the financial panic of 1888; merged with the Phoenix Turnverein in 1889 to form the Concordia Turnverein; formed ladies auxiliary in 1893; built new hall on 9th and G Streets in 1907; had several members relocated by the U.S. government during WWII; lost hall to fire in 1945; changed name to San Diego Turners in 1947; opened new hall on 30th and Date Streets in 1951; sold building due to financial problems in 1969; dissolved in 1985.

Archival Collection

Ca14 San Diego Concordia Turnverein Collection. 1897-1970. 3 linear feet. Finding aid available from repository.
Location: CSDHi
Description: The records include minutes of general meetings, 1944-1969, and

board meetings, 1955-1970; minutes of the *Germania* Building Society, 1945; minutes of the Turner Hall Association, 1957- 1970; gym committee meeting minutes, 1939-1941; minutes of the national bowling conventions 1917, 1972, 1974; reports of the American Turners, 1970-1972; membership materials, 1912-1941, 1971-1976; "*Verfassung des Concordia Turnvereins*," 1897 (includes constitution of the society, inventory of Turner hall, and membership list); handwritten constitution, 1910; constitution of the ladies auxiliary, ca. 1908; financial documents and records, 1950-1976; dues book and receipts, 1944-1948; invoices 1918-1968; tax papers 1917-1974; correspondence, 1940-1968; statistical reports, 1971; a history of the San Diego Turners, 1974; list of major acquisitions and improvements at Turner Hall, 1947-1967; stock journal, 1905-1947; annual reports, 1953-1954; music and holiday songs; catalogs, menus, brochures, and other printed materials.

Publications

Ca15   Concordia Turnverein, Thirty-Five Years of German Society Life in San Diego, Concordia Turnverein. San Diego: Concordia Turnverein, 1907. 46 p.
Location: CSDHi (San Diego Turner Collection).

Ca16   Das Deutsche Heim, San Diego's Deutschthum geschildert in Wort und Bild Heraugegeben zur Erinnerung an die Einweihung des Germania Gebäudes vom Concordia Turnverein. [San Diego]: n.p., [1907]. 46 p.
Location: CSDHi (San Diego Turner Collection).

Ca17   Souvenir Program, 61st Anniversary, San Diego Turners, Dedication of the New Turner Hall, San Diego, Saturday, March 3, 1951. n.p., [1951]. 32 p.
Note: Includes a brief history of the organization.
Location: InIU.

Ca18   Regeln für Bären-Zusammenkünfte nebst Liedern für alte und junge Turner. [San Diego]: n.p., [1904]. 54 p.
Location: CSDHi (San Diego Turner Collection).

Ca19   Verfassung des Concordia Turnvereins, San Diego, California, angenommen am 2. Juli 1930, und Grundsätze und Statuten des Amerikanischen Turnerbundes. San Diego: Deutsche Zeitung, 1930. 23 p.
Note: Constitution and By-laws.
Location: InIU.

Ca20   By-Laws of the San Diego Turners. San Diego: n.p., 1947. 14 p.
Location: CSDHi (San Diego Turner Collection); InIU.

San Francisco: San Francisco Gymnastic Club

Founded as San Francisco Turnverein in 1852; joined by the Orpheus Singing Society in 1853 which formed singing section; built first hall in 1854 on Bush Street but was soon lost due to financial problems; sharpshooters' and Sick and Death Benefit sections founded in 1857; merged with the *Germania* Turnverein in 1860; took part in the funeral service for President Lincoln in 1865; formed dramatic section in 1868; built new hall on O'Farrell Street in 1868; acquired larger hall on Turk Street in 1875 which became the home of many German-American societies; lost hall in the earthquake of 1906; built new hall on Sutter Street in 1911; worked successfully for introduction of physical education in the public schools; changed name to San Francisco Gymnastic Club in 1921; left American Turnerbund, 1931; probably closed in 1940.

Publications

Ca21   75th Anniversary Diamond Jubilee, S.F. Gymnastic Club, formerly San Francisco Turnverein in their Building 2460 Sutter St., Oct. 15th and 16th, 1927. [San Francisco]: Louis Roesch Co., 1927. 32 p.
Note: Includes program, committee members, and brief history of the organization.
Location: InIU.

Ca22   San Francisco Turnverein. 1 print (Chromo lithograph), 1870.
Note: 1 mounted oversized composite print. Group outdoor portrait of members.
Location: PPB.

San Jose: San Jose Turnverein

Organized in 1868; built hall on Third Street in 1885; instrumental in introducing physical education into the San Jose school system in 1891; disbanded in 1906-1907.

Publications

Ca23   Turner Society, San Jose,. Calif., Grand concert! Of Vocal and Instrumental Music, to be Given by the Turner Society, at their Hall, in San Jose, on Sunday... [San Jose]: Owen & Cottle, Printers, San Jose Mercury, [186?].
Location: CU.

COLORADO

Boulder: Boulder Turnverein

Date of organization unknown; joined American Turnerbund with forty members in 1883; suspended from national organization in 1884; closing date unknown.

Publications

Co1   Articles of Incorporation of the Boulder Turnverein, July 9, 1883. [Boulder]: n.p., [1883]. 5 p.
Location: CoB (Carnegie Branch Library for Local History).

Denver: Denver Turnverein, Inc.

Organized in 1865 as East Denver Turnverein; started German school during the same year; formed singing section in 1869, library in 1870, first girl's class in 1872, and ladies auxiliary in 1876; offered first German theater performance in Denver in 1872; built hall on Holladay Street in 1873; made additions to building in 1875 and 1881; successfully worked for introduction of physical education in public schools during 1870s and 1880s; merged with *Gesangverein Concordia* in 1876; built new hall on Arapahoe Street in 1887 when neighborhood declined on Holladay St.; hosted the national convention in 1894 and the national Turnfest in 1913; became one of the most prestigious societies in Denver with U.S. Senator H.A. Tabor and state and local officials as members; lost membership due to anti-German sentiments during WWI; lost building to bank in 1916; merged with the Social Turnverein and *Vorwärts* Turnverein in 1917 to form the Denver Turnverein; purchased the old Coronado Club as new building in 1922 which became known as German House; joined the Federation of German American Societies of Colorado in the 1930s; still active.

Archival Collections

Co2   Denver Turnverein Records.
Location: Denver Turnverein.
Description: Collection reported, but no detailed information available.

Co3   Transcript of proceedings of 80th anniversary celebration, 1946. 49 p.
Location: InIU.
Description: Includes the transcripts of all speeches given during the celebration, held Saturday, October 19, 1946 in Denver. Typed.

Publications

Co4   Souvenir des Denver Turnvereins, Gegründet im Jahre 1866 zur Einweihung der neuen Turn-Halle im Jahre 1890, herausgegeben unter den Auspicien des Vereins von Turner Carl Cazin. Denver: n.p., [1890]. 152 p.
Note: Dedication program for Arapahoe St. hall; program and historical articles are in German followed by English translations.
Location: CoD; PPG.

Co5   Historical Journal of the Denver Turnverein, Published for the Centennial Celebration, October 9th and 10th 1965, Commemorating the First One Hundred Years, 1865-1965. [Denver]: Jefferson Printing Co., 1965. 79 p.
Note: Title page: "Centennial Journal, Denver Turnverein, 1865-1965." Includes a history of the club compiled by Wolfgang Sattler, an article on the first German-American soccer club, membership lists of the society and ladies auxiliary, program, and photographs.
Location: CoD; DLC; InIU.

Co6   Konstitution des Denver Turn-Vereins nebst Platform und Statuten des Nord-Amerikanischen Turnerbundes, und des Rocky Mountain Turnbezirks, sowie die Incorporations-Akte des Vereins. Denver: Colorado Journal, 1866. 35 p.
Location: CoD; IaDP.

Co7   Constitution des Socialen Turn-Vereins nebst Platform und Statuten des Nord-Amerikanischen Turnerbundes und des Rocky Mountain Turnbezirk. Denver: Bischoff, 1900. 24 p.
Note: Cover title: "*Grundsätze und Forderungen, Statuten des Nord-Amerikanischen Turner-Bundes, Statuten des Socialen Turn-Vereins, Statuten des Rocky Mountain Turnbezirks.*"
Location: InIU.

Co8   Exposition of physical education given by the Denver Turnverein, May 13, 1927. n.p., [1927?]. 40 p.
Location: Private collection.

Co9   The Denver Turnverein (Denver Gymnastic Association), (Denver) Constitution and By-Laws as Amended, June 15, 1927. n.p., 1927. 19 p.
Location: InIU.

Co10   Constitution and Statutes of the Denver Turnverein, Inc., Organized 1865. rev. ed. [Denver]: n.p., 1949. 20 p.
Location: InIU.

Co11 Constitution and By-laws of the Denver Turnverein, Inc. (Revised and approved in 1970). Mimeographed. [Denver]: n.p., 1970. 19 p.
Location: InIU.

Co12 Pep and Punch. Official Organ of the Denver Turnverein. Denver: Denver Turnverein, 1927-1950s?
Note: Monthly. Includes national and local Turner news, information on the women's auxiliary and *Arion Gesangverein*, announcements and competition results. Volume 19, no.5 (1946) is also the 80th anniversary publication of the organization. Cover title: "80th Anniversary Program." Includes brief historical overview of the organization and the ladies auxiliary.
Location:
> CoD: vols. 4-6, 8-14, 15-31.
> InIU: v.7, no. 7 (November 1944), v. 19, no. 5 (October 1946).

CONNECTICUT

Hartford: Hartford Turnerbund

Organized in 1878; formed ladies section in 1879; purchased property on Main and Morgan Streets together with other German societies and built hall, later known as *Germania* Hall, in 1888; became member of the German American Alliance in 1900; sold building in 1907 due to disagreements between the German societies sharing the building; built new hall on Park Street in 1911; reached peak membership in the 1920s with approximately three hundred members; probably disbanded in the 1960s.

Publications

Ct1 Golden Jubilee, 1878-1928, Hartford Turnerbund, Friday, Saturday and Sunday, May 18, 19, 20, 1928. n.p., 1928. 64 p.
Note: Includes a detailed history of the society.
Location: CtHi; InIU (photocopy).

Ct2 Statuten des Hartforder Turnerbundes, Gegründet am 19. Mai 1878. Hartford: Connecticut Staatszeitung, 1912. 16 p.
Location: InIU.

Meriden: Meriden Turner Society, Inc.

Organized in 1866 as Meriden Turnverein; formed ladies auxiliary in 1875; operated German school in 1878; dedicated first hall in 1879; acquired larger hall on Pratt Street in 1895 but sold it in 1918; built new hall on Butler street in 1923; changed emphasis from gymnastics to singing in the 1940s; relinquished building to the Meriden Parking Authorities in 1961; dedicated new building on Old Colony Road in 1962; still active as a singing society.

Publications

Ct3   One Century of the Meriden Turner Society, 1866-1966. n.p., 1966. 4 p.
Note: Includes a history of the Meriden Turners.
Location: InIU (photocopy); Meriden Turners.

Ct4   Statuten und Neben-Gesetze des Meriden Turnvereins, Vom 1. März 1898.
New Haven, Conn.: Bußmann, 1899. 27 p.
Location: InIU.

New Britain: Socialer Turnverein

Organized as *Sozialer* Turn Verein in 1853; raised funds for yellow fever victims in New Orleans in 1853, for flood victims in Germany in 1883, for flood victims in Johnstown, PA in 1891, for San Francisco earthquake victims in 1906 and for local hospital; had 23 out of 42 members volunteer during the Civil War; built hall on Arch Street in 1870; established German school in 1885; organized library in 1887; joined German-American National Alliance in 1904; probably closed in 1941.

Publications

Ct5   Statuten und Nebengesetze des New Britain Turnvereins (incorporiert) zu New Britain, Conn., Gegründet am 25. April 1853: Constitution and By-laws of the New Britain Turner's Society (Incorporated) of New Britain, Conn., Founded April 25, 1853. Milwaukee: Freidenker Publishing Co., 1913. 64 p.
Note: Constitution in German and English on facing pages.
Location: InIU.

Ct6   "New Britain Turn Verein, 1853-1912." In Alfred Traute. Connecticut Germans: Historical, Biographical, Industrial. n.p., 1912.
Note: Article written by the New Britain Turnverein's historical committee.
Location: CtHi.

New Haven: New Haven Turnverein

Organized in 1852; reached maximum membership in 1894 with two hundred members; membership dropped from 130 in 1906 to fifteen in 1912; probably closed in 1932.

Publications

Ct7   Reck und Barren: Organ des New Haven Turnvereins. New Haven: New
Haven Turnverein, 1902?-1903?
Note: Years 1902-1903 cited in Pochmann #8751.

Ct8   Statuten des Turn-Vereins in New Haven, Connecticut. n.p., 1903.
Note: Cited in Eldredge, Wentworth "The New Haven German Community." Ph.D.
dissertation, Yale University, 1935.

Rockville: Rockville Turnverein

Organized in 1857; split into two societies due to political disagreements in 1861;
groups reunited in 1863; purchased land in 1864 and built hall in 1865; opened
German school in December 1865; rented hall to *Arbeiter-Liga* (Workers' League)
for meetings; enlarged hall in 1871 and 1875; formed drama section in 1871;
established Turner cemetery in 1875 for members who could not afford to buy plots;
sponsored benefit fair for German flood victims in 1881; changed name to *Socialer*
Turnverein in 1886; built new hall and changed name back to Rockville Turnverein
in 1898; left American Turnerbund with forty members in 1924; probably closed
shortly thereafter.

Publications

Ct9   Souvenir Program of the Golden Jubilee of the Rockville Turn Verein To Be
Held At Turner Hall and Liedertafel Park, June 14, 15, 16, '07. n.p., [1907]. 77 p.
Note: Cover title: "*Fest-Programm für das Goldene Jubiläum des Rockville Turn
Vereins am 14., 15. und 16. Juni '07.*" Includes a history and membership list of the
Rockville Turn Verein, a history of the German societies of Rockville, and the minutes
of the 31st district convention held in Holyoke, Mass., on March 24, 1907.
Location: CtHi; InIU (photocopy).

Waterbury: Turnverein Vorwärts

Founded as the Turnverein *Vorwärts* in 1893 by members of the Waterbury
Turnverein (founded 1871); formed ladies auxiliary in 1900; dedicated hall on North
Main Street in 1910; formed singing section in 1938; withdrew from American
Turners in 1940; affiliated with the Concordia Singing Society to form the Concordia
Turner-Singing Society in 1946-1947; still active.

Publications

Ct10   Treu dem Deutsche Lied: Herzlich Willkommen zum 125ten Jubiläum, Saturday, May 25, 1991, Concordia Society, German-American Club, Waterbury, Connecticut. n.p., [1991]. 78 p.
Note: Includes a history of the Turnverein *Vorwärts*.
Location: InIU.

DELAWARE

Wilmington: Wilmington Turners

Founded as the *Social Demokratischer* Turnverein in 1859; formed singing section in 1861; members joined the 29th Turner Infantry Regiment during Civil War; underwent several name changes including Wilmington Turn Verein (1865), Wilmington Turn Verein Forwards (1882), *Socialer Demokratischer* Turn Verein (1882), and Wilmington *Turn Gemeinde*; purchased building on 6th Street with Delaware *Sängerbund* and Library Association which became known as *Germania* Hall, 1883; moved out due to disagreements between societies; purchased land and built hall on French Street in 1895; sold hall during World War I due to financial problems and purchased smaller one on South Clayton Street; adopted English as official language in meetings in 1936; still active.

Archival Collection

De1   Wilmington Turners Collection, 1880-1969. 13 linear feet.
Finding aid available from repository.
Location: PPB
Description: The collection includes minutes of the Wilmington Turners, 1885-1972; minute books and membership lists from the senior Turners (*Bären*), 1902-1969; minute books from unidentified Turner sections, 1902-1934; minutes of the *Gesang* section (singing section), 1898-1912; minutes of the committee for the German-Day celebration 1913; district minutes, 1930s; minutes and related materials on children's gym classes; library borrowers' records, 1906-1924; membership and dues records, 1916-1924; financial records, 1880-1949; ledgers and notebooks, possibly from the Turner beneficial society, 1897-1957; songbooks; blueprint for change to the lodge building; printed materials; and photographs.

Publications

De2   The Wilmington Turners, One Hundredth Anniversary Centennial Yearbook, 1859[-]1959. Wilmington, Del: Charles Printing Co., 1959. [52 p.]

Note: Includes photographs, articles on American Turners, and history of the society.
Location: InIU; PPB.

De3   The American Turner. Wilmington: Wilmington Turngemeinde, 1912-1917.
Note: Monthly newsletter published by the Wilmington Turngemeinde. Includes national and local Turner news, announcements, and competition results.
Location: Private collection: v. 4, no. 47 (May 1916); v. 5, no. 64 (Nov. 1917).

De4   Charity Bazaar for the Red Cross of the Central Powers, under the Protectorate of his Excellency Count J. Von Bernstorf, German Ambassador, at Wilmington Turn Hall, June 12th to 17th, 1916. n.p., [1916]. [104 p.]
Note: Cover title: "Souvenir Program, Charity Bazaar for the Widows, Orphans and Red Cross of Central Powers of Europe, Turn Hall, Wilmington, Del., June 12-17, 1916." Includes program for events; list of committee members; platform, resolutions, articles demanding United States neutrality in the war, and personal accounts of prisoner-of-war camps to illustrate the horrors of war.
Location: InIU.

ILLINOIS

Alton: Alton Turnverein

Organized in 1864; reached peak membership with 67 in 1890; left American Turnerbund in 1896 and probably closed shortly thereafter.

Publication

Is1   Humbert, Fred. Geschichte der Deutschen von Alton und Umgebung, vorgetragen in der Alton Turnhalle, am 4ten July, 1876. Alton, Ill.: n.p., [1876?].
Note: Cited in Pochmann #5210.

Aurora: Turn Verein Frisch Auf

First Turner activities in Aurora began in 1857 when the Aurora Turnverein was founded; society left American Turnerbund in 1898. Turnverein *Frisch Auf* founded in 1907 but histories do not mention connection to earlier group. Completed building on LaSalle Street in 1922 at which point the society was the largest organization in Aurora; maintained singing section until the 1940s; reduced activities in the 1960s due to financial problems; introduced bingo games in late 1960s which improved financial situation; moved to new location on Mitchell Road in the 1980s; still active as social and gymnastic society.

Archival Collections

Is2   *Frisch Auf* Turners Collection, 1941-1967. 2 volumes.
Location: Private collection.
Description: Minute book of the *Frisch Auf* Turners, Aurora, 1941-1942; membership records for the *Frisch Auf* Turners, Aurora, 1967.

Is3   *Frisch Auf* Turners Collection, 1916-1930s. 4 volumes.
Location: Private collection.
Description: The collection includes minutes of the Turnverein *Frisch Auf*, 1907-1927; records of the national Turnfest from June 1935, principally scores and receipts; correspondence; and part of *Frisch Auf* Turner library.

Publications

Is4   57. Stiftungsfest des Aurora Turnvereins, 1864-1921, am Sonntag, 10. Februar 1921. n.p., [1921]. [15 p.]
Note: Includes a brief history of the society.
Location: WMCHi.

Is5   75th Anniversary, 1907[-]1982, Aurora Turners, Aurora, Illinois. n.p., 1982. 79 p.
Note: Includes brief history of the American and Aurora Turners, list of honorary members, photographs of past and present members and facilities.
Location: InIU; Aurora Turners.

Is6   Vereins-Gesetze des Turn Verein "Frisch-Auf," Aurora, Illinois, Gut Heil! n.p., [1944]. 38 p.
Note: In English and German.
Location: InIU.

Is7   By-laws of the Aurora Turners, December 6, 1979. n.p., [1979]. 18 p.
Location: InIU.

Is8   Aurora Turners Cook Book. Aurora: Arch Printing, 1988. 342 p.
Note: Cook book compiled by the Aurora Turners.
Location: InIU.

Belleville: Belleville Turners

Organized in 1855 as the Belleville Turngemeinde with members drawn from the "Latin Farmers," educated German immigrants, most notably Friedrich Hecker, who took up farming in the area; hosted national Turnfest, 1858; merged with the

Turnverein *Vorwärts* (founded 1866) under the name Belleville *Vorwärts Turngemeinde*, 1885; suspended from American Turnerbund in 1888; reorganized in 1899; changed name to Belleville Turners in 1918; built hall in 1924 that was one of the largest in the country; suspended activities in 1960s but small number of members still hold meetings; hall presently used by Belleville YMCA.

Archival Collection

Is9   Belleville *Vorwärts* Turner Records. 1902-1952. 10 items.
Location: Belleville Turners Room, YMCA Building, Belleville, IL.
Description: The records include four photographs of members and activities 1902-1930s; the architect's plans to the building, 1920s; an undated typewritten constitution and by-laws of the society; financial records from the 1920s and 40s; and a constitution and by-laws of the *Bären* section of the Belleville Turners, 1922.

Is10   Belleville *Vorwärts* Turner Photographic Collection. 25 negatives.
Location: Belleville City Hall.
Description: 25 negatives on Belleville Turners in "Negative File" of Belleville History of the Historic Preservation Committee.

Publications

Is11   The Belleville Turners, Dedication Program, Week of June 1 to 7, 1924. n.p., [1924]. [30 p.]
Location: Private collection.

Is12   50th Anniversary, 1902[-]1952. Belleville: Buechler Publishing Co., 1952.
Location: Private collection.

Is13   Belleville Turner. Belleville: Belleville Turners [1923? - ??].
Subtitle: "Not for Ourselves But for Others."
Note: Newsletter of the Belleville Turnverein. Includes local and national Turner news, announcements, and class schedules.
Location: InIU: v. 4, no. 12 (October 1927). (Photocopies).

Is14   Belleville Turnverein, Scholastic Year, 1908-1909. n.p., [1908]. 30 p.
Note: Includes the class schedules of the scholastic year 1908/09; reasons for becoming a Turner; photographs; written in German and English.
Location: InIU (photocopy).

Is15   Constitution and By-Laws of the Belleville Turnverein, Bärensection. [Belleville]: n.p., 1922.
Location: Private collection.

Bloomington: Bloomington Turnverein

Founded in 1858; reached peak membership in 1890 with approximately sixty-five members; built hall on Front Street; closed between 1955 and 1957.

Publications

Is16 and **Is17** intentionally omitted.

Is18   Principles of the North-American Turner-Bund (Gymnastic Union of North America) and Constitution of the Bloomington Turn-Verein, Bloomington, Illinois. n.p., n.d. 28 p.
Note: In English and German.
Location: InIU.

Chicago

In the years between the end of the Civil War and World War I, Chicago had more Turner societies than any other city in the country, reaching a high point of twenty-eight societies in 1890 and still maintaining nineteen in 1910. The large number of Turner societies was a result of the large influx of working class German immigrants during the 1870s and 1880s. Between twenty-five and thirty percent of the city's population was first or second generation German throughout the period 1860-1900, and about seventy percent of the German population was working class. Turner halls played an important role as community centers in the German neighborhoods, hosting not only athletic activities but also musical and theatrical performances, dances and parties, neighborhood meetings and political rallies. Because of their location in German working class neighborhoods, a number of the societies became closely associated with the radical labor movement. The *Vorwärts* Turner hall hosted numerous labor meetings and rallies and was the scene of notable clashes between German workers and the Chicago police in 1877 and 1891. The Aurora Turnverein was closely associated with the anarchist International Working People's Association, one of whose leaders, August Spies, was the Turnverein's delegate to the 1884 national Turner convention. Spies was also editor of the Chicagoer Arbeiter-Zeitung and was one of the anarchist leaders hung as a result of the Haymarket bombing. Other societies, notably the Chicago Turngemeinde and the Central Turnverein, were more conservative and middle class, and were frequently in opposition to the more radical societies.

In spite of political disagreements, the Turner societies in Chicago were able to work together on a number of issues of mutual interest. During the 1880s they successfully lobbied for the introduction of physical education in the public schools, and many Turner instructors were hired to direct programs, including Henry Suder, who became the school system's supervisor of physical education in 1894. They also worked to establish public parks and playgrounds in their neighborhoods. The

Chicago Turners have been active at the national level of the Turner movement, hosting the national convention in 1888, 1908, 1921 and 1966 and national Turnfests in 1869 and 1921. The number of societies declined sharply after World War I, so that there were only six in 1950 and only three in 1995, one of which, *Eiche*, had moved to Tinley Park.

Chicago: American Turners Northwest Chicago

American Turners Northwest Chicago was formed from the consolidation of the Social Turners, Forward (*Vorwärts*) Turners and Swiss Turners in 1956 following eight years of negotiation; used Social Turner hall as temporary home until new building could be constructed on Belmont Street in 1959-1960; still active as sports organization.

Archival Collection

Is19   American Turners Northwest Chicago Collection, 1956-present.
Location: American Turners Northwest Chicago, Chicago.
Description: The American Turners Northwest Chicago collection includes the complete set of minutes and financial records from 1956 to the present, as well as printed materials from the same period.

Is20   American Turners Northwest Chicago File, 1956-1985. 1 folder.
Location: InIU.
Description: Consists of the consolidation agreement, board of directors minutes from February and March 1956, typed constitution, 1985 membership directory, and miscellaneous papers discussing the consolidation process.

Publications

Is21   Souvenir Program for the Dedication of the New Home of the American Turners Northwest Chicago, 6625 Belmont Avenue, Chicago, Illinois, January 20 through January 24, 1960. [Chicago]: n.p., [1960]. 62 p.
Note: Cover title: "January 1960: American Turners-Northwest Chicago." Includes the histories of the Turnverein *Vorwärts*, the *Sozialer* Turnverein and the *Schweizer* Turnverein before their consolidation into the Northwest Turners. Also includes the principles of American Turners, the dedication program, and photographs.
Location: InIU.

Is22   American Turners Northwest Chicago - Directory. n.p., 1985. 41 p.
Note: Includes names and addresses of members in 1985.
Location: InIU; American Turners Northwest Chicago.

Is23   The Turner. Chicago: American Turners Northwest Chicago, 1956-pres.
Subtitle: Official Publication of the American Turners - Northwest Chicago.
Note: Former publication of the Social Turners which was continued by the new
society after 1956. Includes national and local Turner news, announcements,
competition schedules and results. See also entry **Is80**.
Location: InIU: Aug./Sept., 1958; Summer 1959, April 1978.

Chicago: Aurora Turnverein

Organized in 1864 by German immigrants on the city's Northwest side; built hall at
Milwaukee Ave. and Second St. with financial help from neighborhood residents,
1868; as largest meeting place on the heavily German Northwest side, the hall became
the principal location for plays, concerts, political rallies and labor union and
neighborhood meetings. The society was an active supporter of workers' rights in the
1870s and 1880s. It sponsored rallies and fundraising events on behalf of unions,
striking workers and workers suffering from natural disasters both in the United States
and Germany; banned non-union products from the hall and society events; rented
space to the radical *Land- und Wehr- Verein*; and sponsored the U.S. fundraising and
speaking tour of two representatives of the German Social Democratic Party in 1881.
The Aurora Turnverein was caught up in the Haymarket Affair because one of its
leaders was August Spies, editor of the Chicagoer Arbeiter-Zeitung and one of the
radicals hung as a result of the Haymarket incident. The Aurora Turnverein organized
a defense fund for Spies, contributed support for his family and the family of the other
defendants; and provided 250 marchers for the funeral procession. Because of its
involvement with the radical labor movement, the society was under police
surveillance from 1886 to 1888. The society organized a women's auxiliary in 1878
and started women's physical education classes in 1880; worked for introduction of
physical education in the Chicago public schools in the 1870s; started health insurance
program for members, 1885; gave up hall for financial reasons in 1890 and rented hall
at Ashland Ave. and Division St.; disbanded following destruction of the hall by fire
in 1952.

Archival Collection

Is24   Aurora Turnverein Library.   Ca.100 volumes.
Location: InIU.
Description: Books from the Aurora Turnverein Library, most in German and
published between the late 1860s and 1900. The books were published primarily in
Germany, and include literature, philosophy, history, and a small amount of radical
literature.

Publication

Is25   Verfassung des Aurora Turn-Vereins von Chicago, Illinois, Gegründet am
22. Februar 1864. Chicago: Roessler Printing Co., 1907. 67 p.
Note: Pagination in three sections: pp. 1-36, statutes of North American Turnerbund;
pp. 1-8, constitution of the Chicago *Turnbezirk*; pp. 1-23, constitution of the Aurora
Turn Verein.
Location: InIU.

Chicago: Chicago Turners

Organized as the Chicago Turn Verein in 1852; built first hall on Griswold (Clark St.)
between Van Buren and Jackson Streets in 1853; founded singing section in 1856; lost
group of members who split off to form the *Vorwärts* Turn Verein in mid-1850s;
merged with *Vorwärts* Turn Verein in 1860 and formed the Chicago Turngemeinde;
contributed 105 members to the Turner Union Cadets under the command of Captain
Kowald during the Civil War; Cadets later assigned to the 24th Illinois Regiment
under the command of Friedrich Hecker. Society built new hall on North Clark Street,
between Chicago Avenue and Chestnut Street in 1863-1864; building destroyed in
Chicago Fire in 1871; new hall dedicated on same property in 1873; hall was known
as the North Side Turner Hall and was used as a public assembly hall for political
rallies and hosted public appearances of political figures including Presidents
Cleveland, Hayes and Harrison. Society moved to new three-story building on Wells
Street in 1891; moved back to Clark St. hall later in the 1890s when new building was
lost due to financial problems. Society formed ladies auxiliary in 1879; formed
fencing, bicycling and swimming sections in 1890s. Its gymnastics instructor, Henry
Suder, became supervisor of physical education in the Chicago Public Schools in 1894
and held the position for many years. Turngemeinde had reputation as a conservative
society, and was suspended from the American Turnerbund during 1891-1892 for
expelling from its membership Julius Vahlteich, a labor journalist know for his
socialist views. Moved to Lincoln Ave. in 1937; transferred gymnastic classes and
social activities to Social Turners hall between 1943 and 1949 due to financial
trouble; changed name to Chicago Turners in 1944; moved back to Clark St. hall in
1950; closed in 1970.

Archival Collections

Is26   Chicago Turngemeinde Programs and Photographs, 1889-ca.1940. 3 boxes
(1 linear foot).
Location: InIU.
Description: Includes programs from events at the hall, 1889-1909; programs from
the society's minstrel shows, 1897-1914; certificates; and photographs of society
activities.

Is27   Chicago Turn-Gemeinde, Pioneer Section Records, 1895-1966. ½ box, 9 items.
Location: ICHi.
Description: The records consist of minutes of meetings of the Pioneer section (i.e. Old Settlers Section) of the Chicago Turngemeinde 1895-1931 (7 volumes). Also included is a periodical from Wernigerode, Germany, containing an article on John E. Hochbaum, secretary of the Pioneer section, who emigrated to the United States in 1866. Includes typescript of excerpts. Records are in German.

Is28   Chicago Turn-Gemeinde, Fencing Section. 1909-1915. 1 volume.
Location: ICHi.
Description: Minutes of the Fencing Section of the Chicago Turngemeinde from 1909-1913. Volume also includes the constitution of 1914-1915, list of members, expenses of the Fencing Section, and a few pages of correspondence between club members in 1915. Records are in German and English.

Is29   Frances L. Roberts Collection. 1871-1874. 13 items.
Location: ICHi.
Description: A collection of letters written by Frances Roberts to her mother Sarah L. Roberts; includes references to Turner Hall.

Publications

Is30   Butz, Caspar. "*Prolog zur Eröffnung der neunen Turn-Halle in Chicago, gesprochen von Frau Albertine Kenkel, 31. Dezember 1863*" Deutsch-Amerikanische Monatsheft für Politik, Wissenschaft und Literatur, v. 1 (Jan. 1864), pp. 134-37.
Location: OCU.

Is31   Turn-Halle Souvenir. Chicago: Frederick Hargan, 1869?-??
Note: The Turn-Halle Souvenir was a weekly flyer published by Frederick Hargan under the direction of the Great Western Light Guard Band. It had a circulation of about 1500 copies Includes news of the fine arts around the world and announcements of programs at the Turner hall, including the 1869 Turnfest.
Location: ICHi: June 27, 1869 and August 8, 1869.

Is32   Chicago Turngemeinde: Musenklänge aus dem Leierkasten der Chicago Turngemeinde. Chicago: Justus Loehr, 1877. 120 p.
Note: Includes lyrics of German folksongs.
Location: ICU; InIU; OCU (Fick Collection).

Is33   Suder, Heinrich. Liederbuch der Chicago Turn-Gemeinde. Eine Auswahl von Liedern für die Turn-Schule. Chicago: Max Stern, 1887. 23 p.
Location: OCU.

Is34 Bericht des Sprechers der Chicago Turngemeinde für das Jahr 1891. Chicago: Max Stern, 1892. 20 p.
Note: Report of the president for the year 1892.
Location: InIU.

Is35 Die Entwicklung der Erde: Ein Festnachtstraum in 5 Bildern. Chicago: Max Stern, 1900.
Note: Script for play performed at the Chicago Turngemeinde.
Location: InIU.

Is36 Harmonie: Chicago Turngemeinde, 1852[-]1902, Anniversary Number 3/4 October 1902. [Chicago]: n.p., 1902. [50 p.]
Note: Caption title. Fiftieth anniversary issue of the Harmonie. Includes articles on the history of the Chicago Turngemeinde in English and German.
Location: ICHi.

Is37 Souvenir Program: Benefit for Sufferers from Earthquake and Fire, San Francisco, April 18, 1906 under the auspices of Chicago Turngemeinde at its hall in Chicago, Friday, April Twenty-Seventh, MCMVI. [Chicago]: n.p., [1906]. 4 p.
Note: Program to raise money for earthquake victims.
Location: ICHi; InIU.

Is38 Programm der Chicago Turngemeinde zum Bundes Turnfest in Cincinnati, Juni 1909. n.p., [1909].
Location: InIU.

Is39 Chicago Turngemeinde: Special Train Chicago - Denver to Bundes Turnfest of the North American Gymnastic Union. n.p., 1913.
Location: InIU.

Is40 Chicago Turngemeinde, Musik Section: Souvenir Golden Jubilee Season, 1864-1914. n.p., [1914]. 8 p.
Note: Includes brief history of the choir for its fiftieth anniversary celebration.
Location: InIU.

Is41 Historical Pageant, Commemorating the 75th Anniversary of the Chicago Turngemeinde, Sunday, October 2, 1927, Afternoon and Evening, Medinah Temple, Chicago. [Chicago]: n.p., [1927]. 36 p.
Note: Cover title: "Souvenir Anniversary Program, Chicago Turngemeinde, 1852[-]1927: 75th Anniversary Celebrated by a Historical Pageant, Medinah Temple, Sun. Oct. 2, Two Performances, 2:30 p.m. and 7:30 p.m." Includes a brief history of the club, the complete script of the pageant in which the history of the Chicago Turngemeinde was acted out, and names and photographs of cast members.
Location: ICN; InIU.

Is42   Harmony, Chicago Turngemeinde, 1852[-]1927, Diamond Jubilee Number.
Chicago: Columbia Printing, [1927]. 36 p.
Note: Includes a history of the society, many photographs of members and activities,
classes, and board members.
Location: InIU.

Is43   Souvenir Program, 1852[-]1952, Chicago Turners (Chicago Turn
Gemeinde) One Hundredth Anniversary, October 18th, 1952, Germania Club.
[Chicago]: Mid-States Printing Co.,[1952]. 64 p.
Note: Includes a history of the Chicago Turngemeinde, photographs and officers list.
Location: InIU.

Is44   Gedenkblatt an das Pic-Nic der Chicagoer Alten Ansiedler. Chicago: Max
Stern & Co., 1889-1931. [50 p.]
Note: Cover title: "*Gedenkblatt an das Pic-Nic der Chicagoer Alten Ansiedler
abgehalten am [date] unter den Auspicien der Chicago Turn-Gemeinde.*" Beginning
in 1875 the Chicago Turn Gemeinde sponsored an annual Old Settlers' Reunion.
These booklets include articles about the early settlement of Chicago, lists of
members, and reports on the activities during the event. The picnics were usually held
in August of each year and lasted until the 1950s.
Location:
    IC: 1938;
    ICHi: 1889-1930;
    ICN: 1931;
    MnV: 1903 (microfilm);

Is45   Harmonie. Eine Monatsschrift zur Förderung aller Bestrebungen der
Chicago Turn-Gemeinde Chicago: Chicago Turn Gemeinde, 1900-1931.
 Note: Monthly. English title: "Harmony: A Periodical to promote 'Turnerism' in the
best sense of the word." Began publication in May 1900. Appeared regularly for
twelve years before being discontinued on account of financial problems; appeared
intermittently from 1913 until discontinued in 1931. Included society news, reports by
officers, and local and national Turner news.
Location: ICHi: v.2, no. 41 (Feb. 1904).

Is46   Nibbe, Louis W., Chicago Turngemeinde: Handy Book, 257 Nord Clark
Strasse, Chicago, Ill, USA, 1904-05: Mitglieder Liste für 1904-1905. [Chicago]: n.p.,
[1904]. 80 p.
Note: Calendar for the year 1904/05. Includes a membership list and list of officers.
Location: ICHi.

Is47   ---. Mitglieder Liste der Chicago Turn Gemeinde, Neunzehnhundert und
Sieben. [Chicago]: n.p.,[1907]. 80 p.
Note: Includes membership list of the Chicago Turngemeinde for the year 1907, list

of officers and class participants.
Location: ICHi.

Is48   Verfassung, Nebengesetze und sonstige Verordnungen der Chicago Turn Gemeinde, und Allgemeine Grundsätze des Amerikanischen Turnerbundes, Revidiert im October 1928. [Chicago]: North Chicago Ptg. Co., [1928]. 61 p.
Note: Cover title: "*Verfassung, Nebengesetze vnd sonstige Verordnungen der Chicago Turn Gemeinde, Revidiert im* October 1928, *und Allgemeine Grundsätze des Amerikanischen Turnerbundes*: Constitution, By-laws and Miscellaneous Regulations of the Chicago Turn Gemeinde, Revised in October, 1928 and Declaration of Principles of the American Turner Bund." In German and English.
Location: InIU.

Chicago: Turn Verein Lincoln, Inc.

Organized in 1885 as the Lincoln Turn-Verein; in same year formed gymnastic classes for men, women and children, a singing section and library; moved to Lincoln Turner hall in 1886; lost members who formed the *Sozialer* Turnverein in 1886 and the Washington Turnverein in 1889; joined by members of the LaSalle Turnverein in 1917; among the sections of the society were the *Bären Riege* (1893), the ladies auxiliary (1893), the Sick and Death Benefit Society (1903), Drum and Bugle Corps (1920), dramatic club (1922) and Rainbow Club (1923); purchased building it had been renting on Diversey, 1910; renovated building in 1922 including addition of a swimming pool, gymnasium and meeting rooms; had several women members who made the U.S. Olympic teams; still active as sports organization.

Archival Collection

Is49   Lincoln Turners Collection, 1894-1988. 52 volumes.
Finding aid available from repository.
Location: ICHi.
Description: The Lincoln Turner Collection includes minutes of the regular meetings from 1894-1897, 1902-1909, 1913-1936; minutes of the board of trustees, 1929-1958; minutes of the building committee, 1922-1926; financial records, 1896-1988; membership lists and dues, 1887-1894, 1910-1918; registration book for the use of the building, 1886-1888; student lists for swimming classes, 1933-1937; scrapbooks; and printed materials. Records prior to the 1920s are predominantly in German.

Is50   Lincoln Turners Collection, 1905-1956.
Location: Private Collection.
Description: Correspondence on 1956 tax problems; ten photographs of Lincoln Turners between 1905-1935.

Publications

Is51 Lincoln Turners, Jubiläums-Ausgabe Turn Verein Lincoln, 25 jähriges Jubiläum, Turnverein Lincoln, 1885[-]1910. [Chicago]: n.p., [1910]. [ca. 75 p.]
Note: Twenty-fifth anniversary booklet. Includes a history of the society, a list of members and pictures of members and activities. Written in German and English.
Location: Private collection.

Is52 Souvenir Program, Colonial Fair & Bazaar Given by Turnverein Lincoln, Chicago, Ill., at Lincoln Turner Hall, Oct. 2 to Nov. 2, 1 919. [Chicago]: n.p., [1919]. [ca. 50 p.]
Note: Includes short articles on Turnerism and the Lincoln Turners, and photographs of club activities and individual classes.
Location: Private collection.

Is53 Harvest Festival and Bazaar: Turn Verein Lincoln at Lincoln Turner Hall and Gymnasium, Saturday Nite, October 27, Sunday October 28, 1928. [Chicago]: n.p., [1928]. [ca. 30 p.]
Note: Includes short histories of each class and section of the Lincoln Turners.
Location: ICHi.

Is54 Turn-Verein Lincoln, Fiftieth Anniversary, April Sixth and Seventh Nineteen Thirty-Five. [Chicago]: n.p., [1935]. [48 p.]
Note: Includes a history of the society written in German and English, a list of achievements in athletic competitions, and a list of committee members.
Location: ICHi; InIU; WMT.

Is55 Souvenir Program for the 75th Anniversary Celebration and Banquet of the Lincoln Turners, 1007 Diversey Parkway, Chicago, Illinois, November 13, 1960. [Chicago]: n.p., [1960]. [44 p.]
Note: Cover title: "Lincoln Turners, 75th Anniversary, 1885[-]1960." Includes a history of the society, list of officers, and pictures of members and club activities.
Location: InIU.

Is56 Turn-Verein Lincoln, 100th Anniversary Program, 1885[-]1985, Saturday, October 5, 1985. [Chicago]: n.p., [1985]. 68 p.
Note: Include a history of the society and a list of past presidents.
Location: ICHi; InIU.

Is57 Program of the Lincoln Bears 50th Anniversary, October 13., 1895-1945. [Chicago]: n.p., [1945]. [8 p.]
Note: "The Bears" was the name of the senior class of the Lincoln Turners. The anniversary program includes pictures and a history of the Bears.
Location: InIU.

Is58   Turnverein Lincoln vs. Herbert Paschen. Court Case # 35419 before the
Supreme Court of Illinois: Brief and Argument for Appallent, November 1959.
Mimeographed. n.p., [1959]. Part 1. 38 p., Part 2, 13 p.
Note: Published in two parts. Description of the arguments in the court case between
the Turnverein Lincoln and Herbert Paschen.
Location: InIU.

Is59   Constitution of the Turnverein Lincoln, School of Physical Education, 1019
Diversey Parkway, Chicago 14, Illinois, July 1, 1949. Chicago: Gunthorf-Warren
Printing Co., [1949]. 22 p.
Location: InIU.

Is60   The Lincoln Turner. Chicago: Turnverein Lincoln, 1920-1940s?
Note: Monthly newsletter of the Lincoln Turners. Includes local and national Turner
news, announcements, and schedules.
Location:
　　IC: vol.4, no. 1 (May 1923); vol.10, no.11 (June 1931)
　　ICHi(Lincoln Turner Coll.): scattered issues, 1921-1934
　　Private collection: bound copy of vol. 8 June/July 1928-July/August 1929.

Chicago: Turn Verein Eiche

Organized in 1890 by the merger of the Pullman-Kensington Turngemeinde (1887),
the Turnverein *Eintracht* (1885), and the Pullman *Männerchor* (1884) under the
name Turn Verein *Eiche*; used *Eintracht* Turner hall on Kensington Avenue; hired
Alfred Wild, founder of the Illinois Turner Camp, as instructor in 1902; organized
ladies auxiliary in 1905; purchased land for new hall in 1930 and moved to new
location on 115th Street and Indiana Avenue; sold old hall in 1975; built new hall in
Tinley Park in 1983; still active as gymnastics and social society.

Archival Collection

Is61   *Eiche* Turners Collection, 1955-present. 20 volumes.
Location: Private collection.
Description: The collection consists of twenty scrapbooks put together by a member
of the society. The scrapbooks include photos, programs, and newspaper clippings
which document the activities of the *Eiche* Turners since the mid- 1950s. Also
included are minutes and financial records since 1975, and a small number of
historical photographs.

Publications

Is62   Programme, Die Reise um die Welt in fünf Tagen in der Eiche Turnhalle,

April 5.-9. 1899. n.p., [1899]. [30 p.]
Note: Program to a theater play, written in German.
Location: Private collection.

Is63   Silberes Jubiläum des Turn-Vereins Eiche abgehalten am Samstag, den 16.,
23., und 30. October 1915, in der Eiche Turnhalle, Chicago. n.p., [1915]. [75 p.]
Note: Twenty-fifth anniversary program of the Eiche Turners. Includes a history of the
Turn Verein *Eiche*, a program of events and photographs. Written in German.
Location: Private collection.

Is64   Turnverein Eiche, Dedication Program, 1890[-]1931, Saturday and Sunday,
May 16th and 17th, 1931, The New Turner Hall, 115th Street and Indiana Avenue.
[Chicago]: Holyoke Press, Inc., [1931]. [32 p.]
Note: Includes a brief history of the society, program of events, and photographs of
classes and sections.
Location: InIU; WMT; Turn Verein *Eiche*.

Is65   Souvenir Golden Anniversary, Turn-Verein Eiche, 165 E. 115th St.,
Chicago, October 16, 17, 19, 20, 1940. [Chicago]: n.p., [1940]. 36 p.
Note: Includes pictures of classes, a brief history of the society, and a biographical
sketch of Alfred Wild, the founder of the Illinois Turner Camp.
Location: InIU; Turn Verein *Eiche*.

Is66   Eiche's 75th Anniversary, 1890[-]1965, "A Night in Bavaria." n.p., [1965].
[75 p.]
Location: Private collection.

Is67   Eiche's 80th Anniversary Past Presidents Dinner, December 5, 1970. n.p.,
[1970]. [36 p.]
Note: The event honored the past presidents of the Turn Verein *Eiche*. Includes list
of past presidents; article by Andrea Dzik originally published in Health entitled
"American Turners: A Sound Mind in a Sound Body;" and a brief history of the
American Turners.
Location: InIU; Turn Verein *Eiche*..

Is68   Octoberfest: Eiche's 90th Anniversary, October 18th, 1980, Tolentine
Center. n.p., [1980]. [32 p.]
Note: Includes list of honorary members, and photographs of exercises and activities.
Location: InIU; Turn Verein *Eiche*.

Is69   Souvenir Program, Eiche Turners, 93 Years, Dedication, Sunday, November
27, 1983, Open House, Sunday, December 4, 1983. n.p., [1983]. [44 p.]

Note: Includes a brief history of the Turn Verein *Eiche*, documentation on how the new hall was built, and pictures of the ground breaking ceremony.
Location: InIU, Turn Verein *Eiche*.

Is70	Turnverein Eiche, Celebrating it's 100th Anniversary, 1890-1990, October 20, 1990. n.p., [1990]. [56 p.]
Note: Includes program of events, short biographical sketches of former and present instructors, historical update on the years 1965-1990, and photographs of past and present members and activities.
Location: InIU; Turn Verein *Eiche*.

Is71	Turnverein Eiche, Organized October 16, 1890, Members of the American Turners, Illinois District. [Chicago]: South End Reporter, [1947]. 10 p.
Note: Cover title: "Constitution and By-laws of the Turnverein Eiche, 165 East 115th Street, Chicago 28, Illinois, Comodore 4-9493."
Location: InIU.

Chicago: Turnverein Fortschritt

Organized in 1884; merged with the Almira Turnverein (1888) and the Turnverein *Voran* (1890) to form the *Turnerschaft der Nordseite* in 1906.

Archival Collection

Is72	*Fortschritt* Turnverein Collection, 1884-1888. 1 volume.
Location: Private collection.
Description: Minute book of the Turnverein *Fortschritt*, 1884-1888. Records are in German.

Chicago: Swiss Turners of Chicago

Started by the Sons of Helvetia, a Swiss gymnastic organization, in 1882; officially organized and affiliated with American Turnerbund under the name *Schweizer* Turnverein in 1889; used halls of other Turner societies as meeting places; merged with *Südseite* Turnverein in 1912; merged with Helvetia Turners in 1923; purchased hall on Webster Avenue in 1928 in cooperation with the United Swiss Societies; changed name to Swiss Turners of Chicago in 1939; closed gymnastic program in the 1940s; merged with the Social and Forward Turners to form the American Turners Northwest Chicago in 1956.

Publications

Is73   Statuten und Nebengesetze des Schweizer Turn-Vereins von Chicago, Gegründet am 6. August 1889, Revidiert am 1. January 1929: Constitution and By-laws of the Swiss Turnverein of Chicago, Founded August 6, 1889, Revised and in Force, January 1, 1929. Chicago: North Chicago Ptg. Co., 1929. 32 p.
Note: In German and English.
Location: InIU.

Is74   Grand Festival and Family Gathering arranged by Illinois Turn-Bezirk and Illinois Turn-Bezirk-Senior Classes, Sunday, April 14th, 1929 in all halls of the Swiss Turn Verein, 627 Webster Avenue Near Lincoln Ave. Entertainment & Dance, Schweizer Turnhalle. n.p., [1929].
Location: Private collection.

Chicago: Social Turners

Organized by members of the Lincoln Turnverein under the name *Sozialer* Turnverein in 1886; purchased lot on corner of Belmont and Paulina Streets in 1887 and built hall that opened in 1889; organized ladies auxiliary and Drum and Bugle Corps in 1888; started newspaper, Der Turner, in 1892; hall destroyed by fire in 1901 but rebuilt in same year; started dramatic section in 1924; second fire damaged hall in 1929; changed name to Social Turners in 1939; hall purchased and condemned by the City of Chicago bought and condemned in 1954; merged with Forward and Swiss Turners to form the American Turners Northwest Chicago in 1956.

Publications

Is75   25 Jähriges Jubiläum vom 17-24 März 1912, Sozialer Turnverein, Belmont Ave. & Paulina St., Chicago. [Chicago]: n.p., 1912. [ca. 65 p.]
Note : Twenty-fifth anniversary program. Includes a history of the society and photographs.
Location: IC; ICHi.

Is76   Gut Heil, 50th Anniversary of the Socialer Turn Verein, Chicago, Ill., 1887 [-]1937. Chicago: Cosmopolitan Ptg. & Pub. Co., [1937]. 60 p.
Note: Includes "The Story of Our Past Fifty Years", brief biographies of living charter members, and photographs.
Location: ICHi; InIU.

Is77   Social Turners, Chicago, Fife, Drum and Bugle Corps, 50th Anniversary, 1888[-]1938. Chicago: Northcenter Press, 1938. 40 p.
Location: IC; ICHi.

Is78   Constitution of the Sozialer Turn Verein, Chicago, Illinois, 1932. [Chicago]: n.p., [1932]. 16 p.
Location: InIU.

Is79   Constitution and By-Laws of the Social Turners, Chicago, Illinois, 1945. Chicago: E. Schoenenberger & Son, [1945]. 14 p.
Location: InIU.

Is80   The Turner: Organ des Sozialen Turnvereins. Chicago: Sozialer Turnverein, 1892-1904; 1916-1956.
.**Note:** Monthly newsletter. Began publication in 1901 under the name Der Turner; stopped publication in 1904 when the district paper Gut Heil was published; resumed publication in 1916; continued as The Turner, official organ of the American Turner Northwest Chicago in 1956. Includes local and national Turner news, announcements and schedules. See also entry **Is23**.
Location:
    IC: no. 223 and no. 226 (1940)
    InIU: no. 1 (April 1916).

Chicago: Turnverein Vorwärts

Organized as Turnverein *Vorwärts* in 1867; built hall in 1868; hall served as shelter for the homeless following the Chicago Fire; organized ladies auxiliary in 1878; gained importance among German workers for its socialist views and support of labor party activities; merged with Turnverein *Bahn Frei* erged in 1893; built new hall in 1896; had membership of 391 and 626 students in 1889; involved in establishing the first public playground and natatorium in Douglas Park in 1895; had several members who became municipal playground directors and instructors; changed name to Forward Turners during World War II; sold building to the Mexican Patriotic Committee, Inc. in 1945; merged with the Swiss and Social Turners to form the American Turners Northwest Chicago in 1956.

Publications

Is81   50, Goldenes Jubiläum des Vorwärts Turn-Vereins, 7-8-9 Juni 1917. Vorwärts Turn-Halle, Chicago. Chicago: n.p., [1917]. 48 p.
Note: Cover title: "*50 Jähriges Jubiläum, 7.-8.-9 Juni, 1917. Turnverein Vorwärts*, 2431-33 West 12th Street, Chicago." Includes detailed history of the organization and photographs.
Location: InIU.

Is82   Vorwärts Turnverein, 70th Anniversary Celebration, April 17-18, 1867 [-] 1937. [Chicago]: n.p., [1937]. 32 p.

Note: Includes a brief history of the organization, list of committee members, program, and brief descriptions of each individual class.
Location: InIU.

Is83   Forward Turner Society, 75th Anniversary, 1867[-]1942, October 14th to 18th, 1942. [Chicago]: n.p., [1942]. 40 p.
Note: Includes a brief history of the society, program, and photographs of members.
Location: InIU.

Is84   Meyer, William. History of the Turnverein Vorwärts, Forward Turners of Chicago, Illinois, July 24. 1867-February 12., 1956. [Chicago]: n.p., [1990]. 55 p.
Note: History of the *Vorwärts* Turners. Includes numerous photographs and lists of past presidents and gymnastic teachers.
Location: InIU.

Is85   Constitution of the Turnverein Vorwärts, 2431 W. Roosevelt Road, Chicago, Member of the Illinois Turner District, Affiliated with the American Turner-Bund, Revised April 4th, 1935. [Chicago]: n.p., [1935]. 16 p.
Location: InIU.

Columbia: Columbia Gymnastic Association

Founded as the Columbia Turnverein in 1866; probably changed name to Columbia Gymnastic Association during World War I; affiliated with the American Turnerbund for only a short period in the 1920s when records indicate that it had a membership of over two hundred; still active as a sports organization.

Publication

Is86   Constitution des Columbia Turnverein, Columbia, Illinois, Angenommen von dem Verein am 2. Juni, 1896. Waterloo, Illinois: Republican, 1896. 25 p.
Location: InIU.

Elgin: Elgin Turners

Founded under the name Elgin Turnverein by members of the Concordia singing society in 1883; formed Drum and Bugle Corps (1902), ladies auxiliary (1917) and Turner band (1927); relocated several times before buying the St. Mary's school building on Villa Street in 1925; independent from the American Turnerbund from 1932 to 1973 when it rejoined; still active as gymnastic organization.

Archival Collection

Is87   Elgin Turners Collection, 1891-present. 61 volumes & 7 boxes.
Preliminary inventory available from Indiana Univ. -Purdue Univ. Indianapolis.
Location: Elgin Turner Hall.
Description: The records include the minutes of the organization, 1892-1925, 1938-1956; minutes of the Board meetings, 1948-1971; membership lists, 1891-1960; financial records, 1915-1961; dues records, 1912-1926, 1941-1970; correspondence, 1896-1904, 1930s; bar book, 1962-1966; bingo records, 1964-1970; inventory of the hall, 1929-1945; handwritten, undated constitutions and rules; gym rules, 1942; unidentified paper on Turnerism in Chicago. The collection also includes the records of the Concordia *Männerchor*. Among the papers are a ledger, 1918-1927; a list of songs used by the singers (*Liederverzeichnis*); six boxes of song books, sheet music, and plays. Records prior to the 1930s are predominantly in German.

Publications

Is88   Golden Jubilee of the Elgin Turnverein, Elgin, Illinois, 1883-1933, Fiftieth Anniversary, May 6, 1933. n.p., [1933]. 24 p.
Location: Private collection.

Is89   Elgin Turnverein: 75th Anniversary, 1883[-]1958. n.p., [1958].
Location: IEl.

Is90   100th Anniversary, 1883-1983, Elgin Turners, 112 Villa Street, Elgin, Illinois 60120. n.p., [1983]. 84 p.
Note: Cover title: "Centennial Edition, 1883-1983." Includes a history of the club and photographs of former members, ladies auxiliary, gymnastic classes, the hall, officers, and club activities.
Location: IEl; InIU; Elgin Turners.

Is91   Touring the U.S.A., Jan.-Feb. 1958. West German Gymnastic Teams, Souvenir Program, Elgin High School Gym ... n.p., [1958]. 48 p.
Note: Includes a history of the German and American Turner-Bund, program and list of participants, and photographs of gymnastic exercises.
Location: InIU.

Is92   Elgin Turners, Constitution and By-Laws. n.p., 1973. 15 p.
Location: InIU.

Highland: Highland Gymnastic Association

Founded as the Turnverein Highland in 1853; changed name to Highland Gymnastic

Association during World War I; highest membership reached in the 1920s with approximately 150 members; closed between 1942 and 1944.

Publications

Is93 Constitution des Turnverein-Highland, Highland, Illinois, Glied des Nordamerikanischen Turnerbundes, Revidiert und angenommen in der regelmäßigen Versammlung des Vereins am 1. Februar, 1897. Highland, IL: Highland Union, 1897. 42 p.
Note: Includes the constitution of the Highland Turnverein and the statutes of the North American Turnerbund. The national statutes were printed by the Freidenker Publishing Co. in Milwaukee in 1894. In German.
Location: InIU.

Moline: Moline Turners

Organized under the name Moline Turnverein in 1866; formed ladies auxiliary in same year; changed meeting places several times before moving into hall on Second Street in 1871; merged with the *Concordia Verein*, founded in 1861 as an educational organization, and the *Germania Verein*, founded in 1872 as a singing society, to form the *Concordia-Germania Turnverein* of Moline in 1876; moved to hall on 6th Avenue and 15th Street 1882; purchased tract of land in 1888 for Concordia Park for use in outdoor activities; started ladies gymnastic classes in 1890; lost twenty-five members who withdrew from society to form the *Vorwärts* Turnverein in 1892; merged with the Moline *Männerchor, Plattdeutsche* Verein and the Moline Oral Society in 1894; built new hall on 14th Street in 1898; joined by members of the *Vorwärts* Turnverein after it disbanded in 1909; changed official language to English during World War I; acquired country home in 1931; changed name to Moline Turners in 1938; saw membership drop from 1462 to 366 between 1950 to 1960; lost hall in late 1960s; still active as social organziation.

Publications

Is94 Diamond Jubilee Celebration Commemorating our Seventy-fifth Anniversary, November 1886[-]1941, Moline Turner News. Moline: Moline Gazette, [1941]. 20 p.
Note: Special issue of the Moline Turners' newsletter. Includes national and local Turner news and a brief history of the organization and its sections.
Location: InIU.

Is95 Constitution and By-laws, (Revised May 1934), Concordia-Germania Turnverein, Moline, Illinois, Organized July 22, 1866. n.p., [1934]. 32 p.

Note: Cover title: "Constitution and By-laws, Nineteen Hundred Thirty-four, Concordia-Germania Turnverein."
Location: InIU.

Is96   Constitution and By-Laws, (Revised October 1st, 1941), Moline Turners, Moline, Illinois, Organized July 22, 1866. n.p., 1941. 32 p.
Note: Cover title: "Constitution and By-Laws, Moline Turners, Nineteen Hundred Forty-One."
Location: InIU.

Is97   Souvenir Program of the Mid-West Turnfest at Moline, Illinois, June 24, 25, 26, 1932. n.p.: National Council of American Turners, 1957. 32 p.
Location: St. Paul Turners.

Is98   Fine Foods from Friends: Souvenir from the 33rd National Bowling Tournament Compiled by the Moline Turner's Auxiliary. n.p., n.d. 113 p.
Note: Cookbook.
Location: InIU.

Is99   Moline Turner News: Monthly Publication of the Moline Turner Society. Moline: Moline Turners, 1937-1950s?
Note: Monthly newsletter of the Moline Turners. Includes news of the society, the women's auxiliary and individual families.
Location: InIU: 75th anniversary issue (1941) and September 1945.

Mt. Olive: Mt. Olive Gymnastic Society

Founded as the Mt. Olive Turnverein in 1897; changed name to Mt. Olive Gymnastic Society during World War I; was small society with approximately sixty-five members in the 1920s; probably closed in 1938.

Publications

Is100   Constitution and By-Laws of the Mt. Olive Gymnastic Society of Mt. Olive, Illinois, Adopted July, 1927. Mt. Olive: Herald Print, 1927. [20 p.].
Location: InIU.

Peoria: Peoria Turnverein

Founded in 1851; probably reached its highest membership in the 1890s with 130 members; operated hall on Second Avenue; may have merged with the Peoria *Südseite* Turnverein, founded in 1893, during the 1920s; disbanded in 1950.

Publications

Is101   Plattform and Konstitution des Peoria Turnvereins. Peoria, IL: Druck von Wolf, Brus, Wolfram, 1879.
Location: IP; IU.

Smithton: Smithton Turnverein

Founded in 1867 as the Georgetown Turnverein; organized sick benefit section in 1870; purchased Georgetown brewery in 1879 and turned into Turner hall; built new two-story structure on same location in 1890s; formed ladies section in 1907; organized brass band in 1913; held picture shows in 1920s; probably changed name to Smithton Turners in the 1920s; it still serves as one of Smithton's principal social centers.

Archival Collection

Is102   Smithton Turners Collection, 1881-present. 30 volumes.
Preliminary inventory available from Indiana Univ. - Purdue Univ. Indianapolis.
Location: Smithton Turner Hall.
Description: The collection includes records of the Smithton Turners; its predecessor, the Georgetown Turnverein; and its ladies auxiliary. Records include minutes, 1881-1905, 1922-1948, 1968-1989; membership lists, 1909-1926, 1941-1981; financial records, 1887-1888, 1919-1985; records of the sick and death benefit section, 1906-1947; and ladies section minutes, 1927-1961. Records prior to the 1920s are predominantly in German.

Publications

Is103   Smithton Turner Society, 100th Anniversary, 1867-1967. n.p., [1967]. 32 p. **Note**: Includes a detailed history of the society and photographs of buildings and present and former members.
Location: InIU; Smithton Turners.

Is104   A History of the Smithton Turner Society organized as the Georgetown Turnverein, 125 Anniversary Celebration, Fri., Sat. & Sun., July 10, 11 & 12, 1992, Smithton, Illinois. n.p., [1992]. 36 p.
Note: Includes a history of the society, and pictures of former and present members and activities.
Location: InIU; Smithton Turners.

Is105 Constitution and By-Laws of the Ladies' Section of the Smithton Turner Society . n.p., [1977]. 11 p.
Location: InIU; Smithton Turners.

Is106 Constitution and By-Laws of the Smithton Turner Society. n.p., [1990]. 29 p.
Note: Cover title: "Smithton Turner Society." Constitutions also issued in 1906 (German), 1920, 1939, 1947, 1962, 1973, 1979, 1986 and 1988.
Location: InIU; Smithton Turners.

INDIANA

Evansville: Central Turners

Organized in 1869 as the Turnverein *Vorwärts*; declared bankruptcy, 1897; reorganized as the Evansville Turngemeinde, 1898, then as the Evansville Central Turnverein, ca. 1900; became the Evansville Central Turners, ca. 1940; left the American Turners over financial disagreement, 1954; disbanded, ca. 1983.

Publications

In1 Konstitution des Turnvereins "Vorwärts" von Evansville, Ind., nebst Plattform und Statuten des Nordamerikanischen Turnerbundes. Evansville: Rosenthal & Baumgartner, 1890. 56 p.
Location: NN (microform).

Fort Wayne: Fort Wayne Turners

Organized as Turnverein *Vorwärts* in 1897, at time when the original Fort Wayne Turnverein (1852-ca. 1900) was in decline; joined American Turnerbund and offered classes in 1897; started ladies auxiliary, 1898; successfully lobbied Fort Wayne school board for introduction of physical education into the schools, 1901; purchased building on Superior St. owned by the Fort Wayne Medical College to serve as Turner hall, 1906; changed name to Fort Wayne Turners, 1941; purchased land on Parnell Avenue to serve as summer home, 1950; moved permanently to Parnell Ave. property and sold Superior St. hall, early 1960s; still active.

Archival Collection

In2   Fort Wayne Turners Collection, 1887-1993. 15 boxes.
Preliminary inventory available from Indiana Univ. - Purdue Univ. Indianapolis.
Location: Fort Wayne Turner Hall.
Description: The records of the Fort Wayne Turners include minute books of the
society, 1897-1901; financial records, 1914-1979; records and programs on
entertainment, Christmas dances, Valentine's Day dinners, etc., 1960-1966; records
of national athletic competitions in bowling, golf, and tennis from 1960s and 1970s;
choral group records of the 1950s; women's auxiliary records, 1961-1986; six
scrapbooks of clippings and articles on Fort Wayne Turners activities, 1935-1990;
newsletter from 1935-1943, 1948-1953, 1958-1988; and three boxes of photographs,
awards and plaques, ca. 1900-1980. Records prior to 1922 are in German

Publications

In3   Survey of Fort Wayne Turners, Fort Wayne, Indiana, May 10, 1961.
Mimeograph. n.p., [1961]. [44 p.]
Note: Survey of opinions and attitudes of the members of the Fort Wayne Turners
prepared by Concord Counselors.
Location: InIU.

In4   Constitution and By-Laws of the Fort Wayne Turners, Fort Wayne, Indiana,
Organized June 25, 1897. n.p., [1947]. 18 p.
Note: Cover title: "Constitution and By-Laws, Fort Wayne Turners, 1947."
Location: InIU.

In5   Fort Wayne Turners. Fort Wayne: Fort Wayne Turners, 1935?-present.
Note: Monthly newsletter of the Fort Wayne Turners. Includes national and local
cultural and athletic Turner news, announcements, and schedules.
Location: Fort Wayne Turners: 1935-present. [incomplete]

Indianapolis: Athenaeum Turners

Organized as the Indianapolis Turngemeinde in 1851; merged with the *Socialistische
Turnvereine* (also founded in 1851) to form the *Socialistische Turngemeinde* in 1852;
reorganized as the Indianapolis Turnverein in 1865 after being dormant during the
Civil War; expelled one-quarter of the membership in 1868 for their opposition to the
national platform supporting voting rights for freed slaves (expelled members formed

the *Socialer* Turnverein with the intention of making the society a social rather than a political organization); the two societies merged to form the Indianapolis *Socialer* Turnverein in 1872; adopted the name Athenaeum Turners in 1918 as a result of anti-German sentiment during World War I; changed name to Indianapolis Turnverein, 1922; changed back to Athenaeum Turners, 1938. Opened first Turner Hall in 1853; sponsored building of *Das Deutsche Haus* as a home for the Turnverein and other German-American organizations; building completed in two stages in 1894 and 1898; became the Athenaeum in 1918; ownership transferred to the Athenaeum Foundation, a non-profit corporation created to restore the building in 1991. Related organizations include the *Turnschwestern Verein* (later known as the *Damenverein* and the Women's Auxiliary of the Athenaeum Turners), organized in 1876 to sponsor social, charitable and athletic programs for women; and the *Freidenker Verein* (Freethinkers' Society), made up largely of Turnverein members, which sponsored lectures and discussions in the 1870s and 1880s and a freethinkers' Sunday School for children which lasted into the early twentieth century under the auspices of the *Socialer* Turnverein. Society still active. The society has played a substantial role in the national organization. *Das Deutsche Haus* served as the headquarters of the American Turnerbund from 1898 to 1923, and as the home for the Normal College of the American Gymnastic Union from 1907 until 1970. In addition, the Indianapolis newspaper Die Zukunft served as the national organ for the Turnerbund from 1867 to 1878; the society hosted the *Turnlehrer Seminar* from 1889 to 1891; and the city hosted national Turnfests in 1905, 1983 and 1991.

Archival Collections

In6   Athenaeum Turners, Inc. Collection, 1853-1992. 82.25 linear feet (113 boxes, 180 volumes).
Finding aid available from repository.
Location: InIU.
Description: The collection includes records of the Athenaeum Turners and its predecessors, of a number of other German-American organizations formerly housed in the Athenaeum, and of the American Turners and the Normal College, primarily from the years when they were located in the Athenaeum. Records of the Athenaeum Turners are from the years 1869-1982, and include board minutes, 1894-1904, 1931-1983; correspondence and reports, 1886-1919, 1932-1983; annual reports, 1931-1986; financial records, 1869-1986; membership records, 1876-1917; newsletters, 1919-1931, 1970-1977; programs, invitations and other printed items, 1894-ca. 1990; and records of the restaurant, 1949-1974. The records of the Women's Auxiliary are from the years 1876-1974 and include minutes of meetings, 1876-1947; correspondence, 1904-ca. 1975; membership records, 1887-1962; financial records, 1876-1974; and newspaper clippings, 1917-1986. Other Turner organizations whose

records are in the collection include the *Socialer* Turnverein Stock Association, 1876-1973; the *Turn-Zögling Verein*, an organization for young people set up by the *Socialer* Turnverein, 1872-1882; and the Turner *Bau und Spar Verein* [Turner Building and Savings Association], 1883-1940. Records from 1918 or earlier are predominantly in German.

Local organizations whose records are in the collection include *Der Deutsche Klub*, 1894-1899; *Der Deutsche Klub und Musikverein*, 1899-1938; *Deutsche-Amerikanische Gut-Geld Liga von Indianapolis* [The German-American Sound Currency League of Indianapolis], 1896; *Deutsch-Amerikanischer Schulverein* [German English School Society, 1868-1913; *Freidenker Verein*, including records of its Sunday School, 1870-1898; the Germanistic Society of Indianapolis, 1916-1917; and the *Verband Deutscher Vereine von Indiana* [Alliance of German Societies in Indiana], 1905-1913. For records of the Turner national office and of the Normal College, see the appropriate sections of the guide.

In7 Richard Lieber Collection. 2 scrapbooks, 1892-1901.
Location: In.
Description: Includes two scrapbooks, 1892-1901, containing newspaper clippings and programs for events at the Indianapolis *Socialer* Turnverein and for performances of the Turnverein's drama club.

Publications: Histories & Anniversary Books

In8   Stempfel, Theodor. Fünfzig Jahre unermüdlichen Deutschen Strebens in Indianapolis: Festschrift zur Feier der Vollendung des Deutschen Hauses in Indianapolis. Am 15., 16. und 18. Juni 1898. Indianapolis: Pitts & Smith Publishers, 1898. [ca. 170 p.]
Note: Cover title: "Das Deutsche Haus, Indianapolis, Indiana." History of the Indianapolis Turner societies and of the liberal German element in Indianapolis since 1848, published for the 1898 dedication of the *Socialer* Turnverein's new home, *Das Deutsche Haus*. Stempfel, an Indianapolis banker and leader of the *Socialer* Turnverein, was later president of the American Turnerbund.
Location: In; InHi; InIU.

In9   Stempfel, Theodor. Fünfzig Jahre unermüdlichen Deutschen Strebens in Indianapolis: Festschrift zur Feier der Vollendung des Deutschen Hauses in Indianapolis/ Fifty Years of Unrelenting German Aspirations in Indianapolis: Festschrift Celebrating the Completion of Das Deutsche Haus in Indianapolis., edited by Giles R. Hoyt, Claudia Grossmann, Elfrieda Lang and Eberhard Reichmann. German/English Edition. Indianapolis: German-American Center and Indiana German Heritage Society, Inc., 1991. 150 p.

Note: Republication and translation of the 1898 Stempfel book.
Location: InIU; frequently available in large academic and public libraries.

In10   Indianapolis Turnverein, Seventy-Fifth Anniversary, 1851-1926, November Twelfth and Thirteenth, Nineteen Hundred and Twenty-Six. [Indianapolis]: n.p. [1926]. 26 p.
Note: Includes a history of the society and program for the celebration.
Location: In; InIU.

In11   Athenaeum Turners, 1851-1951, One Hundredth Anniversary.
[Indianapolis]: n.p., [1951]. 20 p.
Note: Includes a history of the society, program of celebration, and photographs.
Location: In; InIU; IaDP.

   Publications: Constitutions & By-Laws

In12   Statuten des Indianapolis Sozialen Turnvereins und Plattform und Statuten des Nord-Americanischen Turner-Bundes, Verbessert und Angenommen am 16. Februar 1876. Indianapolis: *Office der Zukunft*, 1876. 23 p.
Location: MnU.

In13   Constitution und Nebengesetze des Socialen Turnvereins von Indianapolis, Ind., und dessen Damen- und Zöglings-Vereins nebst Regeln für die Turnschule, sowie Platform und Statuten des Nordamerikanischen Turnerbundes und Statuten des Indiana Turnbezirks. Milwaukee: Freidenker Publishing Co., 1889. 69 p.
Location: In.

In14   Constitution und Nebengesetze des Sozialen Turnvereins von Indianapolis, Ind., und dessen Damen=und Zöglings=Vereins nebst Regeln für die Turnschule, sowie Platform und Statuten des Nord=Amer. Turnerbundes und Statuten des Indiana Turnbezirks. Indianapolis: Tribüne Publishing Co., 1897. 64 p.
Location: InIU.

In15   Athenaeum Turners. Constitution and By-Laws. Organized July 28, 1853. Articles of Incorporation of the Social Turnverein as amended to September 1944. [Indianapolis]: n.p., [1944]. 12 p.
Location: InIU.

In16   Athenaeum Turners. Constitution and By-Laws, Organized July 28, 1853. [Indianapolis]: n.p., [1957]. 15 p.
Location: InIU.

In17   Constitution of the Women's Club of the Athenaeum Gymnasium of
Indianapolis, Ind., Organized April 16, 1876. March, 1921. [Indianapolis]: n.p.,
[1921]. 12 p.
Location: InIU.

In18   Das Deutsche Haus: Socialer Turnverein Stock Association, Gegründet
1892. [Indianapolis]: n.p., [1901?]. 32 p.
Note: Includes description of *Das Deutsche Haus*, the *Socialer* Turnverein Stock
Association, and the programs and facilities available in the building; also includes list
of members of the Stock Association. In German and English.
Location: InIU.

In19   Articles of Association of the Turner Building and Saving Association No.2.
[Indianapolis]: n.p., [1890]. 24 p.
Note: In German and English (German title: "*Turner Bau-und Spar-Verein*"). A
savings and home-loan association, operating out of the Turner society. The
Association was created in 1883 and reorganized in 1889.
Location: InIU.

In20   Turner Building and Saving Association of Indianapolis. Articles of
Association, Constitution and By-laws, as amended at the stockholders' meeting,
September 5th, 1896.. Indianapolis: Levey Bros. & Co., 1897.
Location: In.

  Publications: Newsletters

In21   Der Fortschritt; Organ des Socialen Turnvereins, 1887-1888?
Note: Newsletter of the Indianapolis *Socialer* Turnverein. Includes articles and news
of the society, the Turnbezirk and the Turnerbund; schedules of classes and meetings.
Typical issue is 8 pages.
Location: InU: vol. 1, no. 1-10 (1887-1888).

In22   Athenaeum Gym News, 1919-1931?
Subtitle: "Athenaeum Branch of the American Gymnastic Union. Published in the
Interest of Rational Physical Education." (1919-May 1922). Name changed to
Indianapolis Turner: Indianapolis Branch of the American Gymnastic Union.
Published in the Interest of Rational Physical Education, October 1922.
Note: Monthly society newsletter containing local and national Turner news;
announcements, information about the Normal College, and class schedules. Typical
issue is 4 pages.
Location: InIU: 1919-1931 (incomplete).

In23   Athenaeum News. ca.1970-1984?
Note: Title varies: newsletter of the Athenaeum Turners.
Location: InIU: 1970-1984, scattered issues.

In24   Turner Nachrichten, 1984-1990?
Note: Newsletter of the Athenaeum Turners.
Location: InIU: Jan./Feb. 1987.

Publications: Miscellaneous

In25   Feier der Vollendung des Deutschen Hauses 15., 16. und 18. Juni 1898.
Programm für Mittwoch, den 15. Juni. [Indianapolis]: Tribune Publ. Co., 1898. 12p.
Note: Includes program, poetry, and summary of script for the play "German Gifts"
by Konrad Nies, performed as part of the celebration for the dedication of the German
House. In English and German.
Location: In.

In26   Kommers zur Feier der Vollendung des Deutschen Hauses am Samstag, 18.
Juni 1898, Abends 8 Uhr 30 Min. Indianapolis: Tribune Publ. Co., [1898]. 16 p.
Note: Program and lyrics of songs sung for the dedication of the German House.
Location: InIU.

In27   Nies, Konrad. Deutsche Gaben: Fest-Spiel zur Einweihung des Deutschen
Hauses in Indianapolis am 15. Juni 1898. Indianapolis: Tribune Publ. Co., [1898].
26 p.
Note: Script for play performed at the German House Dedication, written by St. Louis
German-American poet Konrad Nies and with prologue, in poetic form, by Philip
Rappaport, editor of the Indiana Tribüne.
Location: InIU.

In28   Germanisches Frühlingsfest des Socialen Turnvereins am Montag den 4.
April 1904 im Deutschen Haus. Unter gest. Mitwirkung des Deutschen Klubs &
Musikvereins. Indianapolis: Gutenberg Co., [1904]. 16 p.
Note: Includes poetry, program and play bill for the *Socialer* Turnverein's German
Spring Festival, organized by the German Club and Music Society.
Location: InIU.

In29   Celebration of Washington's Birthday and fourteenth anniversary of the
dedication of the German House and presentation to the German House of a portrait
of Herman Lieber. [Indianapolis]: n.p., 1908. 31 p.
Note: Cover title: "*Das Deutsche Haus*. February Twenty-second Nineteen Hundred

Eight." Contains toasts and speeches delivered at the German House in celebration of Washington's Birthday, the German House, and the presentation of artist T.C. Steele's portrait of Herman Lieber, one of the principal leaders of the *Socialer* Turnverein. In German and English.
Location: In; InHi.

In30   Athenaeum Turners Women's Auxiliary. Yearbook. [Indianapolis]: n.p., 1963-1966.
Note: Includes list of the elected officers, yearly program of events, and membership list with addresses.
Location: InIU.

Indianapolis: South Side Turners

Organized as the *Südseite* Turnverein in 1893 with the help of the *Socialer* Turnverein to serve the large, working class German population on the city's south side; employed as *Turnlehrer* Kurt Toll, one of the principal physical education instructors in the Indianapolis Public Schools, 1890s-1920s; built hall on Prospect St., 1903; closed building, late 1970s; still active.

Archival Collections

In31   Indianapolis South Side Turners Collection, 1893-1956. 6 boxes.
Finding aid available from repository.
Location: InIU.
Description: The Indianapolis South Side Turner Collection includes minutes of the organization, 1893-1903, 1951-1956; records of the South Side Turnverein Hall Association, 1900-1919; scrapbook of official papers, 1897-1906 (includes correspondence, financial reports, programs and receipts); minutes of Athletic Club meeting, 1927-1931; photographs, 1897-1925. Records prior to the 1930s are in German.

In32   "*Geschichte des Südseite Turn Verein seit dessen Gründung September 1893 bis* October 1900." 71p.
Location: In.
Description: Handwritten, bound history of the South Side Turnverein, written by Turnverein president Henry Victor, October 1900. Includes separate histories of the Women's Section and the Turnverein Hall Association. In German.

Publications

In33   Souvenir zur Einweihungs-Feier der Südseite Turnhalle am 20 und 22 Januar 1901, Indianapolis. Indianapolis: Indiana Tribüne, [1901]. 36 p.
Note: The dedication program for the hall erected by the South Side Turners includes histories of the organizations and sections, description of Turner rules and Turner clothing, program, and photographs.
Location: InIU.

In34   Fest=Programm für das 18. Indiana Bezirks=Turn=Fest unter der Leitung des Südseite Turn=Vereins von Indianapolis, Ind. Den 27., 28., 29. und 30. Juni 1903. Indianapolis: Gutenberg Co., [1903]. 20 p.
Note: Souvenir book for the Eighteenth Indiana District Turnfest in 1903. Includes a brief history of the South Side Turners, list of committee members, list and statistical information on other societies in the district, and brief articles on women's exercises.
Location: InIU.

In35   Constitution and By-Laws of the South Side Turners [Indianapolis]: n.p., 1933. 13 p.
Location: InIU.

In36   South Side Turners of Indianapolis. Constitution and By-Laws, Adopted June 10, 1946. A School of Physical Education. [Indianapolis]: n.p. [1946]. 16 p.
Location: InIU.

In37   South Side Turners of Indianapolis. Constitution and By-Laws, Adopted June, 1950. A School of Physical Education. [Indianapolis]: n.p., [1950]. 19 p.
Location: InIU.

In38   The South Side Turnverein Hall Association, Indianapolis, Ind., Articles of Incorporation. Indianapolis: Indiana Printing and Mfg. Co., 1901. 8 p.
Location: InIU.

South Bend: American Turners South Bend

History

Organized June 1861 as the South Bend Turnverein; remained active during Civil War although numerous members enlisted; built Turner hall on North Michigan St. in 1869; supported singing society, brass band, drama society, masquerades, physical education classes, and other activities throughout late 19th century; organized sick and death benefit society in 1887; employed Eduard Koenig as gymnastics instructor while he also served as supervisor of physical education for the South Bend public schools, 1885-ca.1927; formed women's auxiliary in 1904; raised funds for German and Austrian war relief during the years 1914-1916 and 1919-1920; received new members from large group of German immigrants in 1920s; changed official language to English in 1935; moved to new Turner hall on Ironwood Street in 1974; still active.

Archival Collection

In39   South Bend Turner Records, 1861-present. 27 volumes.
Preliminary inventory available from Indiana Univ. - Purdue Univ. Indianapolis.
Location: Private collection.
Description: The collection includes minute books of the society, 1861-1886, 1902-1918, 1929-1978; statistical reports, 1880-1912; dues payment and membership list, 1864-1929; expenditures and receipts records, 1910-1929; membership ledgers, 1861-present; membership applications since ca. 1880; newspaper articles; president's report for 1960/61; original charter; photographs; minutes of the *Gesangsektion*, 1909-1915, 1926-1942; and minute book of the *Krankenunterstützungs Kasse* (Sick Benefit Society), 1887-1907. Records prior to 1935 are predominantly in German.

Publications

In40   Goldenes Jubiläum: 1861[-]1911, South Bend Turn Verein. [South Bend]: n.p., [1911]. 40 p.
Note: Fiftieth anniversary publication. Includes a history of the society, program, and pictures of members and Turner activities. In German and English.
Location: InIU.

In41   Seventy-Fifth Diamond Jubilee Anniversary, 1861-1936, South Bend Turnverein, June 12th to 14th. [South Bend]: n.p. [1936]. 24 p.
Note: Includes a history of the society and photographs.
Location: InIU.

In42   One Hundred Anniversary: American Turners-South Bend, June 10th-13th-17th. [South Bend]: n.p., [1961]. 30 p.
Note: Includes a history of society, program, and pictures of members and activities.
Location: InIU.

In43   Konstitution und Nebengesetze des South Bend Turnvereins (Gegründet am 13. Juni 1861). Milwaukee: Freidenker Publishing Co., 1911. 32 p.
Note: Contains pasted-in revisions, in German, ca. 1934.
Location: InIU.

In44   South Bend Turners. Constitution and By-laws. Founded June 13, 1861. [South Bend]: n.p., [1948]. 21 p.
Location: InIU.

In45   Turner Times. South Bend: South Bend Turners, 1977?- present.
Note: Newsletter of the South Bend Turners.

Tell City: Tell City Socialer Turnverein

Organized 1859 in town founded by Swiss Colonization Society in 1857; built Turner Hall, 1868; hall later became Opera House and Turner Hall; left national Turnerbund, 1903; closed ca.1904.

Archival Collection

In46   Tell City Socialer Turnverein, 1858-1958. (1 volume).
Location: InIU.
Description: Scrapbook of photocopies of newspaper articles on the Tell City *Socialer* Turnverein complied by Charles Schreiber of the Tell City Historical Society, taken from the local newspapers from 1858 to 1958.

IOWA

Clinton: Clinton Turners, Inc.

Organized as Turnverein *Vorwärts* in 1883; maintained hall on Second Street; changed name to Clinton Turner Benevolent Verein *Vorwärts* in 1937 and to Clinton Turners, Inc. in 1947; reached peak membership with seven hundred members in 1949 but dwindled to fifty-six by 1960; left American Turners in 1962 and possibly closed shortly thereafter.

Publications

Ia1   Articles of Re-Incorporation and By-Laws of the Clinton Turner and

Benevolent Verein Vorwärts of Clinton, Iowa. n.p., 1937. 20 p.
Location: InIU.

Ia2   Articles of Re-Incorporation and By-Laws of the Clinton Turners, Inc.,
Clinton, Iowa. n.p., 1947. 23 p.
Location: InIU.

Davenport: Central Turners

Organized in 1852 as *Socialistischer* Turnverein by exiled revolutionaries who had taken part in the Schleswig-Holstein uprising. Among its founders were Christian Müller, a leader of the *Kieler Turnverein* who was imprisoned for his role in the revolt; Hans Reimer Clausen, a representative at the Frankfurt National Assembly; Theodor Gülich, radical supporter of the Free-Soil party and editor of Davenport's German newspaper Der Demokrat; and journalist Theodor Olshausen. Society built first hall on Fourth Street in 1853; purchased land for new, larger hall on Sixth Street in 1857; changed name to Davenport Turn Gemeinde in 1858. During the Civil War the Turner hall became a military center where volunteers were recruited and drilled by Turners. In 1870 the society bought the *Germania Theater Verein* hall and erected a two-story gymnasium; hall became arts and intellectual center for the city and hosted numerous freethinker and liberal speakers, including Ludwig Büchner, Carl Schurz and Friedrich Hecker. The society led the campaign for physical education in the public schools beginning in the early 1870s; in the following years the Davenport Schools hired a number of Turners, including the society's gymnastic instructor, William Reuter, as physical education instructors. The society built a new hall in 1887-1888 which housed the Davenport Opera House; hosted national conventions in 1884, 1902, and 1952; formed ladies auxiliary in 1890 and Ladies Drum and Bugle Corps in 1925; established Turner Camp along the Mississippi River for outdoor activities in 1932; changed name to Central Turners in 1943; converted opera house to bowling alleys in 1947; closed building due to financial problems in 1959; officially still in existence, but inactive; now located in Rockford, Illinois.

Archival Collection

Ia3   Davenport Turner Collection. 1852-1953.
Finding aid available from repository.
Location: IaDP
Description: The collection includes minutes of the Davenport Turner's Association, 1867-1911; trustee meeting minutes 1871-1912; minutes of the committee for spiritual endeavors, 1873-1885, 1897-1929; minutes of the committee for exhibition

sports, 1876-1925; minutes of the amusement committee, 1896-1926; minutes of the Turner Hall Building Association, 1887-1901; membership lists, 1858-1889, 1903-1908; treasurers' and secretaries' reports, 1887-1891; cash book for choir section, 1883-1908; watch book of the health committee, 1852-1905; guest book, 1899-1912; cash receipts and tax materials, 1889-1937; miscellaneous papers and correspondence, 1887-1908; papers and correspondence of the Davenport Turner Hall Building Association, 1887-1890; histories of the society written in 1874, 1902 and 1927; miscellaneous printed matter such as programs, newspaper articles, manuals and pamphlets of the choir section; proceedings of the Upper Mississippi District, 1921-1953; and national convention minutes and anniversary books of other Turner societies.

Ia4   August Miedke Journal and Scrapbook, 1866-1923. 1 folder
Location: InIU.
Description: August Miedke was a founding member of the Davenport Turngemeinde. Included are photocopies of his journal describing Turner competitions in western Illinois and Iowa in 1859-1860, and of his scrapbook which includes letters and newspaper articles, many relating to Turner activities, from 1866 until his death in 1923.

Publications

Ia5   Benefit Performance for the German Red Cross under the auspices of the Davenport Turngemeinde. Davenport: Lischer Printing Co., 1915. [19 p.]
Note: Includes articles "German Situation" and "*Die Deutschen im amerikanischen Bürgerkrieg*" (The Germans in the American Civil War) and program for the event. In German and English.
Location: IaHi.

Ia6   Richter, August Paul. Die Davenporter Turngemeinde: Gedenkschrift zu ihrem goldenen Jubiläum, 3 August 1902. Davenport: H. Lischer Print Co., [1902]. [118 p.]
Note: Contains extensive history of the Davenport Turnverein and a small number of pictures.
Location: IaDP; IaHI; PPG.

Ia7   Davenport Turn-Gemeinde, Seventy-Fifth Anniversary, 1852-1927, November Twelfth and Thirteenth, Nineteen Hundred Twenty-Seven. [Davenport]: n.p., [1927]. 26 p.
Note: Includes history of the society; program, and small number of pictures.
Location: IaDP.

For 100th anniversary publication, see 44th National Convention, 1952.

Ia8   Constitution and By-Laws of the Davenport Turn-Gemeinde, Including a Copy of the Principles and Statutes of the American Turner Bund. Davenport: n.p., 1931. [61 p.]
Note: Published in two parts: constitution and by-laws of the Davenport Turn-Gemeinde, pp. 1-22; statutes of the American Turnerbund, 1926, unpaged.
Location: InIU.

Ia9   Constitution and By-Laws of the Central Turners at Davenport, Iowa. Davenport: n.p., 1948. 28 p.
Location: InIU; Northwest Davenport Turner Society.

Davenport: Northwest Davenport Turner Society

Organized in 1871; purchased lots and built hall on 16th and Washington Street in 1882; formed ladies auxiliary (1907); sponsored ladies drum and bugle corps (1932-1953); Turner hall routinely used for Republican and Democratic Party rallies since 1884; changing neighborhood caused Turners to sell their hall and purchase old school on Warren Street in 1980s; still active.

Archival Collection

Ia10   Northwest Davenport Turner Society Records, 1872-1972. 2 volumes.
Location: IaBS
Description: The records consist of the society's membership books, including names and addresses of members, 1872-1927. The first volume includes a *Schwarze Liste* (black list) for 1903.

Ia11   Northwest Davenport Turner Society Records, 1924-present.
Location: Northwest Davenport Turner Society.
Description: The records include minutes of the general meetings, 1924-1925 and 1937-1966; trustee minutes, 1940-62; one box of physical education results from the Upper Mississippi District; two scrapbooks with newspaper clippings from the 1940s; approximately fifty historical photographs; and copies of national convention minutes.

Publications

Ia12   Centennial Souvenir Book, 100th Anniversary, 1871-1971, Northwest Turners, Davenport, Iowa. [Davenport]: n.p., [1971]. [16 p.]

Note: Includes a history of the club, short biographies and pictures of long term members, and photographs.
Location: InIU; Northwest Davenport Turner Society.

Ia13   Constitution and By-Laws of the Northwest Davenport Turner Society, Founded August 5th, 1871. [Davenport]: Blackhawk Printing Co., n.d. [1913]. 30 p.
Location: InIU.

Ia14   Constitution and By-Laws of the Northwest Davenport Turner Society, Founded August 5, 1871. [Davenport]: n.p., [1940]. 30 p.
Location: InIU; Northwest Davenport Turner Society.

Ia15   Constitution and By-Laws of the Bears (Senior Class) of the Northwest Davenport Turner Society, Organized July 7, 1905. Davenport: PSC Press, n.d. 8 p.
Location: InIU; Northwest Davenport Turner Society.

Davenport: East Davenport Turners

Organized as *Ost* Davenport Turnverein in 1891 by members of the former Volunteer Fire Department of Davenport; built hall on the bank of the Mississippi River in 1908-1909; expanded hall in 1925; formed ladies auxiliary in 1919; still active as predominantly social society.

Archival Collection

Ia16   East Davenport Turners Records. 1891-present. 12 volumes.
Preliminary inventory available from Indiana Univ.-Purdue Univ. Indianapolis.
Location: East Davenport Turners, Davenport.
Description: Records include minutes of the East Davenport Turners, 1972-present.; membership lists and dues, 1891-1917, 1945-1948; expenses and income, 1945-1969; women's auxiliary: minutes, 1919-1928, 1953-1966, and financial records, 1919-1960; one suitcase of convention minutes and other Turner publications (water damaged); and numerous folders with photographs and newspaper articles. Records are in English.

Publications

Ia17   Souvenir of the East Davenport Turner Society, East Davenport Turner Fair, November 25-29, 1909. [Davenport]: n.p., [1909].
Location: East Davenport Turners.

Ia18   Constitution and By-Laws of the East Davenport Turner Society, Founded in the Year 1891, Revised and Approved Feb. 1932. [Davenport]: Blackhawk Printing Co., [1932]. 25 p.
Location: InIU.

Ia19   By-Laws of the East Davenport Turner Society, Founded in the Year 1891, Revised and Approved November 1949. [Davenport]: n.p., [1949]. 23 p.
Location: InIU.

Garnaville: Garnaville Sozialer Turnverein

Organized in 1869; had fifty-four members in 1872; operated independently from American Turnerbund from 1873 to 1904; rejoined Turnerbund for one year in 1905, at which time there were forty-five members; may have closed shortly thereafter.

Publication

Ia20   Verbesserte Verfassung des Garnaville Sozialen Turnvereins. Garnaville, Iowa: O.E. & W.I. Maurer, Printers, 1895. 18 p.
Location: InIU.

Holstein: Holstein Turnverein

Organized in 1884; built hall in 1889-1890 and addition in 1915; formed ladies auxiliary in 1901; discontinued gymnastic classes during World War I but reorganized them in 1923; allowed hall to be used for community activities, such as city sports tournaments, theater productions, baccalaureate services and band concerts, including Lawrence Welk's; left American Turnbund in 1928 with one hundred members; gave property to town of Holstein in 1959; society continued to meet in building until it dissolved in the 1970s.

Publications

Ia21   Holstein Gymnastic Society, Constitution and By-Laws of the Holstein Gymnastic Society, Organized June 24, 1886. Holstein, Iowa: n.p., 1925. 16 p.
Location: IaHi.

Keystone: Keystone Turners, Inc.

Founded in 1892 as Keystone Turnverein; maintained hall on Second Street; became social center of this rural community; still active as bowling and social society.

Archival Collection

Ia22   Keystone Turners Records, 1892-1982. 25 volumes.
Preliminary inventory available from Indiana Univ. - Purdue Univ. Indianapolis.
Location: Keystone Turners, Inc.
Description: The records include minute books of the society, 1892-1894 and 1923-1974; membership lists and dues, 1936-1981; financial records, 1913-1960; minutes of the ladies auxiliary meetings, 1929-1982; records of the Keystone Turnverein Building Account Fund, 1960; handwritten minutes of the Upper Mississippi Turner convention, April 30-May 1, 1966. All records prior to 1925 are in German.

Publications

Ia23   Constitution and By-Laws of the Keystone Turn-Verein, Keystone, Iowa.
n.p., 1937. 12 p.
Location: InIU.

Ia24   Constitution and By-Laws of the Keystone Turners, Keystone, Iowa.
n.p., 1948. 12 p.
Location: InIU.

Muscatine: Muscatine Turnverein Vorwärts

Organized in 1907;was small society with between twenty and forty members during 1910s; listed as dissolved in American Turnerbund annual report for 1920 but reappeared again in 1930 with eleven members; not listed after 1934 and possibly closed at that time.

Publications

Ia25   Verfassung und Neben-Gesetze des Turnvereins Vorwärts von Muscatine, Iowa, Gegründet am 8. Oktober 1907. Muscatine: Muscatine Herold, 1907. 23 p.
Location: InIU.

Postville: Postville Turnverein

Organized in 1873; was small society with between thirty and forty members in 1890; suspended from Turnerbund in 1901; returned to Bund in 1905 but dropped out in 1906; possibly operated as independent society thereafter; closing date unknown.

Publications

Ia26 Statuten des "Postville Turnvereins," Gegründet den 24. August 1873, Revidiert am 14. Februar 1892. Milwaukee: Freidenker Publishing. Co., 1892. 16 p.
Location: InIU.

KANSAS

Atchison: Atchison Turnverein

Organized in 1859; had numerous confrontations with pro-slavery raiders before and during the Civil War; built hall on corner of Kansas Ave. and Sixth Street in 1880; had average membership of ninety members in the 1890s; dropped out of the American Turnerbund with fifty-one members in 1902; closed in 1917.

Archival Collection

Ks1 Atchison Turnverein Records, 1859-1903. 25 volumes, 3 letter books.
Location: KHi.
Description: The records include minutes of the society, 1866-1899; reports of the officers, 1887; correspondence, 1887; membership and dues records, 1859-1861, 1886-1903; financial records, 1874-1892; accounts of members, 1872-1884, 1892-1897; and minute book of the Kansas Turnbezirk, 1865-1876. The collection also includes the records of the Atchison *Liederkranz*, a singing society, consisting of minutes, 1873-1886, and financial records, 1874-1886. The records are predominantly in German.

Leavenworth: Leavenworth Turnverein

Organized in 1857 and built hall on 6th and Delaware Streets, one of the first buildings in Leavenworth; organized Turnverein militia as a result of encounters with pro-slavery raiders; militia protected voters and ballet boxes from pro-slavery parties to ensure that free-state sympathizers could vote; militia also raided a pro-slavery camp, resulting in capture of artillery and other weapons. Society moved to new hall at Shawnee and Broadway Streets in 1859; organized first regiment in Kansas, the First Kansas Infantry, at the outbreak of the Civil War; played central role in formation of German-American League to fight for women's suffrage and prohibition in 1892; hall destroyed by fire in 1893 and rebuilt in same year; over two hundred members in 1910; disbanded in 1925.

Archival Collection

Ks2　Leavenworth Turnverein Records. 1857-1923; microfilm, 2 reels.
Location: Kansas Historical Society, Topeka.
Description: Records are in German. No further information available.

Publication

Ks3　Verfassung des Leavenworth Turnvereins, Gegründet am 4. Juli 1857.
Leavenworth, KS: Kansas Freie Presse, 1884. 33 p.
Location: InIU.

Seneca: Seneca Turnverein

Organized in 1897; left American Turnerbund in 1903 with eighty-five members; closing date unknown.

Publication

Ks4　Constitution und Neben-Gesetze des Seneca Turnvereins. [St. Joseph]: St. Joseph Volksblatt, 1897. 11 p.
Location: InIU.

Topeka: Topeka Turnverein

Organized in 1867; erected hall on First and Harrison Streets in 1879; built addition in 1882; experienced financial difficulties in the 1880s when drinking came under attack by strong prohibition supporters, including Carrie Nation; held position of one of the most socially prominent societies in Topeka with 200-250 members from 1890s to 1910s; lost hall to fire in 1911; left American Turnerbund in 1917-1918 due to combination of financial losses from fire and anti-German sentiment; possibly closed in the 1920s.

Archival Collection

Ks5   Topeka Turnverein Records, 1904-1922. 4 volumes.
Location: KHi.
Description: No further information available. The Kansas Historical Society also has a number of clippings on the Topeka Turnverein in the Shawnee County clipping file, as well as photographs of the society.

Publications

Ks6   Statuten des Topeka Turn Vereins. Topeka: Kansas Telegraph, 1888. 36 p.
Location: KHi.

KENTUCKY

Covington: Covington Turner Society

Organized in 1855 as Covington Turngemeinde; involved in bloody all-day confrontation between Turners and Know Nothings after picnic in 1856 resulting in the arrest of over thirty Turners and a year-long court case in which all Turners were acquitted; thereafter Turners were guarded by the sharpshooter's section on their picnics. Purchased lot on Pike Street in 1857; lost hall during Civil War; built new hall in 1869-1870; built new hall in 1877; successfully opposed proposed Sunday closing laws in 1905; petitioned the Covington Board of Education for the introduction of German language in the public schools; suffered damage to Turner hall in 1915 tornado; changed name to Covington Turner Society in 1918; allowed use of Turner hall by the Red Cross as relief quarters for flood victims in 1937; still active.

Archival Collection

Ky1   Covington Turner Society Records, 1860-1973. 36 volumes.
Preliminary inventory available from Indiana Univ.-Purdue Univ. Indianapolis.
Location: Covington Turner Society.
Description: The records include minutes of meetings, 1860-1861, 1867-1879, 1942-1973; dues payments, 1927-1935; account books, 1937-1943 and 1962-1967; list of members, 1907; bingo records, 1946-1947; records of the jubilee committee of the Covington Turngemeinde, 1905; guest book to the 75th anniversary, October 18-19, 1930; typewritten history of the Covington Turner Society, 1855 -1977 by Luella C. Roth; scrapbook of the 100th anniversary celebration; and historical photographs, framed documents and banners. Also included are records of the Covington Turners'

women's auxiliary (*Damenverein*) including minutes, 1899-1903, 1916-1925, 1947-1955; membership records and dues records, 1899-1917, 1921-1959; and account book, 1899-1966; and minutes of the *Arion Männerchor* of Newport, KY, 1889-1891, 1902-1926. Records prior to the 1930 are in German.

Publications

Ky2 Covington Turngemeinde, 1855[-]1905: Goldenes Jubiläum Souvenir Programm, September 17.-21., 1905. Covington: n.p., [1905]. [30 p.]
Note: Includes photographs and histories of the Covington Turngemeinde, the *Damenverein*, the choir and *Bärenriege.*
Location: Covington Turner Society.

Ky3 Golden Jubilee Celebration, September 17-21, 1905, Covington Base Ball Park and Turner Hall Auditorium. Official Program and Souvenir. Covington: Press of Standard Printing Works, [1905].
Location: KYLOF.

Ky4 60th Anniversary: Covington Turngemeinde, 1855-1915, Souvenir Program, Gymnastic Exhibition, Field Day and Volksfest of the Combined Societies of the Ohio District of the North American Gymnastic Union, Covington Federal Base Ball Park, Sunday Afternoon & Evening, Sept. 12, 1915. [Covington]: n.p., [1915]. [ca. 20 p.]
Note: Includes pictures of officers, a history of the Covington Turngemeinde, and history of the women's auxiliary. Written in German.
Location: Covington Turner Society.

Ky5 Souvenir Diamond Jubilee, Covington Turners, 1855-1930, October 18-19, 1930, Covington. [Covington]: n.p., [1930]. [36 p.]
Note: Includes a history of the Covington Turner Society and pictures of members.
Location: Covington Turner Society.

Ky6 One Hundredth Anniversary Program of the Covington Turners' Society, Banquet and Dance, Sunday Evening, October 16, 1955 at Turner Hall. [Covington]: n.p., [1955]. 56 p.
Note: Cover title: "The First Hundred Years, Covington Turner Society." Includes history of the club and photographs.
Location: InIU.

Ky7 111 Turner Songs for all Occasions. n.p., n.d. [40 p.]
Note: Compiled by Alban Wolff; songs in German and English.
Location: InIU.

Ky8   Constitution and By-Laws, Rules and Regulations, Covington Turner's Society, Covington, Ky., 1930, Founded September 13, 1855. Covington: Alban Wolff, 1930. 24 p.
Location: Covington Turner Society.

Ky9   Covington Turner Society, Incorporated, Covington, Kentucky, Founded September 13, 1855: Constitution and By-Laws, Rules and Regulations, Revised January 6, 1947. [Covington]: n.p., 1947. 22 p.
Location: InIU.

Ky10   Covington Turner Society, Constitution and By-Laws, Rules and Regulations, Covington, Ky. n.p., n.d. [15 p.]
Location: Covington Turner Society.

Ky11   Turner Echo. Covington: Covington Turngemeinde, 1915-1921.
Note: Monthly newsletter of the society.
Location: Covington Turner Society: scattered issues.

Louisville: American Turners Louisville

Turner activities began in Louisville as early as 1848; society formally organized as Louisville Turngemeinde in 1850; built first Turner hall in 1851; hall threatened with burning by local Know Nothing group, 1855; hall burnt in 1858 and pro-slavery group suspected of arson, thereafter society formed 24-hour guards to protect property. The society discontinued activities during Civil War when most members joined the Union Army and the hall was used as military hospital; built new hall on East Jefferson Street in 1875; absorbed the Louisville Central Turnverein in 1888; lost large number of members to the newly-formed *Männer Turnverein Vorwärts* in 1887 over the unwillingness of the Turngemeinde to publicly support the Haymarket defendants; acquired land for Turner Park in 1912; built new hall on East Broadway in 1917; changed name to Louisville Turners in 1918; changed name to American Turners Louisville in the 1940s; closed Broadway building and moved to Turner Park in 1984; hosted national convention in 1872, 1896, 1919 and 1956, and national Turnfests in 1853, 1926 and 1959; still active as sports organization.

Archival Collection

Ky12   Louisville Turners Records, 1849-1995. app. 50 volumes.
Preliminary inventory available from Indiana Univ.-Purdue Univ. Indianapolis.
Location: American Turners Louisville.

Description: The records of the American Turners Louisville include minutes, 1880-1953; financial records, 1849-1924; membership records, 1849-1901, 1922-1924, 1930s, 1963; two boxes of correspondence, 1930s and 1950s; scrapbook of clippings and newspaper articles, ca. 1925-1940s, including clippings of the 1926 National Turnfest in Louisville. The collection also includes the records of the women's auxiliary, including minutes, 1882-1956; dues records, 1921; and a box of correspondence, 1920s and 1930s; and district records, including financial records of the Cincinnati Turn Bezirk, 1864-1869; minutes of the Indiana Turn Bezirk, 1890-1910; printed minutes of the Indiana and Central States District, 1920s-1950s; and printed annual reports of the American Turnerbund, 1920s to the 1950s. Records before World War I are in German.

Publications

Ky13 Willkommen Zur Neuen Halle. Louisville: Louisville Anzeiger, Turner Nummer, September 2, 1917. 32 p.
Note: An extra edition of the Louisville Anzeiger, a German-language newspaper, to celebrate the dedication of the new Turner hall. Includes a history of the Turner movement in Louisville and detailed descriptions of the society's sections with pictures and personal accounts.
Location: InIU; American Turners Louisville.

Ky14 The Turner: Souvenir Number. Louisville: Louisville Turnverein, 1917. 107 p.
Note: This souvenir edition of The Turner, the monthly publication of the Louisville Turners (v.2, no. 8, October 1917), was published for the dedication of the new Turner hall in 1917. Includes history of organization, reminiscences by long-time members, list of teachers, essays on physical education, and photographs.
Location: InIU; American Turners Louisville.

Ky15 Program, 27th National Convention, North American Gymnastic Union and Turntag Indiana District, June 22 -- 25, 1919, Louisville, KY. Louisville: Anzeiger, 1919. 155 p.
Note: Title taken from page four. Published as a souvenir edition of The Turner, (v. 4, no. 4, June 1919). Includes essays on physical education, the history and future prospects of Turners in the United States, program of event, photographs of the Louisville Turners, and directory of society members in 1919.
Locations: InIU; American Turners Louisville.

Ky16 Diamond Jubilee, Louisville Turngemeinde, 1850 [-] 1925. [Louisville]: n.p., [1925]. 72 p.

Note: Includes a history of the society, description of its activities and photographs. Written in German and English.
Location: InIU; WMCHi.

Ky17 Louisville Turners, A Review of Our First Hundred Years: Louisville Turners, Souvenir Edition. [Louisville]: n.p, [1950]. [47 p.]
Note: Cover title: "100th Anniversary, Louisville Turners." Includes articles on the history of the American Turners Louisville, membership list and photographs.
Location: InIU; American Turners Louisville.

Ky18 Louisville Turners, 310 Broadway. [Louisville]: n.p., n.d. 8 p.
Note: Promotional brochure. Contains photographs and description of activities of the American Turners Louisville.
Location: InIU.

Ky19 Turner Indoor Circus Programs. [Louisville]: n.p., 1950?-1985?
Note: The American Turners Louisville gave an annual gymnastic exhibition called the Turner Circus. Includes programs of events.
Location:
   InIU: 1981.
   Akron Turner Club: 1956
   American Turners Louisville: 1960-1968.

Ky20 Constitution and By-Laws of the Louisville Turners, Incorporated, Louisville, Ky., Adopted in the Meeting of January 7, 1929. [Louisville]: n.p., 1929. 20 p.
Location: InIU.

Ky21 Constitution and By-Laws of the Louisville Turners, Incorporated, Louisville, Ky, Adopted at General Meeting May 19, 1941. [Louisville]: n.p., 1941. 23 p.
Location: InIU.

Ky22 Constitution of the American Turners Louisville, Incorporated, Adopted March 1, 1976. [Louisville]: n.p., [1976]. 28 p.
Location: InIU.

Ky23 Constitution and By-Laws of the Ladies Auxiliary of the American Turners, Louisville, Organized January 22, 1875 at Louisville, Kentucky, Revised and adopted November 7th, 1956. [Louisville]: n.p., [1956]. 8 p.
Location: InIU.

Ky24 The Turner: Official Publication of the Louisville Turners. Louisville: Louisville Turners, 1916-present.
Note: Monthly publication of the Louisville Turners; began publication in 1916. Includes local and national Turner news, announcements, and schedules. Special issues of The Turner were published for events, such as national or district Turnfests or anniversaries.
Location:
American Turners Louisville: 1916-present.
InIU: 1917, 1922-1935, 1947, 1951-present. (incomplete).

Newport: Newport Gymnastic Association

Organized in 1852 as the Newport Turnverein; aided Covington Turners in their confrontation with Know Nothing mob in 1856; was small society with between forty and fifty members in 1890s and early 20th century; reached peak membership with 118 in 1925; changed name to Newport Gymnastic Association during World War I; left American Turnerbund in 1936 and probably closed shortly thereafter.

Publication

Ky25 The Gymnast: Published in the Interest of the Newport Gymnastic Association. Newport: Newport Gymnastic Association, 1922?-1930s.
Note: Monthly publication of the Newport Gymnastic Association of Newport, Kentucky. Includes local and national Turner news and announcements.
Location: InIU: v.5, no. 10 (June 1927).

LOUISIANA

New Orleans: New Orleans Turnverein

Organized in 1851, although Turner activities had taken place a year earlier under the leadership of Forty-eighter immigrants; built hall on Franklin St. near Canal in the early 1850s which became a center for social and cultural events sponsored both by German and non-German groups; sponsored annual *Maifest,* a major New Orleans social event, from 1853 to the Civil War; left national Turnerbund in 1858 over its anti-slavery policy, two years after most of the other Southern societies had withdrawn; had members leave in 1858 and 1860 to form anti-slavery Turner societies, but both closed within a year due to public disapproval; organized military section in early 1861; raised Turner Battalion for the Confederate Army in May 1861; rejoined American Turnerbund after the Civil War; built hall on Clio Street; had become primarily a singing and social organization by the time of World War I; closed its hall and transferred its assets to the New Orleans *Deutsche Haus* in 1928.

Archival Collection

La1   New Orleans Turnverein Records, 1869-1928, 3 volumes.
Finding aid available from repository.
Location: LNHi.
Description: The collection includes a letterbook (*Copier Buch*) for outgoing correspondence, 1869-1877; a book of proceedings, 1912-1928; and the minutes of the Pyramid Section of the New Orleans Turnverein, 1900-1914. The records of the society are part of the archives of the New Orleans *Deutsche Haus*. Records are in German.

MARYLAND

Baltimore: American Turners Baltimore, Inc.

Organized in 1849 as the *Social Democratischer* Turnverein by refugees of the 1848 revolution; among the early members were William Rapp, Johann Straubenmüller and Karl Heinrich Schnauffer; had 278 members by 1850; purchased hall on West Pratt Street by the end of the 1850s and became national headquarters for the *Socialistischer* Turnerbund in 1860; had several encounters with Know Nothing gangs during the 1850s, especially during the 1852 Turnfest when participants were attacked several times; housed the offices of the national newspaper, the Turn-Zeitung, from 1859 until 1861. Most of its members enthusiastically enlisted in the Union Army in 1861 and marched to the defense of Washington; immediately thereafter the Turner hall and Turn-Zeitung offices were destroyed by a mob of southern sympathizers. Played leading role in reactivating the national Turnerbund at the end of the Civil War; lost members who formed the Turnverein *Vorwärts* (1867), Atlantic Turnverein (1872), and Gymnastic Pyramid Club (1882); lost hall during the depression years in the 1870s; consolidated with the Atlantic Turnverein in 1887 and became the Baltimore Turngemeinde; reorganized as the *Germania* Turnverein in 1888 and purchased property on Post Office Avenue; played important role in the introduction of physical education in the public schools in 1895; lost hall and records to fire in 1904; purchased new hall North Gay Street in 1909-1910; rented building to the federal government between 1943 and 1951; merged with the *Vorwärts* Turnverein in 1948 to form the American Turners Baltimore, Inc.; purchased new building in Rossville in 1965; hosted national Turnfest in 1852, 1859 and 1867, and national convention in 1994.

Publications

Md1   100th Anniversary, Century of Health, 1849[-]1949, American Turners Baltimore, A School Of Physical Education, Emerson Hotel, September 24th.
[Baltimore]: Bromwell Press, 1949. [80 p.]

Note: Includes historical sketch of the American and Baltimore Turners and photographs of members.
Location: InIU.

Md2   Historical Sketch of the American Turners Baltimore, Inc., Founded 1849. Baltimore: Bromwell Press, 1949. 20 p.
Note: Compiled by Leroy L. Martin. Reprinted from 100th Anniversary Program, September 24th, 1949.
Location: InIU (photocopy).

Md3   Constitution, By-Laws and Charter of the American Turners-Baltimore, Incorporated, Founded in 1849, Incorporated 1868, Amended 1948. [Baltimore]: Bromwell Press, 1948. 22 p.
Location: InIU.

Baltimore: Baltimore Turnverein Vorwärts

Founded in 1867 by members of the *Social Demokratischer* Turnverein; supported active gymnastic and educational program and sponsored lectures by liberal speakers such as Karl Heinzen, Robert Reitzel, Maximilian Grossmann and Adolph Douai; established drawing school in 1869; formed ladies auxiliary in 1891; purchased building on Lexington Street in 1895; sold property to City of Baltimore during World War II; merged with the Baltimore Turnverein (former *Germania* Turnverein) in 1948 to form the American Turners Baltimore, Inc.

Publications

Md4   Zur Erinnerung an das 25 jährige Stiftungsfest des Turn-Vereins "Vorwärts" zu Baltimore, am 3. und 4. Juli 1892. [Baltimore]: n.p., 1892. 27 p.
Note: Cover title: "*Erinnerungs-Album, 25stes Stiftungsfest, Turnverein Vorwärts, Baltimore, Sonntag, den 3. Juli: Germ. Männerchor-Halle, Montag, den 4. Juli: Darlen-Park.*" Festival book for the twenty-fifth anniversary celebration. Includes a history of the society, membership lists of the society and ladies auxiliary, and list of committee members.
Location: InIU (photocopy); MdBHi.

Md5   Turnverein Vorwärts Gymnastic Ass'n, Baltimore, 734 W. Lexington St. (Bet. Myrtle & Fremont Aves.). [Baltimore]: n.p., [1895]. 32 p.
Note: Title page: "A week in Atlantic City, New Vorwaerts Hall, 734 W. Lexington St., November 25th to 30th, 1895." Includes a history of the society, a description of individual classes and class schedules.
Location: InIU.

Md6   Vorwärts, October 16, 17, 18, 1937, 732-734 West Lexington Street, Baltimore, Maryland. [Baltimore]: n.p., 1937. [20 p.].
Note: Sixtieth anniversary publication. Includes a history of the organization written by Karl A.M. Scholtz, and an appeal for the creation of a German-American archive from the Society for the History of Germans in Maryland.
Location: InIU (photocopy); MdBHi.

Md7   Constitution des Turnvereins Vorwärts in Baltimore, Gegründet am 28. Juni 1867. Baltimore: C. W. Schneidereith & Söhnen, 1893. 24 p.
Note: Paginated in two sections: pp. 1-12 in German, pp. 1-12 in English.
Location: InIU.

Md8   Charter and By-Laws of the Turnverein Vorwärts Baltimore, Md., Founded in 1867, Incorporated 1868, Amended 1898, Revised 1931. [Baltimore]: n.p., [1931]. 30 p.
Note: In English and German.
Location: InIU.

Md9   Vorwärts. Monatsschrift des Turnverein Vorwärts. Baltimore: Turnverein Vorwärts, 1893-1895?
Note: Cited in Arndt/Olson, v.1, p. 197.

MASSACHUSETTS

Adams: Adams Turners, Inc.

Organized as Adams Turn Club in 1889; changed name to Adams Turn Verein Vorwärts during the same year; bought land on North Summer Street (later renamed Turner Avenue), 1901; built hall in 1902 and gymnasium in 1906; renamed Adams Turners, Inc. in 1948; hosted national Turnfest in 1987; still active as gymnastic society in original building.

Archival Collection

Ma1   Adams Turners Records, 1889-present. 19 volumes
Preliminary inventory available from Indiana Univ.-Purdue Univ. Indianapolis.
Location: Adams Turners, Inc.
Description: The records include the minutes of the organization, 1913-1968, 1973-1974, 1977-present; membership records, 1930-1976; financial records, 1889-1929, 1938-1947, 1953-1959; and ladies auxiliary membership records, 1889-1946. The

collection also includes minutes from the *Frauenheim-Loge* no. 15, 1918-1941. Records before the 1930s are in German.

Publications

Ma2   Souvenir Program for the Dedication of New Turner Hall of the Turn Verein Vorwärts, Adams, Massachusetts, Saturday, Sunday and Monday, September 1, 2, and 3, 1906. Adams: Freeman Press, [1906]. 40 p.
Note: Includes articles on physical education, principles of the American Turners, and photographs.
Location: InIU (photocopy); Adams Turners, Inc.

Ma3   Fiftieth Anniversary Souvenir Program Turn Verein Vorwärts, Adams, Massachusetts, Friday, Saturday and Sunday-May 26, 27, 28, 1939. [Adams]: n.p., [1939]. [36 p.]
Note: Includes brief history of the organization and photographs.
Location: InIU.

Ma4   Statuten und Nebengesetze des Turnvereins "Vorwärts" zu Adams, Mass., Incorporiert 1902 unter den Gesetzen des Staates Massachusetts. Angenommen 21. Juli 1925. n.p., [1925]. 40 p.
Note: Constitution and by-laws.
Location: InIU.

Boston: Boston Turnverein

Organized in 1849 by refugees of the 1848 revolution, including Karl Heinzen; provided bodyguard for abolitionist Wendell Phillips; merged with Turnverein *Fortschritt*, 1860; organized two companies during the Civil War; built hall on Middlesex Street in 1875-1876; sponsored lectures by prominent German liberal speakers and Freethinkers, such as Robert Reitzel, Fritz Schütz, Schünemann-Pott, and Ludwig Büchner; lost hall in 1918/19 due to financial difficulties during World War I; moved into hall on Glen Street in Jamaica Plain in 1925; hall destroyed by fire in 1943; used *Arbeiter* Hall on Armory Avenue in Roxbury for meetings until society disbanded in 1956; hosted national conventions in 1868 and 1886.

Publications

Ma5   Einige Blätter aus der Geschichte des Bostoner Turnvereins. Boston: n.p., 1890. 15 p.

Note: In 1890, G. Thomann, a member of the New York Turnverein, mailed questionnaires to all Turner societies in order to collect materials for a proposed English-language book on the Turner movement in the United States. This pamphlet on the society's history was written in response to Thomann's request.
Location: InIU (photocopy); WHi.

Ma6   One Hundredth Anniversary of the Boston Turnverein and the Fiftieth Anniversary of the Boston Turner Frauenverein, Monday Evening, April 18th, 1949, Hotel Lenox, Boston. [Boston]: n.p., [1949]. [24 p.]
Note: Cover title: "100th Anniversary, Boston Turnverein." Includes history of the society and the womens' club.
Location: InIU.

Ma7   Bostoner Turn-Zeitung. Boston: Bostoner Turnverein, 1876-1921.
Note: Title varies: Turner-Zeitung, 1876-1892. The Bostoner Turn-Zeitung was the newspaper of the Boston Turnverein and was published weekly to promote progress, enlightenment, and the interests of the Boston German population.
Location:
    CtY: v.6 (1882) - v.9 (1885).
    In: v.16 (1891) - v.17 (1893).
    InIU: v.11, no.3 (November 1886). Photocopy.
    MBA: v. 11, no. 3 (November 1886).
    NN: v. 28 (1904) - v.32 (1908). Incomplete.

Clinton: Clinton Turn Verein

Organized as Turnverein *Frohsinn* in 1867; bought lot and built hall in 1873-1874; started German school in 1876; completed addition to hall in 1893; introduced physical education into the public schools in 1910; lost hall and all historical records in fire in 1969; completed new building in 1971; hosted national convention in 1982; still active.

Archival Collection

Ma8   Clinton Turn Verein Records, 1973-present.
Location: Clinton Turn Verein.
Description: Records include minutes of the regular meetings, 1973-present, and meeting sign-in books, 1975-1988.

Publications

Ma9   Seventy-Fifth Anniversary, 1867-1942, Clinton Turn Verein, Clinton, Massachusetts, Friday and Saturday, May 22, 23, 1942, Turner Hall, Clinton, Mass., Organized May, 1867, Incorporated October, 1879. [Clinton]: n.p., [1942]. [28 p.]
Note: Includes a history of the American Turner movement, history of the society, and photographs.
Location: InIU.

Ma10   100th Anniversary of the Clinton Turn Verein, 60 Branch Street, Clinton, Mass., May 21st-27th, 1967 [Clinton]: n.p., [1967]. [50 p.]
Note: Includes history of the society and the women's auxiliary, and photographs.
Location: InIU; Clinton Turn Verein.

Ma11   Clinton Turn Verein Corp., 125 Years, 1867-1992. [Clinton]: n.p., [1992]. [56 p.]
Note: Includes brief history of the organization, the women's auxiliary and the American Turners, and contemporary photographs.
Location: InIU; Clinton Turn Verein.

Ma12   Constitution of the Clinton Turn Verein Corporation, Founded in May, 1867, Incorporated 1879, Revised and adopted February 2, 1949. [Clinton]: n.p., [1949]. 28 p.
Location: InIU.

Ma13   Constitution and By-Laws of the Clinton Turn Verein Corporation, Founded in May, 1867, Incorporated 1879, Revised and adopted December, 1978. [Clinton]: n.p., 1978. 28 p.
Location: InIU; Clinton Turn Verein.

Ma14   Constitution and By-Laws of the Clinton Turn Verein Corporation, Founded in May, 1867, Incorporated 1879, Revised and adopted July, 1985, Supersedes Constitution and By-Laws Adopted December, 1978. [Clinton]: n.p., 1985. 27 p.
Location: InIU; Clinton Turn Verein.

Ma15   Constitution and By-Laws of the Clinton Turn Verein Corporation, Founded in May, 1867, Incorporated 1879, Revised and adopted July, 1993, Supersedes Constitution and By-Laws Adopted July, 1985. [Clinton]: n.p., 1993. 27 p.
Location: InIU; Clinton Turn Verein.

Fitchburg: Fitchburg Turners, Inc.

Organized as the Fitchburg Turnverein in 1886; built hall on Frankfort Street in 1893; changed name to *Deutscher Fortbildungs Verein* in 1909; consolidated with the Harugari Lodge and a singing society in 1912; changed name again to Fitchburg Turners, Inc. in 1954; closed due to financial problems in 1983; hall destroyed by fire two days after closing.

Publications

Ma16 Golden Anniversary of the Deutscher Fortbildungs Verein, Turner Hall, 4 Frankfort Street, Fitchburg, Mass., Saturday, Sunday and Monday, October 10, 11 and 12, 1936. Lawrence: Dick & Trumpold, 1936. [32 p.]
Note: Includes poems, jokes, songs, and program.
Location: InIU.

Ma17 Konstitution des Deutschen Fortbildungs-Verein, Fitchburg, Mass.; Constitution and By-Laws of the German Progressive Society, Fitchburg, Mass. Lawrence, Mass.: Dick & Trumpold, n.d. 22 p.
Note: Published in two sections: pp. 1-12 in German; pp. 1-10 in English.
Location: InIU.

Ma18 Constitution and By-Laws, Fitchburg Turners, Inc. Member American Turners, Fitchburg, Mass., Effective January 1, 1970. Fitchburg: 1970. 16 p.
Location: InIU.

Holyoke: Holyoke Turn Verein

Organized in 1871; built hall in 1874; lost members who formed the Springdale *Vorwärts* Turn Verein in 1886; started German school in 1888; remodeled and enlarged hall in 1893; purchased 11 acres of land at Hampton Ponds for a weekend and summer camp in 1912; lost camp buildings to fire in 1930 but rebuilt one year later; Turner hall renovated in 1945; still active as gymnastic society.

Archival Collection

Ma19 Holyoke Turn Verein Records, 1876-present.
Preliminary inventory available from Indiana Univ.-Purdue Univ. Indianapolis.
Location: Holyoke Turn Verein.
Description: The records include minutes of the board, 1893-1902, 1916-1942;

minutes of the general meetings, 1891-1903, 1909-1946; financial records, 1876, 1899, 1902-1924, 1939-1945, 1954-1968; membership and dues records, 1936-1955, 1959-1961; class list (*Turnstundenlist*) 1917-1920; sick and death benefit dues, 1936-1954; and programs to Turner minstrel shows in the 1920s. Ladies auxiliary records include minutes of the meetings, 1878-1891, 1903-1940, 1951-1968. The collection also include minutes of the Connecticut District, 1911-1931. Records before the 1930s are in German.

Ma20   Holyoke Turn Verein Records, 1876-1930. 5 volumes.
Finding aid available from repository.
Location: MHol
Description: The collection includes financial records of the organization, 1876-1909; membership and dues records of the ladies auxiliary, 1892-1894, 1899-1905, 1919-1930; ladies auxiliary financial records, 1913-1921; and newspaper articles.

Publications

Ma21   Souvenir Program Commemorating the 75th Anniversary of the Holyoke Turn Verein, Inc., June 7-8-9, 1946. Holyoke: Kenneth R. Brooks, 1946. [32 p.]
Note: Includes histories of the society and the ladies auxiliary, a summary of gymnastic activities, and contemporary photographs.
Location: InIU.

Ma22   Holyoke Turn Verein, 624 So. Bridge St., Holyoke, Massachusetts, Saturday, October 2, 1971. [Holyoke]: n.p., [1971]. 12 p.
Note: Includes a brief history of the organization.
Location: InIU; Holyoke Turn Verein.

Ma23   Constitution and By-laws of the Holyoke Turn Verein, Effective June 14, 1937. Holyoke: Lehmann Printing Co., 1937. 16 p.
Note: Includes list of members.
Location: InIU.

Holyoke: Springdale Turners, Inc.

Organized by members of the Holyoke Turn Verein under the name of Springdale *Vorwärts* Turn Verein in 1886; built hall on Vernon Street in 1888 and added gymnasium in 1891; discontinued the teaching of gymnastics in the 1930s but sponsored several baseball teams; name changed to Springdale Turners, Inc. in 1940s; still active as social society.

Archival Collection

Ma24   Springdale Turners Records, 1953-present.
Preliminary inventory available from Indiana Univ.-Purdue Univ. Indianapolis.
Location: Springdale Turners, Inc., Holyoke.
Description: The Springdale Turner records include the minutes of the organization,
1953-present, and a dues book, 1960. Also included is "Report of the 3. Atlantic *Kreis*
Turnfest held in the City of Holyoke, Mass, on the 22., 23., 24. days of June 1899
under the auspices of the Turnverein *Vorwärts*, Holyoke, Mass.," which includes a
list of committee members and expenditures for the 1899 Atlantic Circuit festival.

Publication

Ma25   Constitution and the By-Laws of the Turnverein Vorwärts, Springdale Turn
Hall, Vernon St., Holyoke, Mass. [Holyoke]: n.p., 1942. 20 p.
Location: InIU.

Lawrence: Lawrence Turn Verein

Germans in Lawrence organized short-lived Turner societies in 1853 and 1859;
organized Lawrence Turn Verein in 1866; purchased land in 1867 for outdoor
gymnasium; built first hall in 1868 and replaced it with a larger one in 1872; lost hall
to fire in 1894 and constructed new hall in 1895-1896; served as one of the largest
societies in Lawrence with over 500 members in 1900; closed in 1974.

Archival Collection

Ma26   Lawrence Turn Verein Collection, 1944-1958.
Finding aid available from repository.
Location: MLIA
Description: The collection includes correspondence, 1944-1958; list of library
books; minstrel show programs, 1923 and 1934; programs of the Lawrence Turn
Verein Players, 1935-1940; newspaper articles; photographs and printed materials.

Publications

Ma27   Goldenes Jubiläum, Lawrence Turnverein, Lawrence, Massachusetts, den
Vierzehnten, Fünfzehnten und Sechzehnten April Neunzehnhundert und sechzehn.
n.p., 1916.
Note: Festival book for the fiftieth anniversary celebration. Includes history,

photographs, and program.
Location: MLIA.

Ma28   Seventy-Fifth Anniversary, Diamond Jubilee, Lawrence Turn Verein, Friday, Saturday, Sunday, April 18, 19, 20, 1941. Lawrence: Eagle Tribune Printing, [1941]. 44 p.
Note: Includes histories of the organization, the dramatic section, the ladies auxiliary and other sections, and photographs.
Location: InIU; MLIA.

Ma29   100th Anniversary of Lawrence Turn Verein, 1865-1965. [Lawrence]: Eagle Tribune Printing, [1965].
Note: Includes history of the organization and photographs.
Location: MLIA.

Ma30   Kratzbürste: Sonntag, den achten Februar neunzehnhundert und vierzehn, jährliche Karnevalsitzung des kleinen Rats vom Lawrence Turnverein. n.p., [1914].
Note: Program to the annual carnival celebration. Includes program and poems.
Location: MLIA.

Ma31   Statuten and Revidierte Beschlüsse des Turn Vereins zu Lawrence, Mass. gegründet am 30. September 1865, Incorporiert am 8. Dezember 1889. n.p., 1902.
Location: MLIA.

Ma32   By-Laws and Revised Statutes, Lawrence Turn Verein, Member American Turners, Effective January 1, 1950. Lawrence, Mass. Lawrence: Eagle Tribune Printing, 1950. 14 p.
Location: InIU.

Ma33   The Lawrence Turner. Lawrence: Lawrence Turn Verein, 1930-1931?
Subtitle: Monthly Publication issued in the Interest of the Lawrence Turn Verein, its Gym Classes and the N.E. Turner Festival 1931.
Location:
    InIU: v. 1, no. 7 (June 1931);
    MLIA: v.1, no.1 (December 1930) - v.1, no.8 (July 1931).

Malden: Malden Turn Verein

Organized in 1889; purchased land on Forest Street and built hall in 1891; reached peak membership with ninety members in 1915; disbanded in 1942.

Publication

Ma34 Constitution and By-Laws of the Malden Turn Verein, Malden, Massachusetts, 1889-1916. n.p, [1916]. 12 p.
Location: InIU.

Springfield: Springfield Turnverein, Inc.

Organized in 1855; suspended activities during Civil War; rented several locations until erecting own hall on State Street in 1883; started German school in 1890s; purchased land in Longmeadow for Turner park in 1900; discontinued gymnastic and German classes during World War I; sold hall and park in 1926 and bought smaller hall in the Round Hill area; lost hall to state construction projects in 1966; bought new property in Feeding Hills in 1970; active as gymnastic and singing society.

Archival Collection

Ma35 Springfield Turnverein Records, 1884-present. 25 volumes.
Preliminary inventory available from repository.
Location: MSHi
Description: The records of the Springfield Turnverein include the minutes, 1884 - 1921; trustee minutes, 1956-1966, 1974-present; financial records, 1909-1917, 1937-1967; application forms 1890-1893; undated library records; and scrapbook with photographs and newspaper articles. Records prior to the 1920s are in German.

Publications

Ma36 The Souvenir Program of the Seventy-Fifth Anniversary, The Springfield Turn Verein, Springfield, Mass., April 25, 16, and 27, 1930. Holyoke: Wisly Lithograph & Printing Co., Inc., 1930. 55 p.
Note: Cover title: "75 *Jähriges Jubiläum des Springfield Turnvereins, 25-26-27ten* April, 1930." Includes history of the society by August Prizlaf (in German and English), poems, membership list, and photographs.
Location: InIU; MSHi; Springfield Turnverein, Inc.

Ma37 100th Anniversary, Souvenir Program, 1855-1955, Springfield Turnverein, Springfield, Mass., April 1955. [Springfield]: n.p., [1955]. [96 p.]
Note: Includes history of the organization and photographs.
Location: InIU.

Ma38 Springfield Turnverein Inc., Dedication: Our New Home, 176 Garden Street,Feeding Hills, Mass., Saturday, September 19, 1970. [Springfield]: n.p., [1970]. [52 p.]
Location: InIU; Springfield Turnverein, Inc.

Ma39 Gilmore's Court Square Theater, Springfield Turn Verein, Monday 13, 1899. n.p., 1899.
Note: Includes class schedules.
Location: MSHi.

Ma40 Annual Concert and Ball given by the Singing Section of the Springfield Turnverein, Monday Evening, February 8, 1904 at Turner Hall, State Street. n.p., [1904].
Location: MSHi.

Ma41 Constitution and By-Laws of the Springfield Turnverein, Inc., 91 Plainfield Street, Springfield 4, Massachusetts, Amended as of September 29, 1947. [Springfield]: n.p., 1947. [24 p.]
Location: InIU.

Ma42 Constitution and By-Laws of the Springfield Turnverein, Inc., 176 Garden Street, Feeding Hills, Massachusetts 01030, Revised as of April 1974. [Springfield]: n.p., 1974. 18 p.
Location: InIU.

Ma43 The Springfield Turner. Springfield: Springfield Turnverein, 1938-1941?
Note: Monthly publication of the Springfield Turnverein. Includes national and local Turner news, announcements, and articles on physical education.
Location: InIU: v.3, no.3 (March 1941).

Ma44 Turner News. Springfield: Springfield Turnverein.
Note: Monthly newsletter of the Springfield Turnverein. Includes society news and national Turner concerns.
Location: InIU: June 1974.

Westfield: Westfield Turnverein

Organized in 1897; left American Turnerbund with eighteen members in 1906-1907; possibly closed shortly thereafter.

Publication

Ma45   Statuten des Westfield Turnverein zu Westfield, Mass. Holyoke: Aug.
Lehmann, 1898.
Location: MWEA.

Worcester: Worcester Socialer Turnverein

Organized as Worcester *Socialer* Turnverein in 1859; built hall on Southbridge Street
along the shore of Lake Quinsigamond in 1890s; dropped out of the American
Turnerbund in 1900 with 150 members; offered gymnastic classes until 1905 when
apparatus was given to Clark University in Worcester; sold club house in 1921 and
society probably disbanded shortly thereafter.

Publication

Ma46   Turner Picnic auf der Killdeer-Insel bei Webster, Der SocialeTurnverein in
Worcester hält Montag, den 28ten Mai, ein Picnic auf der in dem schönen See
Chaubunagagemoug liegenden Killdeer- Insel. n.p., 1900. 1 broadside.
Location: MWHM.

MICHIGAN

Detroit: American Turners Detroit

Organized as Detroit *Socialer* Turnverein in 1852; erected small building on Russell
Street in 1858; built new hall on Sherman Street, 1862; lost hall in fire in 1864 but
erected new one a year later; sponsored lectures by Freethinkers, such as Friedrich
Schünemann-Pott, Fritz Schütz, and Robert Reitzel; erected three-story building on
East Jefferson Street in 1929; housed national office of the American Turners from
1937 to 1952 during the time Congressman Carl Wiedeman was president of the
American Turners; hosted the national convention in 1938; changed name to the
American Turners Detroit in 1943-1944; society flourished with eighteen hundred
members after World War II, but membership dropped thereafter because of
increasing dues; sold hall in 1962 due to financial troubles; purchased new property
on East Outer Drive, but sold it in 1983; still active as a social society.

Archival Collection

Mi1   American Turners Detroit Collection.
Location: MiU
Description: Collection of printed materials and photographs of the Detroit Turners. See also Carl Wiedeman Papers (**N2**) which include scrapbooks of the Detroit Turners and the American Turner Association, 1933-1939 and 1948.

Publications

Mi2   Goldenes Jubiläum des Detroiter Socialen Turnvereins, 14 & 15 Juni 1903. [Detroit]: Herold Print, [1903]. 55 p.
Note: Includes history and pictures of the society.
Location: InIU.

Mi3   Detroiter Socialer Turnverein, Seventy-Fifth Anniversary, 1853-1928, Detroit, Michigan. [Detroit]: n.p., [1928]. 28 p.
Note: Includes history of the society written in English and German, program of events, and photographs.
Location: InIU.

Mi4   A.T.D. Magazine: 100th Anniversary Festival, 1853-1953, June 26-28, 1953, Detroit, Michigan. [Detroit]: n.p. [1953]. 44 p.
Note: Includes histories of the Detroit Turners and American Turnerism, brief histories of the Buffalo Turners and Milwaukee Turners, and photographs.
Location: InIU.

Mi5   What has the Detroiter Socialer Turnverein to offer you? [Detroit]: n.p., [1930s]. 25 p.
Note: Booklet to advertise the activities and facilities of the *Detroiter Socialer Turnverein*.
Location: InIU.

Mi6   Open House Program, Detroiter Socialer Turnverein, Jefferson at Crance, December 2nd to 8th, 1935. [Detroit]: n.p., [1935]. [20 p.]
Note: Includes a description of the facilities, classes and clubs, a brief history of the society, and photographs.
Location: InIU.

Mi7   Your Health Insurance Policy, Detroit Socialer Turnverein. [Detroit]: n.p., [ca. 1930]. 8 p.

Note: Includes brief history of the society, class schedules, description of activities, and list of Turner societies associated with the American Turners.
Location: InIU.

Mi8   Turnverein Post No. 291, An American Legion Post made up of veterans who are members of the Detroiter Socialer Turnverein. [Detroit]: n.p., 1938. 4 p.
Note: Membership list.
Location: InIU.

Mi9   Turnverein Post No. 291, American Turners Detroit: Membership Roster, 1956. Detroit: Printing Service, Inc., 1956. 32 p.
Note: Membership roster of an American Legion post made up of veterans who were members of the American Turners Detroit.
Location: MiU (Weideman papers).

Mi10   Detroiter Sozialer Turnverein, Constitution and By-Laws, Revised and Accepted October 4, 1922. [Detroit]: William Cornehl & Son, [1922]. 23 p.
Note: In English and German.
Location: InIU.

Mi11   Constitution and By-Laws, Detroiter Socialer Turnverein, Detroit, Michigan. Detroit: n.p., 1931. 16 p.
Location: InIU.

Mi12   Constitution, By-Laws and House Rules, D.S.T.V. (Detroit Turners). [Detroit]: n.p., [1930s]. 39 p.
Location: InIU.

Mi13   Constitution and By-laws and House Rules, American Turners-Detroit, Detroit, Mich. [Detroit]: n.p., [1930s]. 39 p.
Location: InIU.

Mi14   The Detroit Turner. Official Publication of the Detroit Socialer Turnverein. Detroit: Detroit *Socialer* Turnverein, 1923-1946.
Note: Monthly newsletter of the Detroit Turnverein. Includes national and local Turner news, announcements, and articles on health and physical education.
Location: InIU: 1929-1936, 1938-1944 (scattered issues).

Mi15   A.T.D. Mind and Body Culture Magazine. Official Organ, American Turners Detroit. Detroit: American Turners Detroit, 1946-1953

Note: Continuation of The Detroit Turner.
Location: InIU: 1946-1953 (scattered issues).

Mi16   Detroit Turner Time. Detroit: American Turners Detroit, 1953-1959?
Note: Continuation of A.T.D. Mind and Body Culture Magazine.
Location:
    InIU: 1953-1959 (scattered issues).
    MiU (Weideman Papers): v.VIII, no.8, 1953.

Saginaw: Germania Turnverein

Founded as Saginaw Turnverein in 1856; built gymnasium in 1857 and added meeting rooms in 1859; organized German school in 1859 and operated it until 1873 when German was introduced in the public schools; merged with *Liederkranz* to form *Germania Verein* in 1862; returning Civil War soldiers split from the organization to form the East Saginaw Turnverein in 1862; founded Kindergarten in 1875; built new two-story hall in 1877 which became the focal point for German activities in the city; actively opposed law to banish foreign-language teaching from public schools, 1891; merged with East Saginaw Turnverein in 1898; merged with *Teutonia* Turnverein and changed name to Lincoln Club in 1918; was listed as Lincoln *Turnsektion* until society withdrew from American Turnerbund in 1920-1921; *Germania Verein* possibly continued as singing and social society.

Publication

Mi17   Fünfzig Jahre deutschen Strebens, Gedenkblätter zum fünfzigjährigen Jubiläums der Germania von Saginaw, Michigan, 1856-1906. Saginaw: Seemann & Peters, 1906. 88 p.
Note: Festival book for the society's fiftieth anniversary celebration. Includes a detailed history of the organization.
Location: OCU.

MINNESOTA

Minneapolis: St. Anthony Turnverein

Organized in 1857; built first hall on California Street; reduced activities during the Civil War while most members served in the Union Army; had several confrontations with the "Pine Tree Boys," a group of Irish immigrants, during the 1870s; built new hall on Marshall and 6th Streets in 1870; rebuilt hall in 1874 following fire; conducted German-English school from 1886 to 1889; formed ladies auxiliary in 1888; renovated hall in 1913; lost more than half of membership during World War I, dropping from 265 in 1915 to 125 in 1920; sold property in 1930 after most members had left the city for the northern and western suburbs; continued as social society and still officially in operation with a small number of members.

Archival Collection

Mn1   St. Anthony Turnverein Records, 1868-1928, 1942. 6.5 linear feet.
Finding aid available from repository.
Location: MnHi.
Description: The records include society minutes (*Protokoll Bücher*), 1868-1926; minutes of the building committee, 1874-1876; minutes of the education committee (*Versammlung des Schul Vorstandes*), 1877-1879; letterbook and scrapbook of correspondence, 1875-1909, 1911-1916; financial ledgers, 1869-1930 (incomplete); membership and dues records, 1882-1915 (incomplete); address book of members of the St. Anthony Turnverein, ca. 1885; receipt book of the Sick Benefit Fund (*Krankenkasse*), 1868-1915; janitor's record, 1898-1900; financial ledger of the St. Anthony ladies auxiliary, 1888-1903; youth membership ledger (*Zöglings Verein*), 1884-1887; building fund receipt booklets, 1874-1875, 1913-1914; and class registers, 1911-1913, 1934-1935.

The Minnesota Historical Society finding aid indicates that three volumes of St. Anthony Turnverein records from 1910-1940 are also at the Hennepin County Historical Society, Minneapolis.

Mn2   St. Anthony Turner Records, 1938-1979. 1 volume.
Location: Private collection.
Description: The records consist of a minute book, 1938-1978.

Publications

Mn3   St. Anthony Turnverein, 1857-1907, Souvenir zum Goldenen Jubiläum verfasst von August Müller, 27. Januar 1907. Minneapolis: Freie Presse-Herold, 1907. 14 p.
Note: The 50th anniversary publication of the St. Anthony Turners includes a brief history of the society and program of events.
Location: Private collection.

Mn4   Lieder Gesungen beim Kommers des Goldenen Jubiläum des St. Anthony Turnvereins am Samstag Abend, den 26. Januar 1907. [Minneapolis]: n.p., [1907]. 6 p.
Note: German songs from the fiftieth anniversary celebration.
Location: Private collection.

Mn5   Kirmes zum Besten der Notleidenden der alten Heimat, 23.-28. Oktober1916, St. Anthony Turnhalle, Minneapolis, Minnesota: War Relief Bazaar for theBenefit of the Widows and Orphans of the Central Powers, October 23-28, 1916, Minneapolis, Minnesota. [Minneapolis]: n.p., [1916]. [64 p.]
Note: Program for event to raise funds for war relief in Germany and Austria during World War I. The program includes a list of participating societies and songs and poems. In German and English.
Location: InIU.

Mn6   Diamond Jubilee Anniversary, 1857-1932, St. Anthony Turn Verein, Minneapolis, Minn., February 7th, 1932. [Minneapolis]: n.p., [1932]. 24 p.
Note: Includes a history of the society, a brief sketch of the ladies auxiliary (*Damenverein*), an essay on Turnerism, and photographs of members.
Location: InIU; MnHi.

Mn7   Verfassung des Turn Vereins in St. Anthony, Minnesota: Revidiert und in Kraft getreten am 24. Januar, 1857. St. Paul: *Gedruckt in der Office der Minnesota Zeitung,* 1857. 16 p.
Location: MnHi.

Mn8   Verfassung des St. Anthony Turn Zöglings Verein. Minneapolis: *Druck der Minneapolis Freien Presse*, 1885. 12 p.
Location: MnHi.

Mn9   Constitution und Nebengesetze des St. Anthony Turn-Vereins, Sowie Constitution des Unterstützungsfonds der Krankenkasse: Revidiert und in Kraft getreten am 11. Mai 1885. *Ost-Minneapolis: Druck der Minneapolis Freien Presse*, 1885. 16 p.
Note: Constitution of the St. Anthony Turn Verein and the Sick Benefit Society.
Location: MnHi.

Mn10   Constitution und Nebengesetze des St. Anthony Turnvereins: sowie Constitution der Krankenkasse: revidiert und in Kraft getreten am 1. Januar 1915. Minneapolis: n.p., [1915]. 36 p.
Note: Constitution of the St. Anthony Turn Verein and the Sick Benefit Society, in

German with English translation.
Location: MnHi.

Minneapolis: West-Minneapolis Turnverein

Organized in 1866; had over 150 members in 1880s and 1890s; closed in 1900.

Archival Collection

Mn11 West-Minneapolis Turnverein Records in Samuel Hill papers.
Location: MnHi.
Description: The Samuel Hill Papers contain a small number of documents relating to the West-Minneapolis Turnverein from the period 1895-1902.

New Ulm: Ansiedlungsverein des Socialistischen Turnerbundes

At the national convention in 1855, William Pfänder, member of the Cincinnati Turngemeinde, proposed the establishment of a Turner colony. The purpose of the colony was to provide a place where the liberal principles advocated by the *Socialistische* Turnerbund could be put into practice while protecting German workers from interference from nativist groups. Pfänder's ideas found support, with the result that the *Ansiedlungsverein des Sozialistischen Turnerbundes* (Settlement Society of the Socialistic Turnerbund) was formed in 1856. Although the eastern societies declined their support, the Cincinnati Turnverein backed the project financially. Pfänder was elected to draft the charter and look for a suitable location. He found an area along the Minnesota River which had previously been settled by members of the Chicago *Land Verein*, founded in 1853. In 1857 the *Ansiedlungsverein* bought out the Chicago *Land Verein* and reincorporated as the German Land Association. As with many other utopian communities, the Turners' socialist experiment failed because of financial difficulties and disagreements among settlers. The communal mills and shops were soon taken over by private businessmen. Much of the town was destroyed during the Sioux Indian uprising in 1862, but it was soon rebuilt. Although New Ulm did not become an exclusively Turner town the ideology still affected its administration. Most civic figures were prominent Turners, among them William Pfänder who was elected first "president" of New Ulm and later served as a state legislator. German and physical education was a part of the school curriculum from the very beginning, and books for a public library were donated by Friedrich Kapp, one of the leading Forty-Eighters and a liberal from New York. New Ulm still has retained its German character.

Archival Collection

Mn12   New Ulm Ansiedlungsverein Collection, 1855-1880. 2 boxes.
Finding aid available from repository.
Location: MnBCHi.
Description: The collection contains minutes of the society, 1855-1859; settlement records, 1855-1858; early settler registration records, 1868-1880; financial records (*Rechnungsbuch*) of the Chicago Land Society, 1855-1856; record book of the Cincinnati Colonization Society, 1854; and account books. The collection also includes records of the New Ulm Turnverein, including the incorporation papers, 1869; library records (*Protokoll Buch des Bibliothekars*), 1869; diary (*Tage Buch*) of the New Ulm Turners, 1861-1867; and three ledgers, 1857-1860.

Publications

Mn13   *Ansiedlungsverein des Socialistischen Turnerbundes*. Verhandlungen des Convention des Ansiedlungs-Vereins des Sozialistischen Turnerbundes von Nord Amerika in der Turnhalle von Cincinnati am 24. und 25. August, 1856. Cincinnati: The Verein, 1856. 7 leaves.
Note: Convention minutes include a statement by Wilhelm Pfänder, a constitution, and settlement plan (*Ansiedlungsplan*).
Location: MnHi.

Mn14   *Ansiedlungsverein des Socialistischen Turnerbundes von Nord Amerika*. An die Mitglieder des Ansiedlungs-Vereins des Sozialistischen Turnerbundes von Nord-Amerika. New Ulm, MN: New Ulm Pioneer, 1858. 1 broadside.
Note: Broadside signed by William Pfänder and August Wagner, December 1, 1858.
Location: MnHi.

Mn15   An die Verwaltung des Ansiedlungs-Vereins des Sozialistischen Turner-Bundes von Nord-Amerika und an das Direktorium der Globe Mills Co. in New Ulm: Verhandlungen und Beschlüsse, St. Louis, MO, wohnenden Aktionäre des obrigen Ansiedlungs-Verein und der Globe Mills Co. in der am 2ten, Januar 1859 in der St. Louis Turnerhalle gehaltenen Versammlung. St. Louis: n.p., 1859. 1 broadside.
Note: Broadside signed by C.A. Stifel, St. Louis, MO.
Location: MnHi.

Mn16   Stifel, C. A. Ansiedlungs-Verein des sozialistischen Turnerbundes: Am die Aktionäre des Ansiedlungsverein des sozialistischen Turnerbundes, Vierteljärlicher Bericht. New Ulm, MN: n.p., 1859.

Note: Quarterly report to stockholders of the settlement society.
Location: MnHi.

New Ulm: New Ulm Turnverein

Organized in 1856 by members of the *Ansiedlungsverein des Socialistischen Turnerbundes*; built first hall in 1857 which became the social and political center in town; hall was burnt to the ground during Indian attack in 1862 in which Turners who had not joined the Union Army played a vital part in the defense of the town; built new hall in 1866 which was used as school, town hall, and court; maintained close connection with the Freethinkers' Association of Minnesota throughout the nineteenth century; formed ladies auxiliary in 1889; tore down old Turner hall and built new one in its place in 1900-1901; hosted the principal Turner publications, Americanische Turnzeitung (renamed American Turner in 1936) and Mind and Body, 1919-1943; had hall placed on National Register of Historic Buildings in 1978; still active as social and sports organization.

Archival Collections

Mn17   New Ulm Turner Collection. 1858-1993.
Finding aid available from repository.
Location: MnBCHi.
Description: The collection includes newspaper clippings, 1858-1993; 177 photographs, 1876-1956; a history of the New Ulm Turnverein, 1856-1906; and speeches, invitations, programs and other printed items.

Mn18   New Ulm Turnverein Collection, 1875-present.
Preliminary inventory available from Indiana Univ.-Purdue Univ. Indianapolis.
Location: New Ulm Turnverein.
Description: The records include the society's minutes, 1875-1910, 1916- present; financial records: 1879-1955; membership books, 1901-1904; bar books, 1904-1917; records of the building committee, 1900-1901; records of the shooting-competition (*Schützenfest*), 1911; and National Register of Historic Places file, 1980. Records of the ladies auxiliary include minutes, 1889-1916, 1927-1983; financial records, 1890-1979; and membership and dues records, 1896-1897, 1906-1911, 1960-1964. Records of the Minnesota Turn *Bezirk* include financial records, 1889-1934 and convention minutes, 1928-1942. Also included are records of other New Ulm organizations: 1) Shooting section of the New Ulm Hunting Club (*Schützenklub des New Ulmer Jägervereins*), shooting records (*Scheibenregister*), 1909-1911; 2) Records of the Marlitt Lodge, including minutes (*Protokoll der Marlitt Lodge* in

Mankato), 1892-1935 (incomplete); membership records, 1892-1900; and financial records, 1918-1934; 3) Reuter Lodge No. 38, O.D.H.S. (Herman Sisters), New Ulm, membership and dues records, 1901-1930; and 4) Silver Cornet Band membership records and constitution, 1880-1885.

Publications

Mn19   Turnverein New Ulm, 1856-1906, Ein Gedenkblatt zum Goldenen Jubiläum, 11. November 1906. New Ulm: New Ulm Publishing Company, 1906. 34 p.
Note: Includes history of the New Ulm Turnverein written by Eduard Petry and historical photographs. The text was translated by Auguste Kent in 1979. Translations are available at InIU and the Brown County Historical Society, New Ulm.
Location: InIU; MnBCHi; MnHi; WMCHi.

Mn20   New Ulm Turnverein, Diamond Jubilee Anniversary, Nov. 11th, 1931. [New Ulm]: n.p., 1931. [16 p.]
Note: Includes a brief history of the society and membership list.
Location: InIU; MnHi.

Mn21   100th Anniversary: 1856-1956, New Ulm Turnverein, Nov. 10, 1956. [New Ulm]: n.p., [1956]. 37 p.
Note: Includes a translation of the history from the fiftieth anniversary program and an overview of the subsequent fifty years, and membership lists of the New Ulm Turnverein and ladies auxiliary.
Location: InIU; MnBCHi.

Mn22   100th Anniversary, 1889-1989, New Ulm Turner Frauenverein, Turner Ladies Society. New Ulm: n.p., [1989]. [28 p.]
Note: Includes history of the ladies auxiliary and membership list.
Location: InIU; MnBCHi.

Mn23   Verfassung, Nebengesetze, Stehende Beschlüsse. New Ulm: New Ulm Post, 1899. 29 p.
Location: InIU.

St. Paul: St. Paul Turners, Inc.

Organized in 1858 as the St. Paul Turnverein; maintained library, conducted German and drawing classes and held Sunday school programs in 1870s and 1880s; merged with the *Deutsche Gesellschaft* in 1886 to form the *Germania* Turnverein; *Germania*

Turnverein disbanded in 1895 but reorganized as Turnverein St. Paul in 1896; purchased hall on Wabash Street in 1906; formed ladies auxiliary in 1906; merged with *West Seite* Turnverein in 1913; changed name to St. Paul Turners, Inc. in 1940; lost hall to fire in 1943; moved to Ohio Street; built new facility on Lexington Avenue in Mendota Heights in 1990s; still active as gymnastics club.

Archival Collection

Mn24   St. Paul Turners Records, 1896-present.
Preliminary inventory available from Indiana Univ.-Purdue Univ. Indianapolis.
Location: St. Paul Turners.
Description: The records include minutes of meetings, 1896-1907, 1920-1924, 1955-1972; minutes of the building committees (*Protokoll des Bau Komitees des Turnvereins St. Paul*); newspaper clippings; minutes of the Twin City Turners Picnic, 1898-1903; minutes of the Special Picnic Committee, 1906-1919; minutes of the entertainment committee (*Vergnügungskomitee*), 1915-1919; minutes of the active Turner class, 1919-1931; dues and membership records, 1895-1907, 1931-1954; financial records, 1912-1931; class lists for the children's and women's classes, 1897-1920 (incomplete); minutes of ladies auxiliary meetings, 1940-1963; records of the physical education program, 1933-1971; scrapbooks on Turnerism and the St. Paul Turners, 1900-1955; photographs, 1890s - present; file on history of the society by Herman Uebel; district files, 1956; and files with correspondence of Mr. Uebel, 1947-1957. Also included are records of the *West Seite* Turnverein, consisting of financial records, 1896-1902; constitution of the Junior Society of the West Side Turn Verein, 1901-1903; catalog of the music library of the singing society (*Register der Lieder Bibliothek des Gesangvereins Liedertafel des West Side Turnvereins, St. Paul*); and constitution of the singing society. Records before the 1920s are in German

Mn25   St. Paul Turners Collection, 1858-1942. 3.25 linear feet (7 boxes, including 19 volumes).
Finding aid available from repository.
Location: MnHi.
Description: The collection includes minutes 1866-1883; financial records, 1807-1906; membership records, 1879-1883; correspondence and miscellaneous papers, 1896-1956; newspaper clippings, 1906-1952; printed materials, 1912-1942; constitutions and by-laws, 1888-1951; essays on the history of the Turners; and records of the women's auxiliary society, 1906-1935. Also included are records of related organizations: 1) *Deutsch-Amerikanischer Central-Bund* and other German-American organizations' form letters and minutes, 1905-1934; 2) Minnesota Turner District form letters, announcements, and annual meeting minutes, 1902-1942; 3) St.

Paul *Lese Verein* book list, 1857; 4) *Deutscher Verein* minutes, 1871-1875; 5) Turnverein *Germania* membership ledger, 1888-1894. Records prior to 1920s are in German.

Publications

Mn26   Blühender Unsinn: Universal-Mittel gegen alle Gebrechen der Seele, moralischen Katzenjammer, Weltschmerz, Liebeskummer, u.s.w. gebraut in der Hexenküche des Kleinen Raths; herausgegeben unter des Auspicien und im Selbstverlag des St. Paul Turnvereins für den Carneval, 1886. St. Paul: Volkszeitung, 1886. 40 p.
Note: Carnival program.
Location: MnHi.

Mn27   St. Paul Turnverein. Turners Annual Gymnastic Exhibition under the auspices of Turnverein St. Paul, Friday, May 5, 1939, Wilson High School. St. Paul: The Turnverein, 1939. [4 p.]
Location: ICN; MnHi.

Mn28   Turners Annual Gymnastic Exhibition under the Auspices of the Turnverein St. Paul, Auditorium, Friday, April 20, 1928. St. Paul: North Central Publishing Co., [1928]. 16 p.
Note: Program to the annual gymnastics exhibition.
Location: InIU.

Mn29   Turner's Annual Gymnastic Exhibition sponsored by the Turn-Verein St. Paul at the Auditorium, April 5, 1929. St. Paul: North Central Publishing Co., [1929]. 12 p.
Note: Program to the annual gymnastics exhibition.
Location: InIU.

Mn30   Turner's Annual Gymnastic Exhibition under the Auspices of the Turnverein Saint Paul, Friday, April 20, 1930. St. Paul: North Central Publishing Co., [1930]. 15 p.
Note: Program to the annual gymnastics exhibition.
Location: InIU.

Mn31   Constitution und Nebengesetze des St. Paul Turnvereins: Revidiert und Verbessert in der halbjährlichen Generalversammlung vom 12. April 1871. St. Paul: T. Sander, 1871. 16 p.
Location: MnHi.

Mn32   Verfassung und Nebengesetze des Turnverein "St. Paul" von St. Paul, Minnesota. St. Paul: *Volkszeitung* Co., 1908. 19 p.
Location: MnHi.

Mn33   Turner News. [St. Paul]: St. Paul Turnverein, 1926-1927?
Note: Monthly newsletter of the St. Paul Turnverein. Includes local and national Turner news, announcements, and schedules.
Location: MnHi: v.1, no.1 (June 1926) - v.1, no.12 (May 1927). Incomplete.

Mn34   Turner Monthly Bulletin. St. Paul: St. Paul Turnverein, 1951?-1957?
Note: Monthly publication of the organization.
Location: St. Paul Turners: 1951-1957.

St. Paul: West Side Turnverein

Organized in 1888; owned hall on corner of South Wabash and Colorado Streets; joined by a number of members of the dissolved *Germania* Turnverein in 1895; formed ladies auxiliary in 1896; reached peak membership with 90 members in 1905; merged with the St. Paul Turnverein in 1913.

Archival Collection

Mn35   West Side Turnverein Records, 1890-1913, 1981. 2 linear feet, (4 boxes, including 2 volumes)
Finding aid available from repository.
Location: MnHi.
Description: The collection includes minutes of the general business and executive committee meetings, 1891-1913; minutes of the entertainment committee, 1891-1897; minutes of the ladies auxiliary, 1896-1907; membership applications, 1893-1899; correspondence and related papers, 1893-1901, 1911, 1930; financial records, 1892-1913; equipment inventories, 1891-1912; and twelve manuscripts in German, written by Turner George Ehlers, placed in the society library, 1911-1912.

Publication

Mn36   Platform und Constitution des Westseite Turnvereins von St. Paul, Minnesota. St. Paul: Druck der Volkszeitung, 1892. 20 p.
Location: MnHi.

MISSOURI

Boonville: Boonville Turn und Gesang Verein

Organized about 1852 as the Boonville Turnverein; merged with the Boonville *Gesang Verein* in 1867 and became the Boonville *Turn und Gesang Verein*; permanently withdrew from the American Turnerbund in 1873; suspended activities between 1873 and 1883; purchased Baptist Church on Vine Street in 1895 to serve as Turner hall; disbanded and sold building in 1936.

Archival Collection

Mo1   Boonville *Turn und Gesang Verein Records*, 1852-1929. 11 volumes. Finding aid available from repository.
Location: MoU.
Description: The records include constitution and minutes of the *Gesang Verein*, 1852-1858; minutes of the Boonville Turn Verein, 1858-1862; Turnverein roster, 1852-1868; membership records, 1869-1925; account books, 1869-1925; roster and minutes, 1873-1912; miscellaneous reports and legal papers, 1897-1929.

Brunswick: Brunswick Turn Verein

Incorporated on April 17, 1867, but was probably organized in 1866; functioned as an independent society; closing date unknown.

Archival Collection

Mo2   Brunswick Turn Verein records in Chariton County and City of Brunswick Records, part of the Benecke Family Papers, 1860-1869.
Finding aid available from repository.
Location: MoU.
Description: The Brunswick Turn Verein records include incorporation papers; minute book and membership list (*Protokoll Buch*), 1866-1868; account books; accounts and receipts; correspondence; printed materials from other Turner societies in the state; and book lists, 1857 and 1868.

Kansas City: Kansas City Turners

Organized on February 14th, 1858 as the Kansas City *Sozialer Turnverein*; owned first property on Fifteen and Main Streets; involved in the founding of the Kansas City *Schulverein* (School Society) in 1859, seven years before public schools were started in the city; pooled resources to purchase arms and munitions at beginning of Civil War; suspended activities when nearly all members volunteered to joined the Union Army; built new hall on Tenth and Main Streets with a capacity for seating 1200 people in late 1860s; included among its members many of Kansas City's leaders, including August Würz, publisher of the Wöchentliche Kansas City Post and three-term mayor Henry Kumpf; built new and larger Turner hall in 1884 on Twelfth and Oak Streets; played important part in introducing physical education in city schools in 1885, and Turnverein's instructor, Dr. Carl Betz, became the city's director of physical training in 1886; formed ladies auxiliary in 1896; sold hall and purchased smaller building at 1208-1212 East Ninth Street due to the financial crisis of the 1890s; moved to bigger and more modern building at 1325 East Fifteenth Street in 1906 due to rising membership that reached 800 that year; joined by the *Germania Männerchor* in 1951 which formed the singing section of the organization; purchased land outside the city limits in 1955 that became Turner park; added hall, gymnasium, swimming pool, nine hole golf course, playgrounds and tennis courts over following years; hosted the national convention in 1958; still active.

Archival Collection

Mo3   Kansas City Turnverein Collection. 1867-present.
Inventory available from repository.
Location: MoKU
Description: The records include minutes, 1867-1978 (incomplete); dues and membership lists, 1904-1915, 1961-1970; financial records, 1890-1945, 1968-1972; correspondence, 1890-1903, 1972-1982; register of classes, 1920-1932; handwritten by-laws: 1967, 1971-1974; membership list of the death benefit society (*Sterbekasse*), 1915-1918; and papers relating to the Kansas City Turners housing project for Turner Park, 1962, and the Turner Development Company, 1968. Ladies auxiliary records consist of minutes, 1939-1972 and financial records, 1944-1950. Also included are records of the *Germania Männerchor*, including minutes, 1887-1945 (incomplete); Sunday meeting attendance records, 1915-1919; membership and dues records, 1895-1904; and financial records, 1936-1941. Records prior to the 1920s are predominantly in German.

Mo4   Louis Benecke Papers, 1817-1919.
Location: MoU
Description: The Benecke papers include items on the embezzlement of Kansas City Turnverein funds.

Publications

Mo5   Ein Gedenkblatt, 1858-1908, Zum Goldenen Jubiläum des Kansas City Sozialen Turnvereins, 14. Februar 1908. Kansas City: n.p., 1909. 33 p.
Note: Fiftieth anniversary publication of the Kansas City Turners. Includes a history of the organization and many photographs.
Location: DLC; InIU; MnHi; MoKU.

Mo6   60th Anniversary, Kansas City Socialer Turn Verein, 1858[-]1918, February 17, 1918. [Kansas City]: n.p., [1918]. 12 p.
Note: The sixtieth anniversary publication is also v.1, no.7 of The Active, the Kansas City Turners newsletter. Includes an historical sketch, statement of Turner principles, and members' reminiscences.
Location: InIU; MoKU.

Mo7   Souvenir Program, Diamond Jubilee, 1858[-]1933, Kansas City Socialer Turnverein. [Kansas City]: n.p., [1933]. [24 p.]
Note: Includes a history of the club, and photographs.
Location: InIU; MoKU.

Mo8   Souvenir Program, Celebrating 80 Years of Service to Kansas City, Mileposts, 1858-1938, Kansas City Socialer Turnverein. [Kansas City]: n.p., [1938]. 32 p.
Note: Includes a history of the society, a history of the ladies auxiliary, and photographs.
Location: InIU; MoKU.

For 100th anniversary publication, see 47th National Convention, 1958 (**N24**).

Mo9   Kansas City Turners, 125th Anniversary, Since 1858 Part of Kansas City, February 12 & 13, 1983. Kansas City: John Kilgore Printing and Business Forms, Inc., 1983. [24 p.]
Note: Includes a brief history of the Kansas City Turners, and pictures of former and present members and activities.
Location: InIU; MoKU.

Mo10   Booy, Karel. The History of the Kansas City Turners (Kansas City Socialer Turnverein), Years 1857-1973. [Kansas City]: n.p., [1973]. 16 p.
Location: InIU; MoKU.

Mo11   Kansas City Turners. [Kansas City]: n.p., [ca. 1950]. 6 p.
Note: Promotional brochure describing the facilities and activities of the organization.
Location: InIU; MoKU.

Mo12   Song Book, Kansas City Turners. [Kansas City]: n.p., n.d. [ca.100 p.]
Note: Includes 311 songs in German and English.
Location: InIU.

Mo13   Turner's Indoor Circus, Souvenir Edition. n.p., 1956. 20 p.
Location: MoKU.

Mo14   Constitution and By-Laws of the Kansas City Socialer Turn Verein, Founded, February 14th, 1858, Kansas City, Mo, Adopted June 1929. [Kansas City]: n.p., 1929. 18 p.
Location: InIU.

Mo15   The Active. Kansas City: n.p., 1917-1918?
Note: Newsletter of the Kansas City Turners.
Location:
  InIU: v.1, no.7 (1918)
  MoKU: v.1, no.7 (1918)

Mo16   Turner Park News. Kansas City: n.p., 1955-??
Note: Newsletter of the Kansas City Turners, started to report on the developments of the new property and society news. Mentioned in histories, but no issues located.

Lexington: Lexington Turner Society

Founded in June 1859 as the Lexington Turnverein; organized athletic events and competitions, sponsored dances and picnics and operated a bar during 1860s; organized a Turner brass band and chorus with paid directors in 1860; maintained a library in the 1880s and subscribed to several newspapers, including the New York Criminal and the Berliner Kladderadatsch; lost hall to fire in 1875; withdrew from the American Turnerbund in 1867; active through 1960s.

Archival Collection

Mo17   Lexington Turner Records. 1859-1965. 4 vols., 15 folders.
Finding aid available from repository.
Location: MoU.

Description: The records consist of the society's minute books, 1859-1965 (incomplete), with English translations for minutes from 1858-1906. Records prior to 1906 are in German.

St. Louis

St. Louis was one of the principal centers for Turner activities, with large Turner societies scattered throughout the city's German neighborhoods during the late nineteenth and early twentieth centuries. The St. Louis Turnverein, founded in 1850, was the first society. It played a key role in helping to save Missouri for the Union when a majority of its five hundred members formed the nucleus of the volunteer regiment which captured Camp Jackson at the outset of the Civil War. New societies were formed after the war to serve the increasing number of German immigrants. In 1886 St. Louis's Turner societies began working with city authorities on the establishment of parks and playgrounds. By 1890 the Turners had succeeded in introducing physical education into the public school system. During the World's Fair in 1904 visitors were impressed by an exhibition of drills, apparatus work, and games put on by the Turners. When St. Louis hosted the national convention in 1910 the city had twelve societies with a combined membership of approximately 4700 members. Twenty years later, in 1930, the number had dropped to nine societies with 1186 members; in 1950 the number of Turner societies had dwindled to three societies with approximately 400 members. The societies of St. Louis have hosted the national conventions in 1910, 1923, 1972, 1980, and National Turnfests in 1897, 1948, and 1975. Today, only the North St. Louis Turners (founded 1870), the Concordia Gymnastic Society (founded 1874), and the Schiller Turners (founded 1906) remain.

St. Louis: Carondelet Germania Turnverein

Founded in 1875 under the name Carondelet Turnverein; closed in 1887 and reopened in 1890 under the name Carondelet *Germania* Turnverein; changed name to Carondelet *Germania* Gymnastic Society in 1916; sponsored a ladies auxiliary, a drum and bugle corps, and a *Turnschule*; owned property on Michigan Avenue; had membership in 1916 of about 180 members; closed in 1921.

Publication

Mo18 [Summer Night Festival by Carondelet Germania Turnverein, Michigan & Roberts, Saturday, June 3, 1916.] [St. Louis]: n.p., [1916]. [34 p.]
Note: Cover missing; title supplied by handwritten note on first page. Includes

program of events, photographs of the classes, and membership lists.
Location: InIU.

St. Louis: Concordia Gymnastic Society

Founded in December 1874 or January 1875 as the St. Louis Concordia Turnverein by members of the Central Turnverein who wanted a society closer to their home on the south side of the city; built first hall in 1877 at 13th and Arsenal Streets; completed addition to Turner hall in 1884; enlarged and renovated gymnasium after a fire in 1908; sponsored a library (1877), a fife and drum corps (1879), a seniors and *Baers* section (1889), a choir, a dramatic section (1924), a rowing club, a ladies auxiliary (1921), the Concordia band (1922), and the Aeroplane Club; has been the largest Turner society in the St. Louis area since the 1930s; still active.

Archival Collection

Mo19   Concordia Gymnastic Society Records, St. Louis, 1876-1985. 43 boxes. Finding aid available from repository.
Location: MoSHi.
Description: Records include minutes of general and board meetings, 1900-1975; entertainment committee financial reports, 1920-1922; treasurers' report, 1922-1926; financial records, 1876-1979; monthly and annual reports to the board of directors, 1925-1972; correspondence, 1935-1971; library records, 1880s-1905; membership records 1917-1968; class records, 1923-1974; sheet music and Turner song books; and essays and notes on the history of the Concordia Gymnastic Society and Turners. Also included are records of the Concordia Turner Hall Association relating to the building at Arsenal and 13th.

Publications

Mo20   Golden Jubilee, Concordia Turn Verein, Saint Louis, Missouri, January 1925.[St. Louis]: n.p., [1925]. 83 p.
Note: Includes history of the society, its classes and sections. In German and English.
Location: InIU; MoSHi; MoU (Louis Kittlaus Collection).

Mo21   Historical Pageant, Golden Jubilee, Concordia Turner Verein. [St. Louis]: Trio Printing Co., [1925]. 24 p.
Note: Program for pageant celebrating the Concordia Turners' fiftieth anniversary. Includes list of participants and descriptions of scenes. In German and English.
Location: InIU.

Mo22 65th Anniversary of the Concordia Turners of St. Louis, Souvenir Program, 1875-1940, St. Louis, Mo. [St. Louis]: n.p.,[1940]. 10 p.
Note: Includes history of the society and photographs.
Location: InIU; MoSHi.

Mo23 Diamond Jubilee Program, 75th Anniversary, January 14, 1950. [St. Louis]: n.p., [1950].
Location: MoSHi.

Mo24 75th Jubilee Grand Costume Ball Program, February 14, 1950. [St. Louis], n.p., [1950].
Location: MoSHi.

Mo25 100th Anniversary Souvenir Program, 1975, and Invitations to Honorary Members Dinner that Preceded the Anniversary Party (Stiftungsfest), January 10, 1959, January 6, 1967, January 11, 1969, and January 6, 1971. [St. Louis]: n.p., [1975]. 10 p.
Note: Includes brief history of the society and list of past presidents.
Location: MoSHi.

Mo26 Annual Report, 1967, to General Membership, Concordia Gymnastic, 6432 Gravois, St. Louis, Missouri 63116, April 11th, 1968. [St. Louis]: n.p., [1968]. 48 p.
Note: Includes annual reports by all classes and sections of the organization.
Location: InIU.

Mo27 Annual Report, 1969, to General Membership. Concordia Gymnastic. n.p., 1969. 20 p.
Location: InIU.

Mo28 By-Laws of Concordia Gymnastic Society (Concordia Turners). [St. Louis]: n.p., n.d. 12 p.
Location: InIU.

Mo29 Constitution and By-Laws (Revision of 1928), Concordia Gymnastic Society in St. Louis. [St. Louis]: Trio Printing Co., [1928]. 38 p.
Location: InIU; MoSHi.

Mo30 Constitution and By-Laws of the Concordia Turners (Concordia Gymnastic Society), Incorporated 1875, Revision of 1952. [St. Louis]: n.p., [1952]. 16 p.
Location: InIU; MoSHi.

Mo31   Constitution and By-Laws, Concordia Turners (Concordia Gymnastic Society). [St. Louis]: n.p., n.d. 16 p.
Location: InIU.

Mo32   Endowment Fund of Concordia Gymnastic Society (Incorporated 1875) and Founded for the Perpetuation of Concordia's School of Physical Education. [St. Louis]: n.p., n.d. 11 p.
Note: Constitution of the endowment fund.
Location: InIU.

Mo33   Der Concordianer. St. Louis: Concordia Turnverein, 1880-1881.
Note: This publication was the Concordia Turnverein's first newsletter. According to the history written for the fiftieth anniversary of the society, the newsletter did not appear regularly and was discontinued within one year. No issues could be located.

Mo34   Monatsblatt des Turnverein Concordia. St. Louis: Concordia Turnverein, 1897-1914.
Note: The Monatsblatt was the society's monthly newsletter and contained announcements of events and society news. The paper was succeeded by the Concordia Turner in 1914. No issues of the Monatsblatt were located.

Mo35   Concordia Turner. St. Louis: Concordia Gymnastic Society, 1914-1950?
Note: Monthly publication, successor to the Monatsblatt des Turnverein Concordia. Between 1949 and 1951, the Concordia Turner was renamed The Concordian.
Location:
      MoU: June 1944, Nov. 1945.
      MoSHi: 1923-1950 [incomplete].

Mo36   The Concordian. St. Louis: Concordia Gymnastic Society, 1950-present.
Note: Monthly publication, successor to the Concordia Turner. Includes local and national Turner news, announcements, and reports. In the early 1980s, the paper reduced its size and was issued in mimeograph form.
Location:
      InIU: 1950-1980 [incomplete]
      MoSHi: 1950-1985 [incomplete].

St. Louis: North St. Louis Gymnastic Society

Organized in 1868 as the North St. Louis *Turnschule and Kindergarten*; reorganized October 15, 1870 and incorporated in 1874 under the name North St. Louis

Turnverein; started singing section, 1876; built hall at Twentieth and Salisbury Streets in 1879 which became the center for cultural life on the north side; purchased property on North Twentieth Street for use as an open-air playground; sold playground in 1898 and purchased lot east of hall for a playground; reduced activities during World War I and changed the language used in meetings from German to English; ladies auxiliary organized in 1915; merged with the Olympic Turnverein in 1922; renovated hall in 1929 and 1945; still active as predominantly social organization.

Publications

Mo37   Golden Jubilee of the North St. Louis Gymnastic Society, October 15 and 16, 1870-1920. [St. Louis]: n.p., [1920]. 47 p.
Note: Includes history of the North St. Louis Gymnastic Society written by Albert Haesseler, photographs, and membership list.
Location: InIU; MoU (Louis Kittlaus Collection).

Mo38   North St. Louis Turners, 75th Anniversary Program. St. Louis: n.p., 1945. 43 p.
Note: Includes a history of the club, membership list and photographs of classes and facilities.
Location: InIU.

Mo39   In the Supreme Court of Missouri, October Term 1884, No. 1912, North St. Louis Gymnastic Society vs. Nathaniel C. Hudson, Collector, Appeal from St. Louis Court of Appeals, Statement and Brief for Respondent. St. Louis: Central Law Journal, 1884. 11 p.
Location: MoSHi (Concordia Gymnastic Society Collection).

Mo40   Constitution and By-Laws of the North St. Louis Turners, Twentieth and Salisbury Sts, St. Louis, Mo., Organized 1870. St. Louis: Johns & Johns, 1943. 14 p.
Location: InIU.

Mo41   Turner Life of the North St. Louis Turners. St. Louis: North St. Louis Turners, 1934-1950s?
Note: Monthly newsletter of the club, first published under the name North St. Louis Turner. Includes national and local Turner news, announcements, and class schedules.
Location: InIU: v.12, no.10 (October 1945).

St. Louis: Schiller Turners, Inc.

Organized in 1906; purchased property on Weiss Avenue in 1908 and erected small building which was shared with the *Liedertafel*; formed ladies auxiliary in 1908; built new hall due to increasing membership, with loan financed by the Anheuser-Busch brewery in 1909; purchased adjoining land for a picnic area in 1911; remodeled property in 1934 and 1970s; merged with Lindenwood Turners in 1940 and relieved indebtedness by selling Lindenwood property in 1945; formed choral group in 1954; supported large physical education program, primarily for children during the 1970s and 1980s; sponsored cultural activities such as sewing classes, theater groups, choral groups, amateur photography, and painting; still active and serves as community center for the neighborhood.

Archival Collection

Mo42   Schiller Turners Inc. Records, 1914-present.
Preliminary inventory available from Indiana Univ.-Purdue Univ. Indianapolis.
Location: Schiller Turners, St. Louis.
Description: The records include one box of pictures; minutes from the 1980s; ladies auxiliary minutes, 1914-1983; treasurers' book, 1916-1965; membership ledger, 1940s; and youth club financial records, 1976-1986.

Publications

Mo43   Golden Jubilee, 1906[-]1956, Schiller Turners, June 1956, Souvenir Program. [St. Louis]: n.p., [1956]. [48 p.]
Note: Includes history of the society and its sections, an article on physical education and photographs.
Location: InIU; Schiller Turners.

Mo44   Schiller Turners, Diamond Jubilee Anniversary, June 28, 1981, 1906-1981. [St. Louis]: n.p., 1981. [42 p.]
Note: Includes a history of the organization, photographs, and reports on activities and members.
Location: InIU; Schiller Turners.

St. Louis: St. Louis Turnverein

Founded in 1850 as the first Turner society in St. Louis; dedicated first hall on Tenth Street between Market and Walnut Street in 1855; hosted Turnfest in 1860; attained membership of more than five hundred at the outbreak of the Civil War; disbanded and formed military organization for the protection of the Union in 1861; formed four Turner companies under the leadership of prominent Turner members, including Franz Sigel, Nickolaus Schüttner and Charles Stiefel; Turner regiments were involved in the seizure of Camp Jackson which helped to save Missouri for the Union. Resumed activities following the war; moved to new building on Chouteau Avenue in 1888; had membership of approximately seven hundred members by 1898, making it the largest society in St. Louis and one of the largest societies in the country; consolidated with the South Side Turners in 1918; closed in 1940; hall was torn down to make way for the Clinton Peabody housing development.

Archival Collections

Mo45   St. Louis Turnverein Records, 1852-1933. 1 box, 12 volumes.
Finding aid available from repository.
Location: MoSHi.
Description: The records include minute books 1852-1874, 1889-1912; expense book, 1850-1853; two membership ledgers, 1855-1863, 1904-1919; gymnastic hall bookings, 1906-1915; shareholders' account book, 1855-1858; and tax bills, contracts, mortgage papers, and insurance papers.

Mo46   St. Louis Turnverein Records, 1923-1932. 0.4 linear feet.
Finding aid available from repository.
Location: IU.
Description: The collection includes correspondence relating to financial matters, 1923-1932; list of officers, founders, members, and committees; programs and speeches from the Camp Jackson Day celebration, 1932.

Mo47   Eulenhorts Society Records, St. Louis, Missouri, 1907-1961. 1 volume.
Finding aid available from repository.
Location: MoU.
Description: The records consist of the *Goldenes Buch* of the Eulenhorst, the literary branch of the St. Louis Turner Society, 1907-1961. The book includes meeting records, historical sketches, music, poetry, memorials and other records of the society. Records are in German.

Mo48   Louis Kittlaus Collection, 1893-1987. 0.75 linear feet.
Preliminary inventory available from repository.
Location: MoU.
Description: Kittlaus was a long-time member of the Concordia Turnverein, graduate of the Turner Normal College, and teacher in the St. Louis school system. His

collection includes numerous printed materials, 1893-1987, Turnfest and Olympic photographs, Turner medals and membership cards.

Publications

Mo49   St. Louis Turnverein, Goldenes Jubiläum, 1850-1900, May 12th. St. Louis: n.p., 1900. 14 p.
Location: NN.

Mo50   60th Anniversary Celebration of the St. Louis Gymnastic Society, 1850[-] 1910: Grosses Maifest, 12-13-14-15 Mai 1910 zur Feier des 60 Jährigen Jubiläums des St. Louis Turnverein gegründet 1850, betitelt 4 Tage auf Deutschem Boden. [St. Louis]: n.p., [1910].
Location: IU.

Mo51   Einige allgemeine parlamentarische Regeln herausgegeben von dem Turnverein in St. Louis, Mo, 1865. [St. Louis]: n.p., 1865. 16 p.
Note: Rules and advice on organizing a Turner Society.
Location: WMT.

Mo52   St. Louis Turnverein, Gegründet am 12. Mai, 1850. [St. Louis]: n.p., 1893. [40 p.]
Note: Publication for the promotion of the society. Includes class schedules, activities and advertisement for a German-English school.
Location: InIU.

Mo53   St. Louis Turnverein. Katalog der Bibliothek des St. Louis Turnvereins. St. Louis: n.p., 1890. 27 p.
Location: DLC.

Mo54   Retzer, C. and Carl Sauer. Katalog der Bibliothek des St. Louis Turnvereins. St. Louis: August Wiebusch & Son Printing Company, 1895.
Location: MoSW.

Mo55   Program to Lookin' Lovely: A Comedy in Three Acts Given by The Boosters' Club of the St. Louis Turnverein for the Benefit of the Society, Saturday Evening, April 25, 1931. [St. Louis]: n.p., [1931].
Note: Includes program for physical education demonstration.
Location: IU.

Mo56 Commemorating The Surrender and Capture of Camp Jackson, St. Louis, Missouri, May 10, 1861, Sponsored by the St. Louis Gymnastic Society (St. Louis Turnverein), Saturday, May 8, 1932, With a Parade 2 P.M. Sharp from Turner Hall, 1508 Chouteau Avenue to Lyon Park, Ceremonies Lyon Park, 3 P.M., Camp Jackson Day and Campfire Celebration, Tuesday, May 10, 1932, 8 P.M. at Turner Hall, 1508 Chouteau Ave. St. Louis: Trio Printing Co., 1932. 36 p.
Location: DLC; IU (Archives); MoU (Louis Kittlaus Collection).

St. Louis: South St. Louis Turnverein

Founded in 1864 under the name *Süd* St. Louis Turnverein by members of the St. Louis Turnverein; occupied a hall on Ninth and Julia Streets; opened new hall on Carroll and Tenth, 1882; had membership of nearly 750 in 1906 and one of the largest gymnastic schools in the country under the direction of George Wittich; merged with the St. Louis Turnverein in 1918.

Publication

Mo57 Süd St. Louis Turnverein, Souvenir Ausgabe, 1864-1914, Zur Goldenen Jubiläum Feier, October 11, 15, 16, 17 und 18, 1914. [St. Louis]: n.p.,1914. 46 p.
Note: Fiftieth anniversary festival book. Includes photographs, and a history of the society in German and English.
Location: Private collection.

St. Louis: South West Gymnastic Society

Organized in 1893 under the name *Süd-West* St. Louis Turnverein; opened first hall on Cherokee between Texas and Ohio Streets in 1894; began classes for children in 1894 and for ladies in 1895; moved to new hall on Potomac and Ohio Avenues in 1899; formed ladies auxiliary in 1899; invited Emma Goldman to lecture in Turner hall, causing protest from several members, 1900; organized dramatic section, German language classes, and vocational school in 1900; officially changed the language of the society to English in June 1917; merged with Tower Grove Turnverein in 1939; lost hall to fire in 1942; dissolved between 1957 and 1960.

Publication

Mo58 Southwest Turners, Golden Jubilee, 50th Anniversary, 1944. [St. Louis]: n.p., [1944]. 47 p.

Note: Includes history of the society, and numerous photographs.
Location: InIU.

Mo59   Constitution. Mimeographed. n.p., [ca. 1950]. 10 p.
Location: InIU.

St. Louis: Tower Grove Gymnastic Society

Founded in 1906; owned property on Grand Avenue and Juanita Street; replaced simple wooden structure with substantial building in 1911; was largest Turner society in St. Louis between 1912 and 1920, with a membership ranging from approximately 1500 members in 1912 to 685 members in 1920; merged with the Southwest Turners in 1939.

Publication

Mo60   Tower Grove Gymnastic Society, Grand and Juniata Street, Saint Louis, Mo., 1937. [St. Louis]: n.p., 1937. 15 p.
Location: InIU.

St. Louis: West St. Louis Turnverein

Founded as the Schiller Club; incorporated as the West St. Louis Turnverein in 1879; included among the founding members was the German-American poet Zündt; built hall on northeast corner of Morgan and Beaumont Streets in 1881; had membership of 105 by 1898; had largest ladies auxiliary in St. Louis with 122 women; closed between 1911 and 1913.

Publication

Mo61   Silber Jubiläums-Feier des West St. Louis Turnvereins, 16. October, 1879-1904. [St. Louis]: n.p., 1904. 98 p.
Note: Includes detailed history, membership list with addresses, and photographs.
Location: InIU.

Mo62   Turner Fackel. Redigirt für geistige Bestrebungen. St. Louis: West St. Louis Turnverein, 1885?-1909?
Note: Monthly magazine of the West St. Louis Turnverein, published by the committee on intellectual efforts.

Location:
MoHi: v.23 (1907) - v.25 (1909). Incomplete.
MWA: v.24, no.5 (Sept. 1908).

Washington: Washington Turnverein

Founded on December 13, 1859; disbanded during Civil War; reorganized October 9, 1865; dedicated Turner hall on Third and Jefferson Streets on December 26, 1866; joined by theater society (formed 1854) which became the dramatic section in 1868; left American Turnerbund because of disagreements in 1878 but joined again in 1884; closed in 1932.

Publication

Mo63   Washington Turnverein, Washington, Mo. Geschichte des Washington Turnvereins: seit seiner Gründung am 13. Dezember 1859, zusammengestellt und herausgegeben im Auftrage des Vereins von einem historischen Comite. Washington, MO: Pearl Printing Co., 1900. 52 p.
Note: History of the Washington Turnverein.
Location: CtY.

NEBRASKA

Omaha: South Side Turners

Founded as *Süd Seite Turnverein* in 1892; attracted members of the Omaha Turnverein (active 1860-1890) and the Jahn Turnverein (founded 1889); purchased hall on 18th and Vinton Streets in the 1890s; suffered damages to hall in 1930 fire; changed name to South Side Turners in 1946; merged with the *Musik Verein* and the *Plattdeutscher Verein* to form the German-American Society of Omaha in 1966; the German-American Society is still active and offers gymnastics classes.

Publications

Nb1   Dedication Program for the New South Side Turner Hall, 1724 Vinton Street, Omaha, Nebraska. [Omaha]: n.p. [1947]. 24 p.
Note: Includes brief histories of the Omaha Turnverein, and the South Side Turners, and a program of events.
Location: InIU.

Nb2   100 Jahre Bärenbrut: Souvenir Buch, November 20th, 1993: 100 Years
Bärs, 1893-1993. [Omaha]: n.p. [1993]. [24 p.]
Note: Souvenir program to the one hundredth anniversary of the senior men, called the
"Bears." Includes a history of the "Bears," photographs, and list of members.
Location: InIU; German-American Society of Omaha.

Nb3   Constitution and By-Laws of the South Side Turnverein, Omaha, Nebr.,
Founded Nov. 10, 1895, Incorporated on March 6, 1907, Chartered on January 22,
1917. [Omaha]: n.p., [1917]. 16 p.
Location: InIU.

NEW HAMPSHIRE

Manchester: Manchester Turnverein

Founded in 1870; built hall in 1873 on First Street (later renamed Turner Street
because of the society's popularity); founded German school to teach home economics
in 1879; rented hall for use as theater and showing room for funerals; formed
Workers' Relief Association in 1882; organized ladies auxiliary in 1891 (disbanded
in 1965) and Sabre Club in 1929 (still active); lost hall to fire in 1936 but rebuilt it
one year later; sold hall and closed in 1977; former Turner hall burnt down in 1984.

Publications

Nh1   Souvenir Program, Commemorating the 75th Anniversary of the Manchester
Turn Verein Inc., May 4-5-6, 1945. [Manchester]: n.p., [1945].[48 p.]
Note: Includes brief history of the society and women's organization.
Location: InIU.

NEW JERSEY

Carlstadt: Carlstadt Turnverein, Inc.

Founded as *Sozialer Turnverein von* Carlstadt in 1857; purchased hall in 1864 and
second building for public school in 1865; started singing section *Frohsinn* and
Sunday School in 1866; sold hall in 1867; played influential role in establishing first
fire company in 1869; joined by the Calstadt *Schützen* Company in 1875; formed
mixed chorus (1880), dramatic section (1882), fencing section (1887-1902), and
ladies auxiliary (1895); built hall on Monroe and Broad Streets in 1900; played active

role opposing prohibition and supporting war relief for Germany at the end of World War I; supported education programs for newly arrived immigrants in 1910s and 1920s; merged with Carlstadt *Männerchor* in 1933; lost hall to fire in 1952; disbanded gymnastic classes in the 1950s, but restarted in the 1990s; split into gymnastic and singing societies in 1958 but the two stayed under one roof; society still active as social, singing and sports organization.

Archival Collection

Nj1   Carlstadt Turnverein Records, 1856/7-1976. 17 volumes.
Preliminary inventory available from Indiana Univ.-Purdue Univ. Indianapolis.
Location: Carlstadt Turnverein, Inc.
Description: The records include minutes of the organization, 1859-1976; minutes of the Carlstadt Free Sunday School (*Freie Sonntagsschule*), 1897-1911; minutes of the entertainment committee (*Vergnügungs Komitee*), 1882-1888; financial records, 1866-1914; membership and dues records, 1889-1899, 1909-1921; handwritten statutes and first membership list from 1856-1857; district treasurers' reports, 1941-1949. Records prior to 1944 are predominantly in German.

Publications

Nj2   Turnverein of Carlstadt, Carlstadt N. J. Zur Feier des fünfzigjährigen Jubiläums des Carlstadt Turnvereins, 8., 9. Juni, 1907. Carlstadt: Freie Presse Print, 1907. 17 p.
Note: Fiftieth anniversary publication of the Carlstadt Turnverein. Includes history.
Location: DLC.

Nj3   100th Anniversary, 1857-1957, Carlstadt Turnverein, June 8th and 9th. [Carlstadt]: n.p., [1957]. [44 p.]
Note: Includes a history of the society, centennial program, and photographs.
Location: InIU; Carlstadt Turnverein, Inc.

Nj4   125th Anniversary, 1857-1982, Carlstadt Turnverein, June 12th & 13th. [Carlstadt]: n.p., [1982]. [108 p.]
Note: Includes history of the Carlstadt Turnverein and the Mixed Chorus, program of events, and contemporary photographs.
Location: InIU; Carlstadt Turnverein, Inc.

Elizabeth: Elizabeth Turnverein Vorwärts

Founded in 1872 as successor to Turner society active prior to the Civil War; formed bowling section in 1875; merged with *Fortschritt Verein* in 1876; built hall on Hight Street in 1882; merged with singing societies *Germania* and *Lasallia* in 1884; built separate gymnasium in 1905; sold old hall in 1918 and moved into gymnasium; declined during the Depression years but recovered after World War II; left the American Turners in 1940; closed about 1960.

Publications

Nj5 50 Years of the Turnverein Vorwärts, Held at the Turnerhall, Elizabeth, N.J., 1872[-]1922. Elizabeth: Gommel Printing Shop, 1922. [ca. 50 p.]
Note: Includes history of the club.
Location: WMCHi.

Nj6 Elizabeth Turners, Turn-Verein Vorwärts, 1872[-]1947, Diamond Jubilee, Friday evening, December 5 at the Turner's Gymnasium, 719 High St., Saturday Evening, December 6 at the Elks' Auditorium, Union Avenue. [Elizabeth]: Grommel Print Shop, [1947]. [40 p.]
Note: Includes a history of the society, contemporary photographs of classes, and program of events.
Location: InIU.

Nj7 Constitution and By-Laws of the Turn Verein Vorwärts of Elizabeth, N.J., Revised January, 1921. [Elizabeth]: n.p., [1921]. 13 p.
Location: InIU.

Hoboken: Hoboken Turnverein

Founded as Hoboken *Turngemeinde* in 1857 by members of the New York Turnverein; members joined Turner regiment during Civil War; incorporated under the name Hoboken Gymnastic Society in 1868; changed name to Hoboken Turnverein in 1881; purchased hall on Park Avenue in 1883; formed ladies section in 1885; established Jahn Camp, a week-end and summer camp in Monmouth County, in 1907; closed in 1934.

Publications

Nj8 Zur Feier des Fünfzig-Jährigen Jubiläums, Hoboken Turn Verein, 16-22.

Juni 1907, Hoboken, N.J., 1857[-]1907. [Hoboken]: n.p., [1907]. [27 p.]
Note: Fiftieth anniversary publication. Includes a history of the organization, an article on physical education, a program of events and photographs.
Location: InIU (photocopy); NJH; NN.

Nj9   Hoboken Turn Verein. [Hoboken]: n.p., 1903.
Note: Constitution of the Hoboken Turn Verein and women's auxiliary. In German and English.
Location: NN.

Jersey City: Hudson City Turnverein

Founded in 1863 by returning soldiers who had previously belonged to three different Turner societies [*Sozialer* Turnverein (1854); Center Hill Turnverein (1856); and Washington Village Turngemeinde (1860)]; moved to Washington Village in 1866; formed singing section (1873), ladies auxiliary, sick and death benefit, and drama sections (1880); purchased hall on Webster Avenue in 1880; hall destroyed by fire in 1906 and restored by 1908; society probably disbanded in 1939.

Publication

Nj10   Hudson City Turn Verein, Festzeitung für die erste grosse Fair ... 29. Okt.-7. Nov. 1887, Jersey City Hights. Jersey City, NJ: n.p., 1887.
Note: Cited in Pochmann #5187.

New Brunswick: New Brunswick Turnverein

Founded in 1867; changed locations frequently until society built its own hall on Dennis Street in 1884; lost hall due to high maintenance costs; left American Turnerbund to operate as independent society after 1888; purchased new quarters on George Street in 1906; disbanded in about 1960.

Publication

Nj11   Statuten und Neben-Gesetze des New Brunswick Turnverein von New Brunswick, N.J.: Constitution and By-laws of the New Brunswick Turn Verein. New Brunswick: Standard Press, 1948. 36 p.
Note: In German and English.
Location: InIU.

Newark: Newark Turnverein

Formed in 1878 by a merger of the *Sozialistischer* Turnverein (founded 1848) and the *Unabhängiger* Turnverein (founded 1865); established city's first art school (*Zeichenschule*) which later became a public institution; lost hall in fire which killed three people in 1907; built new hall and school, ca.1909; offered education programs in bookkeeping, commercial arithmetic, international law and commercial correspondence in German and English; grew to be the largest society in the New Jersey District in 1930 with 635 members; lost half of membership in early 1930s; lost hall in 1930s due to financial problems; had only fifty members in 1940; closed in the 1960s. The Newark Turnverein hosted national conventions in 1882 and 1906, and the national Turnfest in 1885.

Archival Collection

Nj12   Newark Turnverein School Records, 1894-1918. 2 volumes
Location: InIU.
Description: Minute book of the school committee, 1894-1906; register of the Turner school, 1911-1918. In German.

Publication

Nj13   Newark Turnverein, 25 jähriges Stiftungsfest des Newark Turnvereins. Newark: Heinz Printing Co., 1903. 16 p.
Location: DLC.

North Bergen: Union Hill Turners

Organized in 1872 as the Union Hill Turn Verein; built first hall on the corner of New York Avenue and Lewis Street (38th St.) in 1890; recruited Franz Sigel as guest speaker for cornerstone ceremony; lost hall and all records to fire in 1915; sold property during World War I; built new hall on corner of Hudson Boulevard and Blum Place in 1917; lost hall to financial problems in 1939; discontinued gymnastics classes during World War II; disbanded in 1986.

Publications

Nj14   Eightieth Anniversary, Union Hill Turn Verein, 1872-1952, Schützen Park Hall, North Bergen, N.J. Union City, John Rank, 1952. [56 p.]

Note: Includes a brief history of the organization and contemporary photographs. In German and English.
Location: InIU.

Nj15   Statutes of the Union Hill Turners. typed, [ca. 1955]. 11 p.
Location: InIU.

Passaic: Passaic Turners, Inc.

Founded in 1892 by German workers at the Botany Worsted Mills; formed ladies classes in 1895; built hall on Dayton Avenue in 1909; entertained President Taft during a dinner at Turner Hall in 1910; organized ladies auxiliary in 1910; suffered damage to hall in 1916 fire but restored hall within 40 days; flourished in late 1910s and 1920s, with 450 members in 1920; declined to one hundred members in the 1940s, and to twenty by 1960; inactive with six members in 1994.

Publications

Nj16   50th Anniversary of the Passaic Turnverein, Incorporated, Affiliated with the American Turners - A National Organization, 1892[-]1942. [Passaic]: n.p., [1942]. [122 p.]
Note: Includes a history of the Passaic Turners and the women's auxiliary, list of honorary members, program, and photographs of former and present members.
Location: InIU.

Nj17   Passaic Turn Verein, Incorporated, "Gut Heil!" Gegründet 7 Febr.1892. Passaic: Passaic Wochenblatt, 1927. [30 p.]
Note: German and English versions of constitutions, pages separately. Constitution and by-laws in German, pp.1-19; house rules (*Hausordnung*), pp. 20-21; constitution in English, pp. 1-8.
Location: InIU.

Nj18   The Passaic Turner. Passaic: Passaic Turners, Inc., 1936-1945?
Note: Newsletter of the Passaic Turners. Includes local and national Turner news, class schedule, bowling news, and news of Turners in the service.
Location: InIU: v.9, no.8 (April 1945).

Paterson: Riverside Athletic and Singing Club

Founded in 1867 as the *Socialer* Turnverein; built hall in 1884; changed name to Paterson Turnverein in 1887; reached peak membership in the 1890s with over three hundred members; lost members after turn of the century; lost hall or moved in 1928; had only twenty-five members in 1940; left American Turners in 1950; merged with a singing society to form the Riverside Athletic & Singing Society; possibly closed in 1966.

Archival Collection

Nj19   The Riverside Athletic and Singing Club, 1899-1966. 11 volumes.
Finding aid available from repository.
Location: NJPHi.
Description: The records include minute books of the board meetings, 1925-1934, 1960-1966; reports of the House Committee, 1944-1951; record book of the entertainment committee, 1921-1934; registration and expenses, 1922-1957, 1954-1966; song-list *(Liederverzeichnis)*, October 1940; a silk ceremonial banner, 1899; and 12 photographs and engravings picturing activities and members of the society.

Publication

Nj20   Statuten ... Paterson: 1893.
Note: Cited in Pochmann #8016.

Plainfield: Plainfield Gesang und Turnverein, Inc.

Founded in 1886; operated as independent society; still active as social and singing society.

Publications

Nj21   The German-American Plainfield Gesang und Turnverein, Inc., is Proud to Celebrate its 104th Anniversary, 1886-1990. Concert May 19, 1990, 8:00 p.m. n.p., 1990. 48 p.
Note: Includes concert program and brief history. Listed in 1991 Yearbook of German-American Studies, v.26, no.187.

Nj22   Statuten des Plainfield Gesang und Turn Vereins in Plainfield, N.J. gegründet am 2. Dez. 1886: Einigkeit Macht Stark. New York: Rosswaag's Stuyvesand Press, 1886. 59 p.
Note: In English and German.
Location: NJNHi.

Riverside: Riverside Turners (Turnverein Progress)

Founded in 1860 as Turnverein Progress; changed name to Riverside Turners in 1870; probably closed in 1875.

Archival Collection

Nj23   Progress Turnverein Records, 1865-1875. 2 volumes.
Finding aid available from repository.
Location: PPB.
Description: The records consist of one minute book of the Progress Turnverein, 1860, 1865-1875 which also includes the convention minutes for the 1874 meeting of the Philadelphia Turnbezirk; and the membership list, dues and account book of the Riverside Turnverein *Krankenkasse (Hauptbuch)*, 1869-1875.   Records are in German.

Riverside: Riverside Turners, Inc.

Organized as the Riverside Turngemeinde by members of the *Männerchor* in 1897; built Turner hall on Bridgeboro Street in 1903; discontinued activities during World War I and sold hall; formed ladies auxiliary in 1929; built new hall built on Rancocas Avenue in 1930; still active.

Archival Collection

Nj24   Riverside Turners, Inc. Records, 1902-present. 22 volumes.
Preliminary inventory available from Indiana Univ.-Purdue Univ. Indianapolis.
Location: Riverside Turner Hall, Riverside.
Description: The records include minutes of the organization, 1902-1912, 1932-1940, 1967-present; membership records, 1910-1936, 1967-1973; financial records, 1915-1969; records of the chairman, 1974-1991; correspondence, 1959-1961; guest register, 1935-38; women's auxiliary minutes, 1963-present. Records before the 1930s are in German.

Publications

Nj25 Festschrift zur Einweihung der Halle der Riverside Turn-Gemeinde am 26. November 1903: Souvenir to the Dedication of the Hall of the Riverside Turn-Gemeinde on November 26, 1903. [Riverside]: n.p., [1903]. [ca. 60 p.]
Note: Includes a brief history of the organization, membership list, and photographs.
Location: Private collection.

Nj26 Riverside Turners, 75th Anniversary, Saturday, March 11, 1972, 1897-1972. [Riverside]: n.p., 1972. 20 p.
Note: Includes list of officers, program of events, and a brief history.
Location: InIU; Riverside Turners, Inc.

Nj27 Constitution and By-Laws of the Riverside Turners, Branch of the National American Turners, 300 Rancocas Avenue, Riverside, Burlington County, N.J. [Riverside]: n.p., [1940]. 24 p.
Location: InIU.

Trenton: Trenton Turnerbund

Founded in 1924; reached peak membership in 1930 with seventy-five members; closed in 1948.

Publications

Nj28 Statuten, Trenton Turnerbund, Gegründet Januar 1924, Certificate of Incorporation, Issued July 17, 1924, Statuten angenommen und in Kraft getreten in der Vereins-Versammlung vom 16 Februar 1932. [Trenton]: n.p., [1932]. 7 p.
Location: InIU.

NEW YORK

Buffalo: Buffalo Turn Verein, Inc.

Organized in 1853 as the Buffalo Turn Verein by members of the German-American Workingman's Society; opened first hall on Ellicott Street; formed sharpshooter's section in 1854; added cultural program, singing section, and school in 1855; hosted national convention same year; changed name to *Socialer Männer* Turnverein in 1856 after group of young Turners broke away to form the Turnverein *Vorwärts*; suspended activities during the Civil War when large number of members joined the New York Turner Regiment and Wiedrick Battery; merged with the Turnverein *Vorwärts* to form the Buffalo Turnverein in March 1865; built new hall on Oak Street in 1866 and addition was made in 1870; flourished during the late nineteenth century, including among its members numerous civic leaders, notably Mayors Phillip Becker and Dr. Conrad Diehl; lost hall in 1904 following fire and financial troubles; active in movement to introduce physical education in the public schools, succeeding in 1910; built new hall in 1912 on Oak Street; hosted national Turnfests in 1930 and 1951; lost hall to urban renewal in 1973; purchased new building on Wheatfield Street in 1977, but were forced to sell it in 1980; began renting Lincoln School gymnasium in town of Tonawanda in 1981; still active as a gymnastic organization.

Archival Collection

Ny1   Buffalo Turn Verein Records, 1864-present. 16 volumes
Preliminary inventory available from Indiana Univ.-Purdue Univ. Indianapolis.
Location: Buffalo Turn Verein, Buffalo.
Description: The records include the minutes of the society, 1864-1871, 1885-1904; financial records, 1957-1980; five scrapbooks with newspaper clippings and photographs, 1950s-1970s; annual circus programs, 1947-1968; ladies auxiliary minutes, 1906-1951, 1960-1975; and ladies auxiliary membership list, 1906. Records prior to the 1920s are predominantly in German.

Ny2   Buffalo Turner Collection, 1853-1906, 6 volumes.
Finding aid available from repository.
Location: NBuHi.
Description: The collection consists of minutes of the organization, 1853-1859; committee minutes, 1853-1859; minutes of the ladies auxiliary, 1894-1906; and library records (*Bibliothekar Buch*). Records are in German.

Publications

Ny3   Buffalo Turn Verein, Diamond Jubilee Anniversary, 1853[-]1928. Buffalo: Manhard Printing, [1928]. [20 p.]
Note: Includes a history of the organization, list of officers, and photographs.
Location: InIU.

Ny4   100th Anniversary, Buffalo Turners, 1853[-]1953. Buffalo: n.p., [1953]. 39 p.
Note: Includes a history of the organization, list of active members, photographs, and article "The Turners Introduction of Physical Education in Public Schools."
Location: InIU; WMT; Buffalo Turn Verein.

Ny5   Constitution des Buffalo Turn-Vereins, Gegründet am 29. März 1853, Incorporiert am 13. Mai 1869. Buffalo: *Dampfpressendruck von Bruck und Held*, 1871. 30 p.
Location: NN; NBuU.

Ny6   Constitution des Buffalo Turn-Vereins zu Buffalo, N.Y. Buffalo: Reinecke & Zecht, 1895. 15 p.
Location: InIU.

Ny7   Constitution and By-Laws of the Buffalo Turn Verein, Buffalo, NY. [Buffalo]: n.p., 1929. 24 p.
Location: InIU.

Ny8   Constitution and By-Laws, 1949, Buffalo Turn Verein Inc., Buffalo, New York. [Buffalo]: n.p., 1949. 23 p.
Location: InIU.

Ny9   Ladies Auxiliary Constitution and By-Laws. [Buffalo]: n.p., 1949.
Location: Buffalo Turn Verein.

Ny10   Constitution and By-Laws, Buffalo Turn Verein Inc., Buffalo, New York. [Buffalo]: n.p., 1963. 24 p.
Location: InIU.

Ny11   Constitution and By-Laws of the Buffalo Turners, Inc. [Buffalo]: n.p., 1970.
Location: Buffalo Turn Verein.

Ny12   Constitution and By-Laws of the Buffalo Turners, Inc. [Buffalo]: n.p., 1976.
Location: Buffalo Turn Verein.

Ny13   Roaster. Offizielles Organ für den Jahrmarkt des Buffalo Turn Vereins. Buffalo: Buffalo Turn Verein, 1899--??
Note: Weekly publication of the Buffalo Turn Verein, printed by Reinicke & Zesch.
Location:
   NBuHi: no.1 (Jan. 1899).
   NN: no.1-13 (Jan. 30-April 11, 1899)

Ny14   Buffalo Turner: Buffalo: Buffalo Turn Verein, 1918?-1940s
Note: Monthly newsletter. Includes local and national Turner news, announcements, schedules, and news from the Normal College and other Turner societies.
Location: Buffalo Turn Verein: 1930, 1937-1938 (scattered issues).

Ny15   The Turner Line'R Two. Buffalo Turn Verein Newsletter. Buffalo: Buffalo Turn Verein, 1944?-1957?.
Note: Monthly newsletter of the Buffalo Turn Verein. Includes national and local Turners news, announcements, and schedules.
Location: Buffalo Turn Verein: 1944-1957 (scattered issues).

Ny16   Buffalo Turner Hi-Lites. Buffalo: Buffalo Turn Verein, 1974?-1980s?

Note: Newsletter of the Buffalo Turn Verein.
Location: Buffalo Turn Verein: 1974-1978 (scattered issues).

Newburgh: Newburgh Turnverein

Organized in 1863; reached maximum membership in 1884-1886 with approximately fifty members; left American Turnerbund in 1887; probably closed in 1909.

Publication

Ny17   Statuten des Newburgh Turnvereins, Gegründet den 16. November 1863, Angenommen und in Kraft getreten 7. Jan. 1894. Milwaukee: Germania Publishing Co., 1894. 25 p.
Note: Constitution in German; certificate of incorporation in English.
Location: InIU.

New York City

The Turner societies in New York City have played a prominent role in the movement since its beginnings. Turner activities began in the city in the early 1840s, but they remained informal until 1848 when the New York *Turngemeinde* was formed. During the 1850s the dominant society in the city was the *Sozialistischer* Turnverein, formed in 1850 by men who had been active in the 1848 revolutions in Germany, such as Gustav Stuve, Sigismund Kaufmann and Franz Sigel. This society, along with the *Sozialistischer Turnverein von Brooklyn*, played a leading role in the formation of the national organization, the *Sozialistischer* Turnerbund, and served as its headquarters in the early 1850s. Over the next two decades the Turners in New York continued to be national leaders. Largely because of their influence the Turnerbund sponsored the publication of the gymnastics textbook Das Turnen, by New York instructor Eduard Müller in 1853, and the publication of a series of school books for Turner schools in the late 1860s and early 1870s. New York City Turners were also instrumental in reconstituting the Turnerbund at the end of the Civil War, and in establishing the first training school for physical education instructors, the *Turnlehrer* Seminar, in New York City in 1866. During the Civil War hundreds of New York Turners served in the Union Army, most of them in the 20th New York Regiment, also known as the Turner Rifles, while Franz Sigel and Max Weber, two New York Turners, achieved the rank of general. By the 1890s New York City had eighteen Turner societies. The number declined to fourteen by 1910, and eight by the 1920s. The number of Turners also declined from 1377 in 1920 to approximately 600 in 1950. Today there are only two active societies, the American Turners New York and the Long Island Turners. New York City Turners hosted national conventions in 1850, 1890, 1950, and 1964, and national Turnfests in 1853, 1857, 1871, and 1875.

New York (Bronx): American Turners Bronx, Inc.

Founded in 1881 under the name *Deutsch-Amerikanischer* Turnverein in the Melrose section of the city; joined American Turnerbund in 1889 with seventy members; built Turner hall around 1890; changed name to American Turner Bronx, Inc. in 1948; merged with the Mt. Vernon Turners in 1957.

Publications

Ny18   Festschrift zum 50 jährigen Jubiläeum. New York: n.p., 1931.
Note: Cited in Pochmann #2136.

Ny19   Grand Annual Gymnastic Exhibition and Ball, D.A. Turn-Verein, New York, Ebling's Casino, Saturday Evening, May 3rd, 1941, 60th Anniversary Number. [New York]: n.p., [1941]. [68 p.]
Location: InIU.

Ny20   Statuten ... 6. Sept., 1881, Revised July, 1900. New York: n.p., 1900.
Note: Cited in Pochmann #2137.

New York (Brooklyn): American Turners of Brooklyn, Inc.

Organized as Turnverein *Vorwärts* in 1883 by members of the Brooklyn Labor Lyceum; formed ladies auxiliary in 1889; opened gymnasium built for the Turners by the Brooklyn Labor Lyceum Association, 1891; lost gymnasium to fire in 1900; offered special day classes for night-shift workers employed by local German newspapers from 1900 to 1920 when the major German newspapers went out of business; merged with *Social-Demokratischer* Turnverein in 1901; purchased building on Willoughby Avenue in 1907, later taken over by the Labor Lyceum Association; organized Turner Camp *Vorwärts* on Long Island in 1927; merged with the Brooklyn E.D. Turners to form the American Turners of Brooklyn, Inc. in 1948; sold hall in 1957; society disbanded in 1986.

Archival Collection

Ny21   Turn Verein *Vorwärts* Records, undated. 1 volume.
Location: InIU.
Description: Statutes of the society and membership list, ca. 1885. In German.

Publications

Ny22   Gedenkblatt zum Silbernen Jubiläum, Schauturnen, Bankett und Ball, Turn-Verein Vorwärts, Brooklyn, 30. und 31. Mai 1908, Brooklyn Labor Lyceum.

New York City: n.p., [1908]. [40 p.]
Note: Cover title: "1883-1908, *Silbernes Jubiläum, Turn-Verein Vorwärts,* Brooklyn." Silver jubilee publication. Includes a history of the society and photographs of classes and sections.
Location: InIU.

Ny23   Turn-Verein Vorwärts, Brooklyn, 1833-1933, Golden Jubilee, Gymnastic Exhibition, Saturday, May 6, Banquet and Ball, Sunday, May 14, Brooklyn Labor Lyceum. [Brooklyn]: Bartel, [1933]. [56 p.]
Note: Cover title: "*Turn-Verein Vorwärts*, Brooklyn, N.Y., 1883-1933." Includes a history of the society, articles on gymnastics, photographs of classes and sections, and list of achievements at Turnfests. In German and English.
Location: InIU.

Ny24   Turn-Verein "Vorwärts" Brooklyn, Golden Jubilee, Monster Gymnastic Exhibition and Ball, Saturday, May 6, 1933 at the Brooklyn Labor Lyceum. New York City: n.p., 1933. 8 p.
Note: Includes a brief history of the society, a program for the exhibition, a statement of Turner principles and Turnerism, and chronology of Turnfest achievements.
Location: InIU.

Ny25   American Turners of Brooklyn, Inc., (Formerly Turn Verein Vorwärts), Diamond Jubilee Year, 1883[-]1958. [New York]: n.p.,[1958]. [76 p.]
Note: Includes a brief history of the society, program of events and photographs.
Location: InIU.

Ny26   American Turners of Brooklyn: Annual Anniversary Dinner and Dance. [Programs] [New York]: n.p., 1959-1979.
Note: Cover title includes name of the organization and dates. Programs to annual anniversary celebration of the society.
Location: InIU: 1959-1979. (Incomplete).

Ny27   Statuten des Turn-Verein Vorwärts, Brooklyn. Brooklyn: Bartel, 1911. 27 p.
Location: InIU.

Ny28   Konstitution und Neben-Gesetze, Turnverein Vorwärts of the Borough of Brooklyn, Inc., Angenommen 24. April 1930, In Kraft am 1. Juli 1930. [Brooklyn]: n.p., [1930]. 58 p.
Note: In German and English.
Location: InIU.

Ny29   Constitution and By-Laws of the Turn Verein Vorwärts of the Borough of Brooklyn, Incorporated. New York: n.p., [1939]. 27 p.
Location: InIU.

Ny30   Constitution and By-Laws of the American Turners of Brooklyn, Incorporated, Formerly Turn Verein Vorwaerts of the Borough of Brooklyn, Incorporated, Accepted, March 8th, 1949, In Force, March 9, 1949. Mimeographed. [Brooklyn]: n.p., 1949. [14 p.]
Location: InIU.

Ny31   Turn-Verein Vorwärts Mitglieds-Buch. n.p., [1890?]. 30 p.
Note: Membership booklet, includes "*Statutes des Turnverein Vorwärts*," pp. 1-20. In German.
Location: InIU.

Ny32   Turn-Verein Vorwärts of the Borough of Brooklyn, Inc., 1939. New York: n.p., 1939. [62 p.]
Note: Includes list of committee members, class schedules, and membership list.
Location: InIU.

Ny33   Turn Verein Vorwärts, Brooklyn, Kalender. n.p, 1915?-1919?
Note: Cover title: "Compliments of Turn-Verein *Vorwärts*, Brooklyn." The calendars were published annually and complementary copies were distributed among the members. They included a list of officers for the year, the upcoming events of the organization, general information, class schedules, and a membership list.
Location: InIU: 1915, 1916, 1919.

New York: American Turners New York, Inc.

Founded as the *Sozialistischer* Turnverein by radical members of the New York Turngemeinde in June 1850; included among the founders and early members were numerous exiles from the German revolution, including Sigismund Kaufmann, Germain Metternich; Heinrich Metzner, Franz Sigel, and Gustav Struve; played leading role in the organization of the *Sozialistische* Turnerbund in October 1850; formed school, fencing section and cultural program, including drama section and library, with Franz Sigel as first instructor in 1851; involved in violent confrontation with nativist gangs during Turner picnic, ending in the arrest of twenty-six Turners in 1851; maintained strong ties to the German *Arbeiterbund* in the 1850s; changed name to Turn Verein in the City of New York or New York Turnverein in 1857; purchased first hall in 1859 on Orchard Street and offered free grade school; had approximately two hundred members join the Union Army, most in the 20th New York Regiment, called the United Turner Rifles; organized Cadet Corps in 1864 which lasted until 1921; taught first girls' gymnastic classes in 1864; served as host for the first classes of the national *Turnlehrer* Seminar, 1866-1869 and 1872-1875; dedicated new four story hall in 1872 on Third and Fourth Streets between First and Second Avenues, which became a center for German-American activities; lost hall in fire that killed eight people in 1880, but rebuilt hall the same year; organized first women's class 1889; sponsored school with more than 1,200 students and fifteen teachers in the 1890s; moved to larger facilities on South East Corner of 85th Street and Lexington Avenue in 1898; formed ladies auxiliary in 1915; members attained places on Olympic teams in gymnastics, fencing, and volleyball in 1904, 1920-1936 and 1948-1964; acquired land for summer home along Throggs Neck on Long Island in 1921; merged with the Central Turners in 1956; merged with Mt. Vernon Turners to form the American Turners New York in 1983; moved to summer home on Throggs Neck; society still active as social and athletic organization.

Archival Collection

Ny34   American Turners New York Records, 1849-pres.
Preliminary inventory available from Indiana Univ.-Purdue Univ. Indianapolis.
Location: American Turners New York.
Description: The records include minutes of the general meetings, 1850-present (incomplete);   records of board meetings, 1850-present (incomplete); financial records, 1872-present; dues and membership records, 1860s-1920s; inventories of equipment and supplies, 1881-1918; minutes of school board *(Schulrath)*, 1886-1974 (incomplete); minutes of the *Vorturnerschaft*, 1883-1899, 1957-1977; minutes of committees and clubs, including the singing section (*Liedertafel*), 1881-1917, chess club, 1897-1904, the dramatic section, 1894-1902, the carnival committee, 1890-1899, and the entertainment committee, 1963-1977; Turner passes and letters of recommendation, 1849-1860s; copies of letters written between 1855-1863; ladies auxiliary records, 1908-1914; records of the Jubilee Committee, 1925; and election records, 1939-1980. Also included are issues of the Turnzeitung des Sozialistischen Turnerbundes, Sept. 1853-Oct. 1854; and a regiment book and documents of the 20th New York Volunteer Regiment, ca.1861-1865. Records prior to the 1940s are predominantly in German.

Ny35   New York Turn Verein Papers. 1 folder.
Location: NN
Description: The New York Turn Verein Papers are part of the Gustav Scholar Papers (Box 4, no.7). Scholar was a prominent members of the Turners during the late nineteenth century. The records include Scholar's correspondence and papers as a member of the organization. There are also pages of a scrapbook regarding Franz Sigel and the founding and history of the Turn Verein. The latter includes a draft charter, letters, clippings, and photographs.

Ny36   Venino, Fr. "*Scene aus dem New York Turner-Leben: Turnerleben Excursion*: Composition & Drawn from Nature." 1854 (34.2 x 24.4 cm).

Note: Print showing an outing of the New York Turnverein, with members engaged in beer drinking and playing various musical instruments. Many are equipped with guns for target practice. New York is seen in the distance.
Location: NNM

Publications

Ny37   Zur Feier des Fünfzigjährigen Jubiläms des New Yorker Turn Vereins in der New York Turn-Halle, 1850-1900, 3. bis 6. Juni 1900. New York: Sackett & Wilhelms Litho. and Ptg. Co., 1900. 52 p.
Note: Cover title: "*Zum Goldenen Jubiläum des New York Turn-Vereins.*" Fiftieth anniversary book; includes a detailed history of the club and many photographs. In German
Location: DLC; InIU.

Ny38   Souvenir Programm zur Feier des Fünfzigjährigen Jubiläums der Dramatischen Sektion des New York Turn Vereins in der New York Turn-Halle am Sonntag, den 23. November 1902. New York: Voelcker Brothers, 1902. 16 p.
Note: Cover title: "*N.Y. Turn Verein zum Goldenen Jubiläum der Dramatischen Section. 1952-1902.*" Souvenir program of the fiftieth anniversary of the drama section of the New York Turnverein. Includes a history of the drama club, list of performances and photographs.
Location: InIU.

Ny39   Gedenkschrift zur Feier des Sechzigjährigen Stiftungsfestes des New Yorker Turn-Vereins in der New York Turnhalle, am 4. bis 6. Juni 1910. New York: n.p., 1910. 16 p.
Note: Cover title: "*New York Turn Verein, Zur Feier seines 60 jährigen Stiftungsfestes,* 1850-1910, New York." Includes a detailed history of the society.
Location: InIU.

Ny40   Gedenkschrift zur Feier des Fünfundsiebzigjährigen Jubiläums des New York Turn Vereins, 1850-1925, 6., 7., 13. und 14. Juni 1925. New York: The Co-operative Press, 1925. 80 p.
Note: Cover title: "*New York Turn Verein zur Jubelfeier seines 75-jährigen Stiftungsfestes,* 1850-1925, New York." Seventy-fifth anniversary program. Includes detailed history of the club and photographs of the sections.
Location: InIU.

Ny41   Zur Feier des Neunzigjährigen Jubiläums des New York Turn Verein in der New York Turn-Halle, 1859 - 1940, 6. June 1940. [New York]: n.p., [1940]. 55 p.
Note: Ninetieth anniversary publication. Includes a detailed history of the society and photographs. In German and English.
Location: InIU.

Ny42 Bahn Frei! Historical Journal: A Souvenir of the Centennial Celebration of the New York Turn Verein, January 1st to November 11th, 1950. [New York]: n.p., [1950]. [ca. 160 p.]
Note: Cover title: "One Hundredth Anniversary, New York Turn Verein, 1850-1950." Includes photographs and detailed histories of the society, its school and affiliated groups.
Location: IaDP; InIU.

Ny43 The Commemorative Journal: A Souvenir of the 110th Anniversary of the New York Turn Verein, November 19th, 1960. [New York]: n.p., 1960. 40 p.
Note: Cover title: "One Hundred Tenth Anniversary, 1850-1960, New York Turn Verein." Includes history and photographs.
Location: InIU; MWA.

Ny44 The Commemorative Journal: A Souvenir of the 125th Anniversary of the New York Turn Verein, November 8th, 1975. [New York]: n.p., [1975]. 38 p.
Note: Cover title: "125th Anniversary, 1850-1975, New York Turner Verein." Includes history and photographs.
Location: InIU.

Ny45 Souvenir Journal of the American Turners New York, Inc., Celebrating the Dedication of our New Home, Sunday, September 7, 1986. [New York]: n.p., [1986]. 88 p.
Note: Includes histories of the New York Turnverein and Mount Vernon Turners, a history of Turnerism and photographs.
Location: InIU.

Ny46 Statuten des Socialistischen Turn Vereins in New York. New York: M.W. Siebert, 1855. 11 p.
Location: WMT.

Ny47 Statuten ... 24. Februar 1906. New York, 1906.
Note: Cited in Pochmann #7669.

Ny48 Statuten des New Yorker Turn Vereins, Angenommen in der Generalversammlung vom 27. Oktober 1923 und in Kraft getreten am 1. Januar 1924. New York: Isaac Goldmann Company, [1924]. 32 p.
Location: InIU.

Ny49 Constitution and By-Laws of the American Turners, N.Y. Inc., A Merger of New York Turn-Verein, Founded 1852 and Mt. Vernon Turners, Founded 1891, Merger Date July 14, 1983. [New York]: n.p., [1983]. 29 p.
Location: InIU.

Ny50   Activities of the New York Turn Verein, Founded in 1850. [New York]: n.p., 1933. [20 p.]
Note: Cover title: "A Sound Mind in a Sound Body." Promotional brochure.
Location: InIU.

Ny51   Bahn Frei. Organ des New York Turn Vereins. New York: New York Turn Verein, 1882-present.
Note: Newsletter of the New York Turnverein. It was published twice a month between 1882 and 1910, and monthly since then. The society suspended publication between October and December 1917. From 1882 to 1918 it was edited by Henry Metzner. It includes national and local Turner news, announcements, class schedules, and articles on physical education and health. The issue of February 1950 was the 100th anniversary publication of the society.
Location:
  GyAIZ: 1886.
  ICJ: 1893 -1898. (incomplete).
  NN: 1882-1954. (incomplete).
  American Turners New York: 1889-present. (incomplete).

New York (Bloomingdale): Bloomingdale Turnverein

Organized in the 1850s in Bloomingdale, a town which was later incorporated into New York City; was second largest in the New York District with 359 members in 1891; hosted national convention in 1858; maintained singing section, fencing, ladies auxiliary and library with approximately one thousand volumes; owned hall at 23 West 124th Street; left American Turnerbund with fifty members in 1926 and probably closed shortly thereafter.

Publications

Ny52 intentionally omitted.

Ny53   Bloomingdale Turner. Bloomingdale: Bloomingdale Turnverein, 1888-1894?
Note: Weekly newspaper of the Bloomingdale Turnverein. Cited in Arndt/Olson, v.1, p.346.

New York (Brooklyn): Brooklyn Eastern District Turnverein

Organized in 1853 as the Williamsburgh Turnverein, successor to unsuccessful societies started in 1848 and 1851; built hall in 1857; raised two companies for the 20th New York Volunteers in cooperation with the New York Turnverein during the Civil War; provided members to serve in militia restoring order during the New York

Draft Riots, and provided shelter in hall to African-Americans fleeing the violence; changed name to Brooklyn E.D. in 1884; had largest society in New York at beginning of century with about 700 members; merged with the Turnverein *Vorwärts* and American Turners Brooklyn to form the American Turners of Brooklyn in 1948.

Publications

Ny54 Goldenes Jubiläum des Turnvereins von Brooklyn, E.D., den 21., 27., 28., 29 Juni 1903. Brooklyn: Eagle Press, 1903. [48 p.]
Note: Fiftieth anniversary book of the Brooklyn E.D. Turners. Includes a history of the organization, list of committee members and officers, membership list and photographs. In German with a two-page summary of the history in English.
Location: DLC; NN.

Ny55 Souvenir Program of the Gymnastic Exhibition of the Armory, 13th Regiment, H.A.N.G.N.Y., Brooklyn, given by the Turnverein Brooklyn E.D. under the auspices of Company 13th Reg't, Wednesday, April 20, 1904. [New York]: n.p., [1904].
Note: Includes a program, essay on requirements for physical education in public schools and history of the society.
Location: NN.

Ny56 Statutes des Turnvereins von Brooklyn E.D. Brooklyn: Weidener Printing & Publishing Co., 1909.
Note: In German and English.
Location: NN.

New York: Central Turnverein of the City of New York

Organized in 1886 by members of the New York Turnverein; built hall on 67th Street near Third Avenue in 1889; had 1,406 members in 1887 and 1800 in 1889, although only 289 were active Turners; membership dropped to 1,000 in 1892 and declined constantly thereafter; closed building in 1893 due to financial troubles; affiliated with the New York Turnverein in 1956 when membership numbered only 17.

Archival Collection

Ny57 Central Turnverein of New York City, 1890-1895. 4 volumes.
Finding aid available in repository.
Location: NN.
Description: The records include a private journal, 1890-1895; a cash book, 1891-1893; a membership list, 1892; and records of the *Turnschule* (elementary school) and Kindergarten, 1893-94. Records are in German.

Publication

Ny58 Statuten of the Central Turn-Verein of the City of New York, Incorporated February 12th, 1886, Adopted: October 10th, 1927. New York: n.p., [1927]. 16 p.
Location: InIU.

New York (Long Island): Corona Turnverein

Organized about 1901; had small membership ranging from approximately thirty in 1907 to twelve in 1910; probably disbanded in 1913.

Publication

Ny59 Statuten des Corona Turn-Vereins in Kraft Getreten am 6. August 1902, Corona, N.Y. Corona: A.G. Berhardt, 1903. 19 p.
Location: InIU.

New York (Long Island): Long Island Turners, Inc.

Organized as Long Island City Turnverein in 1875; established a German Free School in 1890; merged with singing society *Frohsinn*; built new hall in 1929; became primarily singing society during the 1940s; reactivated gymnastic section in 1952; renovated hall in 1970 but lost it in 1980s; still active.

Archival Collection

Ny60 Long Island Turner Collection, 1894-present.
Location: Long Island Turners, Inc., New York.
Description: The collection includes minutes of the general meetings, 1968-pres; minutes of the meetings of the Singing and Turning Section, 1968-1974; a society flag, 1888; diplomas, 1894, 1923 and 1930; videotape from the 37th National Turnfest in St. Louis, 1948; and photographs.

Publications

Ny61 Geschichte des Gesang-Vereins "Frohsinn", 1871-1896, zur Erinnerung an das 25. Jährige Jubiläum, 24. und 25. Mai 1896. n.p., 1896.
Note: Includes a history of the organization.
Location: Long Island Turners, Inc.

Ny62 Long Island City Turnverein, 1875-1950, 75th Anniversary, April 29th, 1950 at the Turn Verein. n.p., 1950.

Note: Includes brief history.
Location: Long Island Turners, Inc.

Ny63   100th Anniversary Souvenir Journal, G.V. "Frohsinn" Singing Section of the Long Island City Turnverein, 1871-1971, Concert Ball, Long Island City Turn Hall. n.p., 1971.
Note: Includes brief history and program.
Location: Long Island Turners, Inc.

Ny64   100th Anniversary, Long Island City Turnverein, 1875-1975, Long Island City Turnhall. n.p., 1975.
Note: Includes brief history, program, and two photographs.
Location: Long Island Turners, Inc.

Ny65   Constitution and By-Laws of the Long Island Turners, Inc., June 6, 1991. n.p., 1991. 15 p.
Location: InIU; Long Island Turners, Inc.

New York: Mt. Vernon Turners, Inc.

Organized in 1891 under the name Mt. Vernon Turnverein one year before Mount Vernon attained city status; formed singing section during same year; built Turner hall in 1900 on corner of 10th and Stevenson Ave.; added to building in 1910; lost hall to fire in 1916, but rebuilt it in 1917; reduced activities to a minimum during World War I; organized ladies class in 1919 which remained active until 1968; merged with the Woodstock Turnverein of the Bronx in 1921; changed name to Mt. Vernon Turners, Inc. in 1947; joined by fifty-three members of the American Turners Bronx, Inc. in 1957; lost building in 1981 due to financial difficulties; merged with the New York Turnverein in 1986.

Archival Collection

Ny66   Mount Vernon Turner Records, 1904-1981. 4 volumes.
Location: American Turners New York
Description: Includes membership list, 1904-1967; lists of officers and committees, 1961-1981; minutes of membership and officers meetings, 1978-1983; and correspondence, 1969-1983.

Publications

Ny67   75th Diamond Jubilee and Anniversary, 1891 - 1966, Saturday, May 14th, 1966. n.p., [1966]. [76 p.]

Note: Includes a brief history of the society, list of committee members and officers, contemporary photographs.
Location: InIU.

Ny68   Mt. Vernon Turners, 80th Anniversary, Gala Dinner Dance Celebration held at the Turn Hall, 3 North 10th Avenue in Mount Vernon on Saturday, April 24th, 1971. n.p., [1971]. [64 p.]
Note: Includes a history of the society; program, and contemporary photographs.
Location: InIU.

Ny69   Statuten des Mount Vernon Turn-Vereins. New York: Theo. Gaus's Sons, 1902. 31 p.
Location: InIU.

Ny70   Constitution and By-Laws of the Mount Vernon Turn Verein. Mt. Vernon: Liberty Press, 1931. 25 p.
Location: InIU.

Ny71   Constitution and By-Laws of the Mount Vernon Turners, Inc. Mt. Vernon: Liberty Press, 1947. 29 p.
Location: InIU.

Ny72   The Turner News. Official Organ of the Mt. Vernon Turners, Inc. Mt. Vernon: Mt. Vernon Turners, 1925-1980s?
Note: Monthly newsletter for the society. Published from 1925 to 1937 under the name The Turn Verein News. Discontinued from 1937 to 1944 for financial reasons, then restarted under the name The Turner News. In 1974, the newsletter changed its name to Der Alte in honor of Friedrich Ludwig Jahn.
Location: InIU: May 1981.

Rochester: Rochester Turners, Inc.

Founded in 1852 under the name *Socialer* Turnverein, with drama, debating, and singing sections; started Sunday School in 1853; changed name to Rochester Turnverein in 1854; hosted national convention in 1860; organized day-school in 1861 with two full-time instructors teaching classes in English and German; reorganized school as independent "Real School Society" in 1867; purchased building for first hall on Clinton Ave. in 1869; built larger hall in 1883 to accomodate increased membership; formed ladies auxiliary and training school for girls in 1884; built new facility with swimming pool at 1550 Clinton in 1927; offered classes in lifesaving in cooperation with the Red Cross beginning in 1927; became sponsors of Boy Scout Troop in 1932; closed in 1955 due to financial difficulties brought on by mismanagement; reorganized in 1957; served as host of the American Turners national office from the mid-1950s through the 1960s; turned property over to American Turners in 1981 to settle debts; joined the Federation of German-American Societies in 1983; still active as social club, with activities restricted to the annual picnics and a newsletter which is published four times a year.

Publications

Ny73   Historical Journal, A Souvenir of the Centennial Celebration of the Rochester Turners, Inc., Rochester, N.Y., January 1st to December 31st, 1952. Rochester, n.p., [1952]. [88 p.]
Note: Cover title: "One Hundredth Anniversary, Rochester, New York, 1852[-] 1952." Includes a history of the club and women's auxiliary, articles on physical education, membership list, and photographs,
Location: InIU; NRU.

Ny74   Formal Opening of the Gymnasium and Club Rooms, Saturday and Sunday, December 3 and 4, 1927, The Rochester Turn Verein, Clinton Avenue N. corner Bastian Street. Rochester: Drexler Print, [1927]. [36 p.]
Note: Includes a history and contemporary photographs.
Location: InIU.

Ny75   Constitution of the Rochester Turners, Rochester, N.Y., Adopted February 17, 1941. Rochester: n.p., [1941]. 24 p.
Location: InIU.

Schenectady: Schenectady Turners, Inc.

Organized in 1891 with assistance of the Troy Turnverein; formed dramatic section and Turner *Männerchor* in same year; bought first hall in 1893 on South Center Street (Broadway); organized girls' class in 1896; dedicated new hall on Albany Street in 1904 which became the center of German activities in Schenectady; Turner singing section merged with the Beethoven *Männerchor* in 1911; purchased farm on Alplaus Creek to create a Turner Park in 1931; organized ladies chorus in 1936; suspended physical education activities in 1950s; suffered damage to hall in fire that destroyed the historical records in the 1960s; sold Turner Park in 1958 and the Turner hall in 1986 due to financial difficulties; still active as Turner chorus.

Publications

Ny76   Heck, Oswald E., ed. Geschichte des Schenectady Turnvereins für die Einweihung der neuen Turnhalle am 8., 9. und 10. Januar 1904, zu Schenectady, N.Y. [Schenectady]: n.p., 1905. 78 p.
Note: Dedication program for the new hall of the Schenectady Turnverein. Includes

a detailed history of the organization, and photographs of members and building.
Location: InIU, (photocopy); NSCH.

Ny77   50th Anniversary, Schenectady Turnverein, Gymnastic Exhibition, February 8th, Banquet February 15th, Concert February 22, Turner Hall, Schenectady, N.Y., 1891-1941. [Schenectady]: n.p.,1941. 42 p.
Note: Includes history of the organization, the Ladies Auxiliary, and Männerchor; articles on physical education; poems; and photographs.
Location: InIU.

Ny78   Turner Männerchor, 50th Anniversary, April, May 1948, Schenectady Turnverein, Schenectady, New York. [Schenectady]: n.p., [1948]. 30 p.
Note: Includes the history of the Turner *Männerchor*, the ladies chorus, the Schenectady Turnverein, principles of the American Turners; and contemporary photographs.
Location: InIU.

Ny79   100th Anniversary, 1881-1991, Schenectady Turn-Verein [Schenectady]: n.p., 1991. 12 p.
Note: Includes history of the organization, original charter, proclamation, and photographs.
Location: InIU; Schenectady Turners.

Ny80   Konstitution und Nebengesetze des Schenectady Turnvereins, Schenactady, N.Y., Gegründet den 19, Februar 1891, nebst Plattform, Principielle Beschlüsse und Statuten des Nordamerikansichen Turnerbundes, Revidiert und angenommen in der Vereinsversammlug vom 7. Mai 1929. Schenectady: n.p., 1926. [67 p.]
Note: Published in two sections: 1926 constitution of American Turnerbund, pp. 1-31; constitution of the society, pp. 1-35.
Location: InIU.

Ny81   Constitution and By-Laws of the Schenectady Turn Verein, Inc., Founded 1891 - Incorporated 1902, As Adopted in the Membership Meeting on April 20, 1961. [Rochester]: n.p., [1961]. 20 p.
Location: InIU.

Ny82   Schenectady Turner Topics. Schenectady: Schenectady Turners, 1933-??
Note: Newsletter of the Schenectady Turners. Includes local and national Turner news, class schedules, personal news, and articles pertaining to physical culture and health. No issues located.

Syracuse: Syracuse Turners, Inc.

Organized in 1854 as the *Socialer* Turn Verein, following unsuccessful attempts to start societies in 1848 and 1852; erected first building on Pond Street in 1858; members joined the New York Turner Regiment during the Civil War; built larger hall in 1863 on the corner of Lodi and John Streets; moved again in 1866 to the Center House between the Village of Salina and Syracuse; lost hall in fire in 1867; built new hall on Salina Street in 1869; organized ladies gymnastics classes and ladies auxiliary in 1884; started German school in 1890; hall became well known as a movie theater in the 1940s and 1950s; lost hall in fire in 1952; built new hall in same location in 1954, with bar, dinning hall, meeting rooms and bowling alleys but no gymnasium; still active as social society with bowling and golf as sports activities.

Archival Collection

Ny83   Syracuse Turners Collection, 1943-present.
Location: Syracuse Turners, Inc.
Description: Includes membership records, 1943-present, and minutes, 1961-present. Nearly all records were destroyed in the fire of 1952.

Publications

Ny84   Schmidt, Wilhelm. Fest-Ausgabe zur Fünfzig-jährigen Jubelfeier, 1854-1904, der Gründung des Syracuse Turnvereins und des dreissigsten Bezirks Turnfestes vom West New York Turnbezirk, abgehalten von 2ten bis 5ten Juli 1904, in Syracuse, N.Y. Im Auftrag des Syracuser Turn-Vereins geschrieben von Wilhelm Schmidt. Illustriert von Otto Schweikert. Syracuse: Prinzen Union Publ. Co., 1904. 27 p.
Location: MnV [microfilm]; PPB.

Ny85   125th Anniversary, 1854-1979, Syracuse Turners. [Syracuse]: n.p., 1979. [32 p.]
Note: Includes history of the organization, and many photographs.
Location: InIU; Syracuse Turners, Inc.

Ny86   140th Anniverary of the Syracuse Turners, 1854-1994, 110th Anniversary of the Ladies Auxiliary. [Syracuse]: n.p., 1994. 32 p.
Note: Includes histories of the society and the ladies auxiliary and photographs.
Location: InIU; Syracuse Turners, Inc.

Ny87   By-Laws of the Syracuse Turners, Inc., Organized as Society, May 15, 1854, Incorporated March 14, 1862, Reincorporated September 23, 1942. Syracuse, n.p., 1949. 20 p.
Location: InIU.

Troy: Troy Turnverein

Organized in 1852; split into the Troy *Freie Turngemeinde* and *Socialer* Turnverein in 1853; *Socialer* Turnverein disbanded in 1855; Turngemeinde founded German school; suspended activities during Civil War and resumed in 1866; changed name to Troy Turnverein in 1868; moved locations often until the organization of the *Germania* Hall Association, an umbrella organization for all German societies in Troy; moved into Germania Hall in 1891; played major role in introduction of physical education in the public school system; closed in 1938; Germania Hall Association is still active.

Publications

Ny88   Fest Zeitung zum 50 jährigen Jubiläum des Troy Turn-Vereins (Gegründet 1852) am 16.-18., August 1902. Troy: n.p., 1902.
Note: Cited in Pochmann #10999.

Ny89   Gedenkschrift zur Feier des Fünfundsiebzigjährigen Jubiläums des Troy Turn-Verein in der Germania-Halle, Troy, N.Y., 1., 2. und 3. Oktober 1927. [Troy]: n.p., 1927. 16 p.
Note: Cover title: "Diamond Jubilee Pageant Depicting the History of Physical Education Sponsored by the Troy Turn Verein, Saturday, Sunday, Monday-October 1st to 3rd, 1927, Troy, New York." Festival book for the seventy-fifth anniversary celebration. Includes a history of the society and photographs. In German.
Location: InIU.

Ny90   Program of the Grand Gymnastic and Acrobatic Exhibition sponsored by the Turn und Sport-Verein, Sunday May 19, 1935 at Germania Hall Troy, N.Y., and for. the Participation of the Great New England Turnfestival at Springfield, Massachusetts, June 14,15, 16, 1935. [Troy]: n.p., 1935.
Location: Private collection.

Utica: Utica Turnverein

Formally organized in 1854 following several years of Turner activities in the city; suspended activities during first years of the Civil War; resumed activities in 1863; reorganized in 1874 and 1882 as a result of declining membership; joined the American Turnerbund and incorporated in 1888; formed ladies class in 1893; dedicated first hall at 129-131 Lafayette Street in 1894; merged with *Germania* Turnverein (organized in 1868) in 1894; closed in 1938.

Archival Collection

Ny91   Utica Turnverein Records, 1888-1969. 1 linear foot.
Finding aid available from repository.
Location: NUTHi
Description: The records include minutes of the Utica Turnverein, 1888-1897, 1906, 1908-1917; 1 account book, 1890-1898; a 1969 taped interview with Walter Pietsch, a former president of the Utica Turners; and certificates from 1896-1915. Records prior to 1913 are in German.

Publications

Ny92   Utica Turn-Verein, Golden Jubilee Fair, At Männerchor Hall, October 17, 18, 19, 20, 21 and 22, 1904. Grand Concert with Mass Chorus, German Theatrical Entertainment, Grand Tableaux, Gymnastic Exercises and Fancy Drills. [Utica]: n.p., [1904]. [25 p.]
Note: Includes program of events, list of committees, history of the club. In English and German.
Location: InIU (photocopy).

Ny93   Rules and Regulations of the Utica Turn-Verein of Utica, New York. [Utica]: n.p., n.d.
Location: NUTHi.

Ny94   Utica Turn-Verein, Utica, N.Y., School Year 1913-1914, Opening September Eighth. [Utica]: n.p., [1913]. 4 p.
Note: Class schedule of the Utica Turn Verein for the 1913-1914 school year.
Location: InIU (photocopy).

OHIO

Akron: Akron Turner Club

Organized in 1885 as the Akron Turnverein; built Turner Hall on Grant Street in 1888; started women's auxiliary in 1904; built new hall in 1913; raised funds for German relief after World War I; changed name to Akron Turner Club, ca. 1940; built new hall outside of the city in Springfield Township in 1976; still active. There were two earlier, short-lived Turner societies in Akron: one was formed in the mid-1850s and closed by the beginning of the Civil War; the other was formed in the late 1860s, participated in an 1870 Turnfest in Cleveland, and closed shortly thereafter.

Archival Collection

Oh1   Akron Turner Club Records, ca. 1900-ca. 1976. 2 linear feet.
Preliminary inventory available from Indiana Univ.-Purdue Univ. Indianapolis.
Location: Akron Turner Club.
Description: Included are membership lists and dues records, 1900-1926; scattered
minutes, correspondence, and by-laws, 1930s-1950s; and scrapbooks and photograph
albums.

Publications

Oh2   Silbernes Jubliäum des Akron Turnverein am 24. und 26. Juli 1910.
Cleveland: Chas. Lezius Printing Co., 1910. 32 p.
Note: Cover title: "Festschrift zum Silbernen Jubilaeum des Akron Turnverein, 1885-
1910, am 24. und 26. Juli, 1910." Festival book for the twenty-fifth anniversary
celebration. Includes a detailed history of the Akron Turners and photographs.
Location: InIU; Akron Turners.

Oh3   Festschrift des Akron Turnverein zur Einweihung seiner Neuen Turnhalle
und Vereinsräumlichkeiten, Donnerstag Abend, den 29. Mai und Sonntag, den 1. Juni,
1913. n.p., [1913]. 35 p.
Note: Festival book published for the dedication of the new hall.
Location: Akron Turners.

Oh4   Golden Anniversary of the Akron Turnverein, 1885-1935. n.p., [1935].
39 p.
Note: Includes history of the society and pictures of members and activities.
Location: InIU; Akron Turners.

Oh5   Centennial Anniversary of the Akron Turner Club, 1885 - 1985, Banquet and
Dance, July 27, 1985. n.p., 1985. [55 p.]
Note: Includes history of the club and pictures of members and activities.
Location: InIU; Akron Turners.

Oh6   Constitution of the Akron Turner Club of Akron, Ohio, Founded July 26th
1885 Akron, O., Revised Jan. 7, 1922. Akron: Columbia Printing Co., [1922]. 47 p.
Note: In English and German.
Location: InIU.

204 American Turners Research Guide

Oh7 Constitution of the Akron Turner Club of Akron, Ohio, Founded July 26, 1885 - Akron, Ohio, Revised January 6, 1929. Akron: Exchange Printing Co., [1929]. 49 p.
Note: In German and English.
Location: InIU.

Oh8 Constitution and By-Laws of the Akron Turner Club. Mimeographed. n.p., [1947]. 6 p.
Location: InIU.

Oh9 Constitution, The Akron Turners Club, 547 South Munroe Road, Tallmadge, Ohio, Reprinted 1991. n.p., 1991. 13 p.
Location: InIU.

Oh10 Statuten der Damen Sektion des Akron Turnvereins. n.p., n.d.
Note: In German and English.
Location: Private collection.

Oh11 Statuten der Damen Sektion des Akron Turnvereins, Akron, OH. n.p., 1912. 8 p.
Note: In German.
Location: Private collection.

Oh12 Grand Gymnastic Exhibition of the Akron Turners with the Assistance of the STV of Cleveland at Music Hall, German-American Co. Building, Friday, March 27, 1908, at 8 p.m. n.p., [1908]. 8 p.
Location: Private collection.

Oh13 Quine, C. R. The Old Wolf Ledge. n.p., 1958. 15 p.
Note: Contains a history of the German section of Akron.
Location: Akron Turners.

Oh14 Turners Zeitung. Akron: Akron Turner Club. 1930s?-1960s?
Note: Monthly newsletter of the Akron Turner Club.
Location: Akron Turner Club: 1936-1938 (incomplete); 1956.

Cincinnati

There have been eight Turner societies in Cincinnati since the founding of the Cincinnati Turngemeinde in 1848. At the high point in 1905 there were five societies operating with a total of about 1200 members: the Cincinnati Turngemeinde, the West Cincinnati Turnverein (1881), the North Cincinnati Turnverein (1881), the newly-formed Turnverein Norwood (1905), and the independent Northwest Turnverein, also known as the *Deutsch Ungarische* (German-Hungarian) Turngemeinde (1886). Subsequently two other short-lived societies were formed, the *Allgemeiner Arbeiter Turn & Athletic Club* (1911-1917) and Turnverein Jahn (1923-1925). All but the Cincinnati Turngemeinde had closed by the mid-1930s.

Cincinnati: Cincinnati Central Turners Inc.

Organized as the Cincinnati Turngemeinde in the fall of 1848 during meetings with German revolutionary leader Friedrich Hecker; built first hall in 1850, which became known as the German House because of its role as a major center of German social life; larger building erected on same site on Walnut Street in 1859 and remodelled in 1890; joined national Turnerbund in 1851; played prominent role in the planning of the Turner colony at New Ulm, MN in 1855-1857; members involved in major anti-German riot following Turner picnic near Covington, Kentucky in 1856; established and equipped playgrounds for schools in Cincinnati in late 1850s; members formed Turner Regiment in April 1861, which later became part of the 9th Ohio Regiment, known as the "Turner Regiment;" formed women's society in 1877; maintained theater, choral group, band, shooting section, and commercial school through late 19th century; hosted national Turnfests in 1852, 1889 and 1909; sold downtown building in early 1970s and society relocated to new building on the northern outskirts of the city; still active.

Archival Collection

Oh15   Cincinnati Central Turners, Inc. Records, 1848-1948. 56 vols., 4 boxes. Finding aid available from repository.
Location: OCHi
Description: Included are minutes, 1856-1936 (incomplete); membership records, 1848-1933; financial records, 1867-1927; photographs and newspaper clippings; records of the *Kranken Committee* (Sick Committee), 1869-1874; records of the campaign to save Turner Hall, 1919-1922; and German-language books from the Turners' library. Records prior to 1920 are primarily in German.

Publications

Oh16   Becker, E. *"Das antike und moderne Lustspiel"* Atlantis: Eine Monatsschrift für Wissenschaft, Politik und Poesie. Jan-Juni, 1856.

Note: Subtitle: "*Nach einem in der Cincinnati Turnhalle gebrachten Vortrag von E. Becker, Redacteur der Turnzeitung.*"
Location: OCU.

Oh17   The First Hundred Years, 1848[-]1948, Cincinnati Central Turners, the Oldest Turner Society of the American Turners. [Cincinnati]: n.p., [1948]. 90 p.
Note: Includes history of Cincinnati Turners, articles on the history of Turnerism, and photographs.
Location: InIU.

Oh18   Cincinnati Central Turners 125th Anniversary, Dinner and Dance, November 24th 1973. n.p.: n.p., [1973]. [15 p.]
Note: Includes a history called "Years of Turnerism," and photographs of the board members.
Location: InIU.

Oh19   Konstitution und Nebengesetze des Turner Bauvereins, No. 3, Gegründet am 1. February 1879. Cincinnati: Schweizer & Co., 1879. 30 p.
Note: Principles and by-laws of the Turner Building Association no. 3, in German and English.
Location: OCHi.

Oh20   Verfassung der Cincinnati Turngemeinde, Gegruendet am 21. November 1848. Cincinnati: *Folksblatt* Office, [1914]. 10 p.
Location: OCHi.

Oh21   Katalog der Bibliothek der Turngeimende in Cincinnati, April 1861. Cincinnati: Friedrich Lang & Co., 1861. 48 p.
Note: Catalog of the Cincinnati Turngemeinde library. Includes call numbers and titles of works in the library.
Location: OCHi.

Oh22   Turn-Gemeinde Cincinnati. Liederbücher für Turner. Cincinnati: n.p., 1915. 58 p.
Note: Song book for the Cincinnati Turner Society.
Location: OCU.

Oh23   Turn-Zeitung. Cincinnati: Cincinnati Turngemeinde, 1851.
Subtitle: *Herausgegeben von der Turngemeinde zu Cincinnati.*

Note: Monthly newsletter. Among the editors were Heinrich Esmann, Wilhelm Rothacker and Gustav Tafel.
Location: NN: v.1 no.1 - 10 (January-October 1851).

Oh24   Turner News. Cincinnati: Cincinnati Turngemeinde, ca. 1927-1932?
Note: Newsletter of the Cincinnati Turngemeinde.
Location: InIU: v.5, no.7 (April 1932).

Cincinnati: North Cincinnati Gymnasium

Organized in 1881 as the *Nord* Cincinnati Turnverein; built hall at Vine & Daniels in the 1880s; was the largest society in Cincinnati with 900 members in 1905; changed name to North Cincinnati Gymnasium, ca. 1918; withdrew from national Turnerbund in 1921; closed in mid-1930s.

Publications

Oh25   Nord Cincinnati Turnverein. Silver Jubilee ... Cincinnati: n.p., 1906.
Note: Cited in Pochmann #7739.

Oh26   Nord Cincinnati Turnverein. List of Members, Rules ... for 1903-04. Cincinnati: n.p., 1903.
Location: Cited in Pochmann #7738.

Oh27   Turner Leben, Turner Life. Cincinnati: Nord Cincinnati Turn Verein, 1901-1915?
Subtitle: *Monatlich Herausgegeben vom Nord-Cincinnati Turn Verein.*
Note: Monthly newsletter of the society. Includes local and national Turner news, society news, advertisements and reports of festivals. In English and German.
Location:
    OCHi: v. 1 (1901); November 1914 - October 1915?

Cleveland: Cleveland East Side Turners

Organized in 1849 as the Cleveland Turnverein; occupied series of halls during 1850s; hosted convention of the American Turnerbund in 1853; affiliated with the *Freie Männer* Verein, a free thought society, in mid-1850s; had a number of members join the New Ulm, MN Turner colony in 1856; suspended activities during the Civil War; reorganized in 1864; built new hall on Ohio St. in 1866 which became center for

German theater, music and political rallies into the 1880s; dissolved because of financial problems in 1876, then reorganized as the *Germania* Turnverein and continued to operate the Ohio St. hall; built new hall on Erie St. in 1888; merged with *Vorwärts* Turnverein in 1908 to form the *Germania Turnverein Vorwärts*; sold Erie St. property and invested the funds in enlarging the *Vorwärts* Turner hall on the eastside; changed name to Cleveland East Side Turnverein, ca. 1941; still active.

Archival Collection

Oh28   East Side Cleveland Turner Collection.
Preliminary inventory available from Indiana Univ.-Purdue Univ. Indianapolis.
Location: Cleveland East Side Turners.
Description: Collection includes minutes of board and annual meetings, 1935-1940 (incomplete); instructors' reports, 1943-1952; records of district festivals from the 1930s; typed proceedings of the 1950 Lake Erie District convention; photographs of individual members from the nineteenth century; and German books from the Turnverein library.

Publications

Oh29   Festschrift des Germania Turnvereins "Vorwaerts" zur Einweihung der Neuen Turnhalle und des Neuen Vereinshauses Unter Mitwirkung der Deutschen Gesangvereine Clevelands, Sonntag, 6. November 1910. Cleveland: n.p., 1910. [ca. 50 p.]
Note: Dedication program for the new hall of the Germania Turnverein *Vorwärts*. Includes history of both clubs, pictures, and essay on the value of systematic physical training.
Location: OCIWHi.

Oh30   Souvenir Program, Physical Culture Revue, Sunday Afternoon, April 29, '28, Cleveland, Public Auditorium. [Cleveland]: n.p., [1928]. 72 p.
Note: Includes essays on the beginning of the Turner movement and the history of the *Germania Turnverein Vorwärts*, program for the event, and photographs.
Location: InIU; OCIWHi.

Oh31   Program, Germania Turnverein Vorwaerts, Physical Culture Revue, Sunday Afternoon, April 28, 1929, Cleveland Public Auditorium. [Cleveland]: n.p., [1929].
Location: InIU.

Oh32   Constitution and Nebengesetze, Germania Turnvereins "Vorwärts", Cleveland, Ohio, Revised und angenommen am 4. und 11. Mai 1914: Constitution and

By-Laws, Germania Turnverein Vorwärts, Cleveland, Ohio, Revised and adopted May 4th and 11th, 1914. Indianapolis: Cheltenham-Aetna Press, [1914]. [68 p.]
Note: Published in two sections: *Germania Turnverein Vorwarts* constitution, in German and English, pp. 1-36; constitution of the North American Turnerbund, in German, pp. 1-32.
Location: InIU; OClWHi.

Oh33 Fundamental Principles of the American Turnerbund and Constitution and By-laws of the Germania Turnverein Vorwaerts, Cleveland, O., Revised and Adopted July 13, 1931. [Cleveland]: n.p., [1931]. 20 p.
Note: Cover title: "Constitution and By-Laws of the Germania Turnverein Vorwaerts."
Location: InIU.

Oh34 Fundamental Principles of the American Turners and Constitution and By-laws of the Cleveland East Side Turners, Cleveland, Ohio, January 15, 1947. [Cleveland]: n.p., [1947]. 20 p.
Note: Cover title: "Constitution and By-Laws of the Cleveland East Side Turners, Branch of American Turners, East 55th Street, Cleveland, Ohio."
Location: InIU.

Oh35 Souvenir Program, Golden Jubilee, Cleveland East Side Turners Male Chorus, Sunday, May 5, 1946 at the Cleveland East Side Turners Auditorium. [Cleveland]: n.p., [1946]. 36 p.
Note: Includes a history of the choir and photographs.
Location: OClWHi.

Oh36 G.T.V. Turner. Cleveland: *Germania Turnverein Vorwärts*, 1921?-1930s.
Note: Monthly publication. Includes local and national Turner news, announcements, and schedules.
Location: InIU: December 1936.

Oh37 Cleveland East-Side Turners. [Cleveland]: n.p., [1940]. 12 p.
Note: Promotional booklet for the East Cleveland Turners describing the activities and facilities of the society.
Location: InIU.

Cleveland: Germania Turnverein

See history of the Cleveland East Side Turners.

Publications

Oh38   Germania Turnverein, 1876 [-] 1901, Silbernes Jubilaeum, Donnerstag, den 10, October 1901. Cleveland: Chas. Lezius, Printer, 1901. [32 p.]
Note: Includes history of the organization and numerous photographs.
Location: InIU.

Oh39   Statuten des Germania Turn-Vereins von Cleveland, Ohio. Cleveland: C. Lezius, 1890. 22 p.
Location: InIU.

Cleveland: Swiss Gymnastic Society of Cleveland

Organized in 1891 as the Schweizer Turnverein to serve the Swiss population of Cleveland; operated as independent society rather than joining the North American Turnerbund; changed name to the Swiss Gymnastic Society of Cleveland, ca. 1940; closing date unknown.

Archival Collection

Oh40   Swiss Turner Collection, Cleveland, 1884-1953. (9 volumes).
Finding aid available from repository.
Location: OClWHi.
Description: Includes minutes of the society, 1900-1953 (incomplete); minutes of the Swiss Hall Company, 1930-1939; minutes of the *General Versammlung (*membership meetings*)*, 1895-1940 (incomplete); and minutes of the mutual aid society (*Hülfs-Gesellschaft*), 1884-1910. Records before 1930 are in German.

Publications

Oh41   By-laws of the Turner's Aid of the Swiss American Gymnastic Association. [Cleveland]: n.p., n.d. 7 p.
Location: OClWHi.

Oh42   Constitution of the Swiss Gymnastic Society of Cleveland.[Cleveland]: n.p., n.d. 22 p.
Location: OClWHi.

Oh43   Schweizer American Turnverein, Statuten und Reglemente, Neudruck im April, 1914. West Hoboken, N.J.: Rudolph Grund: [1914]. 36 p.
Location: OClWHi.

Oh44   Statuten der Schweizer American Turners Hülfskasse. Cleveland: Michael und Rank Printers, 1922. 12 p.
Note: Constitution of the Swiss Turners' Benefit Fund.
Location: OClWHi.

Oh45   Schweizer American Turnverein. Statuten und Reglements, Neudruck im April 1932. Midland Park, N.J.: Binz Printing Co., [1932]. 35 p.
Location: OClWHi.

Cleveland: American Turners S.T.V. Cleveland

Organized in 1867 as the *Socialer* Turnverein by members of the Cleveland Turnverein to serve the large German population on the city's westside; started women's auxiliary in 1868 and a singing society in 1872; built first hall by renovating building previously used for the *Schule der Freie Gemeinde* (Free-Thought Society School) in 1872; built new hall on Lorain Ave, 1883; rebuilt hall in 1900 following fire; expanded hall with addition of new gymnasium, 1940; lost hall in fire in early 1980s; purchased old school building on Lawn St. to serve as new hall; still active.

Archival Collection

Oh46   American Turners S.T.V. Cleveland Collection, 1954-present.
Preliminary inventory available from Indiana Univ.-Purdue Univ. Indianapolis.
Location: American Turners S.T.V. Cleveland.
Description: The collection consists of photographs and newspaper clippings on the society; national bowling tournament programs, 1954-present; and scattered issues of the society's newsletter.

Publications

Oh47   Socialer Turnverein, Goldenes Jubiläum, Sonntag und Montag, 8. und 9. April 1917, Cleveland, Ohio, 1867-1917. [Cleveland]: West Side Printing House, 1917. [44 p.]
Note: Includes a detailed history of the society and its sections, lists of members and class participants, and numerous photographs.
Location: InIU.

Oh48   American Turners S.T.V., 100th Anniversary, 1867-1967, Saturday Evening, November 18, 1967. [Cleveland]: n.p., [1967]. 12 p.
Note: Includes history and photographs of the society.
Location: InIU; American Turners S.T.V. Cleveland.

Oh49   Elf Gebote des Bären Riege des Sozialen Turn-Vereins, Cleveland, Ohio. [Cleveland]: Rud. Schmidt, Print, [1904]. 6 p.
Note: Constitution of the *Baer* Section of the Cleveland *Socialer* Turn Verein.
Location: InIU.

Oh50   Constitution and By-Laws of the Socialer Turn-Verein, Affiliated with the American Turner -Bund, Accepted August 23rd, 1934. Cleveland: n.p., [1934]. 12 p.
Note: Cover title: "*Socialer* Turnverein Cleveland: Constitution and By-laws, Effective August 23rd, 1934."
Location: InIU.

Oh51   S.T.V. News. Cleveland: *Socialer* Turn Verein, 1940s?-1950s?
Note: Monthly publication of the *Socialer* Turnverein Cleveland. Includes national and local Turner news, announcements and classs schedules.
Location: InIU: January 1947-December 1948.

Cleveland: Turnverein Vorwärts

See history of the Cleveland East Side Turners.

Publications

Oh52   Constitution des Turnverein "Vorwärts" von Cleveland, Ohio. Cleveland: Carl Lezius, *Deutsch-Englische Buchdruckerei*: 1895. 32 p.
Location: InIU.

Oh53   Statuten der Damen-Sektion des Turnverein "Vorwärts", Angenommen 6 Mai 1902. Cleveleland: C. Lezius, Printer: 1902. 8 p.
Note: Constitution of the ladies auxiliary.
Location: InIU.

Oh54   Turnbezirk Lake Erie, Turnverein Vorwärts, Cleveland, O. [Cleveland]: n.p., 1907. 22 p.

Note: List of members of the Cleveland *Vorwärts* Turnverein and principles of the Turnerbund.
Location: InIU.

Dayton: Dayton Liederkranz Turners

Organized in 1853 as the Dayton Turngemeinde; purchased former school building on Montgomery St. to serve as hall in 1861; had four-fifths of its members serve in the Union Army; built new hall on Commercial and Fourth Streets in 1877; formed women's auxiliary in 1913; changed name to Dayton Turner Association in 1925; merged with the Dayton *Liederkranz*, a singing society, to form the Dayton *Liederkranz* Turners in 1952; dropped out of American Turners in 1962; still active as a singing society.

Archival Collection

Oh55   Dayton Liederkranz Turners Records, 1882-present.
Preliminary inventory available from Indiana Univ.-Purdue Univ. Indianapolis.
Location: Dayton Liederkranz Turners.
Description: The records include minute books, 1899-1934; treasurers' books, 1882-1922; membership records, 1880s-1910s; photographs, certificates, programs and posters from the society's events; and national reports, convention minutes and Turnfest publications, 1920s-1950s. Records prior to 1919 are in German.

Publications

Oh56   The Dayton Turner Association, 75th Anniversary Banquet, Sunday, March 18th, 1928, at 6 p.m., Reception, Monday, March 19th at 8 p.m., Turner Hall.
[Dayton]: n.p., 1928. 8 p.
Note: Includes brief historical account and lists long-term members, members in 1853, and members who served in the Union Army during the Civil War.
Location: InIU:

Oh57   Dayton Turner. Dayton: Dayton Turn-Gemeinde, 1914-1930?
Note: Monthly. Includes local and national Turner news, announcements and schedules.
Location:
    InIU: v.5 (August 1919); v. 11, no.11 (March 1927).
    Dayton Liederkranz Turners: v. 5 (1919); v. 11 (1927)-v. 12 (1929). Incomplete.

Toledo: American Turners Toledo

Organized in 1926 to serve the large German immigrant population that moved to Toledo following World War I; known as the Toledo *Turn und Sport Verein* and the German-American Athletic Club during the 1930s; built first hall on Collingwood Avenue, 1934; joined other German-American organizations and moved to common location on Shawnee in the 1970s; still active as social organization.

Archival Collection

Oh58   American Turners Toledo Records, 1929-present.
Inventory available from repository.
Location: OTU.
Description: The records include scrapbooks of newspaper articles, photographs, and memorabilia, 1929-1986; minute books of the bowling section, 1946-present; films of society activities, early 1940s; and programs for national and local Turner and German-American events, 1930s-1980s.

Publications

Oh59   Toledo Turn und Sportverein, 5. Stiftungsfest, 6 und 7, Juni 1931, Festprogram. [Toledo]: n.p., [1931]. [30 p.]
Note: Program for the fifth anniversary festival. Includes a history of the society and photographs.
Location: OTU.

Oh60   German-American Athletic Club, Turn-und Sportverein, 5th Anniversary, Athletic Festival, Toledo, Ohio, June 6-7, 1931 at the Scott High Stadium, Swiss Hall. [Toledo]: n.p., [1931]. 35 p.
Note: Includes a history and photographs of the Toledo Turners.
Location: Private collection.

Oh61   German-American Athletic Club, Turn und Sport Verein, 10th Anniversary Athletic Festival, Toledo, Ohio, 1936. [Toledo]: n.p., 1936. [15 p.]
Location: OTU.

Oh62   Official Souvenir Book, Toledo Turnverein, June 21-23, 1944. [Toledo]: n.p., [1944]. 25 p.
Location: OTU.

Oh63   Toledo Turner Society Presents, Silver Anniversary Presentation, International Soccer Game, Eintracht Frankfurt A/M vs. Ohio-Michigan All Stars, Toledo Glass Bowl, Sunday, May 13, 1951. [Toledo]: Engray Printing, 1951. [48 p.]
Note: Includes brief history of Toledo Turners, roster of German and American teams and program.
Location: InIU.

Oh64   Constitution and By-Laws, American Turners Toledo, Toledo, Ohio. [Toledo]: n.p., [1965?]. 25 p.
Location: InIU.

Oh65   Constitution and By-Laws, American Turners-Toledo, Ratified & Effective 3/16/75, Toledo, Ohio. [Toledo]: n.p., [1975]. 21 p.
Location: InIU.

Toledo: Toledo Turnverein

Active in the late 1850s; reorganized in 1866; left national Turnerbund in 1893; closed, ca. 1913.

Archival Collection

Oh66   Toledo Turnverein Records, 1858-1866. 2 items.
Location: InIU.
Description: Statutes and description of the Toledo School Turners Class, written by the instructor, E.W.E.(?) Koch, December 1, 1858, 6p. In English. Includes photograph of Koch with women's class, 1866.

Toledo: Toledo Turnverein Vorwärts

Organized in the 1880s; dedicated new hall in 1895; closed in early 1900s.

Archival Collection

Oh67   Toledo Turnverein Vorwärts Memoir, 1974. 5p.
Location: OT; InIU (photocopy).
Description: Memoirs written by Emil C. Konopka (born in 1885) about his childhood and youth at the Turnverein *Vorwärts* in Toledo. Mentions many names of members and teachers; written in 1974.

Publication

Oh68   Kind, Richard, ed. <u>Dedication of the New Turner Hall, March 12, 13, & 14</u>
<u>1895, Under the Auspices of the Toledo Turnverein Vorwärts</u>. [Toledo]: n.p., 1895.
16 p.
Note: Includes the dedication program and a brief description of the new hall of the
Toledo Turner Association. In English and German.
Location: OT; OTU; InIU (photocopy).

OREGON

Portland: Portland Socialer Turnverein

Organized in 1858 as the Portland Turnverein; acquired first hall in 1863; dissolved
and reformed as the Portland *Sozialer* Turnverein in 1871; sponsored art school,
theater, singing section, and sick benefit society by the 1870s; built halls at 4th &
Yamhill Streets in 1875 and on Southwest 13th St. in 1914; advocated German-
American march on Washington to demand American neutrality in 1916; came under
extended surveillance for suspected pro-German activities by the Bureau of
Investigation in 1917-1918; had 250 members in 1908 and nearly 200 in late 1930s;
resigned from American Turnerbund in 1940 and may have closed in the 1950s.

Archival Collection

Or1   Architectural plans of the Portland Turner Hall, S.W. 13th Ave. And S.W.
Main St., Portland. Claussen and Claussen, Architects. 58 plans on 38 sheets.
Location: OrHi.

Publications

Or2   <u>Gedenkblätter zur Feier des Goldenen Jubiläums der Turnverein Portland</u>
<u>und 37jährigen Stiftungsfestes des Portland Sozialen Turnvereins, 1858-1908.</u>
<u>Portland Turnverein, 1858-1871, Portland Sozialer Turnverein, 1871 - 1908,</u>
<u>Portland, Ore., den 20. und 21. September 1908</u>. [Portland]: n.p., 1908. 19 p.
Note: Includes detailed history of Turnerism in Portland, list of officers, and
photographs.
Location: InIU (photocopy).

Or3   <u>Constitution des Portland Socialen Turnvereins (Gegründet den 21. August</u>
<u>1871) nebst Incorporations=Papieren des Vereins. Angenommen den 16. Februar</u>

<u>1899</u>. Portland, Oregon: n.p., 1899. 38 p.
Location: InIU.

PENNSYLVANIA

Ambridge: Harmonie Männerchor, Gesang und Turn Verein

Organized in 1904 as an independent society; joined the American Turnerbund as the Harmony Gymnastic Club in the late 1920s; changed name to Harmonie *Männerchor, Gesang and Turn Verein* in 1930s; became primarily a singing society in following years; left American Turners in late 1960s; possibly still active as singing society in the 1980s.

Publication

Pa1   Constitution and By-Laws of Harmonie Maennerchor, Gesang and Turn Verein of Ambridge, Penna.   Revised and Adopted, November 26, 1945. n.p., 1945. 24 p.
Location: InIU.

Beaver Falls: Beaver Falls Turners

History

Organized in 1871 as the Beaver Falls Turnverein; built first hall in 1880; lost hall to fire and built new one in 1895; suspended gym classes during the Depression; attained membership of 1250 in 1947; still active as social society.

Archival Collection

Pa2   Beaver Falls Turners Collection, 1886-1988. 22 ledgers and 1 box.
Finding aid available from repository.
Location: PPiHi..
Description: The records consist of minutes of meetings, 1886-1944; membership records, 1901-1945; financial records, 1922-1945; and records of the ladies auxiliary, 1944-1988. Records prior to 1918 are predominately in German.

Publications

Pa3   Constitution des Beaver Falls Turnvereins von Beaver Falls, PA. Pittsburgh:
Volz Brothers, 1884. 40 p.
Location: InIU.

Pa4   Constitution and By-Laws of the Beaver Falls Turn Verein, Revised and
Adopted June 5, 1922. n.p., [1922]. 25 p.
Location: InIU.

Pa5   Constitution and By-Laws of the Beaver Falls Turn Verein, Revised and
Adopted January 1, 1944. n.p., [1944]. 22 p.
Location: InIU.

Charleroi: Charleroi Turn Verein

Organized in 1905; had three hundred members in 1925 and an average of two
hundred members throughout the 1940s to 1960s; closed in 1982.

Publication

Pa6   Constitution of the Charleroi Turn-Verein of Charleroi, Pa. Pittsburgh:
Sonntagsbote, 1935. 48 p.
Note: Published in two sections: in English, pp. 1-24; in German, pp. 1-24.
Location: InIU.

Erie: East Erie Turners

Organized in 1874 as the Erie Turn Verein; purchased property on 9th and Parade and
built first hall in 1889; became East Erie Turners in 1919; built current hall in 1926;
opened summer park, Turnwald, in 1950; has been an independent society since its
founding; still active as social oranization.

Archival Collection

Pa7   East Erie Turners. Records, 1911-present.
Preliminary inventory available from Indiana Univ.-Purdue Univ. Indianapolis.
Location: East Erie Turner Hall.
Description: The records include minutes of society meetings, 1914-1981

(incomplete); financial records, 1911, 1974-1992; membership lists, 1974-1989; programs and clippings, 1950s; and building plans, 1920s.

Publication

Pa8 Our 100th Year Centennial, 1880-1980, East Erie Turners. [Erie]: n.p., [1980].
Note: Includes brief history of the society.
Location: PEM; InIU(photocopy); East Erie Turners.

Homestead: Eintracht Music and Turn Hall Association

Founded in 1886 as the *Turn und Gesang-Verein Eintracht von* Homestead; reached peak membership of 380 in 1925; had average membership of two hundred in the 1940s and 1950s; still active as social club.

Publications

Pa9 Revision of By-Laws of the Eintacht Music and Turn Hall Association of Homestead, PA, Adopted June 28, 1921. Pittsburgh: Pittsburgh Printing Co., 1921. 57 p.
Note: In English and German.
Location: InIU.

Pa10 Revision of By-Laws of the Eintacht Music and Turn Hall Association, Homestead, Pennsylvania. n.p.: Weaverling Printing Co., 1950. 17 p.
Location: InIU.

Johnstown: Johnstown Turners

Organized in 1866 as the Johnstown Turnverein by members of the Teutonia Literary Club; Turner hall destroyed and twelve members killed in Johnstown Flood in 1889; rebuilt hall with financial support from the American Turnerbund in 1893; hosted national convention in 1944; still active.

Publications

Pa11 100th Anniversary, Johnstown Turners, July 30 & 31, 1966, Turner Hall, Railroad and Jackson Street. Johnstown: Valley Printing Company, 1966. [36 p.]

Note: Includes a history of the society, and photographs.
Location: InIU.

Pa12   Allgemeine Grundsätze des Amerikanischen Turnerbundes, sowie Statuten,
allgemeine Bestimmungen und Geschäfts-Ordnung des Johnstown Turn-Vereins,
Johnstown, Pa., Gegründet am 27. Juli 1866, Inkorporiert am 8. Juni 1868.
Johnstown: Schubert Press, 1923. 23 p.
Location: InIU.

Pa13   General Principles of the American Turners together with the Statutes, Rules
and Regulations and Order of Business of the Johnstown Turner Society, Johnstown,
PA, Founded July 27, 1866, Incorporated June 8, 1868. Johnstown: W.H. Raab &
Son, Inc., [ca.1940]. 32 p.
Location: InIU.

Pa14   Constitution and By-Laws of the Turn-Verein of Johnstown, PA. n.p., 1983.
16 p.
Location: InIU.

McKeesport: McKeesport Turners

Organized in 1880 and merged with the Harmony Singing Society to form the
McKeesport *Turn und Gesang Verein*; built hall in 1882; hired first permanent
instructor, Adam Doelha, in 1892, and he served as both Turnverein instructor and
Supervisor of Physical Training in the McKeesport Public Schools, 1898-1929; built
Turner Park outside of the city in 1925, but sold it to the city because of financial
problems in 1931; built new hall in 1966; still active.

Publications

Pa15   Golden Jubilee of the McKeesport Turn-und Gesang Verein, 1880[-]1930,
October Eighteenth and Nineteenth Nineteen Hundred and Thirty. n.p., 1930. [16 p.]
Note: Includes a brief history of the society, photographs and lists of officers.
Location: InIU.

Pa16   Dedication Program, McKeesport Turners, Saturday, May 28, 1966. n.p.,
1966. [44 p.]
Note: Includes a brief history of the society.
Location: InIU.

Pa17   Leistungs-Tabellen und Rangordnungen am Schau-und Preis-Turnfest abgehalten am 10. und 11. Juni 1906 in McKeesport, PA. Pittsburgh: Allied Printing, [1906]. 8 p.
Location: InIU.

Pa18   Constitution and By-Laws of the McKeesport Turn-und Gesang- Verein, McKeesport, Pa. Pittsburgh: Fischer & Faeth, 1937. 19 p.
Location: InIU.

Pa19   Constitution and By-Laws of the McKeesport Turn-und Gesang-Verein, McKeesport, PA, Revised May 1, 1949. n.d., [1949]. 27 p.
Location: InIU.

Pa20   Constitution and By-Laws of the McKeesport Turn und Gesang Verein, Revised June 8, 1969. McKeesport: n.p., [1969]. 28 p.
Location: InIU.

Monaca: Monaca Turn Verein

Organized in 1883; built hall at 7th St. and Pacific Ave. in 1880s; opened new hall in 1981; had more than five hundred members in 1980; hosted national convention in 1984; still active.

Publications

Pa21   Constitution and By-Laws of the Monaca Turn Verein, January 1, 1948, 699 Pacific Avenue, Monaca, Pennsylvania. Rochester: Henderson Print,[1948]. 21 p.
Location: InIU.

Pa22   Constitution and By-Laws of the Monaca Turn Verein. July 1, 1982. 1700 Brodhead Road, Monaca, Pennnsylvania. Rochester: Henderson Printing Co., 1982. 21 p.
Location: InIU, Monaca Turn Verein.

Monessen: Monessen Turn Verein

Organized in 1905; built hall in 1909; left American Turnerbund in early 1930s; had average membership of two hundred in the 1950s; closed in 1966.

Publications

Pa23   50th Anniversary of Monessen Turners, Sunday, October 30, 1955, Turner Hall, 2nd Donner Ave., Monessen, Pa. 6:30 p.m. n.p., [1955]. [24 p.]
Note: Includes a brief history of the society and the American Turners.
Location: InIU.

Pa24   Constitution & By-Laws of the Monessen Turn Verein. n.p., 1947. 9 p.
Location: InIU.

Monongahela: Monongahela Turners

Organized as the *Eintracht Gesangverein* in 1889; became the *Turn und Gesang Verein Eintracht* in 1890; built hall on E. Main St., 1900; influential in starting physical education in the public schools, 1904, and provided some of the first instructors; supported singing, drama, debate and mutual benefit sections; changed name to Monongahela Turners in 1945; still active.

Archival Collection

Pa25   Monongahela Turners Records, 1894-1943.
Finding aid available from repository.
Location: PPiHi.
Description: The records include minutes, 1894-1943; membership records, 1899-1923; financial records, 1910-1938; gymnastic class rosters, 1904-1909; and entertainment committee record book, 1916-1917. Records prior to 1920 are predominately in German.

Publications

Pa26   The Fifty-First Anniversary of the Monongahela Turners, Sunday, November 30, 1941, Turner Hall, 127 East Main Street, Monongahela, Pennsylvania, 1980 [-] 1941. n.p., [1941]. [12 p.]
Note: Includes brief history.
Location: InIU.

Pa27   The Sixtieth Anniversary of the Monongahela Turners, 1890-1950, Saturday & Sunday, October 7-8, 1950, Turner Hall, 127 East Main Street, Monogahela, Penna. n.p., [1950]. 8 p.
Location: InIU.

Pa28   Konstitution and Nebengesetze des Turn und Gesang Verein Eintracht zu Monongahela, Pa. Monessen: Daily Independent, 1927. 37 p.
Location: InIU.

Pa29   Constitution der Turner Kranken-Unterstützungs Sektion des Monongahela Turn- und Gesang-Vereins. Grand Rapids: Martin & Wurzburg, Printers, [1920]. 18 p.
Note: In German and English.
Location: InIU.

Pa30   Constitution and By-Laws of the Monongahela Turn Verein, Revised and Adopted, July, 1945. n.p., [1945]. 23 p.
Location: InIU.

Philadelphia

Philadelphia played a prominent role in the early years of the Turner movement in the United States. The first society, the Philadelphia Turngemeinde, was organized in 1849, and over the next few years it served as the host of the first and fourth national Turnfests, of the 1851 meeting at which the national Turnerbund was organized, and of the offices of the national organization and its newspaper, the Turnzeitung, during the years 1853-1855. From the early years the Turner societies had strong radical tendencies. In their 1851 constitution the members of the *Sozialer* Turnverein, nicknamed the *Badische Revolutionäre* because so many of them had been involved in the democratic movement in Baden, pledged themselves to work for the progress, freedom and prosperity of all mankind. The principal society throughout the 1850s was the *Sozialdemokratische* Turngemeinde (predecessor of the Philadelphia Turngemeinde), a name which reflected the political interests of its members. Its members actively supported Fremont in 1856 because of his anti-slavery stand, and had close associations with the Philadelphia *Arbeiterbund*.

The Philadelphia Turngemeinde remained the dominant society in Philadelphia from the end of the Civil War to the Depression, but a number of other societies were formed after the war to serve the growing population of German workers. The Germania Turnverein (founded 1865) served the population of North Philadelphia, and in the late 1880s served as the 19th Ward headquarters for the anarchist *Liga für persönliche Freiheit* (League for Personal Freedom). The Southwark *Turn- und Sonntagschul-Verein* was the product of the merger of the Southwark Turnverein (founded 1879) and the Southwark *Sonntagsschulverein*, a branch of the *Freien Sonntagschule des Arbeiterbundes* (Workers' Union Freethought Sunday School). By 1905 there were seven societies with a total membership of about 2200, almost half of whom were members of the Philadelphia Turngemeinde. In 1925 there were 2800 Turners in the city, but 2400 were members of the Turngemeinde, with the rest spread among four other societies. By 1935 there remained only the Turngemeinde, with one thousand members, and the *Germania Turnverein von* Roxborough, with thirty members. Since the 1960s only the Roxborough Turners have functioned as an active society.

Philadelphia: Philadelphia Turners

Organized in May 1849 as the Philadelphia Turngemeinde; hosted meeting of societies from New York, Baltimore and Boston to discuss the formation of a national organization in October 1850; hosted first national Turnfest in 1851, as well as the meeting following the Turnfest that resulted in the formation of the national Turnerbund; had more than 150 members by 1851; changed name to *Soziale* Turngemeinde in 1851, and lost members who broke away to form new society under the name Philadelphia Turngemeinde; merged with the *Sozialer* Turnverein (founded 1851) to form the *Sozialdemokratische* Turngemeinde; served as headquarters for the national Turnerbund and the national newspaper, the Turnzeitung, under the editorship of Wilhelm Rapp, 1853-1855; hosted the 1854 national Turnfest, which ended in a riot caused by nativist gangs; merged with the Philadelphia Turngemeinde and a new *Soziale* Turngemeinde (founded 1853) under the name *Sozialdemokratische* Turngemeinde in 1854; built hall on 3rd and Willow in 1858; incorporated as the Philadelphia Turngemeinde in 1861; formed a battalion for the Union Army from its shooting section in 1861, and eventually more than 120 members served in the army; reduced activities during the Civil War, but co-sponsored 1864 festival for school children with the Freethinkers School (*Schule der Freien Gemeinde*) and the Workers Association Sunday School *(Sonntagschulen des Arbeiterbundes)*; provided space for union rallies during the strike over the eight-hour work day in 1872; hosted national Turnfests in 1879 and 1900; built new hall on North 6th St. in 1883; sponsored women's organization and sections for fencing, singing and shooting by 1890; served as a leading social and cultural organization for the German community, with approximately one thousand members by 1890 and more than two thousand by 1915; built new hall at Broad and Columbia in 1911; had membership of nearly one thousand in 1935, but dropped to three hundred by 1940 and reported only 57 in 1950; changed name to Philadelphia Turners in late 1930s; sold hall in 1951 and moved to 8400 block of Frankford Ave.; had probable membership of several hundred during 1950s but made no reports to the national organization; remained in business as small social club until 1982.

Publications

Pa31   Philadephia Turngemeinde. Jahresbericht des ersten Sprechers. Philadelphia:
n.p., 1905.
Note: Cited in Pochmann #8234.

Pa32   Philadelphia Turngemeinde, Gegründet, 15. Mai 1849, Incorporiert, 20.
Februar 1861; Founded May 15, 1849, Chartered, February 20, 1861, Corner Broad
Street and Columbia Avenue. Bericht des Ausschusses für Bauplatz und Gebäude,
Report of the Committee on Site and Buildings, 1907-1911. Philadelphia: Walther
Print, [1912]. 45 p.
Note: Report on the building of the new Turner Hall. Includes many photographs
documenting the construction of the building. In English and German.
Location: InIU.

Pa33   The First Hundred Years, 1849[-]1949, Philadelphia Turners, The Second
Oldest Turner Society of the American Turners. Philadelphia: Weiss Printing House,
1949. [24 p.]
Note: Includes brief history of the society, and list of past presidents.
Location: InIU.

Pa34   Constitution der Social-demokrat. Turngemeinde in Philadelphia.
Philadelphia: W. Rosenthal, 1857. 16 p.
Location: PPB.

Pa35   Frei-Brief und Nebengesetze der Philadelphia Turngemeinde, Incorporiert
vom State Pennsylvania am 20. Februar 1861, Revidert und angenommen am 19.
November 1900. Philadelphia: Theos Pfitzmayer, Printer, 1900. 55 p.
Location: InIU.

Pa36   Charter and the By-Laws of the Philadelphia Turngemeinde, Incorporated in
the State of Pennsylvania, February 20, 1861, Revised and Accepted by the Gemeinde
November 1st, 1927. Philadelphia: Rudolph H. Haar, 1928. 16 p.
Location: InIU.

Pa37   The Constitution and and By-Laws and the State Charter of the Philadelphia
Turngemeinde, Founded May 15, 1849, Incorporated in the State of Pennsylvania
February 20, 1861, Revised, Amended and Accepted by the Society, Effective January
5, 1953. Philadelphia: Wm. B. Graf & Sons, 1953. 24 p.
Location: InIU.

Pa38 Bal masque [programs], 1898?-1928?
Note: Programs for the Turngemeinde's annual masked ball. Often includes list of members.
Location: PHi: 1898-1928 (incomplete).

Pa39 Turners' Bulletin. Philadelphia: Philadelphia Turngemeinde, 1911-???
Note: Published on every second and fourth Saturday of every month. Also called The Philadelphia Turners' Bulletin. Includes national and local Turner news, announcements and schedules.
Location: InIU: v.16, no.17 (June 1927); v.30, no.8 (April 1941).

Philadelphia: Roxborough Turners

Organized in 1873 as the *Unabhängige Turner von* Roxborough, an off-shoot of the *Turnverein von* Manayunk, founded in 1854; acquired hall in 1878; joined the national Turnerbund in 1879; merged with the *Germania Sängerbund von* Manayunk to form the *Germania Turnverein von* Roxborough *und* Manayunk in 1886; sponsored women's section, singing group, and gymnastics classes by early 1890s; acquired building on Leverington Ave. to serve as hall in 1890s; had membership of about one hundred from 1890s through 1920s, which dropped to thirty by 1935; changed name unofficially to Roxborough Turners in late 1930s, and officially in 1947; revived following World War II, with 381 members in 1950 and more than two hundred in 1970; still active as social and athletic organization.

Archival Collection

Pa40 Roxborough Turners Records. 1873-1960s. 9 linear feet.
Inventory available from repository.
Location: PPB.
Note: The records include minutes, financial records, membership records, certificates, and photographs. In German and English.

Publication

Pa41 Constitution and By-Laws of the Germania Turn Verein of Roxborough and Manayunk, Organized June 11, 1873, Incorporated April 2, 1888. n.p., n.d. 16 p.
Location: InIU.

Philadelphia: West Philadelphia Turn-und Schul-Verein

Organized in 1904; had 160 members by 1905 and 275 in 1925; closed in 1930s.

Publications

Pa42   Constitution und Nebengesetze des West Philadelphia Turn-und Schul-Verein. Philadelphia: Heymann Printing House, 1904. 31 p.
Location: InIU.

Rochester: Central Turn Verein Rochester

Organized in 1851 as the *Socialer* Turnverein; organized Sunday school in 1853; changed name to Rochester Turnverein in 1854; operated day-school from 1861 until 1867 when it was continued as *Real-Schule* (technical school); built hall on Clinton Avenue in 1867; acquired larger quarters on Clinton Street in 1883; formed ladies auxiliary in 1884 which supported training school for girls; erected new building in 1926 on North Clinton Avenue; began sponsoring Boy Scout Troop in 1932; organized Rochester Turners' Business and Professional Men's Club; had membership of over five hundred in the 1950s; still active.

Archival Collection

Pa43   Rochester Turner Collection. 1934 - present.
Preliminary inventory available from Indiana Univ.-Purdue Univ. Indianapolis.
Location: Central Turn Verein Rochester, Rochester.
Description: The records include minutes of meetings, 1934-1939, 1957-1984; financial and dues records, 1905-1979; scrapbooks containing photographs and newspaper articles, 1950-1955; and women's auxiliary minutes, 1952-1957.

Publications

Pa44   Rochester Turner's Golden Anniversary, 1900-1950, July 14th, 15th, and 16th. n.p., 1950. 12 p.
Note: Includes a brief history of the Rochester Turn Verein.
Location: Rochester Turn Verein, Inc.

Pa45   Constitution and Regulations of the Central Turn Verein of Rochester, PA.
Beaver Valley, PA: n.p., 1941. [22 p.]
Location: InIU.

RHODE ISLAND

Providence: Providence Turnverein

Organized in 1852 as the Providence Turnverein; joined the *Deutsche Gesellschaft* in 1898. The *Gesellschaft* became the Niagara Club in 1918 and closed by 1920.

Archival Collection

Ri1   Providence Turnverein Collection, 1854-1895.
Finding aid available from repository.
Location: RPHi.
Description: The collection includes minute books of the Providence Turnverein, 1854-1857, miscellaneous papers, ca. 1880-1895; applications for membership, 1880; undated memorial poem; and a history of the society written in 1889. Records are in German.

Providence: Providence Turners

Organized as Turnverein *Vorwärts* in 1896; erected hall on Bowlett Street; formed Turner band in 1902; built larger hall on Marino Street (later Glenbridge Avenue) in 1909; changed name to *Deutsche Turnerschaft* for building dedication; formed ladies auxiliary in 1911; changed name to Providence Turners, Inc. in 1940s; joined by former members of the Pawtucket Turners in 1952; still active as gymnastic and social organization.

Archival Collection

Ri2   Providence Turners Collection, 1896-1987.
Finding aid available from repository.
Location: RPHi.
Description: The collection includes minute books of the Providence Turners and its predecessors, the Turnverein *Vorwärts* and *Deutsche Turnerschaft*, from 1898-1976; membership and dues records, 1912-1990; financial records, 1896-1989; bar books, 1904-1986; correspondence from regional and national bodies, 1947-1972; and miscellaneous papers and printed materials. Records prior to 1945 are predominately in German.

Publications

Ri3   Souvenir Program Commemorating The 50th Anniversary of the Providence
Turners, 1896-1946, November 8, 9, 10, 1946. [Providence]: n.p., [1946]. [40 p.]
Note: Includes brief histories of the society, the ladies auxiliary, and the Turner band,
a list of committee members, and program of events.
Location: InIU.

Ri4   Souvenir Program Commemorating The 50th Anniversary of the Providence
Turner Band, 1902[-]1952, October 18,-19, 1952. [Providence]: n.p., [1952]. [18 p.]
Note: Includes brief history of the Turner band and program of events.
Location: InIU.

Ri5   Constitution and By-Laws of the Providnece Turners, September 28, 1959.
Mimeographed. n.p., [1959]. 11 p.
Location: InIU.

TENNESSEE

Chattanooga: American Turners of Chattanooga

Organized as the Chattanooga Turnverein in 1866; dedicated Turner hall on Cherry
Street in 1887; had two hundred members in 1915 but membership decreased rapidly
during World War I to seventy-seven members by 1920; changed name to American
Turners Chattanooga in 1946; left American Turners in 1966; may have closed in
1977.

Publications

Tn1   Chattanooga Turner Club, 100th Anniversary, 1866[-]1966. [Chattanooga]:
n.p., 1966. 10 p.
Note: Includes brief history of the American Turnerbund and photographs of the
Chattanooga Turners.
Location: InIU.

Tn2   Constitution, By-Laws, and House Rules, Chattanooga Turners, Chattanooga,
Tennessee. [Chattanooga]: n.p., [1946]. 32 p.
Location: InIU.

TEXAS

The Turner movement in Texas was started by Forty-Eighters during the 1850s, but its course from that point forward diverged dramatically from that of the Turners in the rest of the country. There is some evidence that Turner activities may have taken place among German immigrants in Galveston as early as the mid-1840s, but there were no formal organizations until the founding of the Galveston Socialer Turnverein in 1851 and the San Antonio Turnverein in 1852. More than ten societies were formed in Texas during the 1850s, most of them in the small German settlements such as New Braunsfeld and Fredericksburgh. Whatever Forty-eighter principles came with the new Turners were largely abandoned under pressure from the pro-slavery climate and physical isolation from the rest of the Turner movement. One of the few Turner leaders who stayed in step with the national movement was Adolf Douai, one of the founders of the San Antonio Turnverein and editor of the anti-slavery San Antonio Zeitung. Following several threats on his life, though, he left San Antonio in 1856 for the more hospitable New York City. After his departure the San Antonio Turnverein was moribund until after the Civil War. A more typical and successful accommodation to Texas life was made by E.B.H. Schneider, one of the founders of the Houston Turnverein and veteran of a revolutionary Turner regiment in Germany in 1848. Schneider became captain of the Houston Turner Rifles, and led the outfit into the Confederate Army at the outset of the Civil War.

Following the Civil War the Turner movement flourished briefly in Texas, reaching a total of approximately thirty societies by the late 1870s. The Texas societies became the center of the German communities and frequently provided schools, sick and death benefit societies and even volunteer fire departments. In 1871 the Turner societies of Texas established the Texas district (Texas Turn *Bezirk*) and joined the American Turnerbund. The association was short-lived, though. None of the Texas societies appears to have participated in either a national convention or Turnfest, and the continued political radicalism of the national Turnerbund seems to have found few supporters in Texas. By 1877 the Texas *Turnbezirk* had disappeared, but was replaced by an independent Texas State Turnerbund which attempted to sponsor state Turnfests and other cooperative activities. Neither the *Bezirk* nor the state Turnerbund could overcome the problems of rural poverty, distance and lack of railroad connections which prevented most societies from sending representatives to festivals or conventions, and so by 1880 the state Turnerbund was gone as well. By the mid-1870s the Texas societies had already largely abandoned their interest in physical education and were becoming nothing more than local social clubs. While the northern societies were successfully lobbying for the introduction of physical education in the public schools, the Texas societies were ignoring the issue. Perhaps as a result, Texas did not require physical education until the mid-1920s, long after it was a common requirement throughout the rest of the country. Most of the societies that had been active in the 1870s were closed by 1900, and the remaining societies became social, singing or bowling clubs. There are about a half-dozen societies still in existence, including ones in Houston and San Antonio. Due to the early closing dates and the independent nature of Texas societies, only a few records have been located.

Belleville: Piney Concodia Turnverein

Organized about 1870; built hall in 1872; belonged to American Turnerbund in 1871 and 1872 with 140 members; closing date unknown.

Publication

Tx1 Seventy-Fifth Anniversary Celebration, Piney Concordia, May 26, 1935, Turnverein Park, Belleville, Texas. Belleville, TX: Belleville Times Job Print, [1935]. **Location**: TxU.

Fredericksburg: Fredericksburg Sozialer Turnverein

Organized in 1871; joined American Turnerbund one year later with sixty-two members; left American Turnerbund before 1877; still active as independent society.

Publication

Tx2 Statuten des Fredericksburger Sozialen Turn-Vereins, Fredericksburg, Texas. Fredericksburg: Penniger's Printery, 1910. 15 p. **Location**: InIU (photocopy).

New Braunsfeld: New Braunsfeld Turnverein

Organized in 1853; established volunteer fire department after Civil War; probably closed between 1874 and 1883.

Publication

Tx3 Rules, Regulations and By-Laws of the Gymnastic Association of New Braunsfeld. San Antonio: Druck von Siemering and Company, 1874. **Note**: Cited in Mary Lou LeCompte, "German-American Turnvereins in Frontier Texas, 1851-1880," Journal of the West 26 (1987), p.25.

WEST VIRGINIA

Morgantown: Turnverein Concordia

Organized in 1897; had more than one hundred members between 1905 and 1913; suspended from American Turnerbund in 1914; closing date unknown.

Publication

Wv1   Verfassung des Turnvereins Concordia, Morgantown, W. Va. Milwaukee: Freidenker Publishing Co., 1904. 23 p.
Location: InIU.

WISCONSIN

Farmington: Farmington Turner Society

Organized in August 1862 as the Farmington Turn Verein; suspended activities because of the Civil War until 1866; joined the national Turnerbund in 1867; built Turner hall in 1868; operated German Sunday school, 1869-1876; left the national Turnerbund for financial reasons in 1894; changed name to Farmington Turner Society in 1930; still in operation as independent society.

Publications

Wi1   Farmington Turnverein/Farmington Turner Society, Inc., 1862-1962. n.p., [1962]. 80 p.
Note: Includes a history and historical photographs of the society and the Farmington area.
Location: InIU; WMCHi; WMT.

Wi2   Constitution and By-Laws of the Farmington Turner Society, effected July 1, 1933. n.p.; 1933. 15 p.
Location: WMT.

Fond Du Lac: Fond Du Lac Turnverein

Organized in April 1855 as the *Sozialer Turnverein von Fond du Lac*; acquired first hall on Marr Street, ca. 1856; joined the national Turnerbund in 1857; members joined Franz Sigel's company in St. Louis at outbreak of Civil War, then formed Fond du Lac Turner Company in August 1862, later becoming part of the 26th Wisconsin Regiment; purchased Plymouth Church for new hall in 1866; joined by the *Harmonie Gesangverein* which became the Turners' singing section in 1868; changed name to Turnverein Fond du Lac in 1871; formed ladies auxiliary in 1888; active in efforts to introduce physical education in Fond du Lac public schools in early 1900s; left the national Turnerbund in 1914; closing date unknown.

Publications

Wi3   Goldenes Jubilaeum des Turnvereins Fond Du Lac, 1855 - 1905, 13, 14, 15 Mai. n.p., [1905]. 97 p.
Note: Includes a history of the club and pictures of the city and society.
Location: WM.

La Crosse: La Crosse Turnverein

Organized in 1865 as the La Crosse Turnverein; merged with the *Liederkranz* Society in 1874 to form the *Deutscher Verein*; known as the Pioneer Club after about 1918; disbanded in 1937.

Archival Collection

Wi4   *Deutscher Verein* Records, 1859-1937. 0.4 linear feet (1 box).
Location: WLC
Description: The records consist primarily of the legal and financial records for the *Deutscher Verein*, but also include records of the *Liederkranz* and Turner societies. The early records are in German.

Madison: Madison Turners

Organized in 1855 by members of the Madison *Gesang-Verein* as the Madison Turnverein; joined national Turnerbund in 1857; built hall with theater and library on Butler Street in 1858; started sick benefit society that lasted from the late 1850s to 1937; lost hall in fire, then rebuilt it in 1863; Turner Hall served as meeting place for the Wisconsin Democratic Party and other groups, and as one of Madison's leading theaters during 1870s and 1880s; introduced physical education program for the Madison public schools under director of Turner instructor Jacob Riettich in 1892, and classes continued under leadership of the Madison Turnverein until about 1900;

provided collection center for clothing and other relief supplies for German and Austrian civilians during World War I; changed official language of the society to English in 1937; changed name to Madison Turners during World War II; lost hall in fire in 1940 but rebuilt it in 1941; still active. Among the members was William Vilas, Secretary of the Interior and Postmaster General under Grover Cleveland, and U.S. Senator from Wisconsin, 1891-1897.

Archival Collections

Wi5   Madison Turners Records, 1855-present. Approx. 5 linear feet.
Finding aid available from repository.
Location: WHi.
Description: The records include minutes of board of directors and general meetings, 1855-1859 and 1935-present; minutes of the *Schützen-Club* (Shooting Club), 1887-1892; minutes of the Bears Club, 1918-1965; minutes of the Physical Training Committee, 1956-1978; minutes of the Young Turner Social Club, 1934-1945; membership records, 1858, 1952-1966; gym class roll books, 1915-1953; treasurers' reports, bank statements and other financial records, 1921-1987; health and death benefit records, 1906-1926; entertainment reports, 1949-1966; newsletters, 1977-1990; scrapbooks, 1935-1954; and secretary-treasurers' book of the Wisconsin Turner District, 1939-1946. Records prior to 1926 are predominantly in German.

Wi6   Madison Turners Papers, 1855-1950. 6 boxes and 17 vols.
Finding aid available from repository.
Location: WHi.
Description: The papers include three boxes of correspondence 1855-1950; financial reports 1889-1940; physical education committee reports, 1944-1948; membership records, 1901-1940; sixteen volumes of scrapbooks containing minutes, clippings and memorabilia, 1855-1934; and minutes of meetings, 1942-1951. Records prior to the 1930s are predominantly in German.

Publications

Wi7   A Century of Health, 1855-1955, Madison Turners 100th Anniversary Souvenir Booklet. n.p., [1955]. 32 p.
Location: InIU; WHi; WMT; Madison Turners.

Wi8   125th Anniversary, 1855-1980, Madison Turners. n.p., [1980]. [36 p.]
Location: InIU; Madison Turners.

Wi9   Verfassung des Madison Turnvereins, nebst Freibrief des Vereins und

Statuten der Unterstützungssektion sowie allgemeine Grundsätze des North American Turnerbund. Madison: n.p., 1923. 38 p.
Note: Constitution and charter of the Madison Turnverein, by-laws of the society's mutual benefit section, and general principles of the North American Turnerbund. In German and English.
Location: WHi.

Wi10   Platform and Constitution of the Madison Turnverein, Madison, Wisconsin. n.p., 1937. 19 p.
Location: InlU; WHi.

Milwaukee

At the height of the Turner movement in the late nineteenth century, Milwaukee had six Turner societies affiliated with the North American Turnerbund, along with a Bohemian Turnverein (active in the 1880s) and a Swiss Turnverein (founded in 1903 and still active). The Turnverein Milwaukee, established in 1853, was the first and largest of the societies, and new societies were formed after the Civil War to serve the increasing population of German immigrants. The Southside (*Südseite*) Turnverein, formed in 1868, was particularly important in the labor and socialist movement, and it became known as the *roter* (red) Turnverein after one of its members, Victor Berger, was elected to Congress as a Socialist in 1910. In 1893, the year of the national Turnfest in Milwaukee, there were six societies: Turnverein Milwaukee, Turnverein *der Südseite*, Turnverein *der Nordseite* (founded 1869), *Vorwärts* Turnverein (founded 1879), Turnverein *Bahn Frei* (founded 1890) and Humboldt Turnverein (founded 1891). All of the societies had their own halls, and between them they had approximately 1600 members and approximately 1600 children enrolled in physical education classes. The societies began to merge or close shortly thereafter. By 1915 there were only three societies, and by 1940 only the Milwaukee Turners remained. With the founding of the East Side Turners in 1980, there are now two Turner societies in Milwaukee.

Milwaukee: Turnverein Bahn Frei

Organized in 1890 as an off-shoot of the North Side Turnverein; dropped out of national Turnerbund in 1929; merged with the Turnverein Milwaukee in 1939.

Publications

Will   Constitution and by-laws of Turnverein Bahn Frei, revised and adopted January 8, 1925. Milwaukee: Krüger Printing Co., 1925. 18 p.
Location: WMCHi.

Milwaukee: Milwaukee Turner Foundation

Organized in 1853 as the *Socialer* Turn Verein, under the influence of exiled German revolutionary leader August Willich; built hall on Fourth and State Streets in 1855; started annual Thomas Paine celebration, a singing society, gymnastics classes for girls, and a mutual benefit society in mid-1850s; changed name to Turnverein Milwaukee and left national Turnerbund in late 1850s in reaction to political disputes; rejoined national Turnerbund in 1859; members formed Turner Rifle Company to support the Union cause in April 1861, then became part of the 5th Wisconsin Regiment; built new Turner hall and hired George Brosius as first paid gymnastics instructor in 1864; organized women's auxiliary in 1868; played active role in overturning of Milwaukee's Sunday laws, ca. 1870; began offering course in physical education in Milwaukee public schools in 1874; served as host society for the North American Turnerbund's *Turnlehrer-Seminar* (Normal College), 1875-1888; built new Turner hall in 1883; hosted national Turnfests in 1857 (for western Turners), 1877 and 1893; sent first American team to compete in German Turnfest, at Frankfurt am Main, in 1880; changed official language to English in 1918; changed name to Milwaukee Turners in 1940; became the Milwaukee Turner Foundation, ca.1990.

   The Milwaukee Turnverein had extensive connections with socialist and freethinker activists in the city. The first leader of the *Socialer* Turnverein, Heinrich Loose, was also the editor of the radical newspapers Der Humanist (1853) and Der Arbeiter (1855). Joseph Brucker, who worked out of the Turner hall during much of the 1870s, was editor and publisher of Der Freidenker (1874-1877) and Der Socialist, organ of the *Internationalen Arbeiter Association*. Publication of Der Freidenker was taken over by Turner Karl Dörflinger in 1878, followed by the Freidenker Publishing Co., 1883-1916, with Dörflinger and Turner leader Carl Hermann Boppe as editors for much of that time. Dörflinger and the Freidenker Publishing Co. were also responsible for publishing the Amerikanische Turnzeitung and its predecessor supplements to Der Freidenker, along with the North American Turnerbunds' annual reports and convention proceedings, 1878-1916. The Turner hall was a principal meeting place of the Social-Democratic party in the early part of the twentieth century, and one of the Turnverein's members, Emil Seidel, was elected the city's first Socialist mayor in 1910. The Social Democratic Party moved to the Turner hall in 1939 and remained there for a number of years. Members of the party who were also active members of the Milwaukee Turners included Walter Palm, Milwaukee Deputy Commissioner in the the late 1930s, Carl Zeidler, Mayor of Milwaukee, 1940-1942, and Frank Zeidler, Mayor of Milwaukee, 1948-1960.

Archival Collections

Wi12   Milwaukee Turners Records, 1852-1944. 9 boxes and 4 packages (includes 36 vols.)
Finding aid available from repository.
Location: WMU
Description: The records include correspondence, 1928-1936; financial reports, 1928-1932; printed histories; records of the recording secretary, 1855-1944, the financial secretary, 1855-1934, and the corresponding secretary, 1854-1859; membership rolls, 1852-1887; and scrapbooks of memorabilia, 1857-1928, including one for the Milwaukee Turners participation in the 1880 German Turnfest in Frankfurt am Main, and one for the 1914 George Brosius fiftieth anniversary celebration. Records prior to 1915 are predominantly in German.

Wi13   Milwaukee Turners Foundation, Inc. Records, 1855-1993. 3.5 file drawers.
Partial finding aid available from repository.
Location: WMT
Description: The records consist primarily of financial, membership, and committee records of the Milwaukee Turners. Includes minutes of society meetings, 1949-1982; minutes of the building committee meetings, 1881-1882; minutes of the children's costume contest, 1905-1919; membership records, 1853-1937; financial records, 1854-1958; cash book of the *Unterstützungsverein*, 1874-1910; account book of the *Wirtschafts Committee*, 1877-1882; cash book of the Milwaukee Gymnastic Association records, 1934-1936; women's auxiliary membership list, 1919-1936; women's auxiliary correspondence, 1912-1935; roll call books, 1936-1942; photographs, 1888-1959; member and subject files, including files on George Brosius; scrapbooks with newspaper articles and memorabilia, 1948-present; and scrapbook of the Swiss Turners Helvetia, 1883. Records prior to 1915 are predominantly in German.

Wi14   Milwaukee Turners Collection, 1852-1965. 2 cubic feet (5 boxes).
Finding aid available from repository.
Location: WMCHi
Description: Includes incorporation document, 1855; scrapbooks, 1880-1893; minute books, 1889-1893, 1957-1969; photographs, 1853-1969; membership roster, 1919-1928; statistics and membership lists; correspondence; account book, 1851-1858; committee records; and miscellaneous folders on social activities, the

women's auxiliary, the Normal College, and the 1938 Turnfest. Records prior to 1915 are predominantly in German.

Wi15   Olga L. (Dolge) Wiedemann Papers, 1884-1991. 4 boxes.
Finding aid available from repository.
Location: WMT.
Description: The bulk of the material dates from the years 1981-1988 when Wiedemann was president of the Milwaukee Turner Foundation, Inc., and concerns both Milwaukee Turner activities and activities of the American Turners. The collection includes secretary's notes, 1980-1988; membership information, 1970-1988; financial and legal papers, 1894-1986; anniversary booklets, 1953-1979; women's auxiliary convention minutes, 1970-1982; papers from national conventions, 1966-1987; district reports, 1950-1983; brochures from various festivals and conventions, 1941-1987; newspaper clippings, 1950-1988; photographs, 1936-1967; and minutes of the mixed chorus, 1943-1949.

Wi16   John C. Gregory Collection.
Location: WM
Description: Included in collection is a history of seven Turner societies that were active in Milwaukee in 1885, along with illustrations of Turner activities in the nineteenth century.

Publications: Histories & Anniversary Books

Wi17   Das 25. Jährige Stiftungsfest des Turnvereins Milwaukee, Juli, den 17ten 1878. Milwaukee: n.p., 1878. unpaged.
Note: Festival book for the twenty-fifth anniversary of the founding of the Milwaukee Turnverein.
Location: WM.

Wi18   Turnverein Milwaukee, Souvenir, October 17th und 18th, 1896. Milwaukee: Breithaupt & Sonntag, Printers, 1897. 21 p.
Note: Includes short history of the society's early years, and pictures of interior of the Turner hall.
Location: WHi; WM; WMCHi.

Wi19   Turnverein Milwaukee Souvenir, Eröffnungsfeier, 14. Oktober 1899. [Milwaukee]: n.p., [1899]. 15 p.
Note: Published for the dedication of the Turnhall. Includes pictures of the building.
Location: WM.

Wi20   Goldenes Jubiläum des Turnvereins Milwaukee, 1853-1903, am 12, 13, und 14 Juni 1903. [Milwaukee]: n.p., [1903]. 51 p.
Note: Cover title: "*Festschrift zum goldenen Jubiläum des Turnvereins Milwaukee.*" Includes history of the club and the women's society, photographs, and articles on the founders of the Turner movement.
Location: NN; WHi; WM; WMCHi.

Wi21   Diamond Jubilee of the Turnvereins-Milwaukee, 1853-1928. [Milwaukee]: n.p., [1928]. 40 p.
Location: InIU; WHi; WMCHi;WMT.

Wi22   90 Years of Service: 1853-1943. [Milwaukee]: n.p., 1943. 48 p.
Note: Special issue of The Milwaukee Turner, October 1943. Includes history of the society, brief sketches of the choir and the women's auxiliary and photographs.
Location: InIU; WMCHi; WMT.

Wi23   The Milwaukee Turners 100th Anniversary Centennial Banquet Program, Saturday, June 13th, 1953. [Milwaukee]: n.p., [1953].
Note: Includes photographs and histories of the society, the womens auxiliary and Turners in the United States.
Location: WMCHi.

Wi24   Milwaukee Turners: One Hundredth Anniversary, 1853-1953. [Milwaukee]: n.p., [1953]. 48 p.
Note: Alternate title page: "Souvenir program: The Milwaukee Turners: Show of the Century, 1853-1953." Souvenir program for the one hundredth anniversary celebration, April 12, 1953. Includes history of the society and its sections, a history of Turners in the United States and photographs.
Location: InIU; WHi; WMCHi; WMT.

Wi25   Milwaukee Turners: 140th Anniverary, 1853-1993. [Milwaukee]: n.p., [1993]. 32 p.
Location: InIU; WHi.

Publications: Constitutions & By-Laws

Wi26   Verfassung des Milwaukee Turn-Vereins gegründet am 17. Juli, 1853. Milwaukee: *Office vom Banner und Volksfreund*, 1864. 16 p.
Location: WMT.

Wi27   Verfassung des Turnvereins Milwaukee nebst Platform und Statuten des Nord- Amerikansichen Turnerbundes und des Turnbezirks Wisconsin, sowie Freibrief (Charter) des Vereins und Statuten der Unterstützungssektion. Milwaukee: Freidenker Publishing Co., 1884. 51 p.
Note: Contains constitution of the Milwaukee Turnverein, platform and regulations of the North American Turnerbund and the Wisconsin Turner District, charter of the Milwaukee Turnverein, and regulations of the society's mutual benefit section.
Location: WM.

Wi28   Verfassung des Turnvereins Milwaukee nebst Grundsätzen und Forderungen und Statuten des Nord Amerikanischen Turnerbundes und des Turnbezirks Wisconsin sowie Freibrief (Charter) des Vereins, Hausregeln und Statuten der Unterstützungssektion. Milwaukee: Freidenker Publishing Co., 1903. 82 p.
Note: Contains constitution of the Milwaukee Turnverein, principles and regulations of the North American Turnerbund and the Wisconsin Turner District, charter of the Milwaukee Turnverein, and rules and regulations of the society's mutual benefit society.
Location: WM.

Wi29   Constitution and By-laws of the Turnverein Milwaukee, Organized 1855. n.p., [1927]. 32 p.
Note: In German and English.
Location: InIU; WHi; WM.

Wi30   Constitution and By-laws of the Turnverein Milwaukee, Organized 1855, Milwaukee, WI, revised 1939. n.p., [1939?]. 32 p.
Location: WM; WMT.

Wi31   Constitution and By-laws of the Turnverein Milwaukee, Organized 1855, Milwaukee, WI, July, 1943. n.p., [1943?]. 32 p.
Location: WMT.

Wi32   Constitution and By-laws of the Milwaukee Turners, Organized July 18, 1853, Incorporated February 14, 1855, Milwaukee, Wisconsin, Revised January 1, 1944. n.p., [1944?]. 23 p.
Location: InIU; WM; WMCHi; WMT.

Wi33   Constitution and By-laws of the Milwaukee Turners, Organized July 18, 1853, Incorporated February 14, 1855, Milwaukee, Wisconsin, Revised June 20, 1961. n.p., [1961?]. 23 p.
Location: InIU; WMT.

Wi34   Constitution and By-laws of the Milwaukee Turners, Organized July 18, 1853, Incorporated February 14, 1855, Revised May 1, 1980. n.p., [1981?]. 24 p.
Location: InIU; WMT.

Wi35   Constitution and By-laws of the Milwaukee Turners' Mixed Chorus Founded June 18, 1943. n.p., [1950?].
Location: WMT.

Publications: Newsletters

Wi36   Milwaukee Turner. 1939 - present.
Note: Newsletter of the Milwaukee Turners. Published monthly until the late 1980s, then published quarterly. During its first years the editor was Frank Zeidler, later Socialist mayor of Milwaukee. In 1990-1991 the Turner Foundation also published the newsletter The Link as a fund-raising tool; it was discontinued after one year.
Location:
  InIU: June 1955.
  WM: 1939-1968 (incomplete).
  WMCHi: 1939-1968 (incomplete).
  WMT: 1939 - present.
  WULC: 1939-1963.

Publications: Miscellaneous

Wi37   Brown, James S. Arguments of Hon. James S. Brown and R.N. Austin, Esq.: also Opinion of the Court Relating to Ordinances of the City against Sunday Dancing, in the Cases of the City of Milwaukee vs. Milwaukee Turn Verein, also City of Milwaukee vs. Franz Bader and Peter Crass. Milwaukee: Keogh & Corbitt, 1870. 52 p.
Location: WHi.

Wi38   Historische Skizze des Turnvereins Milwaukee und offizieller Wegweiser nach den Dells des Wisconsin Flusses. Milwaukee: King, Fowle & Katz, 1886. 43 p.
Note: Itinerary for trip to the Wisconsin Dells sponsored by the Milwaukee Turnverein. Includes historical sketches of the society.
Location: WHi.

Wi39   Katalog der Bibliothek des Turnvereins Milwaukee. Milwaukee: Freidenker Publishing Co., 1895. 206 p.
Note: Catalog for the Milwaukee Turnerverein's library.
Location: WHi; WM.

Wi40   Grosses Schauturnen, Concert und Ball des Turnvereins Milwaukee zum Benefit der Philadelphia Fest Riege, Samstag, den 28. April 1900. Milwaukee: n.p., 1900. 81 p.
Note: Program for events held to raise funds for the society's team to attend the national Turnfest in Philadelphia. Chiefly advertising and program information.
Location: WHi.

Wi41   Forkmann, Hans H. Festspiel zum Goldenen Jubiläum des Turnvereins "Milwaukee". Milwaukee: Freidenker Publishing Co., 1903. 15 p.
Note: Play performed at the Milwaukee Turnverein's fiftieth anniversary celebration.
Location: WMCHi.

Wi42   Die Turnschule des Turnvereins Milwaukee, 1853-1907. Milwaukee: Freidenker Publishing Co., 1907. 40 p.
Note: History of the society's gymnastics school.
Location: WM.

Wi43   Turnverein Milwaukee, 1927-28: Schedule for the School of Educational Gymnastics, Calendar for the Season 1927-28, Sociable Events of the Turnverein Milwaukee. n.p., [1927]. [25 p.]
Location: WM.

Wi44   Tested Recipes: Cook Book Published by the Frauen-Verein of the Turnverein Milwaukee, Milwaukee, Wis. n.p., 1929. 160 p.
Location: WMT.

Wi45   Gesang Sektion der Milwaukee Turner, Sunday, Nov. 3, 1857-1957, Westseite Turnhalle. n.p., [1957]. 75 p.
Note: Program for the one hundredth anniversary celebration of the Milwaukee Turners' Singing Section. Includes history of the organization.
Location: WMT.

Wi46   The Milwaukee Turners 108th Annual Gymnastic Exhibition: "A Salute to Brosius." n.p., [1961]. [28 p.]
Note: Includes brief history of the society, biographical information on George Brosius, exhibition program and contemporary photographs.
Location: InIU.

Milwaukee: Turnverein der Nordseite

Organized in 1869 as the West Hill Turning Society; changed name to Turnverein *der Nordseite* by 1870; built Turner hall on W. Walnut between 10th and 11th Streets in 1871; closed in 1905.

Publications

Wi47   Verfassung des Turnvereins der Nordseite nebst Platform und Statuten des Nordamerikanischen Turner=Bunds und des Turnbezirks Wisconsin sowie Freibrief (Charter) des Vereins. Milwaukee: Hugo Schubel, 1890. 87 p.
Note: Constitution of the Northside Turnverein, with platform and statutes of the North American Turnerbund and the Wisconsin Turner District.
Location: InIU.

Sheboygan: Sheboygan Turners, Inc.

Organized in 1854 as the *Socialer* Turnverein, one year after the founding of Sheyboygan; name changed to Turnverein Sheboygan by 1860; occupied a series of buildings until permanent building constructed at St. Clair and N. 9th St. in the late nineteenth century; offered classes in history, science, and the arts during the 1880s; started ladies auxiliary and singing society in 1890; changed name to Sheboygan Gymnastic Society in 1919 and to Sheboygan Turners, Inc. in 1965; still active.

Archival Collections

Wi48   Sheboygan Turners Records, 1885-present.
Preliminary inventory available from Indiana Univ.-Purdue Univ. Indianapolis.
Location: Sheboygan Turners, Inc.
Description: Includes minutes of meetings, 1885-1899, 1925-1976; scrapbooks, 1936-present; class schedules for 1932-1933 and 1935-1936; the Sheboygan Turner, the monthly newsletter, 1931-1932; historical photographs; and programs, flyers, and other Turner publications. Records prior to 1900 are predominantly in German.

Publications

Wi49   Goldenes Jubiläum des Turnvereins Sheboygan 1854 - 1904, Festschrift und Programm für die Feier des Goldenen Jubiläums des Turnvereins Sheboygan zu Sheboygan, Wisconsin, am 17, 18, und 19. Juni 1904. n.p., [1904]. [ca. 100 p.]
Note: Program and festschrift for the fiftieth anniversary celebration of the Sheboygan

Turners. Includes list of members, history of the society, photographs, program for the festival, and the script for the festival play.
Location: WSCHi; Sheboygan Turners, Inc.

Wi50   Diamond Jubilee Program of the Sheboygan Gymnastic Society 1854 - 1929. Souvenir program dedicated to the Diamond Jubilee Celebration of the Sheboygan Gymnastic Society, April 27th, 28th, and May 4th, 1929. Sheboygan: Sheboygan Printing Co.; 1929. 48 p.
Location: WSCHi; Sheboygan Turners, Inc.

Wi51   100th Anniversary Sheboygan Gymnastic Society, 1854-1954. n.p., [1954]. [48 p.]
Location: InIU; WMT; Sheboygan Turners, Inc.

Wi52   Constitution and By-laws of the Sheboygan Gymnastic Society, Sheboygan, Wisconsin, January 1, 1925. n.p.; 1925. 24 p.
Location: InIU.

Wi53   Sheboygan Gymnastic Society, 1931-32, Turner Social Calendar. n.p., 1931. 27 p.
Location: WHi.

Chapter 4

Normal College of the American Gymnastic Union

The national Turnerbund began discussing the need for a school to educate competent physical education teachers at the national convention in Pittsburgh in 1856. Further discussions and the Civil War delayed the implementation of the plan until 1866 when the *Turnlehrer Seminar* (Turner Teacher School) was established in New York City. The six-month course offered night classes so students could work during the day to support themselves. Gymnastics classes were taught by E. Heeseler, the physical education teacher at the New York Turnverein, and lectures were given by Henry Metzner, a prominent member of the New York Turnverein, and Eduard Müller, a political refugee of the 1848 revolution, former publisher of the <u>Mainzer Turnzeitung</u> and author of the <u>Das Turnen</u>, the first Turner gymnastics manual published in the United States. The *Seminar* stayed in New York City for two courses, from November 1866 to July 1869, and then moved to Chicago where it came under the direction of George Brosius. On October 6, 1871, the course in Chicago ended abruptly when the city was destroyed by fire. The school relocated again to New York City and opened its fourth course on October 27, 1872. Three years later, in 1875, it moved to Milwaukee where the Milwaukee Turnverein assumed responsibility for it. Gymnastics classes were taught by George Brosius, who had moved to Milwaukee following the Chicago Fire. During that same year, the course was changed from a six-month night course to a three-month day course. Although enrollment dropped because of the increased financial burden on students, the quality of the course improved. In 1875, the school graduated its first female student, Laura Gerlach, who was later employed as a teacher by the Milwaukee School Board.

In 1878 academic classes were added to the curriculum. By 1888, the school offered a ten-month full-time term to its students. During the same year, the Milwaukee Turnverein asked to be relieved of the burden of housing the school. Furthermore, George Brosius left Milwaukee to accept a position as teacher at the New York City Turnverein. For the next two years the school was housed by the

Socialer Turnverein in Indianapolis while negotiations proceeded in Milwaukee to house the *Turnlehrer Seminar* in a new building with the German-English Academy and the German-American Teacher's Seminary. In 1891 an agreement was reached among the three institutions to share facilities and exchange teachers. When the school reopened in Milwaukee, again under the direction of George Brosius, its new facilities and extended program attracted more students to the school. In 1894 the one-year course was expanded to a two-year course to give students a more sophisticated education. In 1906, problems arose between the *Turnlehrer Seminar* and the German-American Teachers Seminary which led the Turners to seek other arrangements.

In 1907 the school moved again to Indianapolis where the Indianapolis Turnverein's *Deutsche Haus* became its new home. In Indianapolis it was officially renamed the "Normal College of the North American Gymnastic Union" and Karl Kroh became its director. The school prospered under able leadership and again extended its program. By 1914 it had been accredited by the state of Indiana to award one-, two-, and five-year teacher licenses in both elementary and secondary schools. Along with the physical education classes, students were taught history, foreign languages, health, sociology, political science, economics, and literature. In 1921, the college purchased land at Lake Elkhart in Wisconsin for a summer camp which became known as "Camp Brosius." By 1931 the school faced serious financial troubles caused by the nationwide depression and rising requirements for teachers. In order to stay open, it made arrangements with Indiana University in 1933 which allowed the college to keep its identity and permitted students to attend Indiana University during their fourth year to receive a Bachelor of Science degree.

Continuing financial problems finally led to the merger of the Normal College and Indiana University on 1941. All property was transferred to Indiana University and beginning with the 1941-1942 academic year the school was known as the "Normal College of the American Gymnastic Union of Indiana University." The school remained autonomous until 1946 when it became part of the newly organized School of Health, Physical Education and Recreation of Indiana University. The school continued to operate from the Turner hall in Indianapolis until 1970, when building code violations forced it to move to instructor Walter Lienert's camp on 1010 W. 64th Street. In 1972 the program became the School of Physical Education of Indiana University-Purdue University at Indianapolis. Since 1982 it has been housed in the Natatorium/ Physical Education Building on the IUPUI campus.

As one of the country's first schools for gymnastics instructors, the Normal College played an influential role in the development of physical education and recreation programs for schools and parks during the late nineteenth and early twentieth centuries. Although the college was founded to provide instructors for the Turner societies, most of the students pursued careers in the public schools or public parks. Particularly during the 1890s, the college's graduates frequently found themselves in the position of starting a school system's physical education program, and for many years Normal College graduates were in charge of physical education in the school systems of major midwestern cities, including Chicago, Milwaukee, St. Louis, Indianapolis and Fort Wayne.

Turnlehrer Seminar (1866 to 1907)

<u>Archival Collection</u>

T1 *Turnlehrer Seminar* Records, 1877-1902. 1 box.
Finding aid available from repository.
Location: InIU.
Description: Includes records of student and teacher participation at the fourth and fifth *Turnlehrer Seminar* held in Milwaukee (*Stundenverzeichnis des Turnlehrer-Seminars während des 4ten und 5ten Curses, 1877/78-1878/79*); report by Hermann Boppe on project to combine the Teacher's Seminar and the Turner Teachers' School, 1889; Articles of Indenture, Incorporation, and Articles of Organization, 1901-1902; correspondence, deeds and other legal documents, including papers documenting the controversies between the *Turnlehrer Seminar*, the German-English Academy, and the National German-American Teacher's Seminary.

<u>Publications</u>

T2 Arnold, E. H. <u>Das Turnlehrerseminar. Eine Zeit-und Streitschrift</u>. n.p., [1886].
Note: Cited in Eldredge, Wentworth "The New Haven Community." Ph.D. Dissertation, Yale University, 1935.

T3 <u>Extracts from Rules and Regulations for the Normal School for Teachers of Gymnastics</u>. Milwaukee: Freidenker Publishing Co., 1889. 23 p.
Location: WHi.

T4 <u>Festschrift zur Einweihungsfeier der neuen Heimstätte deutsch-amerikanischer Erziehung in Milwaukee, gestiftet von den hochherzigen Frauen Elizabeth Pfister und Louise Vogel</u>. Milwaukee: Freidenker Publishing Co., 1891. 64 p.
Note: Publication to accompany the dedication of the school building shared by the German-English Academy, the German-American Teacher's Seminary, and the *Turnlehrer* Seminar. Includes article by Hermann Boppe: *"Das Turnlehrerseminar des Nord-Amerikanischen Turnerbundes,"* pp. 45-64.
Location: OCU.

T5 <u>Summer School for Physical Training to be held under the Auspices of the North American Gymnastic Union at Milwaukee, Wisconsin, Six Weeks, July 1st to August 10th, 1895</u>. n.p., 1895. 8 p.
Note: Includes a list of faculty members teaching summer school, description of the classes, synopses of lectures and practical information.
Location: InIU.

T6   Lehrplan des Turnlehrer-Seminars des Nordamerikanischen Turnerbundes.
Normal School of the North-American Gymnastic Union. Milwaukee: Freidenker
Publishing. Co., [1897]. 48 p.
Note: Includes brief historical overview of the school, its constitution, lesson plans,
list of graduates from 1868-1898, and photographs of the institution.
Location: InIU.

T7   Kurzgefasste Geschichte der Deutsch Englischen Akademie des Nationalen
Deutsch-Amerikanischen Lehrerseminars und des Turnlehrerseminars des Nord-
amerikanischen Turnerbundes, 21.-25. Mai 1901. Milwaukee: *Festausschuss des
Jubiläums der Engelmannschen Schule*, [1901]. 124 p.
Note: Title translation: "Brief history of the German English Academy of the National
German-American Teacher Seminar and the Turnteacher Seminar of the North
American Turnerbund."
Location: InIU; OCU; PPG; WMCHi.

Normal College (1907 to 1966)

Archival Collection

T8   Normal College of the American Gymnastic Union Collection, 1907-1941.
7 boxes.
Finding aid available from repository.
Location: InIU.
Description: The records include Board of Trustee Minutes, 1907-1941 (in German
into the 1920s); drafts of the Trust Indenture, Building and Endowment Fund for the
Normal College, 1939; papers on teachers' instruction, 1920s and 30s; bibliography
on principles of teaching; freshman handbook, (1930s?); newspaper clippings, 1936-
1961; miscellaneous correspondence and papers, 1900-1970; and files of Theodore
Stempfel, board of trustee member, 1931-1936. The collection also includes Student
Alliance minutes, 1909-1918; Student Council minutes, 1922-1933; records of the
Alumni Association, including minutes of the secretary, 1911-1935, 1939-1975;
typescript copy of the Normal College Alumni Association constitution, 1917; and
records of Camp Brosius, including financial papers, song books, plays and pageants,
instructions on sports activities and promotional brochures.

Publications

T9   Normal College of the American Gymnastic Union. [Bulletin]. Indianapolis:
Hollenbeck Press, 1907-1941.
Note: Annual catalog for the Normal College. Typical issues included college
calendar, history of the college, list of faculty members, description of courses and
facilities, requirements for admission and graduation, and a list of graduates. No

catalogs were issued for the 1934-1935 and 1936-1937 academic years. After 1941 information about courses was published in Indiana University Bulletins.
Location:

> In: 1907/08, 1925/26, 1927/28-1933/34, 1935/36, 1937/38-1940/41
> InIU: 1907/08, 1911/12, 1918/19, 1925/26-1933/34, 1935/36, 1937/38-
> 1940/41,
> PPB: 1917/18, 1920/21
> Dayton Liederkranz Turners, Dayton: 1926/27.

T10   Articles of Incorporation. [Indianapolis]: n.p., 1907. 3 p.
Location: In; InIU.

T11   By-Laws of the Normal College of the North American Gymnastic Union.
[Indianapolis]: n.p., [1907]. 8 p.
Location: In.

T12   Normal College of the North American Gymnastic Union. "Commencement Programs." n.p. 1908-1941.
Note: The programs include the schedule of events for the graduation ceremonies. After 1913 they also include a list of graduates.
Location: InIU: 1908-1910, 1913-1916, 1920, 1922-1941.

T13   By-Laws of the Normal College of the North American Gymnastic Union.
[Indianapolis]: n.p., [1909]. 6 p.
Location: InIU.

T14   Summer Session at Indianapolis, Indiana. Indianapolis: Normal College of the American Gymnastic Union, [1912-1920].
Note: Class schedules and general information for summer sessions.
Location:

> In: 1913, 1916.
> InIU: 1912-1917, 1919-1920.

T15   The Gymnast. Indianapolis: Senior Class of the Normal College N.A.G.U., 1913-1941.
Note: Yearbook published by the senior class of the Normal College of the North American Gymnastic Union. All yearbooks include photographs of the students and the fraternal organizations, reports about campus activities and athletic teams, and a student directory.
Location:

> In: 1918-1919.
> InIU: 1913-1941.
> MoSHi: 1921-1930.
> PPB: 1923, 1925, 1927.

WMCHi: 1923.
WMT: 1914, 1937-1939.

T16 Ankündigungen für das Studienjahr 1913-14. Milwaukee: Freidenker Publishing Co., 1913. 11 p.
Note: Cover title: "*Turnlehrerseminar des Nordamerikanischen Turnerbundes. Incorporiert als Normal College of the North American Gymnastic Union. Akkrediert vom Erziehungsrat des Staates Indiana. Ankündigungen für das Studienjahr* 1913-14." Normal College catalog in German. Includes application information, faculty list, and description of courses.
Location: In.

T17 Proposed Constitution and By-laws for the Amalgamation of the Alumni Association of the Normal College of the North American Gymnastic Union (N.A.G.U.) and the Turnlehrerschaft of the N.A.G.U., and Proposed Constitution and By-laws for the Reorganization of the Death Benefit Branch of Such Organization. [Indianapolis]: n.p., 1914. 16 p.
Note: Submitted to the joint convention of the *Turnlehrerschaft* and the Alumni Association of the N.A.G.U. at Indianapolis, Ind., July 4, 1914.
Location: InIU.

T18 Physical Education's Call for Trained Men. Indianapolis: Normal College of the North American Gymnastic Union, [ca. 1914]. 15 p.
Note: Promotional brochure for the Normal College. Includes photographs of activities.
Location: In.

T19 Ankündigungen für das Studienjahr 1916-17. Minneapolis: Turner Publishing Co., 1916. 12 p.
Note: Cover title: "*Turnlehrerseminar des Nordamerikanischen Turnerbundes. Incorporiert als Normal College of the North American Gymnastic Union. Akkrediert vom Erziehungsrat des Staates Indiana in den Klassen A, B und C. Ankündigungen für das Studienjahr* 1916-17." School catalog in German. Includes application information, faculty list, and description of courses.
Location: InIU.

T20 Summer Session in Camp at Elkhart Lake, Wisconsin. Indianapolis: Normal College of the American Gymnastic Union, [1921-1941].
Note: Class schedules and general information for summer sessions.
Location:
     In: 1923, 1926-1932.
     InIU: 1921-1925, 1931-1935.

T21   Declaration of Trust Building and Endowment Fund of the Normal College of the American Turners. Detroit: Executive Office, [1939]. 19 p.
Note: Includes biographical sketches of the trustees, and principles and articles of the building and endowment fund.
Location: InIU.

T22   Homecoming, Celebrating the One Hundredth Anniversary of the Normal College A.G.U., Indiana University, November 24-26, 1966. Indianapolis: n.p., 1966. 8 p.
Note: Includes the program of events and photographs of university and Turner officials.
Location: InIU.

Camp Brosius

After the Normal College's move to Indianapolis, the board of trustees discussed the need for a summer camp program for students. For the 1921 summer session the College rented a camp site at Elkhart Lake, 60 miles north of Milwaukee and 20 miles west of Sheboygan. After a successful season, the College decided to purchase the camp in the fall of 1921, renaming it Camp Brosius after George Brosius. The College used the camp to train students for outdoor recreation programs. Besides the daily academic program, the students participated in various programs, including camp fires, outdoor and indoor games, stunt night, treasure hunts, cookouts, and overnight camping. In addition to the regular camp program, the students were also assigned chores, such as camp maintenance, and kitchen and dining room duties. The summer program was required for first and second year students. The camp was also used to host several national Turner activities including the national conventions in 1925, 1931, 1933, and 1940. When the Normal College became part of Indiana University, Camp Brosius was taken over by Indiana University and has been used both for physical education programs and other university purposes.

Publications

T23   Camp Brosius, Elkhart Lake, Wisconsin, A Summer Camp for Boys, Season 1935, July 1 to August 10. n.p., 1935. 15 p.
Note: Promotional brochure for the camp describing its facilities, activities, rules, and application materials.
Location: InIU.

T24   Camp Brosius, Elkhart Lake, Wisconsin, A Summer Camp for Boys, Season of 1937. n.p., 1937.

Note: Promotional brochure for the camp describing its facilities, activities, rules, and application materials.
Location: Akron Turner Club.

T25   Elkhart Lake Wisconsin's Beauty Spot. n.p., [ca.1930]. 50 p.
Note: Promotional brochure about the Turner camp at Elkhart Lake.
Location: InIU.

Normal College Alumni Association

The Normal College Alumni Association was established on June 8, 1908. Its objectives at the time of establishment were to maintain a close connection between graduates and the college, the discussion of physical education and related topics, the publication of data, and the establishment of a network among graduates.

Publications

T26   Alumni Bulletin. Indianapolis: Alumni Association of the Normal College of the American Gymnastic Union, [1917-present].
Note: From 1917 to 1961, the Alumni Bulletin was published three times a year; since 1961 it has been published twice a year. Includes news on activities, teachers, students, and alumni of the Normal College and Indiana University School of Physical Education.
Location: InIU: 1917-1995 (incomplete).

T27   Normal College of the American Gymnastic Union. List of Graduates. Issued periodically.
Note: List of all Normal College alumni, their addresses, and positions, arranged alphabetically and geographically.
Location: InIU: 1925, 1927, 1931, 1937.

T28   Songs of the Normal College A.G.U. [Indianapolis]: Alumni Association Normal College, [1927]. 40 p.
Location: InHi.

T29   Alumni Directory, Normal College of the American Gymnastic Union. [Indianapolis]: Alumni Association, 1938. 32 p.
Note: List of all Normal College alumni, their addresses, and positions arranged alphabetically and geographically.
Location: InIU.

T30   Alumni Newsletter: Normal College A.G.U. of Indiana University. Mimeographed. Indianapolis: n.p., 1951-1957?

Note: Published twice a year in May and October. Contains news on school activities and alumni.
Location:

> In: v.3 (1953) - v.6 (1957). Incomplete.
> InIU: v.2 (1953) - v. 6 (1957).

T31   Indiana University. Normal College of the American Gymnastic Union. Alumni Directory, October 15, 1966. [Indianapolis]: Alumni Association, 1966. 73 p.
Note: Alphabetical list of all Normal College alumni.
Location: InIU.

T32   "The Oldest in the Country." Indiana Alumni Magazine v.29 (1967), pp. 6-11.
Note: Article written for the centennial anniversary of the Normal College. Includes commentary on Emil Rinsch's History of the Normal College (1966).

Chapter 5

Publications on Physical Education

When the *Socialistische* Turnerbund asked Eduard Müller to write the first guidelines on conducting exercise classes in 1853, it was the beginning of a tradition of Turner publishing on physical education. The rising numbers of Turner societies and the introduction of physical education in public schools in the late nineteenth century increased the demand for literature on gymnastics, health and recreation, with the result that graduates and faculty members of the *Turnlehrer Seminar* and the Normal College became well-known authorities in the field. Instructors and faculty members gave lectures at national conferences, wrote articles in national physical education magazines, and published outlines of exercises and lesson plans, essays on the value of physical education, and manuals and textbooks to be used by public schools and Turner societies in the teaching of gymnastics. The list of instructors and faculty members connected with the American Turner movement is very long. Some faculty members only taught a few courses while continuing their careers as physicians, language teachers, or directors of physical culture programs.

This chapter includes works by key figures in the movement reflecting Turner ideas on physical education. Only works published separately as books or pamphlets are included. Writers such as Carl Betz, Emil Rath and William Stecher also published extensively in physical education journals such as <u>Mind and Body,</u> but those works have not been included. The English-language, commercially-published works from the 1910s through the 1940s were widely distributed at the time and can still be found in many large academic and public libraries.

G1   Barrows, Isabel Chapin. <u>Physical training: a full report of the papers and discussion of the conference held in Boston in November, 1889</u>. Boston: Press of George H. Ellis, 1890. 135 p.
Note: Includes an article by Henry Metzner, principal of the school of the New York

Turnverein, on "The German System of Gymnastics." Other articles discuss the German and the Swedish systems of gymnastics.
Location: CLU; CSt; IU; MdBG; MnM; MnU.

G2   Betz, Carl. A system of physical culture designed as a manual of instruction for the use of schools. Kansas City: Kansas City Presse, 1887. 4 volumes.
     v.1: Free Gymnastics, 1887; 2nd. rev. ed., 1893.
     v.2: Gymnastic Tactics, 1887; 2nd. rev. ed., 1894.
     v.3: Light Gymnastics, 1887; 2nd rev. ed., 1892.
     v.4: Popular Gymnastics: Athletics and Sports of the Play-Ground, 1887.
        2nd. rev. ed., 1893.
Note: Carl Betz was a graduate of the *Turnlehrer* Seminar in Milwaukee in 1876. While he was the instructor for the *Soziale* Turnverein of Kansas City he played a leading role in introducing physical education into the Kansas City public school system. He was later appointed Kansas City's director of physical training, and in this capacity wrote numerous training manuals. Later editions of the publications were published in Chicago by A. Flanagan Co.
Location: DLC; InIU.

G3   ---, ed. Work and play: a magazine devoted to the interest of American boys and girls at home, in school and abroad. Chicago, May 1893-February/March 1894.
Note: Carl Betz was managing editor of this short-lived magazine.
Location: MoK.

G4   Doering, Leo J. and Mrs. Leo J. Doering. The possibilities of different musical rhythms in Turnverein work. n.p., n.d. [1900?]. 14 p.
Note: Leo Doering was the instructor for the *Socialer* Turnverein Detroit; his wife, Cyrilla Doering, was the pianist for the society. Includes lesson plans and examples of children's dances.
Location: InIU.

G5   Du Bois-Reymond, Emil. Swedish gymnastics and German gymnastics: from a physiological point of view. Milwaukee: Freidenker Publishing Co., n.d. [1880s]. 13 p.
Note: Fifth essay in the series Essays concerning the German system of gymnastics, sponsored by the American Turnerbund. Emil du Bois-Reymond, a professor at the University of Berlin, compares the German and Swedish systems of gymnastics.
Location: InIU.

G6   Essays concerning the German system of gymnastics.   Milwaukee: Freidenker Publishing Co., n.d. [1880s]. [58 p.]
Note: Title page: "Essays Concerning the German System of Gymnastics. Translated from the German by A.B.C. Biewend. Published by the Executive Committee of the North American Turnerbund." Collection of nine essays on physical education by

German and American scholars, including C.F. Koch, J.C. Lion, Emil DuBois-Reymond, and Adolf Spieß. Each essay was also published separately by the Freidenker Publishing Company.
Location: InIU.

G7   Fischer, Robert. Course in fencing, foil, saber and single stick arranged by Dr. Robert Fischer. Indianapolis: Normal College of the North American Gymnastic Union, 1908. 29 p.
Note: Fischer was the supervisor of physical training and school hygiene for the Indianapolis Public Schools and served as dean of the Department for Anatomy, Physiology, and Hygiene for the Normal College.
Location: ICRL; ICU; MnU; NBuU; WHi.

G8   Grohe, Ed. Kurzgefasste Geschichte der Leibes-Übungen. Milwaukee: Carl Dörflinger, 1877. 34 p.
Note: Essay on the history of physical exercises from the time of the Greek and Roman empires to 1877. Grohe was a Turner instructor.
Location: InIU.

G9   Grundriss für Vorturnerkurse im Nordamerikanischen Turnerbund. Milwaukee: Freidenker Publishing Co., 1914. 11 p.
Note: Title page: "*Grundriss für Vorturnerkurse im Nordamerikanischen Turnerbund. Angenommen vom Bundesvorort am* 7. November 1914." *Vorturner*, or class-leaders, were members of Turner societies who were permitted to instruct children and adults in certain exercises and mass drills following the completion of a 6-month course. *Vorturner* played a particularly important role at smaller societies that were unable to hire professional instructors. This outline for the *Vorturner's* course includes general rules, a class schedule, and work plans for men and women.
Location: InIU.

G10   Heintz, George. Theory of fencing with the foil in form of a catechism. Milwaukee: Freidenker Publishing Co., 1890. 52 p.
Location: CU.

G11   Koch, C. F. Courage, independence, presence of mind and a cheerful disposition as a result of gymnastic exercises. Milwaukee: Freidenker Publishing Company, [1900]. [7 p.]
Note: First essay in the series Essays concerning the German system of gymnastics, sponsored by the American Turnerbund.
Location: InIU.

G12   Kroh, Karl. Fete Gymnastique, Music Hall, March 1887. The Turner's Association For the Advancement of Physical Education, Cincinnati Deutsche Turngemeinde, organized 1848. [Cincinnati]: n.p., 1887. 15 p.

Note: Karl (Charles) Kroh was a graduate of the *Turnlehrer* Seminar in 1879. He taught physical education in Dayton and Cincinnati, Ohio, as well as at Chicago University before he became the director of the Normal College of the American Gymnastic Union in 1907. Publication includes outline of exercises and games.
Location: OCHi.

G13   ---. Gymnastics: synopsis of the German system. St. Louis: Executive Committee of the North American Gymnastic Union, printed by Shullcross-McCallum Printing Company, 1897. 39 p.
Note: Includes outline of gymnastic exercises, games and plays, and fencing, foil and sword exercises.
Location: CLAA; InIU.

G14   Lang, August. ed. A. Lang's Turntafeln. Chicago: Shoer & Co., 1876. 121 p.
Note: Full title page: "A. Lang's Turntafeln: Illustrationen, frei bearbeitet nach J.C. Lion und August Ravenstein, herausgegeben von August Lang, Turnlehrer der Chicago Turngemeinde." August Lang was the instructor of the Chicago *Turngemeinde*. His *Turntafeln* are illustrations of physical exercises described in Dr. J.C. Lion's Leitfaden für Ordnungs-und Freiübungen und gemischten Sprung and August Ravenstein's Volkesturnbuch. The Turnerbund had made both works obligatory handbooks for gymnastic instructions in each Turner society. Lang's illustrations were meant to aid in the understanding of the often complicated explanations of exercises. The Turntafeln were financially supported by the Turnerbund.
Location: C; InIU.

G15   Liebold, Anton. Manuals of physical culture for schools, gymnastic associations, and private use. Louisville: Bradley & Gilbert Company, 1888. 47 p.
Note: Anton Liebold graduated from the *Turnlehrer* Seminar in 1877 and became supervisor of physical culture in the Columbus, OH public schools.
Location: DLC; NcGU.

G16   ---. Manuals of physical culture for public schools. 3rd rev. ed. Columbus, OH: Crescent, 1899. 122 p.
Location: CtRP.

G17   ---. Manuals of physical culture for public schools. rev. ed. Columbus, Ohio: Poland Co., Printers, 1908. 136 p.
Location: MSC.

G18   ---. Official handbook of the public recreation commission of Columbus, Ohio, governing athlectics under its jurisdiction. Columbus, Ohio: n.p.,1911. 28 p.
Note: "The outline and rules ... [were] prepared by the secretary of the Public

Recreation Commission [Edgar S. Martin] and by Prof. Anton Liebold, supervisor of physical culture in the public schools." p. 28.
Location: CU.

G19   ---. Physical games for our youth. Columbus, OH: Press of L. Hirsch, 1902. 51 p.
Note: Descriptions of games for use in physical education programs.
Location: MSC.

G20   Lion, Justus Carl. Concerning the method of teaching gymnastics in our gymnastic societies. Milwaukee: Freidenker Publishing Co., n.d. 6 p.
Note: On cover: "From the German by A.B.C. Biewend." The ninth essay in the series Essays concerning the German system of gymnastics, sponsored by the American Turnerbund. Lion was the author of numerous physical education books in Germany.
Location: InIU.

G21   ---. Concerning the nature of gymnastics and gymnastics in school. Milwaukee: Freidenker Publishing Co., n.d. 13 p.
Note: On cover: "From the German by A.B.C. Biewend." The ninth essay in Essays concerning the German system of gymnastics, sponsored by the American Turnerbund.
Location: InIU.

G22   Müller, Eduard. Das Turnen. Ein Leitfaden für die Mitglieder des socialistischen Turnerbundes und Freunden der Leibesübungen im Auftrag des Vorortes dargestellt durch Eduard Müller, Turnlehrer. New York: John Weber, 1853. 371 p.
Note: Title translation: "Guidelines for members of the socialist Turnerbund and friends of physical education." Contains 340 pages text, 31 pages of illustrations. Eduard Müller, a refugee of the 1848 revolution and former editor of the Mainzer Turnzeitung, was instructor in New York City where he aided in the establishment of the *Turnlehrer Seminar* in 1866. This work was commissioned by the Turnerbund in the early 1850s in order to provide a text book for Turner societies and the planned *Turnlehrer Seminar*. Includes outline of physical exercises.
Locations: IaDP; InIU; PPG.

G23   Ocker, W.A. Bulletin on physical education: a manual of games, rhythmic steps and exercises in physical training for the public schools of Indianapolis, grades 3 to 8. [Indianapolis]: n.p., 1928. 116 p.
Note: W.A. Ocker graduated from the *Turnlehrer* Seminar in 1892. He was later director of physical education and hygiene for the Indianapolis public schools and a professor at the Normal College. This work consists of fifty-four lesson plans for physical training lessons to be taught in grades three through eight.
Location: InIU.

G24   ---. Physical education for primary schools: informal gymnastics in lesson form with piano accompaniment. New York: A.S. Barnes and Company, 1926. 83 p.
Note: Includes lesson plans, songs, and games.
Location: InIU.

G25   ---. Physical education for the second grade. New York: A.S. Barnes and Company, 1928. 37 p.
Note: Includes lesson plans, songs and games.
Location: InIU.

G26   Outline for class leader's courses of the North American Gymnastic Union. Indianapolis: Bookwalter-Ball Printing, 1915. 12 p.
Note: Title page: "Outline for Class Leader's Courses of the North American Gymnastic Union. Adopted by the Twenty-Sixth Convention Nineteen-Fifteen." Includes general rules and outlines of gymnastic exercises for men and women.
Location: InIU.

G27   Passow, Franz. Teaching gymnastics: a state affair. Milwaukee: Freidenker Publishing Co., n.d. 6 p.
Note: On cover: "Translated from the German by A.B.C. Biewend." The seventh essay in the series Essays concerning the German system of gymnastics, sponsored by the American Turnerbund. Discussion on the value of physical exercises in education.
Location: InIU.

G28   Rath, Emil. Aesthetic dancing. New York: A.S. Barnes Co. 1914.   136 p.
Note: Emil Rath was director of the Normal College of the American Gymnastic Union from 1910 until 1934. Under his leadership the college expanded to a nationally recognized institution. In 1934, Rath became Director of Physical Education and Health in the Indianapolis public schools. During his career Rath published numerous books on physical education and health. This work covers the philosophy and techniques of aesthetic dancing, and includes photographs of exercises.
Location: Frequently available at large public and academic libraries.

G29   ---. Aesthetic dancing. rev. ed. New York: A.S. Barnes Co. 1928.   136 p.
Location: PU.

G30   ---. Folk and school dances. 3rd rev. ed. Indianapolis: Normal College of the American Gymnastic Union, 1929. 25 p.
Note: First edition was published in 1916. Includes music and dance steps.
Location: InIU; NIIC.

G31   ---. The folk dance in education. Minneapolis: Burgees Pub. Co., 1939. [51p.]
Location: Frequently available at large public and academic libraries.

G32   --. Graded apparatus work for men: lower grade. Indianapolis: Normal College of the North American Gymnastic Union, 1916. 92 p.
Location: CLAA; MSC; InIU; WULC.

G33   ---. Graded apparatus work for men. rev. ed. Indianapolis: Normal College of the North American Gymnastic Union, 1923. 92 p.
Location: CLU; DLC.

G34   ---. Gymnastic dancing for girl's and women's classes. Indianapolis: Normal College of the N.A.G.U., 1913. 32 p.
Location: DLC; NJNC.

G35   ---. Outlines of educational gymnastics. Indianapolis: Normal College of the North American Gymnastic Union, 1916. 143 p.
Location: DLC; NALU.

G36   ---. Outline of some physical education activities. rev. ed. Indianapolis: Normal College of the American Gymnastic Union, 1926. 207 p.
Note: First edition was published in 1916 and was sold out by 1922.
Location: InIU.

G37   ---. "A program of physical education for boys in secondary schools of Indiana." M.A. Thesis, Indiana University, 1929. 172 p.
Location: InIU.

G38   ---. Theory and practice of physical education. Indianapolis: Normal College of the North American Gymnastic Union, 1915-1916. 3 vols.
      v.1: Gymnastic dancing, 1915. 132 p.
      v.2: Free exercises without and with hand apparatus, 1916. 265 p.
      v.3: Apparatus, track and field work for girls and women, 1915. 160 p.
Location: Frequently available at large public and academic libraries.

G39   ---. Theory and practice of physical education. 2nd ed. Indianapolis: Normal College of the North American Gymnastic Union, 1920-1923. 3 vols.
      v.1: Gymnastic dancing, 1923. 160 p.
      v.2: Free exercises without and with hand apparatus, 1920. 265 p.
      v.3: Apparatus, track and field work for girls and women, 1921. 209 p.
Location: Frequently available at large public and academic libraries.

G40   ---. Theory and practice of physical education: open order work. 3rd ed. Indianapolis: Normal College of the American Gymnastic Union, 1927. 189 p.
Note: "Open order work" is the 3rd revised edition of volume two "Free exercises without and with hand apparatus."
Location: ICU; IEdS; InIU; MnU; OCI; PS.

G41   Rice, Emmett. A brief history of physical education. New York: A.S. Barnes and Co., 1929.
Note: Rice was vice-principal at Shortridge High School in Indianapolis and lecturer on the history of education and anthropology at the Normal College. A revised and enlarged edition was published in 1936.
Location: InIU.

G42   Richter, H. E. How may we preserve our youth? Milwaukee: Freidenker Publishing Co., [ca. 1885]. 7 p.
Note: The second essay in the series Essays concerning the German system of gymnastics, sponsored by the American Turnerbund. Essay describes the importance of physical culture for developing moral strength in the young.
Location: InIU.

G43   Royal Prussian Deputation of the Medical Department. Exercises on the parallel bars: from a medical point of view. An opinion by the Royal Prussian Deputation of the Medical Department, Berlin, Prussia. Milwaukee: Freidenker Publishing Co., [ca. 1885]. 8 p.
Note: The sixth essay in the series Essays concerning the German system of gymnastics, sponsored by the American Turnerbund. Translation of report written in 1862 on the physical value of exercises on the parallel bars.
Location: InIU.

G44   Schmidt, Frederick A. Physical exercises and their beneficial influence: a short synopsis of the German system of gymnastics and all friends of physical culture. 3rd ed. St. Louis: North American Gymnastic Union, 1894. 41 p.
Note: On cover: "Translated from German by A.B.C. Biewend."
Location: MnU; WHi; WMCHi.

G45   Schmidt, Ferdinand A. and Wolfgang Kohlrausch. Physiology of exercise. Translated by Carl B. Sputh with assistance from Emil Rath and Leopold Zwarg. Philadelphia: F.A. Davis Co., 1931. 216 p.
Note: Translated from the fourth edition of Dr. Schmidt's Physiologie der Leibesübungen. Includes chapters describing concepts of physical education, medical analysis of physical exercises, influence of physical education on specific body parts and exercises for different age groups. Includes photographs and illustrations. The translator, Carl Sputh, was president of the Normal College.
Location: Frequently available at large public and academic libraries.

G46   Spieß, Adolf. About gymnastics in the schools: selections from Spiess' works. Milwaukee: Freidenker Publishing Co., [ca. 1885]. 16 p.
Note: On cover: "Translated from the German by A.B.C. Biewend." The eighth essay in the series Essays concerning the German system of gymnastics, sponsored by the American Turnerbund. Adolf Spieß was the author of numerous works on physical

education in Germany in the mid-nineteenth century.
Location: InIU.

G47   Sputh, Carl. <u>Outline: educational gymnastics</u>. n.p.: 1915. 129 p.
Note: Cover title: "Arranged for the students in the School of Physical Education, State Normal, La Crosse, Wis." Carl Sputh, graduate of the Normal College class of 1905, organized the Physical Education Department at the State Teachers College, La Crosse, Wisconsin. He began teaching at the Normal College in 1916 and served as its president from 1934 until 1941.
Location: WULC.

G48   Stecher, William A. <u>Games and dances: a selected collection of games, song-games and dances suitable for schools, playgrounds, gymnastic associations, boy's and girl's clubs, etc</u>. Philadelphia: McVey, 1912. 165 p.
Note: Stecher graduated from the *Turnlehrer* Seminar in 1881 and became the supervisor for physical education in the Philadelphia Public Schools and nonresident lecturer at the Normal College.
Location: Frequently available at large public and academic libraries.

G49   ---. <u>Games and dances</u>. 2nd ed., rev. and enl. Philadelphia: McVey, 1916. 265 p.
Location: Frequently available at large public and academic libraries.

G50   ---. <u>Games and dances</u>. 3rd ed., rev. and enl. Philadelphia: McVey, 1920. 357 p.
Location: Frequently available at large public and academic libraries.

G51   ---. <u>Games and dances</u>. 4th ed., rev. and enl. Philadelphia: McVey, 1926. 405p.
Location: Frequently available at large public and academic libraries.

G52   ---. <u>Games and dances for exercises and recreation: a selection of worth while games, athletics, stunts, and dances for teachers colleges, schools, recreation centers, playgrounds, boy's and girl's clubs, camps, picnics, etc</u>. Philadelphia: Theodor Presser Company, 1941. 392 p.
Location: Frequently available at large public and academic libraries.

G53   ---. <u>The German system of physical education. A paper read at the seventh annual meeting of the American Association for the Advancement of Physical Education, held in Philadelphia, Pa., April 7, 8 and 9, 1892</u>. St. Louis: Press of A.C. Clayton & Son, 1892. 14 p.
Note: The same paper was also published by the Freidenker Publishing Company in Milwaukee in 1892, 14 p.
Location: DHEW; DNLM (Freidenker Pub. Co.); OO.

G54   ---. A guide to track and field work contests and kindred activities: a supplement to the handbook of lessons in physical training and games for the Philadelphia Public Schools. Philadelphia: J.J. McVey, 1912. 47 p.
Location: CLAA; ICU; IEN; MiEM; NB; RPB; TxU.

G55   ---. ed. Gymnastics: a textbook of the German-American system of gymnastics: specially adapted to the use of teachers and pupils in public and private schools and gymnasiums. Boston: Lothrop, Lee and Shepard Publishers, 1896. 348p.
Note: A collection of essays on gymnastics written by sixteen teachers of the Normal College of the North American Gymnastic Union.
Location: Frequently available at large public and academic libraries.

G56   ---. ed. Gymnastics: a textbook of the German-American system of gymnastics: specially adapted to the use of teachers and pupils in public and private schools and gymnasiums. London: Gay & Bird, 1896. 348 p.
Location: ICRL; ICU.

G57   ---. Handbook of graded lessons in physical training and games for primary and grammar grades. Philadelphia: McVey, 1908-1910. 3 vols.
        v.1: For 1st and 2nd grades.
        v.2: For 3rd and 4th grades.
        v.3: For 5th, 6th, 7th & 8th grades.
Location: Frequently available at large public and academic libraries.

G58   ---. Handbook of graded lessons in physical training and games for primary and grammar grades. Philadelphia: McVey, 1919-1921. 3 vols.
        v.1: For 1st and 2nd grades, 5th rev. ed, 1921.
        v.2: For 3rd and 4th grades, 3rd rev. ed., 1919.
        v.3: For 5th, 6th, 7th & 8th grades, 3rd rev. ed, 1921.
Location: Frequently available at large public and academic libraries.

G59   ---. "Has school gymnastics an appreciable effect upon health?" International Congress on School Hygiene v. 5 (1914), pp. 560-565.
Location: NN.

G60   ---. Lesson in physical training. Indianapolis: Indiana Public Schools, 1904. 40 p.
Location: PPT; WULC.

G61   ---. Lessons in physical training in three grades of difficulty for mentally retarded pupils in the special classes of the elementary schools. Philadelphia: Board of Public Education, 1920. 40 p.
Location: PPT.

G62   ---. Physical training lessons in three grades of difficulty for backward classes. Philadelphia: McVey, 1923. 38 p.
Location: CL; DLC; MiEM; OCI; PPiU.

G63   ---. Physical training lessons, including games, dances, stunts, track and field work: an illustrated handbook for the class room teacher, with seventy-six halftone illustrations, fifteen line drawings and five song games with music. Philadelphia: McVey, 1924. 149 p.
Location: Frequently available at large public and academic libraries.

G64   ---. "Physical welfare work with school children in war times: principles underlying minimum essentials of exercises." National Education Association of the United States, address and proceedings (1913), pp. 677-683.

G65   ---. School tactics for the use of schools and gymnastics associations. Cincinnati, n.p., 1887. 46 p.
Location: Frequently available at large public and academic libraries.

G66   ---. The theory and practice of educational gymnastics, embracing free exercises, rhythmic steps, track and field work, games, apparatus work. Philadelphia: McVey, 1915. 188 p.
Location: Frequently available at large public and academic libraries.

G67   ---. Theory and practice of educational gymnastics for boys' and girls' high schools. Philadelphia: McVey, 1918. 104 p.
Location: Frequently available at large public and academic libraries.

G68   ---. Theory and practice of educational gymnastics for junior high schools; also for boys' and girls' clubs and all associations having gymnasium and playground work. Philadelphia: McVey, 1918. 145 p.
Location: Frequently available at large public and academic libraries.

G69   Suder, Henry. Chicago public schools: manual of exercises in physical education; light gymnastics for elementary schools. Chicago: n.p., 1912. 214 p.
Note: Suder graduated from the *Turnlehrer Seminar* in 1875. He was later superintendent of physical culture of the Chicago public schools and a nonresident lecturer on physical education for the Normal College.
Location: CLAA; NALU.

G70   ---. Chicago public schools: manual of exercises in physical education; light gymnastics for elementary schools. rev. ed. Chicago: n.p., 1926. 214 p.
Location: CU.

G71   ---. Gymnastics with special apparatus for elementary grades. Chicago. n.p., 1902. 60 p.
Location: DLC (microfilm).

G72   ---. Manual of gymnastics on apparatus for elementary schools. Chicago: Board of Education of the City of Chicago, 1911. 115 p.
Note: Revised edition in 1916.
Location: CLAA; DLC.

G73   ---. Program of exercises in physical training: first to fourth grades. rev. ed. Chicago: Board of Education of the City of Chicago, 1902. 126 p.
Location: ICHi.

G74   ---. Song-roundels and games. Chicago: Board of Education, 1904. 76 p.
Note: Children's songs and games, for use by teachers.
Location: Frequently available at large public and academic libraries.

G75   ---. Song-roundels and games. rev. ed. Chicago: Board of Education, 1918. 146 p.
Location: Frequently available at large public and academic libraries.

G76   ---. Teachers' manual of physical culture for public schools: second series, part 1, fifth grade. Milwaukee: Freidenker Publishing Co., 1891. 56 p.
Location: OCU; WULC.

G77   Viehweg, Ernst. The necessity of physical culture: with a series of illustrated practical exercises. Milwaukee: Freidenker Publishing Co., [ca.1895] 41 p.
Note: Cover title: "Issued by the Wisconsin District, N.A. Gymnastic Association." Ernst Viehweg graduated from the *Turnlehrer Seminar* in 1890 and became a teacher of physiology and physical culture in Sheboygan, WI. Discusses the value of physical education and includes lesson plans.
Location: InIU.

G78   Wittich, George. Elements of strength and weakness in physical education as taught in public schools. n.p., 1908.
Note: Reprinted in the National Education Association of the United States's Journal of Proceedings and Addresses, 1908. George Wittich was the supervisor of physical training at the Milwaukee public schools and nonresident lecturer at the Normal College.
Location: MnU.

G79   ---. Manual of physical training for the primary and grammar grades of the Milwaukee public schools. Milwaukee: n.p., 1914. 172 p.
Location: CU.

G80   Zwarg, Leopold F. Apparatus work for boys and girls: a course of graded instruction, with illustrations in the use of horizontal bars, parallel bars, horses, rings, ladders, stall bars, giant strides, climbing poles, bucks, mats. Philadelphia: J.J. McVey, 1923.
Note: Leopold Zwarg was an instructor of physical education at the University of Pennsylvania, Department Head of Physical and Health Education for Germantown High School, Philadelphia, and member of the National Committee of the American Turnerbund.
Location: Frequently available at large public and academic libraries.

G81   ---. Apparatus & tumbling exercises for boys and men in high schools, colleges, clubs and playgrounds. Philadelphia: J.J. McVey, 1928. 316 p.
Location: Frequently available at large public and academic libraries.

G82   ---. "A study of the history, uses, and values of apparatus in physical education." M.A. Thesis, Temple University, 1929.
Location: CSt; LU; MiU.

G83   ---. A study of the history, uses, and values of apparatus in physical education. Philadelphia: Westbrook Publishing Co., 1930. 139 p.
Note: Includes a historical review of the development of apparatus exercises and six experimental studies in the use of apparatus.
Location: Frequently available at large public and academic libraries.

G84   ---. A guide to officials & competitors: the judging and evaluation of competitive exercises. Philadelphia, n.d. 16 p.
Note: Includes score tables and guidelines for judging gymnastic competitions.
Location: InIU.

Chapter 6

Writings on the American Turners

The Turner movement has attracted the attention of many scholars working in fields ranging from physical education to labor history. To list all sources where Turner activities have been mentioned would be impossible. Instead, this chapter includes only those books, articles, Ph.D. dissertations and M.A. theses which are focused on the Turners and book-length works which have separate sections or chapters on the Turners. Unpublished student papers, newspaper articles, or works which only briefly mention Turner activities have not been included. For more specific information on individual societies, consult local newspapers, county histories, and city directories. General scholarly works on the Forty-eighters, German immigration, or the history of physical education will usually include information on the American Turners as well.

In order to distinguish works written during the height of the movement from more current academic scholarship, the publications have been divided into two groups: pre-1920 publications and publications from 1920 to the present. Within each group the publications are arranged alphabetically by author. Because most of these works are generally available, locations have not been listed.

Pre-1920 Publications

W1   "*Anglo-Amerikaner über deutsches Turnen*." <u>Der Deutsche Pionier</u> 14 (1862): 303-04.

W2   Cronau, Rudolf. <u>German Archievements in America</u>. New York: Rudolf Cronau, [1916].
Note: Includes the article, "The North American Turnerbund and its Influence on Physical Development of the American Nation," pp. 121-124.

W3   [*Deutsch-Amerikanischer National-Bund*]. Das Buch der Deutschen in Amerika. Herausgegeben unter den auspicien des Deutsch-Amerikanischen National-Bundes. Philadelphia: Walther's *Buchdruckerei*, 1909. 982 p.
Note: Includes the article, "*Der Nord-Amerikanische Tunerbund*," pp. 736-747.

W4   "*Die deutsche Ansiedlung* New Ulm in Minnesota." Der Deutsche Pionier 3, no.1 (1871): 12-17.

W5   "*Die deutsche Turnerschaft im Jahre* 1885." Der Deutsche Pionier 17 (1885): 372-75.

W6   Eiboeck, Joseph. Die Deutschen von Iowa und deren Errungenschaften: Eine Geschichte des Staates, deren deutsche Pioniere und ihre Nachkommen. Des Moines: Iowa Staats-Anzeiger, 1900.
Note: Includes a history of the *Obere Mississippi Turnbezirk* (Upper Mississippi District), pp. 289-292.

W7   "*Die ersten Jahre der Philadelphia Turngemeinde*." Mitteilungen des Deutschen Pionier Vereins von Philadelphia 22 (1911): 29-36.

W8   Euler, Carl. Encyklopädisches Handbuch des gesamten Turnwesens und der verwandten Gebiete. Vienna and Leipzig: *Verlag von A. Pichler's Witwe & Sohn*, 1894-96. 3 vols.
Note: Euler was a professor at the training school for physical education instructors in Berlin. His three volume encyclopedia on Turner history and practice includes a lengthy entry on the Turners in the United States, part of which was written by Heinrich Metzner, and part by Euler. The entry is under "*Nord-Amerika, Vereinigte Staaten*," vol. 2, pp. 194-206. Included are biographical sketches of a number of leaders of the Turner movement in America.

W9   Fritsche, Louis Albert, M. D. History of Brown County Minnesota: its people, industries and institutions. Indianapolis: B.F. Bowen & Company, Inc., 1916.
Note: Chapter 18, "The City of New Ulm," describes the involvement of the Turners in the founding of the town.

W10   George, Adolph. "*Aus der Geschichte der Chicago Turngemeinde*." Deutsch-Amerikanische Geschichtsblätter 5 (1905): 42-51.

W11   Goebel, Julius. "Karl Follen." Jahrbuch der Deutschen in Chicago und im Staate Illinois für das Jahr 1917, edited by Michael Singer, pp.171-176. Chicago: n.p., 1917.

W12   Gorbach, August B., ed. Deutscher Vereins-Wegweiser von Cincinnati. Cincinnati: Rosenthal & Co., 1915. 274 p.

Note: Includes a general over-view of several Cincinnati Turner societies, including the *Allgemeine Arbeiter Turn-und Athleten Verein*, the Cincinnati Turngemeinde, and the *Nord*-Cincinnati Turnverein.
Location: OCU.

W13   Grebner, Constantin. Ohio Infantry, 9th Regiment, 1861-1864: Die Neuner, Eine Schilderung der Kriegsjahre des 9ten Regiments Ohio Vol. Infantries, vom 17. April 1861 bis 7. Juni, 1864 mit einer Einleitung von Oberst Gustav Tafel. Cincinnati: S. Rosenthal & Co., 1897. 290 p.
Note: History of the Ninth Ohio Infantry Regiment, a German regiment with large numbers of Turners.

W14   Hoehn, G.A. Der Nordamerikanische Turnerbund und seine Stellung zur Arbeiterfrage. 1882.
Note: Cited in William Frederic Kamman, Socialism in German American literature. Philadelphia: Americana Germanica Press, 1917.

W15   Huch, C.F. "*Das erste allgemeine Turnfest in* [Philadelphia]." Mitteilungen des Deutschen Pionier Vereins von Philadelphia 22 (1911): 20-23.

W16   ---. "*Der Sozialistische Turnerbund.*" Mitteilungen des Deutschen Pionier-Vereins von Philadelphia 23 (1912): 1-15.

W17   Hyde, William and Howard Conrad, eds. Encyclopedia of the history of St. Louis. 4 vols. New York: The Southern History Company, 1899.
Note: The encyclopedia includes a lengthy article on the Turners in St. Louis, pp. 2314-2318.

W18   Kallmeyer, Otto. "*Das Turnwesen, seine Entwicklung und dessen Bedeutung für Missouri.*" Deutsche Geschichtsforschung für Missouri (German Historical Researches of Missouri) 1 (October 1913): 7-14.
Note: Article on the St. Louis Turners during the 1850s and their activities at the beginning of the Civil War, including the formation of a military organization in 1861 to prepare for war in the event of succession and actions to preserve Camp Jackson for the Union.

W19   Kamman, William F. Socialism in German-American literature. Philadelphia: Americana-Germanica Press, 1917.
Note: See Chapter 4: "The Turner and Socialism."

W20   Kansas City und sein Deutschthum im 19. Jahrhundert. Cleveland: German-American Biographical Publishing Company, 1900. 350 p.
Note: Includes a history of the Kansas City *Socialer* Turnverein.

W21 Knortz, Karl. Das Deutschtum der Vereinigten Staaten. Hamburg: *Verlagsanstalt und Druckerei A.G.*, 1898. 83 p.
Note: Includes an overview of the history of Turners in the United States, *"Deutsche Turnkunst in den Vereinigten Staaten,"* pp. 55-64. Knortz is identified on the title page as the superintendent of schools for Evansville, Indiana.

W22 Learned, Marion Dexter. The German-American Turner lyric. Baltimore: C.W. Schneidereith & Son, 1897. 58 p.
Note: Study of Turner poetry and songs. Reprinted in the 10th annual report of the Society for the History of Germans in Maryland (1897): 79-134.

W23 ---. "The German-American Turner lyric." Deutsch-Amerikanische Geschichtsblätter 11 (1911): 47-48.

W24 Mannhardt, Emil. "Henrich Metzner's *verdiente Ehrung.*" Deutsch Amerikanische Geschichtsblätter 11, no. 4 (1911): 301-02.

W25 "New Britain Turn Verein, 1853-1912." In Connecticut Germans: historical, biographical, industrial, edited by Alfred Traute. n.p., 1912.
Note: Historical overview of the New Britain Turnverein.

W26 *"Der New York Turnverein."* Der Deutsche Pionier 17, no. 3, 1886: 270-2.

W27 Nix, Jacob. Der Ausbruch der Sioux-Indianer in Minnesota, im August 1862. New Ulm, Minn.: *Verlag des Verfassers*, 1887. 71 p.
Note: Account of the Sioux uprising in Minnesota in 1862, with particular attention to the attack upon New Ulm.

W28 Paul, A. *"Der Einfluß der deutsch-amerikanischen Turner auf die Kultur der Vereinigten Staaten."* Körper und Geist 22 (1913/14): 7-12.

W29 Pfaefflin, Hermann. Hundertjährige Geschichte des Deutschtums von Rochester. [Rochester]: *Deutsch-Amerikanischer Bund von Rochester und Umgebung*, 1915. 255 p.
Note: Includes a history of the Rochester Turnverein, pp. 150-158.

W30 *"Die Pionier-Turngemeinde Amerika's."* Der Deutsche Pionier 17, no. 5 (July 1875): 178-187.

W31 Ruetenik, Herman Julius. Berühmte Deutsche Vorkämpfer für Fortschritt, Freiheit und Friede in Nord-Amerika von 1626-1898. Cleveland: Forest City Bookbinding Co., 1899.
Note: Contains 150 biographical sketches of leading Germans in America, including a number with strong Turner and Forty-eighter connections including Karl Follen,

Franz Lieber, Karl Heinzen, Karl Daniel Adolph Douai, Gustav von Struve, Freidrich Hecker, August Willich and Franz Sigel.

W32   Schem, Alexander J. Deutsch-Amerikanisches Konversations-Lexicon: Mit spezialler Rücksicht auf das Bedürfniss der in Amerika lebenden Deutschen mit Benutzung aller deutschen, amerikanischen, englischen und französischen Quellen und unter Mitwirkung vieler hervorragender deutscher Schriftsteller Amerika's. New York: Steiger, 1869-1874.
Note: Contains entries on *"Turnen," "Turners,"* and *"Turnwesen"* in the U.S."

W33   Schlüter, Hermann. Die Anfänge der deutschen Arbeiterbewegung in Amerika. Stuttgart: *Verlag von J.H.W. Dietz Nachfolger*, 1907.
Note: See Chapter 6: *"Der Sozialistische Turnerbund,"* p. 199-214.

W34   "Springfield Turn Verein." In "Historical sketches and brief accounts of clubs, societies, fraternal organizations, etc., in Springfield, written on the occasion of the 275th anniversary of the settlement of the city." Unpublished manuscript. Springfield, MA, 1911.
Location: MSHi.

W35   Strasser, J. H. Chronologie der Stadt New Ulm, Minnesota. New Ulm: New Ulm Post, 1899. 91 p.
Note: This work was translated into English by Kay Sierass in 1978. Translation available at MnHi.

W36   Tiling, Moritz Philip Georg. History of the German element in Texas from 1820-1850, and historical sketches of the German Texas Singer's League and Houston Turnverein from 1853-1913. Houston: n.p., 1913. 225 p.

W37   Tilton, Rev. H.C. The Turn-Fest, its teachings and practices. A discourse, delivered in Appleton August 1, 1875. Fond du Lac, Wl.: Reporter Job Office, 1875. 18 p.
Note: Publication critical of Turner activities.
Location: NN; WHi.

W38   Traute, Alfred. Connecticut Germans: historical, biographical, industrial. n.p., 1912.
Note: Includes a brief history, "The Connecticut Turn *Bezirk*: the Connecticut German Gymnastic Union," written by Moritz F. Kemnitzer.

W39   Der Turner: illustrierte Zeitschrift für das Vereins-Turnen. Berlin, 1886-1914.
Note: Magazine published for the German Turners; frequently includes news of Turner activities in the United States.

W40 25th National Convention, Order of Hermann's Sons, San Francisco, September 14. to 21., 1913. San Francisco: The Hansen Co., [1913].
Note: Includes an article on "*Deutsche Turnerei*" in San Francisco and histories of the San Francisco Turn Verein and Mission Turn Verein in San Francisco.
Location: Private collection.

W41 "*Zum Sechzigsten Jubiläum des New York Turnvereins.*" Deutsch-Amerikanische Geschichtsblätter July (1903).

Publications: 1920 -- present

W42 Ables, Emil. "The German element in Wilmington from 1850-1914." Master's thesis, University of Delaware, 1948.
Note: Includes a chapter on the Wilmington Turners.

W43 Adams, Paul. "The Topeka Turn Verein." Bulletin of the Shawnee County Historical Society October (1953): 5-10.

W44 Beaver Falls area centennial: historical salute to the centuries, 1868-1968. Beaver Falls, Pa.: Tribune Printing Co., 1968. 199 p.
Note: Includes a brief history of the Beaver Falls Turners.
Location: PBF.

W45 Baumgaertner, Rainer. "The immigration press and Americanization: a comparative study of the German communities in Tell City and Indianapolis, 1856-1882." Master's thesis, Indiana University, 1987.
Note: Includes substantial amount of information on the Indianapolis Turnverein.

W46 Barney, Robert Knight. "An historical reinterpretation of the forces underlying the first state legislation for physical education in the public schools in the United States." Research Quarterly 44 (1973): 146-360.

W47 ---. "German Turners in America: their role in nineteenth century exercise expression and physical education legislation." In History of Physical Education and Sport in the United States and Canada, edited by Earle F. Zeigler. Champaign, Ill.: Stripes Publishing Co., 1975.

W48 ---. "German Turners in 19th century North America: their role in exercise expression and physical education legislation." In The history, evolution and diffusion of sports and games in different cultures, edited by Ronald Renson et al. Brussels: *Bestuur voor de Lichamelijke Opvoeding*, 1976.

W49   ---. "German Turners in American domestic crisis: Jahnistic ideals in clash with southern sentiment during the Antebellum and Civil War periods." Stadion 4 (1978): 344-357.

W50   ---. "Friedrich Ludwig Jahn revisited: a report on the International Jahn Symposium." Journal of Physical Education and Recreation 50, no.3 (1979): 58.

W51   ---. "Mary E. Allen: thought and practice in 19th century American gymnastics." Journal of Physical Education and Recreation 51, no.4 (1980): 82-86.

W52   ---. "Knights of cause and exercise: German Forty-Eighters and Turnvereins in the United States during the Antebellum period." Canadian Journal of History of Sport 13 (1982): 62-79.

W53   ---. "Notes, documents, and queries. America's first Turnverein: commentary in favor of Louisville, Kentucky." Journal of Sport History 11, no. 1 (1984): 134-137.

W54   ---. "German-American Turnvereins and socio-politico-economic realities in the Antebellum and Civil War upper and lower south." Stadion 10 (1984): 135-181.

W55   ---. "For such Olympic games: German-American Turnfests as prelude to the modern Olympic games." Proceedings: Sport, The Millennium Congress, Quebec City, 1990. 10 p.

W56   ---. "The German-American Turnverein Movement: its historiography in North America." In Turner and sport: the cross-cultural exchange, edited by Roland Naul. Münster and New York: Waxmann, 1991, pp. 3-20.

W57   ---. "Forty-eighters and the rise of the Turnverein movement in America." In Ethnicity and sport in North American history and culture, edited by George Eisen and David K. Wiggins. Westport, CT: Greenwood Press, 1994, pp.20-41.

W58   Bean, Phillip A. Germans in Utica: an exhibition held at Utica College of Syracuse University, October 10-November 2, 1990. Utica: Utica College of Syracuse University, 1990. 18 p.
Note: Includes information on the Utica Turnverein.

W59   Beran, J.A. "The Turners in Iowa, USA: promoters of fitness and shapers of culture." In Turnen and sport: the cross-cultural exchange, edited by Roland Naul. Münster and New York: Waxmann, 1991, pp. 83-106.

W60   Berghold, Alexander. "The German settlement of New Ulm in Minnesota." unpublished paper, n.d. 7 p.

Note: Discusses the New Ulm settlement society of the *Sozialistischer* Turnerbund, and its merger with the Chicago Land Society.
Location: MnHi.

W61 Binz, Roland. "German gymnastic societies in St. Louis, 1850-1913: emergent socio-cultural institutions." Master's thesis, Washington University, 1983.

W62 Bowen, Elbert Russell. Theatrical entertainment in rural Missouri before the Civil War. Columbia, MO: University of Missouri Press, 1959.
Note: Includes a chapter on Turner theaters in Missouri.

W63 Chambers, Robin L. "Chicago's Turners: inspired leadership in the promotion of public physical education, 1860-1890." Yearbook of German-American Studies 24 (1989): 105-114.

W64 ---. "The German-American Turners: their efforts to promote, develop, and initiate physical culture in Chicago's public schools and parks, 1860-1914." Yearbook of German-American Studies 22 (1987): 101-110.

W65 Cobb, Francis T. "Origin and development of the Turnverein." Master's thesis, George Peabody College for Teachers, 1936.

W66 Der deutsche Einfluß im Staate Michigan (The history of the Germanic influence in the state of Michigan), Festschrift zum 6. Deutschen Nationalfest, Sonntag, 19. Juni 1938, Carpathia Park. Detroit: Detroit Abend Post, 1938. 96 p.
Note: Articles on the history and activities of Germans in Michigan, published for the sixth German national festival, held in Detroit. Includes a history of the Detroit *Socialer* Turnverein and an article on the Turner movement in the United States written by the Turner's national president Carl Wiedeman.
Location: InIU.

W67 Donaldson, Randall. "The role of the German-American social groups in the assimilation of German immigrants." The Report: A Journal of German-American History 41:33-41.
Note: Focuses on the role of Turner societies.

W68 Duke, Julia L. "History of German gymnastics." Master's thesis, George Peabody College for Teachers, 1936.

W69 Dyer, Robert. Booneville: an illustrated history. Booneville, MO: Pekitanoui Publications, 1987.
Note: Includes section on the Booneville Turner Society.

W70   Dzik, Andrea. "American Turners: a sound mind in a sound body." Health November (1970): 43-47.
Note: Reprinted in the 80th anniversary publication of the *Eiche* Turners, Chicago, Illinois.

W71   Ehlert, Edward. The Turnverein, the Turner hall, and other early day recreational activities. Manitowoc, WI: Manitowoc County Historical Society, 1978. 12 p.

W72   Ehrenreich, Carol J. "Sheboygan Turners, Inc., part I: 1854-1904, from German roots to the golden jubilee; part II: 1904-1929." unpublished manuscript, 1994.
Location: WSCHi.

W73   Faust, Albert Berhardt. The German element in the United States, with special reference to its political, moral, social and educational influence. 2 vols. Boston: Houghton Mifflin, 1909.
Note: See section in Chapter 16: "The influence of Germans in St. Louis and Missouri; the Turners, the Arsenal, Camp Jackson, Sigel's campaign, etc." Faust's work was reprinted by Arno Press in 1969.

W74   Funck, Erwin, et al. (eds.). Festschrift 150 Jahre, 1844-1994. Kiel: Kieler Männer Turnverein, 1994.
Note: Includes a chapter by Joachim Reppmann comparing the German and the American Turner movement.

W75   Geldbach, Erich. "Emigration of the German gymnastic movement to America: Beck, Follen, Lieber." Stadion: Journal of the History of Sport and Physical Education 1, no. 2 (1975): 331-376.

W76   ---. "The beginning of German gymnastics in America." Journal of Sport History 3 (1976): 236-272.

W77   Gems, Gerald R. "Not only a game." Chicago History 18 (June 1989): 9-11.
Note: Includes illustrations of the Chicago Turners, p. 9-11.

W78   Gerhard, Elmer Schultz. "Library of the Davenport Turngemeinde." The American-German Review June (1946): 33-37.

W79   Glasrud, Clarence A. and Diana M. Rankin, eds. A heritage deferred: the German-Americans in Minnesota. Moorhead, MN: Concordia College, 1981. 168 p.
Note: Turner activities in Minnesota mentioned throughout the book, plus three pages of Turner photographs.

W80   Godbersen, Bruce L. A History of Ida County. Ida Grove, IA: Midwest Industries, Inc., 1977.
Note: Chapter 22 in this county history includes pictures and accounts of the Holstein Turnverein, Iowa.

W81   Goff, Nancy. Springfield's ethnic heritage: the German community. Springfield, MA: USA Bicentennial Committee of Springfield, Inc., 1976.
Note: Includes a chapter on the Springfield Turnverein.

W82   Goldberg, Bettina. *"Deutsch-Amerikanische Freidenker in Milwaukee 1877-1890: Organization und gesellschaftspolitische Orientierung."* Staatsarbeit, *Ruhr Universität Bochum*, 1982.
Note: Discusses the relationship and ties between the Freethinkers and Turners in Milwaukee.

W83   Gray, Wendy. "The origin and evolution of the German-Canadian Turnverein movement: a study of Waterloo County, Canada West, 1855- 1875." Master's thesis, University of Western Ontario, 1990.

W84   Grebner, Constantin. We were the ninth: a history of the ninth regiment, Ohio Volunteer Infantry, April 17, 1861, to June 7, 1864. Translated and edited by Frederic Trautmann. Kent, OH: Kent State University Press, 1987. 322 p.
Note: Translation of Grebner's Ohio Infantry, 9th Regiment, 1861-1864: Die Neuner, Eine Schilderung der Kriegsjahre des 9ten Regiments Ohio Vol. Infantries, vom 17. April 1861 bis 7. Juni, 1864 mit einer Einleitung von Oberst Gustav Tafel. Cincinnati: S. Rosenthal & Co., 1897. See **W13**.

W85   Grossbroehmer, Rainer. "German influences on the North American system of gymnastics teachers' training: the NAGU Normal College." In Turnen and sport: the cross-cultural exchange, edited by Roland Naul. Münster and New York: Waxmann, 1991, pp. 107-119.

W86   Gurt, Megan. "The Turner society of Keystone, Iowa." American Schleswig Holstein Heritage Society Newsletter (ASHHS). Sept./Oct. 1992, pp. 9-11.

W87   Harzig, Christine. Familie, Arbeit und weibliche Öffentlichkeit in einer Einwanderungsstadt: Deutschamerikaner in Chicago um die Jahrhundertwende. St. Katharinen: *Scripta Mercaturae Verlag*, 1991.
Note: Includes a description of Turner ladies auxiliaries in Chicago.

W88   Hofmann, Annette R. *"Bahn Frei: Das deutsch-amerikansiche Turnen von seinen Anfängen bis Ende des Bürgerkrieges."* Master's thesis, Eberhard-Karls-Universität Tübingen, 1993.

W89   The Holstein centennial book, 1882[-]1982. Odebolt, IA: Miller Printing and Publishing, 1981.
Note: Includes a history of the Holstein Turnverein and a number of historical photographs of the Turner hall, Turnfests, and its members on pages 102-110.

W90   Hoyt, Dolores. "The role of libraries in the American Turner organization." Ph.D. dissertation, Indiana University, 1993.

W91   Hübner, Theodore. The Germans in America. Philadelphia: Chilton Company, 1962.
Note: The section on "Labor Relationships" in Chapter 8 called "Building the Nation," talks about the *Sozialistischer* Turnerbund and its involvement in the labor movement.

W92   ---. " The German school of the New York Turnverein." The American-German Review. 16 (1950): 14-15.

W93   Iverson, Noel. Germania, U.S.A.: social change in New Ulm, Minnesota. Minneapolis: University of Minnesota Press, 1966.
Note: Examines the history and social structures of the Turner community of New Ulm, Minnesota.

W94   John, H. G. "German gymnastics association and the German Turners in the U.S.A. between 1848-1914." In Documents du Seminaire international d'histoire du sport et d'education physique comparee organise en cooperation avec HISPA, SHPESA et AAPE, Universite du Quebec a Trois-Rivieres. Trois Rivieres, Quebec: *Universite de Quebec*, 1976.

W95   Johnson, Hildegard Binder. "German Forty-Eighters in Davenport." The Iowa Journal of History and Politics 44 (1946): 3-53.

W96   ---. "List of lectures and debates given before the Davenport Turngemeinde." Iowa Journal of History and Politics 44 (1946): 54-60.

W97   Johnstone, Lizzi. "Camp Brosius." Wisconsin Magazine of History 10 (1929): 170-174.

W98   Jones, W. D. "Cincinnati German society of a century ago." Historical and Philosophical Society of Ohio Bulletin 20, no 1 (1962): 39-43.

W99   Karl, John A. "A history of the Saint Louis Turnverein societies, 1849 to 1948." Master's thesis, Northeast Missouri State Teachers College, Kirksville, Missouri, 1966.

W100 Keil, Hartmut, ed. German workers' culture in the United States 1850 - 1920. Washington D.C.: Smithsonian Institution Press, 1988.
Note: Turners mentioned throughout the book. See especially Chapter 10 by Ralf Wagner, "Turner Societies and the Socialist Tradition."

W101 Keil, Hartmut and John Jentz. German workers in Chicago: a documentary history of working-class culture from 1850 to World War I. Urbana, Chicago: University of Illinois Press, 1988.
Note: See especially Chapter 4: "Church and Turnverein - two contrasting neighborhood institutions." Also available in German: Deutsche Arbeiterkultur in Chicago von 1850 bis zum Ersten Weltkrieg: Eine Antologie. Ostfielden: *Scripta Mercaturae Verlag*, 1984.

W102 Kierschner, Alfred P. "New York Turn-Verein 100th anniversary." American- German Review 16 (1950): 7-13.

W103 Kiessling, Elmar C. Watertown remembered. Watertown, WI: Watertown Historical Society, 1976.
Note: History of Watertown which includes a chapter on the Watertown Turners, describing their activities and influences, pp. 81-84.

W104 Knoche, Karl Heinz. The German immigrant press in Milwaukee. Columbus: Ohio State University, 1969.
Note: Reprinted by Arno Press in New York in 1980. Chapter 8, "The Freethinker and Socialist Press," discusses the Amerikanische Turnzeitung.

W105 Koester, Leonard. "Early Cincinnati and the Turners: from Mrs. Karl Tafel's autobiography." Bulletin of the Historical and Philosophical Society of Ohio 7 (1949): 18-22.
Note: Excerpt from Mrs. Karl Tafel's autobiography in which she describes the journey from Germany to the United States with her family, her first years in Cincinnati, the founding of the Cincinnati Turnverein by her brothers and cousins and the early activities of the club.

W106 Kramer, William M. and Norton Stern. "The Turnverein: a German experience for western Jewry." Western States Jewish History 16, no.3 (1984): 227-229.

W107 LeCompte, Mary Lou. "German-American Turnvereins in frontier Texas, 1851-1880." Journal of the West 26 (1987): 18-25.

W108 Leonard, Fred E. History of physical education. Philadelphia: Lea and Febinger, 1923.
Note: Includes historical information on Turners, pp.109-119.

W109   ---. Pioneers of modern physical training. New York: Associate Press, 1919.
Note: Reprinted in 1922. Includes biographies of Friedrich Ludwig Jahn, Charles Beck, Charles Follen, Francis Lieber, George Brosius, and Carl Betz.

W110   ---. A guide to the history of physical education. Westport, CT: Greenwood Press, 1971.
Note: See chapter 11, "Friedrich Ludwig Jahn, and popular gymnastics in Germany," pp. 83-108; chapter 21, "The first introduction of the Jahn gymnastics into America," pp. 231-254; and chapter 24, "German- American gymnastic societies and the North American Turnerbund," pp. 294-315.

W111   Lipsitz, George. The sidewalks of St. Louis: places, people and politics in an American city. Columbia, MO: The University of Missouri Press, 1991.
Note: In the chapter, "The Friedrich Jahn statue: the Turnverein legacy in St. Louis," Lipsitz describes the Turner movement in general and the St. Louis societies.

W112   Marquette, Bud. "American Turner organization and history." International Gymnast, 1985-86.
Note: Includes history and one-page reviews of the work and activities of contemporary Turner societies in the United States. See issues for May, June, August, October, December, 1985, and January, March, May, and October, 1986.

W113   McCaffery, Robert Paul. "Islands of *Deutschtum*: German-Americans in Manchester, New Hampshire and Lawrence, Massachusetts, 1870-1942." Ph.D. dissertation, University of New Hampshire, 1994.
Note: Includes chapters on the Manchester and Lawrence Turners.

W114   McCune, Gill. Turnvereins. St. Louis: Title Insurance Corporation of St. Louis, n.p. 10 p.
Note: Discusses the history of the Turners in St Louis.
Location: InIU.

W115   McMorrow, Elizabeth. "The nineteenth century German political immigrant and the construction of American culture and thought." Ph.D. dissertation, New School for Social Research, New York City, 1982.

W116   Miller, Eugene. "The contribution of German immigrants to the Union cause in Kentucky." Filson Club History Quarterly 64, no. 4 (1990): 462-478.

W117   Miller, Eugene and Forrest Steinlage. Der Turner: a Turner soldier in the Civil War, Germany to Antietam: a biographical narrative of a German immigrant who served as a private in the 20th Regiment, New York Volunteers, the United Turners Rifles. Louisville: Calmar Publications, 1988. 118 p.

Note: The story of Eberhard Futterer, a private in Company B of the United Turner Rifles.

W118   Moonen, Alida Joyce. "The missing half: the experience of women in the Indianapolis Turnverein Women's Auxiliary, 1876-1919." Ph.D. dissertation, Ohio State University, 1993.

W119   Müller, Theodore. "Milwaukee's German cultural heritage." Milwaukee History 10, no. 3 (1987): 95-108.
Note: Describes the cultural activities of the Milwaukee Turners.

W120   ---. "Milwaukee Turners, a century of gymnastic activity." Unpublished paper, March 10, 1953. 21 p.
Location: WMCHi.

W121   Naul, Roland, ed. Turner and sport: the cross-cultural exchange. Münster, New York: Waxmann Verlag, 1991.
Note: Includes four essays on the American Turners written by international physical education scholars.

W122   Neumann, Hannes. Die deutsche Turnbewegung in der Revolution 1848/49 und in der amerikanischen Emigration. Schondorf bei Stuttgart: Verlag Karl Hofmann, 1968.

W123   Park, Roberta. "German associational and sporting life in the Greater San Francisco Bay area, 1850-1900." Journal of the West 26; no.1 (1987): 47-64.
Note: Includes a discussion of the San Francisco Turners.

W124   Pelton, B. C. and J. C. Wendt. "Sport international: fitness renaissance or the Turnverein revisited." International Journal of Physical Education 22, no. 2 (1985): 31-33.

W125   Pesavento, Wilma Jane. "A historical study of the development of physical education in the Chicago public schools, 1860-1965." Ph.D. dissertation, Northwestern University, Chicago, 1966.
Note: Includes a discussion of the influences of Chicago's Turner societies on the introduction of physical education into the public schools.

W126   Pilger, Celina. "The settlement of New Ulm." unpublished manuscript, 1931. 21 p.
Note: The paper discusses the settlement of New Ulm and the Turner settlement society.
Location: MnHi.

W127   Piotrowski, Thaddeus. The German-American heritage in Manchester, N.H. [Manchester]: n.p., 1976.
Note: Includes a chapter on the Manchester Turnverein, the Turn Sisters, and the Turners' Sabre Club.

W128   Prahl, Augustus J. "The ideological background of the American Turners." Comparative Literature News-Letter 3, no 2 (1944): 11-13.

W129   ---."History of the German gymnastic movement of Baltimore." Report of the Society for the History of the German in Maryland 26 (1945): 16-29.

W130   ---. "The beginning of the gymnastic movement in America." German-American Review 14, no. 5 (1948): 12-15.

W131   ---. "The Turner." In The Forty-Eighters: political refugees of the German revolution of 1848, edited by Adolf Eduard Zucker. New York: Columbia University Press, 1950.

W132   Pumroy, Eric. "Historical records of Turners in America." In Das Ohio Tal-the Ohio Valley: the German dimension, edited by Don Heinrich Tolzmann, pp. 65-75. New York: Peter Lang Publishing, Inc., 1993.

W133   Pumroy, Eric and Katja Rampelmann. "A sound mind in a sound body: Turner societies in the United States." Humanities 15, no. 2 (1994): 34-38.

W134   Rampelmann, Katja. "Small town Germans: the Germans of Lawrence, Kansas, from 1854 to 1918." Master's thesis, University of Kansas, 1993.
Note: Includes a chapter on the Lawrence Turnverein.

W135   Rentschler, Thomas B. "Some American Bowie bayonets." The Gun Report April (1965): 6-14.
Note: Article about guns and bayonets produced and used by Turners before and during the Civil War.

W136   Reppmann, Joachim. Freiheit, Bildung und Wohlstand für Alle!: Schleswig-Holsteinische Achtundvierziger in den USA, 1847-1860. Wyk auf Föhr: *Verlag für Amerikanistik*, 1994.
Note: Includes information on the Davenport Turnverein.

W137   Rice, Emmett. "The American Turners." Journal of Health and Physical Education 5, no. 4 (1934): 3-6.
Note: Reprinted in International Gymnast no. 9 (July 1982).

W138   Rice, Emmett, John L. Hutchinson and Mabel Lee. A brief history of physical education. 6th ed. New York: The Roland Press Company, 1969.
Note: Originally published by Barnes and Company in 1926; revised and enlarged editions published in 1929, 1930, 1952, and 1958. Chapter 2 describes the Turner movement in the United States.

W139   Riemer, Shirley. "Sacramento Turners." Der Blumenbaum 11, no. 2 (1993); 11, no. 3 (1994); 11, no. 4 (1994); 12, no.1 (1994).
Note: Series of articles in Der Blumenbaum, the publication of the Sacramento German Genealogy Society in which the author lists the membership records of the Sacramento Turnverein, 1874-1907, 1931-1945. Records include place of birth, date of birth, occupation, previous affiliation with other Turner societies, marriage status, and date of initiation. Also included are articles about the society and the American Turners.

W140   Rinsch, Emil. History of the Normal College of the American Gymnastic Union of Indiana University, 1866-1966. Bloomington: Indiana University Publication, 1966. 182 p.
Note: Describes the foundation and development of the *Turnlehrer Seminar* and Normal College from 1866 to 1966. Includes photographs and school schedules.

W141   Ripley, La Vern J. "Status versus ethnicity: the Turners and Bohemians of New Ulm." In The German Forty-eighters in the United States, ed. by Charlotte L. Brancaforte. New York: Peter Lang, 1989.

W142   Rudnic, O.H. Das Deutschthum in St. Paul in Wort und Bild: eine historische Beleuchtung deutsch-amerikanischer Tätigkeit in St. Paul. St. Paul: n.p., 1924.
Note: German societies, including the Turner societies, described on pages 47-64.

W143   Russell, Mary Landon. "A history of the music of Williamsport, Pennsylvania." Master's thesis, Pennsylvania State University, 1957.
Note: Includes the chapter, "German Choruses," which describes the *Liederkranz* of the Williamsport Turnverein, and discusses several of its music directors.

W144   Savering, William A. "A history of the American Turnerbund and its influence and contributions to physical education in the United States." Master's thesis, Pennsylvania State University, 1961.

W145   Schild, Richard. "A brief history of gymnastics in the La Crosse, Wisconsin, Turnverein." Master's thesis, Wisconsin State College, La Crosse, 1960.

W146   Schlüter, Hermann. Die Anfänge der deutschen Arbeiterbewegung in Amerika. Edited by Carol Poore. New York; Frankfurt a/M: Peter Lang, 1984.

Note: Originally published in 1907 in Stuttgart. Includes a chapter on the *Sozialistische* Turnerbund and its relationship to the Socialist Party before 1865.

W147   Schwendener, Norma. A history of physical education in the United States. New York: A.S. Barnes Company, 1942.
Note: See section: "The Turnverein in the United States," pp. 45-52.

W148   Sickinger, Raymond L. and John K. Primeau. The Germans in Rhode Island: pride and perseverance, 1850-1985. Providence, R.I.: The Rhode Island Heritage Commission and The Rhode Island Publication Society, 1985.
Note: Includes a chapter on the Providence Turners (Turnverein *Vorwärts*).

W149   Spelker, Henriette E. "Education policy and the political role of the German-American gymnastic societies." Master's thesis, University of Pittsburgh, 1927.

W150   Steinhauser, Frederic R. "Settlement of New Ulm, Minnesota." Unpublished paper, 1978. 19 p.
Note: Unpublished paper on the Turners and their settlement of New Ulm.
Location: MnBCHi.

W151   ---. "New Ulm Minnesota Germans: adults of German birth settled in New Ulm and Surrounding Areas, 1860." Unpublished paper, 1979. 25 p.
Note: Statistics on German population of New Ulm in 1860, giving information on the age of resident, birth and death date, birth place, occupation, arrival in New Ulm, if member of the Chicago Land Society, Cincinnati Land Society, and/or New Ulm Turnverein.
Location: MnHi.

W152   Steinhauser, Frederic and John Hickey. "The German settlement of New Ulm, Minnesota: a case study in Minnesota's ethnic history." Unpublished paper, n.d. [24 p.]
Location: InIU (photocopy); OCU.

W153   Streit, W.K. "Normal College of the American Gymnastic Union." The Physical Educator 20, no 2 (1963): 51-55.
Note: Brief historical overview on the development and history of the Normal College.

W154   "The Turnverein." Annals of Iowa 36, no. 1 (1961): 50.
Note: Short historical abstract on the Holstein Gymnastic Society.

W155   Tyler, Alice Felt. "William Pfänder and the foundation of New Ulm." Minnesota History 30, no 1 (1949): 24-35.

W156   Ueberhorst, Horst. *"Der deutsche Beitrag zur Leibeserziehung in den USA."* Deutsches Turnen 22 (1975): 468 ff.

W157   ---. *"Die Anfänge der deutsch-amerikanischen Turnbewegung und ihre Bedeutung für die amerikanische Gesellschaft."* In Forschen, Lehren, Handeln. Sportwissenschaft Beiträge, edited by Hermann Andrecs, Sepp Redl and Hans Groll, pp. 163-190. Wien: Österreichischer Bundesverlag, 1976.

W158   ---. Friedrich Ludwig Jahn, 1778-1978. Bonn-Bad Godesberg: Inter Nations, 1978.
Note: Biography of Friedrich Ludwig Jahn. Includes discussions of Jahn's historical significance and of Turner societies outside Europe; available in German and English.

W159   ---. "German gymnastics movement and German history: Friedrich Ludwig Jahn and thereafter." Aus Politik und Zeitgeschichte 28 (1978): 3-15.

W160   ---. *"Jahnsches Turnen in den* USA." Deutsches Turnen 16 (1978): 374-377.

W161   ---. Turner unterm Sternenbanner: Der Kampf der deutsch-amerikanischen Turner für Einheit, Freiheit und Soziale Gerechtigkeit. München: Heinz Moos, 1978.

W162   ---. "Jahn's historical significance." Canadian Journal of the History of Sport and Physical Education 10 (1979): 7-14.

W163   ---. *"Die nordamerikanischen Turner und ihr Jahnbild."* In Internationales Jahn-Symposium in Berlin, edited by Bernett, Denk, Goehler, Lämmer, Ueberhorst, pp. 358-364. Köln/Leiden, 1979.

W164   ---. Turner und Sozialdemokraten in Milwaukee: Fünf Jahrzehnte der Kooperation, 1910-1960. Bonn: Friedrich Ebert Stiftung, 1980.

W165   ---. *"Turnverein Milwaukee, ein Zentrum deutsch-amerikanischer Kulturarbeit im 19. Jarhundert."* In Sportwirklichkeit: Beitrag zur Didaktik, Geschichte und Soziologie des Sports. Festschrift zum 70. Geburtstag von Univ. Prof. Dr. Erwin Niedermann, edited by Rainhard Bachleitner and Sepp Redl, p. 120-132. Wien: Österreichischer Bundesverlag, 1981.

W166   ---. *"Cincinnati und der erste deutsch-amerikanische Turnverein."* Deutsches Turnen 10 (1986): 26 ff.

W167   ---. "Turners and Social Democrats in World War I: division and decline of the Social Democratic Party." Canadian Journal of History of Sport 18, no. 1 (1987): 76-85.

W168   ---. "Texas-Deutsche und ihre Turnvereine." Deutsches Turnen 3 (1987): 36ff.

W169   ---. "Franz Lieber - Turner pioneer, scholar, politician." Canadian Journal of History of Sport 22 (1991).

W170   Valentine, Michael Frank. "The contribution of the American Turners to physical education in the United States." Master's thesis, De Paul University, Chicago, 1962.

W171   Van Dalen, Deobold, Elmer Mitchell and Bruce Bennett. A world history of physical education: cultural, philosophical, comparative. New York: Prentice Hall, Inc., 1953.

W172   Vodges, Walter. "*Volksgeist*, German nationalism, Turnvater Jahn, and 4F Beer Steins-or-Why I like 'Em." Prosit September (1993): 216-222.
Note: Article on Turner beer steins.

W173   Wagner, Martin. "The contribution of the German Turnvereins to physical education in San Francisco Public Schools, 1850-1900." Master's thesis, University of California, Berkeley, 1968.

W174   Wagner, Ralf. "Turner societies and the Socialist tradition." In German workers' culture in the United States, 1850 to 1920, edited by Hartmut Keil. Washington: Smithsonian Institution Press, 1988, pp. 221-239.

W175   ---. Zwischen Tradition und Fortschritt: Zur gesellschafts- politischen und kulturellen Entwicklung der deutsch-amerikanischen Turnbewegung am Beispiel Milwaukees und Chicagos, 1850-1920. Ph.D. dissertation, Ludwig-Maximilians Universität, München, 1988.

W176   Wamsley, Kevin. "Loyal to the Confederacy: Galveston, Texas, Turners and national Turnerbund ideology, 1840-1865." Master's thesis, University of Western Ontario, 1987.

W177   ---. "A home in the South: the Turners of Galveston, Texas, 1840-1865." In Ethnicity and sport in North American history and culture, edited by George Eisen and David K. Wiggins. Westport, CT: Greenwood Press, 1994, pp. 43-53.

W178   Wandel, Joseph. The German dimension of American history. Chicago: Nelson Hall Inc., 1979.
Note: See Chapter 9, "The Forty-Eighters and the Turner societies."

W179　Wild, Robert. "Chapters in the history of the Turners." Wisconsin Magazine of History. December (1925): 123-139.

W180　Wildt, Klemens C. Auswanderer und Emigranten in der Geschichte der Leibesübungen. Schorndorf bei Stuttgart: Verlag Karl Hofmann, 1964.

W181　Wilkinson, James. "The influence of the German Turnverein in American physical education." Unpublished paper, 1991.
Location: InIU.

W182　Williams, Vera Estelle. "The contribution of Hans Christopher Reuter to physical education at La Crosse and in the state of Wisconsin." Ph.D. dissertation, Ohio State University, 1969.

W183　Wittke, Carl. The Ninth Ohio volunteers: a page from the Civil War record of the Ohio German Turners of Ohio. Columbus: The F.J. Heer Printing Company, 1926. 18 p.

W184　---. "The Ninth Ohio Volunteers: a page from the Civil War record of the Ohio German Turners of Ohio." Ohio Archeological and Historical Quarterly 35 (April 1926): 402-417.

W185　---. Refugees of revolution: the German Forty-eighters in America. Philadelphia: University of Pennsylvania Press, 1952.
Note: See Chapter 11: "The Turner."

W186　Zechetmayr, Monica. "*Deutsches Turnen in Kanada*." Stadion 4 (1978): 365-377.

W187　Zeigler, Earle F. "Clearing up some confusion about the first teacher training program in physical education in the United States." Canadian Journal of History of Sport and Physical Education 5 (1974): 38-48.

W188　---. "Professional preparation concerns of the Normal College of the American Gymnastic Union (1866-1919)." Canadian Journal of History of Sport 18, no 1 (1987): 19-35.

W189　Zucker, Adolf Eduard, ed. The Forty-Eighters: political refugees of the German revolution of 1848. New York: Columbia University Press, 1950.
Note: Turner activities are mentioned throughout the book; see especially Chapter 4: "The Turner," by Augustus Prahl.

Appendix 1

List of Turner Societies

There have been over 700 Turner societies in the United States since 1848. Some of them have left numerous records behind while the existence of others can only be proved by notices in city directories or nineteenth century newspapers . The following is an initial attempt to identify all past and present Turner societies in the United States. This list does not claim to be definitive. Because of the ephemeral nature of many societies, some have undoubtedly been overlooked while others may have information that is either incomplete or inaccurate. Even in its current state, though, the list should be useful for indicating the extent of the Turner movement in the United States, as well as for indicating the level of activity in individual cities and states.

The list is organized alphabetically by state and city, and within cities by founding date. The list is divided into five columns consisting of (1) the name of the city, (2) the last known official name of the society, (3) approximate beginning dates, (4) approximate ending dates and (5) notes on name changes and mergers with other societies. Smaller towns which were later absorbed by neighboring cities are listed under the city of which they are presently a part, in so far as we have been able to determine, and their former locations have been recorded in the note. Societies are listed by their last known official name, but their previous or alternative names are indicated in the notes.

Beginning and ending dates for societies were drawn from the listings in the American Turner annual reports, from society publications, or from other historical sources, including information provided by local libraries and historical societies. Dates with a question mark indicate that these were the earliest or latest times when references to the the society were found, but they may not be beginning and ending dates. If beginning and ending dates are identical and both have a question mark, then references to the society were only found during the one year. The dates should be regarded with caution since so many societies had such a history of closings, reorganizations, defections and mergers that tracing lineage was a difficult matter, and certainly would have required more time and access to sources than was possible for this project. Dates are particularly difficult for independent societies since, by definition, they were not a part of a larger group that collected information about them.

The following abbreviations were used for the list of societies:

Ab.	=	*Abteilung*
Am.	=	American
Assoc.	=	Association
Cincin.	=	Cincinnati
Co.	=	County
d.	=	*der/des*
D.B.	=	*Deutscher Bund*
Demok.	=	*Demokratischer*
E.D.	=	East District
Germ.	=	German
GV	=	*Gesangverein*
Gym.	=	Gymnastic
Inc.	=	Incorporated
L.I.	=	Long Island
N.	=	North
N.W.	=	North West
N.Y.	=	New York
pres.	=	Present
S.F.	=	San Francisco
Soc.	=	Society
St.	=	Saint
S.T.V.	=	*Socialer* Turnverein
TG	=	Turngemeinde
TS	=	*Turnsektion*
TV	=	Turnverein
V	=	*Verein*

State/ Town	Society Name	Beg. Date	End Date	Note
Alabama				
Birmingham	*Deutscher* TV	1887	1915	
Helena	Helena TV	1874	1874?	
Mobile	TV *Vorwärts*	1851	1915?	Founded as Mobile TV; changed name in 1906
Arkansas				
Fort Smith	Fort Smith TV	1892	1901?	
Hot Springs	Hot Springs TV	1891	1894	
Little Rock	Little Rock TV	1867	1902?	
Little Rock	Westend TV	1909	1911	
California				
Alameda	Alameda TV	1886	1912?	
Anaheim	Anaheim TV	1892	1927?	
Berkeley	West Berkeley TV	1885	1888?	
Berkeley	Berkeley TV	1927	1937	Possibly also known as Berkeley *Turn & Sportverein*
Boise City	Boise City TV	1870	1875?	
Joplin	Joplin TV	????	1917?	
Los Angeles	Los Angeles TV	1870	1871	Merged with *Teutonia Concordia V.* to form TV *Germania*
Los Angeles	*Teutonia Concordia* TV	1870	1871	Merged with Los Angeles TV to form TV *Germania*
Los Angeles	Los Angeles Turners	1871	pres.	Founded as TV *Germania* by merger of *Teutonia* Concordia V. and TV *Germania* in 1871; renamed Los Angeles Turners in 1943
Marysville	Marysville TV	1856	1918?	
Napa	Napa TV	1871	1917?	Became Napa *Gesangverein*
Oakland	Oakland TV	1867	1952	

State/ Town	Society Name	Beg. Date	End Date	Note
Petaluma	Petaluma TV	1875?	1899	
Sacramento	Sacramento TV	1854	pres.	
San Bernardino	San Bernardino TV	1888	1895	
San Diego	San Diego Turners	1890	1985	Founded as *Concordia* TV by merger of San Diego TV & Phoenix TV; changed name to San Diego Turners, 1947
San Diego	*Teutonia* TV	1873	1875	
San Diego	San Diego TV	1884	1890	Founded as *Eintracht* TV; changed name to San Diego TV, 1886; merged with Phoenix TV to form *Concordia* TV in 1890
San Diego	Phoenix TV	1889	1890	Merged with TV *Eintracht* to form *Concordia* TV in 1890
San Francisco	*Germania* TV	1850s	1860	Joined S.F. TV in 1860
San Francisco	S.F. Gymnastic Club	1852	1940?	Founded as S.F. TV; absorbed *Germania* TV in 1860; changed name to S.F. Gymnastic Club in 1921
San Francisco	TV *Eintracht*	1857	1905?	
San Francisco	Eureka TV	1863	1875?	
San Francisco	TV *Vorwärts*	1880	1905?	
San Francisco	Mission TV	1881	1927?	
San Francisco	S.F. *Turn Abt.* *Deutscher V*	1924	1940?	Possibly same as S.F. Gymnastic Club
San Jose	San Jose TV	1868	1907	Closed officially in 1907 but might have become the *TS d. Germania Vereins*
San Luis Obispo	San Luis Obispo TV	1875?	1895?	
Santa Cruz	TV Santa Cruz	1894	1921	Merged with *Arion* Society, 1921
Sonoma	Sonoma TV ?	1875?	1883?	
St. Helena	St. Helena TV	1883?	1895	
Stockton	Stockton TV	1856	1917?	

State/ Town	Society Name	Beg. Date	End Date	Note
Woodland	Woodland TV	1856?	1856?	

Colorado

State/ Town	Society Name	Beg. Date	End Date	Note
Boulder	Boulder TV	1883?	1884?	
Canon City	Canon City TV	????	????	Mentioned briefly as a 19th century Colorado society in the <u>Amerikanische Turnzeitung</u> and <u>Pep & Punch</u> (Denver TV) in 1949
Central City	Rocky Mountain TV	1868	1903?	
Cripple Creek	Cripple Creek TV	1903?	1905?	
Denver	TV *Vorwärts*	1860s	1917	Also known as West Denver TV; merged with East Denver TV & *Socialer* TV in 1917 to form the Denver TV
Denver	East Denver TV	1865	1917	Merged with *Socialer* TV & TV *Vorwärts* to form Denver TV in 1917
Denver	Central TV	1891	????	
Denver	*Socialer* TV	1901	1917	Merged with East Denver TV & TV *Vorwärts* to form Denver TV in 1917
Denver	Denver TV	1917	pres.	Formed by merger of East Denver TV, *Socialer* TV and TV *Vorwärts*
Georgetown	Georgetown TV	1880?	1895?	
Grand Junction	TV Grand Junction	1893	1894?	
Leadville	Leadville TV	1879	1934	
Pueblo	*Germania Turn & GV*	1881	1891?	
Sugar City	Sugar City TV	1895?	1895?	
Trinidad	Trinidad TV	1888	1890	

Connecticut

State/ Town	Society Name	Beg. Date	End Date	Note
Bridgeport	Bridgeport Turner Assoc.	1856	1986	Founded as *Socialer* TV

State/ Town	Society Name	Beg. Date	End Date	Note
Bristol	Bristol TV	1912?	1912?	
Collinsville	*Socialer* TV	1889	1891?	
Danbury	TV *Vorwärts*	1890	1892?	
Derby	Derby TV	1880	1940s?	
Hartford	*Socialer* TV	1858?	1877?	
Hartford	Hartford Turnerbund	1878	1960s	
Meriden	Meriden Turner Society	1866	pres.	Founded as Meriden TV; currently a singing society
New Britain	New Britain TV	1853	1941?	Founded as *Socialer* TV
New Haven	New Haven TV	1852	1932?	
Norwich	Norwich TV	1869	1872	
Rockville	Rockville TV	1857	1924?	Founded as Rockville TV; changed name to *Socialer* TV in 1886 and back to Rockville TV in 1898
Stamford	Stamford Turner *Liedertafel*	1890	1963?	Founded as *Socialer* TV but known as Stamford Turner *Liedertafel* since 1899
Waterbury	Waterbury TV	1871	1917?	
Waterbury	TV *Vorwärts*	1893	1946/47	Merged with *Concordia* Singing Society to form the *Concordia* Turner Singing Society in 1946/47

Delaware

Wilmington	Wilmington Turners	1859	pres.	Also known as *Socialer Demokratisches* TV (1859), Wilmington TV (1865), TV Forwards (1882), *Social-Demok.* TV (1882), and Wilmington TG

State/ Town	Society Name	Beg. Date	End Date	Note
District of Columbia				
Washington	Columbia TV	1852	1913	
Washington	Georgetown TV	1866	1868	
Florida				
Gotha	Gotha TV	1885	1903?	
Miami	Miami *Turn & Sport Verein*	1926?	1929	
Georgia				
Atlanta	TV Atlanta	1873	1921	
Atlanta	TV *Germania*	1896?	1896?	
Savannah	Savannah TV	1852	1895	
Idaho				
Boise	Boise TV	1870	1916?	
Illinois				
Alton	Alton TV	1864	1896?	
Aurora	Aurora TV	1857	1898?	
Aurora	TV *Frisch Auf*	1907	pres.	Also known as the Aurora Turners
Belleville	Belleville TG	1855	1885	Merged with TV *Vorwärts* to form Belleville *Vorwärts* TG in 1885
Belleville	TV *Vorwärts*	1866	1885	Merged with Belleville TG to form the Belleville *Vorwärts* TG
Belleville	Belleville Turners	1885	pres.	Founded as the Belleville *Vorwärts* TG by the merger of the Belleville TG and the

State/ Town	Society Name	Beg. Date	End Date	Note
				TV *Vorwärts*; changed name to Belleville Turners in 1918; currently a social society
Belleville	*Germania* TV	1890?	1892?	
Berlin	Berlin TV	1874?	1874?	
Bloomington	Bloomington TV	1858	1957?	
Cairo	Cairo TG	1862	1870s?	
Centralia	Centralia TV	1859	1924?	
Champaign	Champaign TV	1867	1870s?	
Chatsworth	*Germania & Sänger Verein*	1867	1873	
Chicago	Avondale TV	????	1896	Joined TV *Gut Heil* in 1896
Chicago	TV *Vorwärts*	1850s	1860	Merged with Chicago TV to form Chicago TG in 1860
Chicago	Chicago TV	1852	1860	Merged with TV *Vorwärts* to form the Chicago TG in 1860
Chicago	Chicago Turners	1860	1970	Founded as Chicago TG; renamed Chicago Turners in 1944
Chicago	Union TG	1861	1896	
Chicago	Aurora TV	1864	1952	In 1886 members split off over Haymarket affair to form *Centraler* TV
Chicago	TV *der Westseite*	1864	????	
Chicago	TV La Salle	1864	1917	Joined TV Lincoln in 1917
Chicago	TV Columbia	1866	1928?	
Chicago	Forward Turners	1867	1956	Founded as TV *Vorwärts*; joined by TV *Bahn Frei* in 1893; changed name to Forward Turners during WWI; merged with Social Turners and Swiss Turners to form the American Turners Chicago Northwest in 1956
Chicago	TV *Concordia*	1871	1897	Located in Blue Island
Chicago	Grand Crossing TV	1878	1937	
Chicago	TV *Fortschritt*	1884	1906	Merged with Almira TV & TV *Voran* to form the *Turnerschaft der Nordseite*

State/ Town	Society Name	Beg. Date	End Date	Note
Chicago	*Südseite* TV	1885	1912	Merged with *Schweizer* TV in 1912
Chicago	TV *Eintracht*	1885	1890	Merged with Pullmann-Kensington TG to form TV *Eiche*
Chicago	TV *Germania*	1885	1894	
Chicago	TV Lincoln, Inc.	1885	pres.	Also known as the Lincoln TV; in 1886 members split and formed *Socialer* TV; another split in 1989 produced TV Washington; joined by TV LaSalle in 1917
Chicago	*Centraler* TV	1886	1935	Founded by members of the Aurora TV in debate over Haymarket affair
Chicago	Social Turners	1886	1956	Founded as *Socialer* TV by members of the TV Lincoln; changed name to Social Turners in 1939; in 1956 merged with Forward Turners and Swiss Turners to form the American Turners Chicago Northwest
Chicago	*Südseite* TG	1886	1891	Merged with Lakeside TV to form Calumet TV
Chicago	Garfield TV	1887	1913	
Chicago	Pullmann-Kensington TG	1887	1890	Merged with TV *Eintracht* to form TV *Eiche*
Chicago	*Teutonia* TV	1887	1931?	
Chicago	Almira TV	1888	1906	Merged with TV *Voran* & TV *Fortschritt* to form the *Turnerschaft der Nordseite*
Chicago	National TV	1888	1900	
Chicago	*Nordwest* TV	1888?	1897	
Chicago	TV *Freiheit*	1888	1934	
Chicago	Lake View TG	1889	1892	
Chicago	Lakeside TV	1889	1891	Merged with *Südseite* TG to form Calumet TV
Chicago	Swiss Turners	1889	1956	Founded as *Schweizer* TV;

State/ Town	Society Name	Beg. Date	End Date	Note
				Südseite TV joined in 1912; merged with Forward Turners and Social Turners in 1956 to form the American Turners Chicago Northwest.
Chicago	TV *Einigkeit*	1889	1920	
Chicago	TV *Gut Heil*	1889	1902	Joined by Avondale TV in 1896
Chicago	TV *Nordwest*	1889	1907	
Chicago	TV Washington	1889	1896	Formed by split of Lincoln TV
Chicago	Riverdale TV	1890	1894	
Chicago	TV *Bahn Frei*	1890	1893	Merged with TV *Vorwärts*
Chicago	TV *Eiche*	1890	pres.	Formed by merger of TV *Eintracht* & Pullmann- Kensington TG
Chicago	TV *Voran*	1890	1906	Merged with TV Almira and TV *Fortschritt* to form the *Turnerschaft der* *Nordwestseite*
Chicago	Calumet TV	1891	1896	Founded by the merger of the *Südseite* TG & Lakeside TV
Chicago	TV *Vater* Jahn	1891	1917?	Possibly also known as Physical Training Club Jahn
Chicago	Westside Chicago TV	1891	1906	
Chicago	Harlem TV	1892	1940	Located in Oak Park
Chicago	TV Cleveland	1893	1894	
Chicago	TV Englewood	1894	1924?	
Chicago	TV *Süd*-Chicago	1895	1928	
Chicago	TV Chicago Heights	1901	1902	
Chicago	*Turnerschaft der* *Nordwestseite*	1906	1911	Formed by a merger of the Almira TV, TV *Voran* & TV *Fortschritt*
Chicago	American Turners Chicago N.W.	1956	pres.	Formed by the merger of

State/ Town	Society Name	Beg. Date	End Date	Note
				Forward Turners, Social Turners and Swiss Turners
Coal Valley	Coal Valley TV	1870	1870s?	
Columbia	Columbia Gym. Assoc.	1866	pres.	Founded as Columbia TV.
Danville	*Socialer* TV	1874	1916?	
Decatur	Decatur TV	1867?	1901?	
Dixon	Dixon TV	1871	1870s?	
East St. Louis	East St. Louis TG	1884	1894	
Edwardsville	Edwardsville TV	1883?	1886?	
Elgin	Elgin Turners	1871	pres.	Also known as the Elgin TV or TG Elgin
Freedom	Freedom TV	1867	1869	
Freeport	*Socialer* TV	1855	1870s	
Freeport	*Turnsektion d.* *Germania V*	1890	1901?	
Highland	Gym. Society Highland	1853	1943?	Founded as TV Highland; reorganized in 1866; changed name in WWI
Jacksonville	Jacksonville TV	1858	1905?	
Joliet	Joliet TV	1874	1924	
Marine	Marine TV	1869	1904	
Mascoutah	Central TV	1860	1836?	
Mendota	*Germania* Soc.	1875	1914	Founded as Mendota TV; renamed *Germania* Soc. in 1891
Millstadt	Millstadt TV	????	????	
Moline	Moline Turners	1866	pres.	Founded as Moline TV; in 1876 merged with *Concordia* *V. & Germania V.* to form *Concordia-Germania* TV; renamed Moline Turners in 1938
Moline	TV *Vorwärts*	1892	1909	Formed by members of the *Concordia-Germania* TV
Monee	Monee TG	1865	????	
Mt. Olive	Mt. Olive Gym. Soc.	1897	1938?	Founded as Mt. Olive TV; changed name in WWI

State/ Town	Society Name	Beg. Date	End Date	Note
Nashville	Nashville TV	1879?	1893?	
Ottawa	Ottawa TV	1856	1877?	
Pekin	Pekin TV	1865	1902?	
Peoria	Peoria TV	1851	1950	Possibly absorbed *Südseite* TV
Peoria	Union TV	1868	1869?	
Peoria	*Südseite* TV	1893	1923?	Possibly joined Peoria TV
Peru	Peru TV	1863	1927	
Pontiac	Pontiac TV	1864	????	
Quincy	Quincy TV	1856	1900?	
Red Bud	Red Bud TV	1866	1869	
Rock Island	Rock Island TV	1857	1938	
Rockford	Central Turners	1852	pres.	See Davenport, IA
Smithton	Smithton TV	1867	pres.	Founded as Georgetown TV; probably changed name in the 1920s
Springfield	Springfield TV	1857	1880s	
St. Jacob	St. Jacob TV	1888?	1889?	
Staunton	TV *Turnertreu*	1909	1918	
Streator	Streator TV	1888	1890?	
Trenton	Trenton TV	1866	1890	
Waukegan	TV *Germania*	1901	1945?	Founded as TV *Gut Heil*, renamed TV Germania in 1914
Wellston	*Turn & Schulverein*	1907	????	

Indiana

Alexandria	TV *Vorwärts*	????	????	
Evansville	Central Turners	1864	1983?	Founded as TV *Vorwärts*; reorganized as Evansville TG in 1898; changed name to Central TV, ca. 1900, and to Central Turners in 1940s
Fort Wayne	Fort Wayne TV	1865	1872	
Fort Wayne	Fort Wayne Turners	1897	pres.	Founded as TV *Vorwärts*; successor of Fort Wayne TV;

State/ Town	Society Name	Beg. Date	End Date	Note
				renamed Fort Wayne Turners in 1941
Hammond	*Socialer* TV	1891	1893	
Hammond	TV Hammond	1901	1906	
Huntingburgh	Huntingburgh TV	1868?	1868?	
Indianapolis	Indianapolis TG	1851	1853	Merged with *Socialistischer* TV to form *Socialistische* TG
Indianapolis	*Socialistischer* TV	1851	1852	Merged with Indianapolis TG to form *Socialistische* TG
Indianapolis	Indianapolis TV	1853	1872	Founded as *Socialistische* TG; formed by merger of Indianapolis TG and *Socialistischer* TV; reorganized in 1865 as Indianapolis TV; merged with *Socialer* TV in 1872 to form Indianapolis *Socialer* TV
Indianapolis	*Socialer* TV	1868	1872	Merged with Indianapolis TV to form Indianapolis *Socialer* TV
Indianapolis	Athenaeum Turners	1872	pres.	Founded as Indianapolis *Socialer* TV; renamed Athenaeum Turners in 1918
Indianapolis	*Unabhängiger* TV	1879	1939	Founded by members of *Socialer* TV; became Hoosier Athletic Club
Indianapolis	South Side Turners	1893	pres.	Founded as *Südseite* TV
Jeffersonville	Jeffersonville TV	1872	1875?	
La Porte	La Porte *Männerchor*	1870	1884	
Lafayette	Lafayette TV	1863	1884?	
Logansport	*Germania* TV	1867	1873	
Madison	Madison TV	1853	1869?	
Mt. Vernon	Mt. Vernon TV	1868?	1868?	
New Albany	*Deutsch-Amerikanischer* TV	1853	1892?	Possibly also known as New Albany TG
Richmond	Richmond TV	1868?	1868?	

State/ Town	Society Name	Beg. Date	End Date	Note
Shelbyville	Shelbyville TV	1853	1873	
South Bend	Am. Turners South Bend	1861	pres.	Founded as South Bend TV
Tell City	*Socialer* TV	1859	1904?	
Terre Haute	Terre Haute TV	1852	1903	In 1884 merged with the *Männerchor* to form *TS* of the *Germania* Soc.
Versailles	Versailles TV	1869?	1869?	
Vevay	Vevay TV	1868?	1868?	

Iowa

Avoca	Avoca TV	1875	1879?	
Belle Plaine	Belle Plaine TV	1871	1879?	
Bellevue	Bellevue TV	1867	1879?	
Boone	Boone TV	1886	1888?	
Buffalo	Buffalo TV	1869	1912?	
Burlington	Burlington TG	1852	pres.	Absorbed TV *Bahn Frei* in 1899
Burlington	TV *Bahn Frei*	1853	1899	Joined the Burlington TG in 1899
Cedar Rapids	Cedar Rapids TV	1877	1878?	
Cedar Rapids	TV *Germania*	1896?	1899	
Charles City	TV *Concordia*	1892?	1892?	
Clinton	Clinton Turners	1883	1962?	Founded as TV *Vorwärts*; in 1937 name changed to Clinton Turner and Bene-volent *V. Vorwärts*; renamed Clinton Turners, Inc. in 1947
Communia	Communia TV	1883	1906?	
Council Bluffs	Council Bluffs TV	1870	1870?	
Davenport	Central Turners	1852	pres.	Founded as *Socialistischer* TV; renamed Davenport TG in 1858 and Central Turners in 1943; moved to Rockford, IL, in 1971
Davenport	N.W. Davenport Turner Society	1871	pres.	Founded as the N.W. Davenport TV

State/ Town	Society Name	Beg. Date	End Date	Note
Davenport	East Davenport Turner Society	1891	pres.	Founded as the *Ost Davenport* TV
Denison	Denison TV	1881	1881?	
Des Moines	*Socialer* TV	1866	1917?	
Des Moines	*Concordia* TV	1936	1938	
Dubuque	*Sozialer* TV	1863	1896?	Possibly also known as *Germania* TV from 1863-67?
Durant	Durant TV	1874	1889?	Also called Durant TG
Eldridge	*Sozialer* TV	1869	1942?	
Guttenberg	Guttenberg TV	1868	1904?	
Holstein	Holstein TV	1884	1970s?	
Keokuk	Keokuk TV	1850s?	1889?	Conflicting beginning dates of 1852, 1859 & 1863
Keystone	Keystone Turners, Inc.	1892	pres.	Founded as Keystone TV
Le Claire	Le Claire TV	1877	1877?	
Lansing	Lansing TV	1868	1875?	
Manning	TV Manning	1896	1899?	
Marshalltown	Marshall TV	1884?	1885?	
Muscatine	TV *Vorwärts*	1907	1934?	Dissolved in 1920; reorganized in 1930
Muscatine	Muscatine TV	1866	1894	
Ottumwa	Ottumwa TV	1867	1920	
Postville	Postville TV	1873	1906?	
Reinbeck	Grundy & Tacoma County TV	1899	1912?	
Rock Island	Rock Island TG	1857	1938	
Sioux City	Sioux City TV	1882	1980?	Possibly known as TV *Eiche* from 1882-95
Walcott	Walcott TV	1875?	1894?	
Waterloo	Waterloo TV	1870s?	1904?	Conflicting beginning dates of 1873 & 1878

Kansas

State/ Town	Society Name	Beg. Date	End Date	Note
Atchison	Atchison TV	1859	1917	
Baker	Baker TV	1893	1898?	
Baxter Springs	Baxter Springs TV	1870	1875?	
Bern	TV Bern	1891	1927?	

State/ Town	Society Name	Beg. Date	End Date	Note
Brunswick	Brunswick TV	1866	1867	
Chetopa	Chetopa TV	1871	1873	
Coffeyville	Coffs TV	1901	1903	
Denton	TV Doniphan Co.	1895	1897?	
Eudora	Eudora TV	1864	1889?	
Everest	Everest TV	1893	1896?	
Fort Scott	Fort Scott TV	1863	1917	
Hanover	Hanover TV	1872	1920	
Hiawatha	Hiawatha TV	1895	1898?	
Home City	TV Home City	1893	1911	
Horton	Horton TV	1891	1898?	Possibly also known as *Vorwärts* TV
Junction City	Junction City TV	1866	1873	
Kansas City	TV Columbus	1894?	1897?	
Lawrence	Lawrence TV	1866	1938	
Leavenworth	Leavenworth TV	1857	1925	
Marysville	Marysville TV	1874	1925?	
Newton	Newton TV	1883	1889?	
Ottawa	Ottawa TV	1868	1875?	
Parico	Parico TV	1888	1890	
Pittsburgh	Pittsburgh TV	1890	1893?	
Seneca	Seneca TV	1897	1903?	
Severance	Severance TV	1893	1903	
St. Joseph	St. Joseph TV	1858	1920	
Summerfield	Summerfield TV	1890	1920	
Topeka	Topeka TV	1867	1920s?	
Valley Falls	Valley Falls TV	1878	1914	
Weir	*Harmonie* TV	1895	1898?	Possibly also known as Weir City TV
Wichita	TV *Vorwärts*	1885	1896?	
Willis	Willis TV	1895	1896?	
Wyandotte	Wyandotte TV	1866	1887	

Kentucky

Covington	Covington Turner Society	1855	pres.	Founded as Covington TV; changed name to Covington Turner Society in 1918

State/ Town	Society Name	Beg. Date	End Date	Note
Falmouth	Henderson TV	1894	1894?	
Louisville	Am. Turners Louisville	1850	pres.	Founded as Louisville TG; absorbed *Centraler* TV in 1888; changed name to Louisville Turners in 1918 and to Am. Turners Louisville in 1940s
Louisville	*Centraler* TV	1880?	1888	Joined Louisville TG in 1888
Louisville	*Männer* TV *Vorwärts*	1887?	1899?	
Louisville	River City Turners, Inc.	1894	pres.	
Newport	Newport Gym. Assoc.	1852	1936?	Founded as Newport TV; changed name during WWI
Paducah	Paducah TV	1868?	1868?	

Lousiana

New Orleans	New Orleans TV	1851	1928	Became member of the "*Deutsche Haus*" in 1928

Maryland

Baltimore	Locust Point TV	????	????	
Baltimore	Social Democratic TV	1849	1887	Merged with Atlantic TV to form the Baltimore TG
Baltimore	TV *Vorwärts*	1867	1948	Merged with *Germania* TV to form Am. Turners Baltimore
Baltimore	Atlantic TV	1872	1887	Merged with Social Democratic TV to form Baltimore TG in 1887
Baltimore	Gymnastic *Pyramiden* Club	1882	1900?	
Baltimore	*Germania* TV	1887	1948	Founded as Baltimore TG from merger of Social

State/ Town	Society Name	Beg. Date	End Date	Note
				Democratic TV and Atlantic TV; reorganized in 1888 as *Germania* TV; merged with TV *Vorwärts* in 1948 to form Am. Turners Baltimore
Baltimore	Labor Lyceum *TS*	1901	1907	
Baltimore	Am. Turners Baltimore	1948	pres.	Formed by the merger of *Germania* TV and TV *Vorwärts*

Massachusetts

Adams	Adams Turners, Inc.	1889	pres.	Founded as Adams Turn Club; changed name to TV *Vorwärts* during same year; during 1890s possibly also known as *Germania* TV; renamed Adams Turners, Inc. in 1948
Boston	*Germania* TV	????	1952	Located in Rosendale
Boston	Boston TV	1849	1956	Absorbed TV *Fortschritt* in 1860
Boston	TV *Fortschritt*	1850s	1860	Joined Boston TV
Boston	*TS d. Bostoner*?	1882	1927?	
Boston	*TS d. GV Harmonia*	1883?	1898?	Located in Roxbury/Dedham
Boston	*Deutscher Arbeiter* TV	1887	1938	Absorbed TV *Vorwärts*; located in Roxbury
Boston	TV *Vorwärts*	1894	1900	Joined *Deutscher Arbeiter* TV; located in Roxbury
Boston	Schiller TV	1935?	1942?	Located in Roxbury
Cambridge	Cambridge TV	1891?	1898?	
Clinton	Clinton TV	1867	pres.	Founded as TV *Frohsinn*
Easthampton	TV Easthampton	1897	1916	
Fair View	*Turn & GV Frohsinn*	1901?	1902?	

State/ Town	Society Name	Beg. Date	End Date	Note
Fitchburg	Fitchburg Turners, Inc.	1886	1983	Founded as Fitchburgh TV; changed name to *Deutscher Fortbildungsverein* in 1909 and to Fitchburgh Turners, Inc. in 1954
Greenfield	Greenfield TV	1867	1875?	
Holyoke	Holyoke TV	1871	pres.	Group split to form Spingdale *Vorwärts* TV in 1886
Holyoke	Springdale Turners, Inc.	1886	pres.	Split from Holyoke TV in 1886 and organized as Springdale *Vorwärts* TV; changed name to Springdale Turners, Inc. in 1940s
Lawrence	Lawrence TV	1866	1974	
Lynn	*Deutscher* TV	1916	1924?	
Malden	TV Malden	1889	1942	
New Bedford	*Socialer* TV	1855	1856?	
Norwood	Norwood TV	1894	1897?	
Pittsfield	*Germania* TV	1862	1938	
Shelburne Falls	Shelburne Falls TV	1864	1875?	
Springfield	Springfield TV Inc.	1855	pres.	Today located in Agawam
Taunton	TV *Germania*	1889?	1963	
Webster	TV *Vorwärts*	1887	1922	
Webster	Webster TV	1883	1921?	
Westfield	Westfield TV	1897	1907?	
Worcester	*Socialer* TV	1859	1921?	

Michigan

Adrian	Adrian TV	1871	1874?	Possibly also known as *Socialer* TV
Ann Arbor	Ann Arbor TV	1869	1886	
Dearborn	Dearborn TV	1934?	1938	
Detroit	American Turners Detroit	1852	pres.	Founded as *Socialer* TV; changed name in 1943/44

State/ Town	Society Name	Beg. Date	End Date	Note
Detroit	*Freier* TV	1869?	1873?	
Detroit	TV *Sachsenbund*	1886	1888?	
Detroit	*Ostseite* TV	1889	1898?	
Detroit	West-Detroit TV	1889	1900?	
Grand Rapids	*Deutscher* TV	1870	1931	
Jackson	Jackson TV	1881	1892	
Kalamazoo	Kalamazoo TV	1871?	1917	First local TV mentioned in city directory of 1871/72, in other sources by 1879
Lansing	Lansing TV	1884	1896?	
Manistee	Manistee TV	1868	1892	
Menominee	Menominee TV	1886	1932	
Saginaw	Saginaw TV	1856	1862	Merged with *Liederkranz* to form *Germania* TV
Saginaw	East Saginaw TV	1862	1898	Split from *Germania* TV and merged with it again in 1898
Saginawa	*Germania* TV	1862	1918	Formed by merger of Saginaw TV and *Liederkranz*; absorbed East Saginaw TV in 1898; merged with *Teutonia* TV to form Lincoln Club in 1918
Saginaw	*Teutonia* TV	1869	1918	Merged with *Germania* TV in 1918 to form Lincoln Club
Saginaw	German Club	1918	pres.	Founded as Lincoln Club; formed by merger of *Germania* TV and *Teutonia* TV; reorganized as social society with former TV renamed Lincoln *TS*; left American Turnerbund in 1921; today known as German Club

Minnesota

Duluth	Duluth TV	1882?	1900?	
Hastings	Hastings TV	1870	1873	
Jordan	Jordan TV	1894?	1894	

State/ Town	Society Name	Beg. Date	End Date	Note
Mankato	Mankato TV	1872	1872?	
Minneapolis	St. Anthony TV	1857	pres.	Present address Balsam Lake, WI
Minneapolis	West Minneapolis TV	1866	1900	
New Ulm	New Ulm TV	1856	pres.	
Osseo	Osseo TV	1876	1906?	
Owatonna	Owatonna TV	1866	1887?	
Red Wing	Red Wing TV	1866?	1868?	
Rochester	Rochester TV	1868	1896	
St. Paul	St. Paul TV	1858	1886	Merged with *Deutscher V.* to form *Germania* TV
St. Paul	*Westseite* TV	1888	1913	Joined St. Paul TV in 1913
St. Paul	N. St. Paul TV	1890?	1890?	
St. Paul	St. Paul Turners, Inc.	1886	pres.	Founded as *Germania* TV; formed by merger of St. Paul TV and *Deutscher V.*; reorganized as St. Paul TV in 1896; absorbed *Westseite* TV in 1913; renamed St. Paul Turners in 1940
Stillwater	Stillwater TV	1872	1893?	
Wabasha	Wabasha TV	1885?	1886	
Winona	*TS d. Philarm. Vereins*	1868	1899	
Winona	*Germania* TV	1883?	1883?	

Missouri

Barthold Valley	St. Louis Co. TV	1895	1897	
Bluffton	Bluffton TV	1867?	1867	
Boonville	Boonville Turn & GV	1852	1936	Organized as Boonville TV
Brunswick	Brunswick TV	1866?	1869?	
Cape Girardeau	Cape Girardeau TV	1883?	1886?	
Hannibal	Hannibal TV	1870	1876?	
Hermann	Hermann TV	1860	1917?	

State/ Town	Society Name	Beg. Date	End Date	Note
Jefferson City	Jefferson City TV	1867	1875?	
Kansas City	Kansas City Turners	1858	pres.	Founded as *Socialer* TV
Kansas City	TV *Vorwärts*	1884	1896	
Lexington	Lexington TV	1859	1965?	
St. Charles	St. Charles TV	1864	1875?	
St. Joseph	St. Joseph TV	1855	1938	
St. Louis	St. Louis TV	1850	1940	Absorbed Southside TV in 1918
St. Louis	*Schweizer* National TV	1859	1947	Conflicting founding date of 1887
St. Louis	Southside TV	1865	1918	Founded as *Süd* St. Louis TV; joined St. Louis TV in 1918
St. Louis	North St. Louis Gymnastic Soc.	1870	pres.	Also known as *Nord* St. Louis TV; absorbed Olympic TV 1922
St. Louis	*Socialer* TV	1872	1912?	Possibly merged or reorganized as Olympic TV in 1912
St. Louis	*Concordia* Gymnastic Soc.	1874	pres.	Founded as *Concordia* TV
St. Louis	Carondelet *Germania* Soc.	1875	1921	Founded as Carondelet TV; closed 1887; reopened 1890 as Carondelet *Germania* TV; renamed Carondelet *Germania* Soc. in 1917/18
St. Louis	West St. Louis TV	1879	1911?	
St. Louis	Rock Spring TV	1887	1940	
St. Louis	*Nordwest* TV	1892	1897	
St. Louis	Southwest Turners	1893	1958?	Also known as *Süd-West* TV; absorbed Tower Grove TV in 1939
St. Louis	TV Humbolt	1894	1909	
St. Louis	TV Columbia	1896	1896?	
St. Louis	Humboldt TV	1898?	1898	
St. Louis	Schiller Turners, Inc.	1906	pres.	Founded as Schiller TV;

State/ Town	Society Name	Beg. Date	End Date	Note
				absorbed Lindenwood TV in 1939
St. Louis	Tower Grove TV	1906	1939	Joined Southwest Turners in 1939
St. Louis	TV Forest Park	1909	1918?	
St. Louis	Lindenwood TV	1910	1940	Joined the Schiller Turners in 1940
St. Louis	Olympic TV	1912	1922	Joined North St. Louis TV in 1922
Sedalia	*Harmonie* TV	1871	1894	
Warrensburg	Warrensburg TV	1868	1875?	
Washington	Washington TV	1859	1932	

Montana

Anaconda	Anaconda TV	1893	1902?	
Butte City	Butte City TV	1886?	1899	Possibly also known as *Germania*-American TV
Great Falls	Great Falls TV	1891?	1894?	
Helena	TV *Vorwärts*	1880s?	1901?	
Philipsburg	Philipsburg TV	????	????	

Nebraska

Fremont	Fremont TV	1883	1920	
Lincoln	Lincoln TV	1889	1896	
Millard	Millard TV	1894	1907	
Nebraska City	Nebraska City TV	1890	1896	
Norfolk	Norfolk TV	1883?	1892?	
Omaha	Omaha TV	1860	1890	
Omaha	Jahn TV	1889	1893	Merged with *Südseite* TV
Omaha	South Side Turners	1892	1966	Founded as *Süd Seite* TV; joined by Jahn TV in 1893; changed name to South Side Turners in 1946; merged with other German-American societies in 1966
Plattsmouth	Plattsmouth TV	1870	1922	

State/ Town	Society Name	Beg. Date	End Date	Note
West Point	West Point TV	1890	1892?	
Wilber	Wilber TV	1893?	1893?	

Nevada

Virginia City	Virginia City TV	1874?	1883	

New Hampshire

Manchester	Manchester TV	1870	1977	Sabre Club offshoot still meets today

New Jersey

Atlantic City	Atlantic City TV	1889	1902?	
Bloomfield	TV *Germania*	1883	1885	
Camden	Camden TV	1890	1901?	
Carlstadt	Carlstadt TV, Inc.	1857	pres.	Founded as *Socialer* TV
Egg Harbor City	*Vorwärts* TV	1858	1875?	
Elizabeth	TV *Vorwärts*	1872	1906?	
Fairview	Am. Gym. Soc.	1935	1953	
Greenville	Greenville TV	1867	1957	
Hackensack	Hackensack TV	1864	1875?	
Hoboken	Hoboken TV	1857	1934	Founded as Hoboken TG; changed name to Hoboken Gymnastic Society in 1868 and to Hoboken TV in 1881
Irvington	National TV	1883	pres.?	
Jersey City	Jersey City TV	1854	1897	Founded as *Socialer* TV
Jersey City	Centre Hill TV	1856	1861	
Jersey City	Washington Village TV	1860	1861	
Jersey City	Hudson City TV	1863	1939?	
Keansburg	Turner *Männerchor*	1914	1919	
Milltown	Milltown TV	1867	1873	
New Brunswick	New Brunswick TV	1867	1960?	

State/ Town	Society Name	Beg. Date	End Date	Note
Newark	*Socialistischer* TV	1848?	1878	Merged with *Unabhängiger* TV to form Newark TV
Newark	*Unabhängiger* TV	1865	1878	Merged with *Socialistischer* TV to form Newark TV
Newark	Newark TV	1878	1967?	Formed by members of the *Unabhängige* TV & *Socialer* TV
Newark	TV *Vorwärts*	1882	1913	
Newark	*Nordseite* TV	1892	1897	
North Bergen	Union Hill Turners	1872	1986	Founded as Union Hill TV
Orange	Orange TV	1856	1898	Possibly also known as *Socialer* TV
Pakson	*Socialer* TV	1854	1885	
Passaic	Passaic Turners, Inc.	1892	pres.	Founded as Passaic TV
Paterson	Riverside Athletic & Singing Club	1867	1966?	Founded as *Socialer* TV; changed name to Paterson TV in 1887 and to Riverside Athletic & Singing Club after 1950
Paterson	*Schweizer* TV	1890?	1980	
Plainfield	Plainfield *Gesang* & TV, Inc.	1886	pres.	Possibly founded as *Arbeiter* TV
Rahway	*Socialer* TV	1867	1904?	
Riverside	Riverside Turners	1860	1875?	Founded as TV Progress; changed name to Riverside Turners in 1870
Riverside	Riverside Turners, Inc.	1897	pres.	Founded as Riverside TG
Trenton	*Socialer* TV	1855	1895?	
Trenton	Turnerbund	1924	1948	

New Mexico

State/ Town	Society Name	Beg. Date	End Date	Note
Albuquerque	Albuquerque TV	1891	1900?	
Fort Bayard	*Germania* TV	1885	1887	
Union City	Swiss Turners	????	????	

State/ Town	Society Name	Beg. Date	End Date	Note
New York				
Albany	*Socialer* TV	1851	1867?	
Albany	Capitol TV	1869	1890	
Albany	Albany TV	1896	1901?	
Amsterdam	TV *Fortschritt*	1911	1913?	
Atica	*Socialer* TV	1874?	1874?	
Auburn	Auburn TV	1870	1946	
Buffalo	Buffalo TV, Inc.	1853	pres.	In 1856 the society split into TV *Vorwärts* and *Sociale Männer* TV; in 1865 both societies reunited to form the Buffalo TV
Buffalo	*Sociale Männer* TV	1856	1865	Founded by members of the Buffalo TV; rejoined the Buffalo TV in 1865
Buffalo	TV *Vorwärts*	1856	1865	Founded by members of the Buffalo TV; rejoined the Buffalo TV in 1865
Buffalo	East Buffalo TV	1874?	1874?	
Buffalo	TV Columbia	1900	1916?	
Buffalo	*Eiche* TV	1927	1938	
Camillus	TV Camillus	1913	1916?	
College Point	College Point TV	????	1887	
Dolgeville	Dolgeville TV	1885	1901?	
Dunkirk	Dunkirk TV	1867	1875?	
Elmira	Elmira TV	1866	1873	
Fort Plain	Fort Plain TV	1887	1890?	
Long Island	Green Point TV	1871	1893	
Long Island	Long Island Turners, Inc.	1875	pres.	Founded as Long Island City TV
Long Island	Corona TV	1901	1913?	
Mt. Morris	Mt. Morris TV	1891	1896?	
Newburgh	Newburgh TV	1863	1909?	
New York	Maspeth TV	????	????	
New York	New York TG	1848	1852	
New York	New York TV	1850	1983	Founded as *Socialistischer* TV; in 1857 changed name

State/ Town	Society Name	Beg. Date	End Date	Note
				to New York TV; Central TV joined in 1956; merged with Mt. Vernon Turners in 1983 to form the Am. Turners New York, Inc.
New York	*Socialer* TV	1851	1939?	Also known as *Socialistischer* TV of Brooklyn or Brooklyn TV
New York	Brooklyn E.D. TV	1853	1948	Founded as Williamsburgh TV; changed name to Brooklyn E.D. in 1884; merged with TV *Vorwärts* to form Am. Turners of Brooklyn in 1948
New York	Morrisania TV	1853	1873?	Located in the Bronx
New York	New Brooklyn TG	1854	1903	
New York	Strattonport TV	1855	1869	
New York	East N.Y. TV	1859	1893	
New York	Bloomingdale TV	1862	1926?	
New York	Harlem TV	1867	1897?	
New York	Brooklyn Central TV	1869?	1886	
New York	Gowanus TV	1869	1890?	Located in Brooklyn
New York	*Arbeiter* TV d. *Westseite*	1870	1875?	
New York	Melrose TV	1874	1913	
New York	South Brooklyn TV	1875	1908?	
New York	American Turners Bronx, Inc.	1881	1957	Founded as *Deutsch-Amerikanischer* TV; changed name in 1848/49; joined Mt. Vernon Turners in 1957
New York	TV *Vorwärts*	1883	1948	Joined by *Social Demokratischer* TV in 1901; merged with Brooklyn E.D. TV to form the Am. Turners Brooklyn in 1948
New York	*Sozial demo-kratischer* TV	1884	1901	Joined TV *Vorwärts* in 1901

State/ Town	Society Name	Beg. Date	End Date	Note
New York	Central TV	1886	1956	Merged with New York TV
New York	National TV	1890?	1890	Located in Brooklyn
New York	West End TV	1890	1903	
New York	Mt. Vernon Turners, Inc.	1891	1986	Founded as TV Mt. Vernon; joined by TV Woodstock in 1921; changed name to Mt. Vernon Turners, Inc. in 1947; Am. Turners Bronx joined in 1957; in 1986 merged with New York TV to form Am. Turners New York, Inc.
New York	*Rheinpfälzer* TV	1891?	1894	
New York	Columbia TV	1892	1946	Located in Brooklyn
New York	Bronx TV	1905	1906?	
New York	TV Woodstock	1907	1921	Joined Mt. Vernon TV in 1921
New York	American Turners Brooklyn, Inc.	1948	1986	Formed by merger of TV *Vorwärts* and Brooklyn E.D. TV
New York	American Turners New York, Inc.	1983	pres.	Formed by merger of New York TV and Mt. Vernon Turners
Oneida	Oneida TV	1895	1898	
Poughkeepsie	*Socialer* TV	1854	1875?	
Rochester	Rochester Turners, Inc.	1852	pres.	Founded as *Socialer* TV; changed name to Rochester TV in 1854 and to Rochester Turners, Inc, in 1940s
Rome	Rome TV	1889	1898	
Rondout	*Socialer* TV	1867	1875?	
Schenectady	Schenectady Turners, Inc.	1891	pres.	Founded as *Socialer* TV
Springfield	Columbia TV	1939	1947	
Staten Island	Staten Island TV	1869	1875?	Also known as *Männer* TV
Suspension Bridge	Suspension Bridge TV	1869	1873	

State/ Town	Society Name	Beg. Date	End Date	Note
Syracuse	Syracuse Turners, Inc.	1854	pres.	Founded as Syracuse TV
Troy	Troy TV	1852	1938	In 1853 Troy TV split into the *Freie* TG and *Socialer* TV; *Freie* TG changed name back to Troy TV in 1868
Troy	*Socialer* TV	1853	1855	
Troy	TV *Vorwärts*	1893	1896?	
Utica	Utica TV	1854	1938	Absorbed *Germania* TV
Utica	*Germania* TV	1868	1894	Joined Utica TV in 1894
Utica	Union TV	1870?	1870?	
Yonkers	Yonkers TV	1875	1908?	

North Dakota

Jamestown	Jamestown TV	1879	1891?	
New Salem	New Salem TV	1890s?	1920s?	
Wahpeton	TV *Vorwärts*	1885	1920s?	

Nevada

Carson City	Carson City TV	1862	1866?	

Ohio

Akron	Akron Turner Club	1885	pres.	Founded as Akron TV; changed name in the 1940s
Alliance	Alliance TV	1894	1895	
Bellaire	Belmont TV	1876	1894	
Canton	*Germania* TV	1873	1913?	
Cincinnati	Cincin. Central Turners, Inc.	1848	pres.	Founded as Cincin. TG
Cincinnati	Lick Run TV	1881	1889?	
Cincinnati	North-Cincin. Gymnasium	1881	1930s	Founded as *Nord* Cincin. TV; changed name in ca. 1918

State/ Town	Society Name	Beg. Date	End Date	Note
Cincinnati	West-Cincin. TV	1881	1910	
Cincinnati	North West TV	1886	1929	Also called *Deutsch Ungarische* TG
Cincinnati	TV Norwood	1905	1938	
Cincinnati	*Allgemeiner Arbeiter* TV	1911	1917?	
Cincinnati	TV Jahn	1923	1925?	Located in Norwood
Cleveland	Cleveland TV	1849	1876	Reorganized as *Germania* TV in 1876
Cleveland	Cleveland Turners S.T.V.	1867	pres.	Founded as *Socialer* TV
Cleveland	Stern TV	1873	1910	In 1910 Stern TV and *Fortschritt* TV merged to form the *Deutscher* Club Cleveland
Cleveland	*Germania* TV	1876	1908	Merged with TV *Vorwärts* to form *Germania* TV *Vorwärts*
Cleveland	TV *Vorwärts*	1890	1908	In 1908 merged with *Germania* TV to form the *Germania* TV *Vorwärts*
Cleveland	Swiss Gymnastic Society	1891	1950s	Founded as *Schweizer* TV; changed name to Swiss Gymnastic Society in 1940s
Cleveland	TV *Fortschritt*	1897	1910	Merged with Stern TV to form *Deutscher* Club Cleveland
Cleveland	East Side Turners	1908	pres.	Founded as *Germania* TV *Vorwärts* by merger of *Germania* TV and TV *Vorwärts*; changed name to East Side Turners ca. 1941
Cleveland	*Deutscher* Club	1910	1917?	Formed by the merger of Stern TV and *Fortschritt* TV
Columbus	Columbus TV	1867	1937	
Columbus	*Deutsche Turn-gesellschaft*	1913?	1913?	
Cumminsville	Cumminsville TV	1871	1896?	
Dayton	Dayton *Liederkranz* Turners	1853	pres.	Founded as Dayton TG;

State/ Town	Society Name	Beg. Date	End Date	Note
				changed name to Dayton Turner Assoc. in 1925; joined Dayton *Liederkranz* to form the Dayton *Liederkranz* Turners in 1952
Dayton	TV *Vorwärts*	1884	1898	
Findlay	Findlay TV	1890	1918?	
Findlay	TS d. Germania Verein	1893	1895	
Fostoria	*Concordia* TV	1895	1898?	
Hamilton	*Deutscher* TV	1852	1898	Possibly identical with Hamilton TG
Hamilton	Hamilton TV	1891?	1894?	
Hamilton	Hamilton TG	1893	1898?	Possibly identical with *Deutscher* TV
Lima	Lima TV	1888	1894	
Liverpool	Kraft Liverpool TV	????	????	
Liverpool	TV East Liverpool	1884	1939	
Lorain	TV *Vorwärts*	1905	1908	
Newark	Newark TV	1889	1896	
Piqua	Piqua TV	1858	1879?	
Portsmouth	Portsmouth TV	1881	1887?	
Ripley	Ripley TV	1860	1873	
Salem	Salem TV	1926?	1929	
Sandusky	Sandusky TV	1868	1868?	
Sandusky	*Activ* TV	1876	1889	Merged with *Socialer* TV to form Sandusky TG
Sandusky	*Socialer* TV	1882	1889	Merged with *Activ* TV to form Sandusky TG
Sandusky	Sandusky TG	1889	1895	Formed by the merger of *Socialer* TV and *Activ* TV
Springfield	Springfield TV	1885	1894	
Steubenville	*Germania* TV	1874	1926?	
Tiffin	Tiffin TV	1868	1896?	
Toledo	Toledo TV	1866	1913?	
Toledo	TV *Vorwärts*	1880s	1900?	
Toledo	*Sozialer* TV	1904	1908?	
Toledo	Am. Turners Toledo	1926	pres.	Also known as *Turn & Sport V.* or Germ.-Am. Gym. Club

State/ Town	Society Name	Beg. Date	End Date	Note
Warren	TV *Bahn Frei*	1894	1898	
Oklahoma				
Muskogee	Muskogee TV	1907?	1908?	
Oregon				
Portland	*Socialer* TV	1858	1950s?	Founded as Portland TV; in 1871 reorganized as Portland *Socialer* TV
Salem	Salem TV	1872?	1872?	
Pennsylvania				
Allentown	TV & *Liederkranz*	1889	1928?	
Altoona	*Concordia* TV	????	????	
Altoona	Altoona TV	1882	1928?	Possibly also known as Altoona TG
Ambridge	Harmony *Männerchor, Gesang* & TV	1904	1990s	Founded as Harmony Gymnastic Club; changed name in 1930s
Beaver Falls	Beaver Falls Turners	1871	pres.	Founded as Beaver Falls TV
Birmingham	Birmingham TV	1890?	1929	
Braddock	Central Turn & *GV*	1882	1937	
Chambersburg	*Socialer* TV	1885	1888?	
Charleroi	TV Charleroi	1905	1982	
Chester	Turn & *Sonntags Schulverein*	1891	1894?	
Duquesne	Turn & *GV Vorwärts*	1890	1920	
Erie	South Erie Turners	1868	pres.	Founded as *Süd* Erie TV

State/ Town	Society Name	Beg. Date	End Date	Note
Erie	East Erie Turners	1874	pres.	Founded as Erie TV; renamed East Erie Turners in 1918
Erie	Central TV	1890	1892	
Homestead	*Eintracht* Music & Turn Hall Assoc.	1886	pres.	Founded as Turn & GV *Eintracht*
Jeanette	Jeanette TV	1890	1931?	Possibly also called Jeanette Gymnastic Union
Johnstown	Johnstown Turners	1866	pres.	Founded as Johnstown TV; renamed Johnstown Turners in 1940s
Kensington	*Germania* TV	1866	1879?	
Kensington	N. Kensington TV	1892	1899	Joined East Pittsburgh TV in 1899
Lancaster	*Germania* TV	1889	1894?	
Mansfield	Mansfield Valley TV	1885	1889?	
McKees Rocks	McKees Rocks *Männerchor* & TV	1892?	1892?	
McKeesport	McKeesport Turners	1880	pres.	Founded as McKeesport *Turn & GV*
Monaca	Monaca TV	1883	pres.	
Monessen	Monessen TV	1905	1966	
Monongahela	Monongahela Turners	1889	pres.	Founded as *Eintracht GV*; in 1890 became *Turn & GV Eintracht*; renamed Monongahela Turners in 1945
Philadelphia	*Schweizer* TV	????	????	
Philadelphia	Philadelphia Turners	1849	1982	Founded as Philadelphia TG
Philadelphia	*Germania* TV	1866	1928?	
Philadelphia	Manayunk TV	1866	1873	Merged with Roxborough TV to form *Germania* TV of Roxborough and Manayunk
Philadelphia	Roxborough TV	1872	1873	Merged with Manayunk TV

State/ Town	Society Name	Beg. Date	End Date	Note
Philadelphia	Roxborough Turners	1873	pres.	to form *Germania* TV of Roxborough and Manayunk Founded as *Germania* TV of Roxborough and Manayunk; formed by merger of Roxborough TV and Manayunk TV; changed name to Roxborough Turners in the 1940s
Philadelphia	Southwark TV	1886?	1886?	
Philadelphia	West Turn & *Schulverein*	1887	1932	
Philadelphia	*TS d.* Cambrinus	1890	1890?	
Philadelphia	Columbia TV	1895	1932	
Philadelphia	TV Tioga	1903	1908	
Philadelphia	*TS d.* Labor Lyceums	1916	1928	
Pittsburgh	Allegheny TV	1850	1939	
Pittsburgh	Pittsburgh TV	1852	1946	
Pittsburgh	Birmingham TV	1867	1929	
Pittsburgh	Lawrenceville TV	1867	1922	
Pittsburgh	*Germania* TV	1869	1879?	
Pittsburgh	Central TV	1871	1933	Possibly same as Central *Turn & GV*
Pittsburgh	Central *Turn & GV*	1882	1936	Possibly same as Central *Turn & GV*
Pittsburgh	*Südseite* TV	1882	1929	
Pittsburgh	Allentown TV	1884	1940	
Pittsburgh	TV Manchester	1886	1919	
Pittsburgh	Mt. Olive *Turn & GV*	1891	1930	
Pittsburgh	Troy Hill TV	1891	1891?	
Pittsburgh	TV *Bahn Frei*	1893	1900	Possibly merged with Allegheny TV
Pittsburgh	Columbia TV	1894	1901	
Pittsburgh	TV Esplen	1894	1914?	
Pittsburgh	Schiller's *Glocke Turn & GV*	1895?	1928	

State/ Town	Society Name	Beg. Date	End Date	Note
Pittsburgh	East Pittsburg TV	1897	1947	Absorbed N. Kensington TV in 1899
Pittsburgh	Lincoln TV	1897	1898	
Pittsburgh	*Concordia* TV	1904?	1904?	
Reading	TV Reading	1891	1913?	
Rochester	Rochester TV	1851	????	Founded as *Socialer* TV; changed name to Rochester TV in 1854
Rochester	Central TV	1900	pres.	
Scranton	Scranton TV	1867	1898?	
Vandergrift	Kiski Valley *Turn & GV*	1904	1920	
Wilkes-Barre	TV Wilkes-Barre	1867	1924?	
Williamsport	TV *Vorwärts*	1886	1921?	

Rhode Island

State/ Town	Society Name	Beg. Date	End Date	Note
Pawtucket	Pawtucket Turners	1939	1952	Founded as Pawtucket TV; joined ProvidenceTurners in 1952
Providence	Providence TV	1852	1898	Became part of *Deutsche Gesellschaft* in 1898
Providence	TV & *TS d. GV Harmonie*	1889?	1889?	
Providence	Providence Turners, Inc.	1896	pres.	Founded as TV *Vorwärts* in Johnstown, a part of Providence since 1898; renamed *Deutsche Turnerschaft* in 1909; changed name to Providence Turners in 1940s; Pawtucket Turners joined in 1952

South Carolina

State/ Town	Society Name	Beg. Date	End Date	Note
Charleston	Charleston TV	1852	1917?	

State/ Town	Society Name	Beg. Date	End Date	Note
South Dakota				
Hartford	Hartford TV	1896?	1897	
Sioux Falls	TV *Fortschritt*	1892	1899?	
Yankton	Yankton TV	1885?	1899?	
Tennessee				
Chattanooga	Chattanooga Turners	1866	1977?	Founded as Chattanooga TV; changed name in 1946/47
Knoxville	Knoxville TV	1867	1879?	
Memphis	Memphis TV	1874?	1874?	
Memphis	*Germania* TV	1885	1920s?	
Nashville	Nashville TV	1865	1880?	
Texas				
Alamo City	Alamo City TV	????	????	
Austin	Austin TV	1870	1872?	
Belleville	TV *Gut Heil*	1870?	1937?	Possibly also known as Piney *Concordia* TV
Boerne	Boerne TV	1890	pres.	Currently a bowling society
Comfort	Comfort TV	????	1974	
Dallas	Dallas TV	1874?	1900?	Also known as *Concordia* TV
Fredericksburg	*Socialer* TV	1871	pres.	
Galveston	*Socialer* TV	1851	1900	Possibly later known as Tin Pen Club
Gruenau	Gruenau *Turn & Schützenverein*	1897	pres.	Merged with Gruenau *Schützenverein* to form the Gruenau *Turn & Schützenverein*
High Hill	High Hill TV	1871	1872?	
Houston	Houston TV	1853	pres.	Joined by Jahn TV in 1878; currently a bowling society
Houston	Jahn TV	1875	1878	Joined Houston TV in 1878

State/ Town	Society Name	Beg. Date	End Date	Note
La Bahia	La Bahia TV	1879	pres.?	
Mill Creek	West Mill Creek TV	1877?	1877?	
New Braunfels	New Braunfels TV	1853	1880s?	
Qiutu	Qiutu TV	1877?	1877?	
Round Top	Round Top TV	1878?	1885?	
San Antonio	San Antonio TV	1853	pres.	
Schulenburg	Schulenburg TV	1880s?	1913?	

Utah

Ogden	Ogden TV	1890?	1890?	
Salt Lake City	Salt Lake City TV	1895	1920?	

Virginia

Norfolk	Norfolk TV	1866	1866?	
Richmond	*Unabgängiger* TV	1850	1917?	Founded as *Socialer* TV; reorganized in 1885 as *Unabhängiger* TV

Washington

Centralia	Centralia TV	1891	1893	
Seattle	Seattle TV	1885	1950	
Spokane	Spokane TV	1890	1920?	
Tacoma	Tacoma TV	1886	1894?	Possibly also known as *Germania TS* from 1893/94
Vancouver	*Socialer* TV	1896	1896?	

West Virginia

Martinsburg	Martinsburg TV	1866	1866?	
Morgantown	TV *Concordia*	1897	1914?	
Wheeling	Wheeling TV	1853	1937	
Wheeling	*Südseite* TV	1890	1891	
Wheeling	Beethoven Society & Turn Society	1925?	1925?	

State/ Town	Society Name	Beg. Date	End Date	Note
Wisconsin				
Appleton	Appleton TV	1869	1895?	
Beaver Dam	Beaver Dam TV	1885?	1885?	
Buffalo City	TG of Buffalo City	1858	1863	Possibly founded as Buffalo City TV; reorganized as TG of Buffalo City in 1859
Cassville	Cassville TV	1889	1890?	
Cedarburg	Cedarburg TV	1867?	1867?	
Cedarburg	*Concordia* TV	1867	1870?	
Fillmore	Farmington Turner Society	1862	pres.	Founded as Farmington TV; changed name in 1930
Fond du Lac	Fond du Lac TV	1855	1914?	Founded as *Socialer* TV; renamed Fond du Lac TV in 1871
Fountain City	Fountain City TV	1858	1872	Became part of *Germania* Society in 1872
Green Bay	Green Bay TV	1860	1924?	
Hartford	Hartford TV	1878	1899?	
Kenosha	TV *Vorwärts*	1897	1903?	
Kenosha	TV *Germania*	1915	1936	
LaCrosse	*TS d. D.B.*	1855	1910?	
La Crosse	La Crosse TV	1865	1874	In 1874 merged with *Liederkranz* to form the *Deutscher V.*
Madison	Madison Turners	1855	pres.	Founded as Madison TV; changed name in 1930s
Manitowoc	Manitowoc TV	1866	1898	
Marinette	TV Marinette	1894	1896?	
Mayville	TV *Eintracht*	1868	1946	Also known as TV Mayville
Medford	Medford TV	1886	1888?	
Menomonee Falls	Swiss Helvetia Turners	????	pres.	
Menomonie	Menomonie TV	1877	1931	
Mequon	Mequon TV	1853	1853?	
Milwaukee	TV *Teutonia*	1852	1853	
Milwaukee	Milwaukee Turner Foundation	1853	pres.	Founded as *Socialer* TV; changed name to Milwaukee

State/ Town	Society Name	Beg. Date	End Date	Note
				TV in 1850s; absorbed TV *Bahn Frei* in 1939; became Milwaukee Turners in 1940, and Milwaukee Turner Foundation ca. 1990.
Milwaukee	TV *d. Südseite*	1868	1928	
Milwaukee	TV *d. Nordseite*	1869	1905	Founded as West Hill TV; renamed TV *d. Nordseite* by 1870
Milwaukee	TV *d. Ostseite*	1869	1889	
Milwaukee	Bohemian TV	1885?	1885?	
Milwaukee	TV *Bahn Frei*	1890	1939	Merged with Milwaukee TV in 1939
Milwaukee	TV Humbolt	1890	1896	
Milwaukee	TV Jahn	1895	1914	
Milwaukee	TV *Vorwärts*	1895?	1900	
Milwaukee	Swiss Turners	1903	pres.	Founded as *Schweizer* TV
Milwaukee	East Side Turners	1980	pres.	Founded as Greater Metropolitan Turners
Monroe	Monroe TV	1859	1918?	
New Berlin	M & M Turners	1980	pres.	Split from Swiss Turners
New Holstein	New Holstein TV	1867	1948	
Oconto	Oconto TV	1869	1915?	
Oshkosh	Oshkosh TV d. *Nordseite*	1869	1917?	Also known as Oshkosh TV
Oshkosh	TV d. *Südseite*	1885	1915?	
Plymouth	Plymouth TV	1872	1887	
Port Washington	Port Washington TV	????	????	
Princeton	Princeton TV	1874	1920	
Racine	*Socialer* TV	1855	1898?	Possibly also known as Racine TV
Sauk City	Sauk City TV	1871?	1871?	
Sheboygan	Sheboygan Turners, Inc.	1854	pres.	Founded as *Sozialer* TV; changed name to Sheboygan TV by 1860, to Sheboygan Gymnastic Society in 1919 and to Sheboygan Turners, Inc. in 1965

State/ Town	Society Name	Beg. Date	End Date	Note
Sheboygan	*Concordia* TV	1860?	1872?	
Thiensville	Thiensville TV	1893	1893?	
Two Rivers	Two Rivers TV	????	????	
Watertown	Watertown TV	1860	pres.	
Wausau	Wausau TV	1883	1890?	Possibly also known as TV *Vorwärts*
West Bend	West Bend TV	1867	1867?	

Wyoming

State/ Town	Society Name	Beg. Date	End Date	Note
Cheyenne	Cheyenne TV	1868	1900?	
Laramie	Laramie TV	1868	1868?	

Appendix 2

Turner Addresses

NATIONAL ADDRESSES

American Turners National Office, 1127 E. Kentucky St., P.O. Box 4216, Louisville, KY 40204. Telephone: (502) 636-2395.

Ruth Lilly Special Collections and Archives, IUPUI University Library, 755 W. Michigan St., Indianapolis, IN 46202. Telephone: (317) 274-0464. (Repository for the American Turners' archives).

CENTRAL STATES DISTRICT

American Turners Louisville, 3125 Upper River Rd., Louisville, KY 40207
American Turners South Bend, 53666 N. Ironwood Rd., South Bend, IN 46635
American Turners Toledo, 3126 Shawnee, Toledo, OH 43613
Athenaeum Turners, 401 E. Michigan St., Indianapolis, IN 46204
Cincinnati Central Turners, 2200 Piney Ln., Cincinnati, OH 45231
Covington Turner Society, 447 Pike St., Covington, KY 41011
Fort Wayne Turners, 3636 Parnell Ave., Ft. Wayne, IN 46895
River City Turners, 8009 Terry Rd., Louisville, KY 40258
South Side Turners, 3702 Raymond St., Indianapolis, IN 46203

ILLINOIS DISTRICT

American Turners Northwest Chicago, 6625 West Belmont Ave., Chicago, IL 60634
Elgin Turners, 112 Villa St., Elgin, IL 60120

Turn Verein Eiche, 16767 S. 80th Ave., Tinley Park, IL 60477
Turn Verein Frisch Auf (Aurora), 1335 Mitchell Rd., Aurora, IL 60504
Turn Verein Lincoln, Inc. 1019 W. Diversey Parkway, Chicago, IL 60614

LAKE ERIE DISTRICT

American Turners Detroit, 26214 Virginia, Warren, MI 48091
Akron Turner Club, 547 S. Munroe Falls Rd., Tallmadge, OH 44278
Cleveland East Side Turners, 1616 East 55 St., Cleveland, OH 44103
Cleveland Turners STV, 7412 Lawn Ave., Cleveland, OH 44103

MIDDLE ATLANTIC DISTRICT

American Turners Baltimore, 9124 Lennings Ln., Baltimore, MD 21237
Riverside Turners Inc., 300 Rancocas Ave., Riverside, NJ 08075
Roxborough Turners, 418 Leverington Ave., Philadelphia, PA 19138
Wilmington Turners, 701 S. Claymont St., Wilmington, DE 19805

MINNESOTA DISTRICT

New Ulm Turnverein, 102 South State St., New Ulm, MN 56073
St. Anthony Turnverein, P.O. Box 276, Balsam Lake, WI 54810
St. Paul Turners, Inc., 2500 Lexington Ave. So., Mendota Hts., MN 55120

NEW ENGLAND DISTRICT

Adams Turners, Inc., 6 Turners Ave., Adams, MA 01220
Clinton Turnverein, 60 Branch St., Clinton, MA 01510
Holyoke Turn Verein, 624 S. Bridge St., Holyoke, MA 01040
Providence Turners, 118 Glenbridge Ave., Providence, RI 02909
Springdale Turners, Inc. 2 Vernon St., Holyoke, MA 01040
Springfield Turnverein, 176 Garden St., Feeding Hills, MA 01030
Syracuse Turners, Inc., 619 N. Salina St., Syracuse, NY 13208

NEW JERSEY DISTRICT

Carlstadt Turnverein, Inc., 500 Broad St., Carlstadt, NJ 07072
Passaic Turners, Inc. 13 Gray St., West Caldwell, NJ 07006

NEW YORK DISTRICT

American Turners New York, 748 Clarence Ave., Bronx, NY 10465
Long Island Turners Inc.: Contact American Turners National Office for current
address.
Schenectady Turn Verein, P.O. Box 3157, Schenectady, NY 12303

ST. LOUIS DISTRICT

Concordia Gymnastic Society, 6432 Gravois Rd., St. Louis, MO 63116
Kansas City Turners, 7620 E. 79th St., Kansas City, MO 64138
North St. Louis Turners, 1928 Salisbury St., St. Louis, MO 63107
Schiller Turners, 200 Weiss Ave., St. Louis, MO 63125

UPPER MISSISSIPPI DISTRICT

Central Turners of Rockford: Contact American Turners National Office for
current address.
East Davenport Turners, 2113 East 11th St., Davenport, IA 52803
Keystone Turners, 91 2nd Ave., Keystone, IA 52249
Moline Turner Society, 3119 15th St., Moline, IL 61265
Northwest Davenport Turner Society, 1430 Warren St., Davenport, IA 52804

WESTERN NEW YORK DISTRICT

Buffalo Turn Verein, 3200 Elmwood Ave., Buffalo, NY 14217
Rochester Turners, Inc. : Contact American Turners National Office for current
address.

WESTERN PENNSYLVANIA DISTRICT

Beaver Falls Turners, 615 8th St., Beaver Falls, PA 15010
Central Turn Verein Rochester, 338 Pennsylvania Ave., Rochester, PA 15074
Eintracht Music and Turn Hall Assoc., 218 E. 11th Ave., Homestead, PA 15120
Johnstown Turnverein, 632 Railroad St., Johnstown, PA 15901
Mckeesport Turners & Gesang Verein, Mckeesport, PA 15132
Monaca Turn Verein, 1700 Brodhead Rd., Monaca, PA 15061
Monongahela Turners, 127 E. Main St., Monongahela, PA 15063

WESTERN STATES DISTRICT

Denver Turnverein, Inc., 1570 Clarkson St., Denver, CO 80030
Los Angeles Turners, 4950 Wilshire Blvd., Los Angeles, CA 90010

WISCONSIN DISTRICT

Madison Turners, Inc. 21 S. Butler St., Madison, WI 53703
Milwaukee Turners Foundation, Inc., 1034 N. 4th St., Milwaukee, WI 53203
Sheboygan Turners. Inc., 3714 N. 15th St., Sheboygan, WI 53083

INDEPENDENT SOCIETIES

California: Sacramento Turners, 3349 J Street, Sacramento, CA 95816
Connecticut: Concordia Turner and Singing Society, 1181 North Main Street, Waterbury, CT 06704
Connecticut: Meriden Turner Society Inc., 800 Old Colony Road, Meriden, CT 06450
Illinois: Belleville Turners, YMCA Building 15 N 1st Street, Belleville, IL 62220
Illinois: Columbia Gymnastic Association, E. Cherry Street, Columbia, IL 62236
Illinois: Smithton Turners, P.O.Box 73, Smithton, IL 62285
Ohio: Dayton Liederkranz Turners, 1400 E. Fifth Street, Dayton, OH 45402
Pennsylvania: East Erie Turnerhall, 829 Parade Street, Erie, PA 16503
Pennsylvania: South Erie Turners, 2663 Peach St., Erie, PA 16508
Wisconsin: Watertown Turners, 4th Street, Watertown, WI 53094
Texas: Boerne Turn Verein, P.O.Box 711 Boerne, TX 78006
Texas: Houston Turn Verein, 7800 Westglen (Suite 190) Houston, TX 77063
Texas: San Antonio Turner Club, 120 Ninth Street, San Antonio, TX 78215

Appendix 3

Repository Codes

The repository codes are based upon those established for the National Union Catalog. In many cases the Turner items will be found in the special collections or local history sections of the listed institution, rather than in the main library collection.

ALABAMA

AB	Birmingham Public Library, Birmingham
AM	Mobile Public Library, Mobile
AMU	University of South Alabama, Mobile
AU	University of Alabama, Tuscaloosa

ARKANSAS

ArU	University of Arkansas, Fayetteville

CALIFORNIA

C	California State Library, Sacramento
CL	Los Angeles Public Library, Los Angeles
CLAA	Amateur Athletic Foundation of Los Angeles, Los Angeles
CLU	University of California, Los Angeles
CSDHi	San Diego Historical Society, San Diego
CSDS	San Diego State University, San Diego
CSFS	San Francisco State University, San Francisco

CSJS	San Jose State University, San Jose
CSmH	Huntington Library, San Marino
CSt	Stanford University, Stanford
CU	University of California, Berkeley
CUI	University of California, Irvington
CU-SB	University of California, Santa Barbara

COLORADO

CoB	Public Library of Boulder, Boulder
CoD	Denver Public Library, Denver
CoDU	University of Denver, Denver
CoFS	Colorado State University, Fort Collins

CONNECTICUT

Ct	Connecticut State Library, Hartford
CtHi	Connecticut Historical Society, Hartford
CtNHHi	New Haven Colony Historical Society, New Haven
CtY	Yale University, New Haven

DELAWARE

| DeU | University of Delaware, Newark |

DISTICT OF COLUMBIA

DGW	George Washington University
DHEW	US Department of Health, Education & Welfare Library
DLC	Library of Congress
DS	Smithsonian Institute Library

FLORIDA

FTaSU	Florida State University, Tallahassee
FTU	University of Tampa, Tampa
FU	University of Florida, Gainesville

ILLINOIS

IC	Chicago Public Library, Chicago
ICD	De Paul University, Chicago
ICN	Newberry Library, Chicago
ICHi	Chicago Historical Society, Chicago
ICRL	Center for Research Libraries, Chicago
ICU	University of Chicago, Chicago
IDEKN	Northern Illinois University, De Kalb
IEdS	Southern Illinois University, Edwardsville
IEl	Gail Border Public Library, Elgin
IEN	Northwestern University, Evanston
IHi	Illinois State Historical Library, Springfield
INS	Illinois State University, Normal
IP	Peoria Public Library, Peoria
IU	University of Illinois at Urbana-Champaign, University Archives

INDIANA

In	Indiana State Library, Indianapolis
InFA	Allen County Public Library, Fort Wayne
InHi	Indiana Historical Society, Indianapolis
InIB	Butler University, Indianapolis
InIU	Indiana University-Purdue University Indianapolis
InND	University of Notre Dame, South Bend
InU	Indiana University, Bloomington

IOWA

IaBS	Scott Community College, Bettendorf
IaCFT	University of Northern Iowa, Cedar Rapids
IaDa	Davenport Public Library, Davenport
IaDP	Putnam Museum, Davenport
IaHi	State Historical Society of Iowa, Iowa City
IaU	State University of Iowa, Iowa City

KANSAS

KHi	Kansas State Historical Society, Topeka
KMK	Kansas State University, Manhattan
KU	University of Kansas, Lawrence

KENTUCKY

KYHi	Kentucky Historical Society, Frankfort
KYLoU	University of Louisville, Louisville
KYU	University of Kentucky, Lexington
KYLOF	Filson Club, Louisville

LOUISIANA

LN	New Orleans Public Library, New Orleans
LNHi	Historic New Orleans Collection, New Orleans
LU	Louisiana State University, Baton Rouge

MARYLAND

MdBG	Goucher College, Baltimore
MdBHi	Maryland Historical Society, Baltimore

MASSACHUSETTS

MAC	Amherst College, Amherst
MB	Boston Public Library, Boston
MBA	Boston Athenaeum, Boston
MBU	Boston University, Boston
MH	Harvard University, Cambridge
Mhol	Holyoke Public Library, Holyoke
MLIA	Immigration City Archives, Lawrence
MSC	Springfield College, Springfield
MSHi	Conneticut Valley Historical Museum, Springfield
MWA	American Antiquarian Society, Worcester
MWHM	Worcester Historical Museum, Worcester
MWeA	Westfield Athenaeum, Westfield

MICHIGAN

MiD	Detroit Public Library, Detroit
MiEM	Michigan State University, East Lansing
MiMN	Northern Michigan University, Marquette
MiU	University of Michigan, Bentley Library, Ann Arbor

MINNESOTA

MnBCHi	Brown County Historical Society, New Ulm
MnHi	Minnesota Historical Society, St. Paul
MnM	Minneapolis Public Library, Minneapolis
MnSH	Hamline University, St. Paul
MnSU	Mankato State University, Mankato
MnU	University of Minnesota, Minneapolis
MnV	Immigration History Research Center, University of Minnesota, Minneapolis

MISSOURI

MoK	Kansas City Public Library, Kansas City
MoKU	Univesity of Missouri - Kansas City
MoSHi	Missouri Historical Society, St. Louis
MoSM	St. Louis Mercantile Library Association, St. Louis
MoSW	Washington University, St. Louis
MoU	University of Missouri, Western Historical Manuscript Collection, Columbia

NEBRASKA

NbU	University of Nebraska, Lincoln

NEW HAMPSHIRE

NhD	Dartmouth College, Hanover

NEW YORK

NALU	State University New York, Albany
NB	Brooklyn Public Library, Brooklyn
NBuHi	Buffalo and Erie County Historical Society, Buffalo
NBuU	State University of New York, Buffalo
NIIC	Ithaca College, Ithaca
NN	New York Public Library, New York City
NNM	Museum of the City of New York, New York
NRU	University of Rochester, Rochester
NSCH	Schenectady County Historical Society, Schenectady
NUTHi	Oneida County Historical Society, Utica

NEW JERSEY

NJH	Hoboken Public Library, Hoboken
NJNC	Free Public Library at Newark, Newark
NJHi	New Jersey Historical Society, Newark
NJPHi	Passaic County Historical Society, Passaic
NJR	Rutgers University, New Brunswick

NORTH CAROLINA

NcD	Duke University, Durham
NcGU	University of North Carolina, Greensboro

OHIO

OB	Bluffton College, Bluffton
OBGU	Bowling Green State University, Bowling Green
OCHi	Cincinnati Historical Society, Cincinnati
OCI	Cleveland Public Library, Cleveland
OClWHi	Western Reserve Historical Society, Cleveland
OCU	University of Cincinnati, Blegen Library, Cincinnati
OH	Ohio Historical Society, Columbus
OkentC	Kent State University
OO	Oberlin College, Oberlin
OOxM	Miami University, Oxford
OT	Toledo-Lucas County Public Library, Toledo
OTU	University of Toledo, Toledo
OU	Ohio State University, Columbus

OREGON

OrHi	Oregon Historical Society, Portland
OrP	Library Association of Portland, Portland
OrU	University of Oregon, Eugene

PENNSYLVANIA

PBF	Carnegie Free Library, Beaver Falls
PEM	Mercyhurst College, Erie
PHi	Historical Society of Pennsylvania, Philadelphia
PP	Free Library of Philadelphia, Philadelphia

PPB	Balch Institute for Ethnic Studies, Philadelphia
PPG	German Society of Pennsylvania, Philadelphia
PPiHi	Historical Society of Western Pennsylvania, Pittsburgh
PPiU	University of Pittsburgh, Pittsburgh
PS	Pennsylvania State University, College Park
PSC	Swarthmore College, Philadelphia
PPT	Temple University, Philadelphia
PU	University of Pennsylvania, Philadelphia
PWCS	West Chester State College, West Chester

RHODE ISLAND

| RPB | Brown University, Providence |
| RPHi | Rhode Island Historical Society, Providence |

TEXAS

| TxSMS | Southwest Texas State University, San Marcos |
| TxU | University of Texas, Austin |

UTAH

| UPB | Brigham Young University, Provo |

VIRGINIA

| Vi | Virginia State Library, Richmond |
| ViU | University of Virginia, Charlottesville |

WASHINGTON

WaSp	State College of Washington, Pullman
WaT	Tacoma Public Library, Tacoma
WaU	University of Washington, Seattle

WISCONSIN

| WHi | State Historical Society of Wisconsin, Madison |
| WLC | La Crosse Public Library, La Crosse |

WM	Milwaukee Public Library, Milwaukee
WMCHi	Milwaukee County Historical Society, Milwaukee
WMT	Milwaukee Turner Foundation, Milwaukee
WMU`	University of Wisconsin, Milwaukee
WSCHi	Sheboygan County Historical Society, Sheboygan
WULC	University of Wisconsin, La Crosse
WUO	University of Wisconsin, Oshkosh

GERMANY

GyAIZ	Internationales Zeitungsmuseum, Aachen, Germany

Index

The index contains two types of references: 1) item numbers for information included in a bibliographical entry, and 2) page numbers for information found in the introductory essays and historical notes. The item numbers always appear first, and consist of both a letter designation and a number. The letter designations are **N** for National Publications (Chapter 1), **C** and **D** for Circuit and District Publications (Chapter 2), **T** for *Turnlehrer-Seminar*/Normal College Publications (Chapter 4), **G** for Turner publications on physical education (Chapter 5), and **W** for writings on the American Turners (Chapter 6). Designations for the entries in Chapter 3, Society Publications, consist of a two-letter state code (Ny for New York, for example), followed by a number. Page numbers are separated from the item numbers by a semicolon and the abbreviations 'p.' or 'pp.' The list of societies found in Appendix 1 has not been indexed since its geographical arrangement makes it self-indexing.

About the Compilers

ERIC L. PUMROY is Director of the Library and Archives at the Balch Institute for Ethnic Studies. He is the author of *A Guide to Manuscript Collections of the Indiana Historical Society and the Indiana State Library* (1986).

KATJA RAMPELMANN is a doctoral student at the Ruhr University Bochum. She was Project Archivist for the American Turners Historical Records Survey Project, funded by the National Endowment for the Humanities.

ISBN 0-313-29763-0

90000>

EAN

9 780313 297632

HARDCOVER BAR CODE